STUDENT ACTIVITIES MANUAL

Enric Figueras
Boise State University

Lisa Nalbone
University of Central Florida

to Accompany

Comunicación y cultura

Fifth Edition

Eduardo Zayas-Bazán
Emeritus, East Tennessee State University

Susan M. Bacon
University of Cincinnati

Holly J. Nibert
Western Michigan University

Upper Saddle River, New Jersey 07458

Publisher: *Phil Miller*
Editorial Supervisor/Assistant Development Editor: *Debbie King*
Director of Marketing: *Kristine Suárez*
Director of Editorial Development: *Julia Caballero*
Development Editor: *Janet García-Levitas*
Development Editor for Assessment: *Melissa Marolla Brown*
Production Supervision: *Nancy Stevenson*
Composition/Full-Service Project Management: *Natalie Hansen and Sandra Reinhard, Black Dot Group*
Assistant Director of Production: *Mary Rottino*
Supplements Editor: *Meriel Martínez Moctezuma*
Senior Media Editor: *Samantha Alducin*
Prepress and Manufacturing Buyer: *Christina Amato*
Prepress and Manufacturing Assistant Manager: *Marianne Gloriande*
Interior Design: *Black Dot Group*
Cover Art Director: *Jayne Conte*
Art Manager: *Maria Piper*
Marketing Coordinator: *William J. Bliss*

This book was set in 11/14 Meridian Roman by Black Dot Group and was printed and bound by Bind-Rite Graphics. The cover was printed by Bind-Rite Graphics.

Printed in the United States of America
10 9 8 7

ISBN: 0-13-239746-3/978-0-13-239746-9

Pearson Education LTD., *London*
Pearson Education Australia PTY, Limited, *Sydney*
Pearson Education Singapore, Pte. Ltd.
Pearson Education North Asia Ltd., *Hong Kong*
Pearson Education Canada, Ltd., *Toronto*
Pearson Educación de Mexico, S.A. de C.V.
Pearson Education—Japan, *Tokyo*
Pearson Education Malaysia, Pte. Ltd.
Pearson Education, *Upper Saddle River*, New Jersey

CONTENTS

PREFACE

Drawing on the organization, pedagogy, and special features of the student text, the Student Activities Manual to accompany *¡Arriba! Comunicación y cultura*, Fifth Edition, is a completely integrated manual that offers a wide range of practice opportunities for the vocabulary, grammar, and culture topics presented in the student textbook. It includes traditional "workbook" activities as well as audio- and video-based activities. All activities in each section follow a progression from mechanical exercises to fill-in exercises to activities that require more open-ended responses.

This edition of the activities manual has been carefully crafted so that it is completely coordinated with the student textbook, an improvement that makes it stand out from previous editions. Its organizational structure is now exactly parallel to that of the text, making it easier for students and instructors alike to find all of the practice materials on a given topic. Each chapter of the manual is divided into three sections: *Primera parte, Segunda parte,* and *Nuestro mundo.* Each *parte* is further subdivided according to the sections of the text, with *¡Así es la vida!* and *¡Así lo decimos!* to strengthen vocabulary usage and *¡Así lo hacemos!* to practice grammar points in the order in which they appear in the chapter. We have gone to great lengths to ensure that the practice activities in the manual correspond not only in sequence, but also in scope and difficulty to the topics introduced in the parallel sections of the student text.

Other features new to this edition of the manual include the following:

- A new section entitled *Letras y sonidos* provides additional practice of the Spanish accentuation and pronunciation topics introduced in the text.
- A *¿Cuánto sabes tú?* assessment section after each *parte* coordinates with the communicative goals outlined in the text. The *¿Cuánto sabes tú?* activities provide students with the ability to review the material introduced in the text and track their progress toward reaching the stated goals.
- A new *Observaciones* section offers a series of activities relating to the new *¡Arriba!* episodic video, *¡Pura vida!* These activities follow the process approach, providing pre-viewing, during-viewing, and post-viewing activities to increase student comprehension of each of the video segments.
- An expanded *Nuestro Mundo* section now parallels the corresponding section of the text. The *Panoramas* section challenges students to develop their knowledge of the cultural topics presented in the textbook. The *Ritmos* section correlates with the musical group or ethnic sound introduced in the textbook, while the *Páginas* section allows the student to experience more information about the writers or writing styles found in the text. The activities in these two sections also include Internet discovery components in which students journey outside the textbook to enhance their understanding. To complete the integration, the *Taller* permits students to synthesize their own ideas about topics explored in the chapter while expanding their writing skills through guided composition.
- Section headings in the manual now include the corresponding textbook pages as a direct reference for the student.
- Many art- and realia-based activities have been added to this edition to provide students with additional visual context.

Nombre: ______________________________ Fecha: ______________________

1 Hola, ¿qué tal?

PRIMERA PARTE

¡Así es la vida!

CD 1, Track 1

1-1 Conversaciones. Listen to the following conversations using expressions of greeting. Then, write the letter of the conversation that takes place between each of the persons listed below. Finally, listen to the conversations again and indicate whether they are formal or informal.

	CONVERSACIÓN	FORMAL	INFORMAL
1. La señora Cárdenas y Paco Ureña	____	____	____
2. El profesor Pérez y Francisco Fernández	____	____	____
3. Luis y Carmen	____	____	____
4. Eduardo y María	____	____	____
5. Cristina y Manolo	____	____	____

1-2 Saludos y despedidas. Complete the following dialogue by filling in the blanks with the most appropriate word from the word bank. You can use the dialogues on page 4 of the textbook as models.

bien	buenos	mucho	llama
pronto	menos	encantado	llamo

Sr. Pérez: Hola, (1) ______________ días. ¿Cómo se (2) ______________ usted?

Eduardo: Me (3) ______________ Eduardo Orozco.

Sr. Pérez: (4) ______________ gusto. Soy el señor Pérez.

Eduardo: (5) ______________. ¿Cómo está usted?

Sr. Pérez: Muy (6) ______________, gracias. ¿Y usted?

Nombre: ____________________ Fecha: ____________________

Eduardo: Más o (7) menos________. Adiós, Sr. Pérez.

Sr. Pérez: Hasta (8) pronto________.

CD 1, Track 2

1-3 Más conversaciones. Complete the sentences formally or informally by selecting the appropriate words based on the prompt you hear. Then, listen and repeat as the speaker gives the correct answer.

Modelo: You see: ¿Cómo está________ (estás/está) usted________? (tú/usted)
You hear: Formal
You write, then say: *¿Cómo está usted?*

1. Buenas tardes, profesora. ¿Cómo ____________ (estás/está) ____________? (tú/usted)
2. ¡Hola! ¿Cómo ____________ (estás/está) ____________? (tú/usted)
3. Me llamo Natalia. ¿Y ____________? (tú/usted)
4. ¿Cómo ____________ (te/se) ____________ (llamas/llama) ____________? (tú/usted)
5. ¿Y ____________? (tú/usted)
6. Soy Pablo Figueroa. ¿Y ____________? (tú/usted)
7. ¿Cómo ____________? (estás/está)

Nombre: ______________________ Fecha: ______________________

¡Así lo decimos! Vocabulario (TEXTBOOK P. 5)

1-4 ¿Saludos o despedidas? Decide if each expression should be used as a *saludo* or *despedida* and select the letter of the correct answer.

1. Adiós.
   a. Saludo
   b. Despedida
2. Hasta pronto.
   a. Saludo
   b. Despedida
3. Hasta mañana.
   a. Saludo
   b. Despedida
4. Hasta luego.
   a. Saludo
   b. Despedida
5. Buenos días.
   a. Saludo
   b. Despedida
6. Buenas noches.
   a. Saludo
   b. Despedida
7. ¿Qué pasa?
   a. Saludo
   b. Despedida
8. ¡Hola!
   a. Saludo
   b. Despedida

1-5 ¿Formal o informal? Decide if each expression should be used in a formal or informal social setting and choose the letter of the correct answer.

1. ¿Cómo estás?
   a. Formal
   b. Informal
2. ¿Y tú?
   a. Formal
   b. Informal
3. ¿Cómo se llama usted?
   a. Formal
   b. Informal
4. ¿Qué pasa?
   a. Formal
   b. Informal
5. ¿Y usted?
   a. Formal
   b. Informal
6. ¿Cómo te llamas tú?
   a. Formal
   b. Informal

Nombre: ______________________ Fecha: ______________________

1-6 Respuestas. Look at the following drawings and choose the letter of the most logical answer to complete each conversation.

1. a. Buenos días.

   b. Más o menos.

   c. ¿Y tú?

2. a. De nada.

   b. Hasta luego.

   c. Mucho gusto.

3. a. ¿Y usted?

   b. Adiós.

   c. Buenos días, profesora.

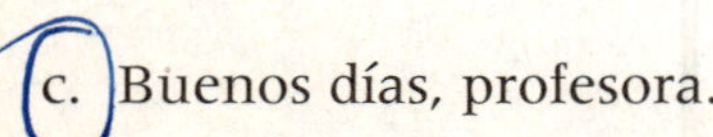

4. a. Hola.

   b. Hasta pronto.

   c. Muy bien, ¿y usted?

5. a. ¡Buenos días!

   b. No muy bien.

   c. Hasta mañana.

6. a. Más o menos.

   b. De nada, María Luisa.

   c. ¿Y tú?

Nombre: ______________________ Fecha: ______________________

1-7 ¡Hola! ¿Qué tal? Based on what you hear, select the letter that corresponds to the most logical response. Then listen and repeat as the speaker gives the correct answer.

CD 1, Track 3

1. a. Mucho gusto. Yo soy Alfredo Rivera.
   b. De nada.
   c. Estoy bien.
2. a. Buenas noches.
   b. Encantado.
   c. Bien, gracias.
3. a. Encantada.
   b. Gracias.
   c. Muy bien, gracias.
4. a. Muchas gracias, soy Felipe.
   b. Es Felipe.
   c. Me llamo Felipe.
5. a. Adiós. Hasta mañana.
   b. Muy bien.
   c. Bien, gracias.

1-8 Diálogos. Complete the following conversations with the appropriate questions or answers, in response to the prompts from Sr. Morales and Carlos.

Sr. Morales: Buenos días. ¿Cómo se llama usted?

~~My name is~~ Good moring. What is your named?

Sr. Morales: Muy bien, gracias. Hasta pronto. See you soon

very good thank you. See you soon

Carlos: Hola.

Hi

Carlos: Me llamo Carlos. ¿Y tú?

my name is Carlos. And you?

Carlos: Más o menos. ¿Y tú?

So, so and you?

Carlos: Hasta pronto.

See you soon

Nombre: ______________________ Fecha: ______________________

Letras y sonidos (Textbook p. 7)

CD 1, Track 4

1-9 La vocal *a*. You will hear a series of Spanish words. Select all letters corresponding to the words that contain the *a* sound.

1. a b c d

2. a b c d

3. a b c d

CD 1, Track 5

1-10 La vocal *e*. You will now hear a different series of Spanish words. Select all letters corresponding to the words that contain the *e* sound.

1. a b c d

2. a b c d

3. a b c d

CD 1, Track 6

1-11 La vocal *i*. Now listen to another series of Spanish words. Select all letters corresponding to the words that contain the *i* sound.

1. a b c d

2. a b c d

3. a b c d

CD 1, Track 7

1-12 La vocal *o*. You will hear another series of words. Select all letters corresponding to those that contain the *o* sound.

1. a b c d

2. a b c d

3. a b c d

CD 1, Track 8

1-13 La vocal *u*. For this final series, select all letters corresponding to the words that contain the *u* sound.

1. a b c d

2. a b c d

3. a b c d

Nombre: ______________________ Fecha: ______________________

¡Así lo hacemos! Estructuras

1. The Spanish alphabet (Textbook p. 8)

1-14 Letras y palabras. Match the Spanish letter with the word that contains it.

1. e ge
2. g equis
3. a eñe
4. b y griega
5. d zeta
6. c uve
7. h cu
8. f hache

a. señor
b. muy
c. verdad
d. López
e. luego
f. hasta
g. México
h. que

1-15 Ciudades del mundo hispano. Give the name of each city that is spelled out below.

1. ce, a, ere, a, ce, a, ese — Caracas
2. eme, a, de, ere, i, de — Madrid
3. eme, o, ene, te, e, uve, i, de, e, o — Montevideo
4. ce, u, zeta, ce, o — Cuzco
5. ge, u, a, de, a, ele, a, jota, a, ere, a — Guadalajara
6. ese, e, uve, i, ele, ele, a — Sevilla
7. uve, e, ere, a, ce, ere, u, zeta — Veracruz
8. ge, u, a, y griega, a, cu, u, i, ele — Guayacuil

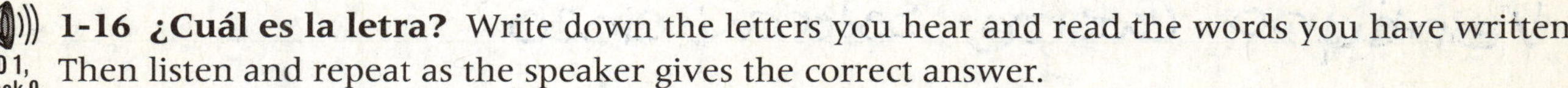

CD 1, Track 9

1-16 ¿Cuál es la letra? Write down the letters you hear and read the words you have written. Then listen and repeat as the speaker gives the correct answer.

1. h a s _ _ / m a n a n a.
2. m u c h o / g u s t o.
3. ¿q u e / t a l?

Nombre: ______________________ Fecha: ______________________

1-17 Letras y expresiones. Write the letters you hear. Then unscramble the letters to form expressions related to meeting new friends. Finally, listen and repeat as the speaker gives the correct answer.

CD 1, Track 10

LETRAS	EXPRESIONES
1. ___ ___ ___ ___ ___ ___ ___	______________
2. ___ ___ ___ ___ ___ ___ ___ ___ ___	______________
3. ___ ___ ___ ___ ___ ___ ___ ___ ___ ___	______________
4. ___ ___ ___ ___ ___	______________

2. The numbers 0–100 (Textbook p. 10)

1-18 Números de teléfono. Look at the following business cards and spell out the phone numbers listed below.

Eduardo Soto España
Director Ejecutivo
Comisión de Intercambio Educativo
Entre Estados Unidos y Venezuela
(Fullbright Commission)
Palomo 305 - 3º
Tel. 392-4971/3855
2013 - 6047
Caracas

José Sigüenza Escudero
Tomasa Miranda de Sigüenza
C/ El Molino, 11
Teléfono 39 21 37
QUEL (Logroño)

José Bernardo Fernández

Aníbal Ruiz Pérez
Departamento de Matemáticas
Universidad de Puerto Rico,
Río Piedras

SERVICIO DE VIAJES RODRÍGUEZ TRAVEL SERVICE
Antonio Rodríguez
DIRECTOR GENERAL
PASEO DE CABALLOS 371
58300 MONTERREY,
MÉXICO
TELS. 21-14-75 Y
21-14-93
TELEX 4902384 HOTME

1. José Sigüenza y Tomasa Miranda:
Treintaynueve veintiuno treinta y ~~seite~~ siete

2. Eduardo Soto España:
trescientos noventa y dos - cuatrocientos noventaysiete

3. Antonio Rodríguez:
Veintiuno catorce setenay cinco
veintiuno catorce noventa y tres

Nombre: ______________________ Fecha: ______________________

1-19 Matemáticas. Imagine that Pedro is practicing his math facts. How would he complete each of the following? Write the missing number in Spanish.

1. Once – nueve = dos.
2. Treinta + setenta = noventa.
3. Ochenta – Setenta = diez.
4. Tres x ______________ = cuarenta y ocho.
5. Quince ÷ ______________ = cinco.
6. Dos x ______________ = cuarenta.
7. Cien – ______________ = cuarenta y nueve.
8. Doce ÷ ______________ = dos.
9. Once + ______________ = treinta y dos.
10. Ocho ÷ Qutaro = dos.

CD 1, Track 11

1-20 Más matemáticas. Write the numbers you hear and complete the math problem according to the cue. Then read each equation. Finally, listen and repeat as the speaker gives the correct answer.

+ (más) – (menos) x (por) ÷ (entre) = (son)

1. ________ + ________ = ________
2. ________ – ________ = ________
3. ________ x ________ = ________
4. ________ x ________ = ________
5. ________ ÷ ________ = ________
6. ________ + ________ = ________

3. The days of the week, the months, and the seasons (TEXTBOOK P. 13)

1-21 ¿En qué mes del año...? Match the list of events with the month of the year when they take place.

1. e el día de la Independencia de los Estados Unidos
2. f *Halloween*
3. A el día de San Valentín
4. B la Navidad (*Christmas*)
5. D el día de Acción de Gracias (*Thanksgiving*)
6. G el día de Martin Luther King
7. H el día de la Madre (*Mother*)
8. C el día del Padre (*Father*)

a. febrero
b. diciembre
c. junio
d. noviembre
e. julio
f. octubre
g. enero
h. mayo

Nombre: ______________________ Fecha: ______________________

1-22 Los días, los meses y las estaciones. Circle all the days of the week, the months, and the seasons in the puzzle.

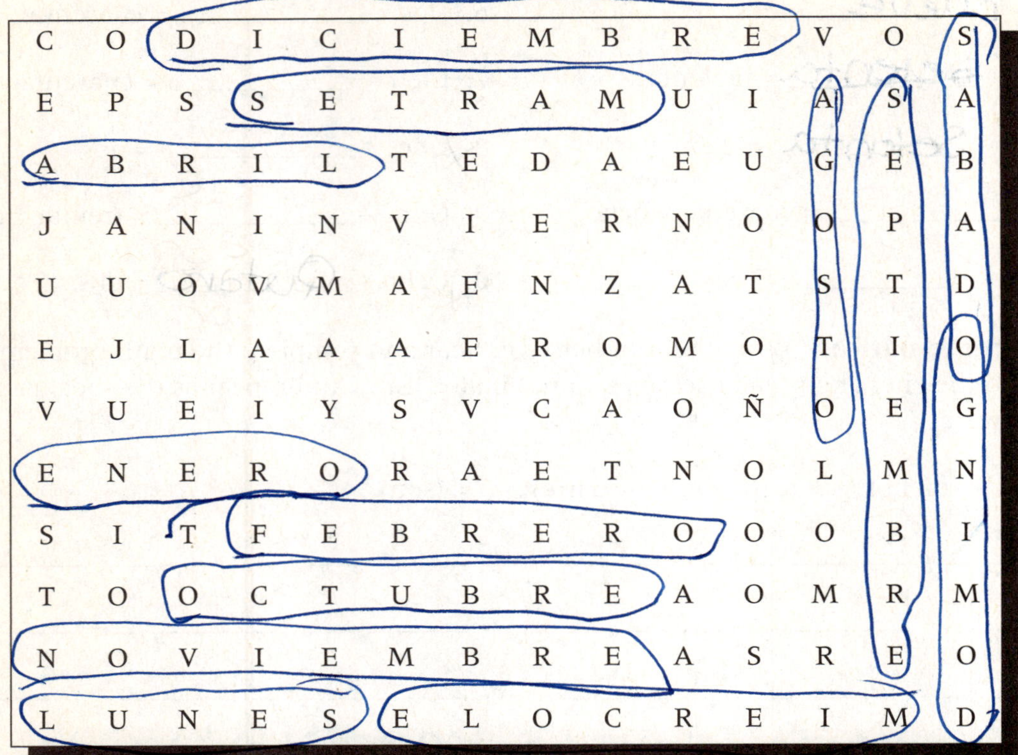

Nombre: ______________________ Fecha: ______________________

1-23 Las estaciones y las fechas importantes. Look at the list of events and other dates and write each one under the drawing that represents the season in which it takes place.

el invierno

el Año Nuevo

Hanukkah

la primavera

el Cinco de mayo

la Pascua

el verano

el otoño

el día del Trabajo

el día de Cristóbal colón

1. el día del Trabajo (*Labor Day*)
2. el Cinco de Mayo
3. la Pascua (*Easter*)
4. Hanukkah
5. el Año Nuevo (*New Year's Day*)
6. el día de Cristóbal Colón (*Columbus Day*)

Nombre: ______________________ Fecha: ______________________

1-24 Los días de la semana. Write in Spanish the day that completes the sequence.

1. martes, miércoles, jueves — monday
2. domingo, lunes, martes — tues
3. miércoles, jueves, viernes — wed
4. lunes, martes, miércoles — thurs
5. jueves, viernes, sábado — fri
6. sábado, domingo, lunes — sat
7. viernes, sábado, domingo — sun

CD 1, Track 12

1-25 El calendario de Paola. You will hear some important dates on Paola's calendar. Write the day of the week that corresponds to the events taking place according to her planner below. Then listen and repeat as the speaker gives the correct answer.

lunes	día de los Presidentes
martes	clase de español
miércoles	examen de literatura
jueves	día de San Valentín
viernes	concierto (*concert*)
sábado	fiesta de Ricardo
domingo	restaurante con la familia

1. Hoy es ______________________.
2. Hoy es ______________________.
3. Hoy es ______________________.
4. Hoy es ______________________.
5. Hoy es ______________________.
6. Hoy es ______________________.

Nombre: ______________________ Fecha: ______________________

1-26 ¿Cuándo es? Write the month you hear and its corresponding season. Then listen and repeat as the speaker gives the correct answer.

CD 1, Track 13

	MES	ESTACIÓN
1.	______	______
2.	______	______
3.	______	______
4.	______	______
5.	______	______
6.	______	______

1-27 ¿Cuál es la fecha? You will hear certain dates of the year in Spanish. Write them in numerals in the spaces below.

CD 1, Track 14

Modelo: You hear: treinta de octubre
You write: *30/10*

1. 2 / 11
2. 12 / 9
3. 20 / 12
4. 4 / 3
5. 5 / 7
6. 16 / 1

¿Cuánto sabes tú?

1-28 La conversación de Alberto y Victoria. Complete each sentence by selecting the letter of the correct answer according to the conversation you hear.

CD 1, Track 15

1. Alberto está…

   a. mal. b. más o menos. c. bien.

2. Victoria está…

   a. muy bien. b. mal. c. bien.

3. Hoy es…

   a. jueves. b. martes. c. miércoles.

Nombre: ______________________ Fecha: ______________________

4. Hoy es el...

a. 30 de julio. b. 25 de marzo. c. 30 de septiembre.

5. Hoy es un día de...

a. otoño. b. primavera. c. verano.

1-29 ¿Sabes matemáticas? Solve the following calculations and write out the answer in Spanish.

1. 53 + 14 = sesenta y siete.
2. 66 – 33 = treinta y tres.
3. 33 x 3 = noventa y nueve.
4. 10 + 14 = veinticuatro.
5. 20 x 5 = cien.

CD 1, Track 16

1-30 ¿Sabes los días, los meses y las estaciones? You will hear the names of days of the week, months, or seasons spelled out. Fill in the blank with the corresponding word.

1. ______________________ 4. ______________________
2. ______________________ 5. ______________________
3. ______________________ 6. ______________________

CD 1, Track 17

1-31 ¿Qué tal? Give an appropriate response to the following questions or situations.

1. ______________________
2. ______________________
3. ______________________
4. ______________________
5. ______________________
6. ______________________

Nombre: ______________________ Fecha: ______________________

Segunda parte

¡Así es la vida!

1-32 En la clase. Choose the letter of the word that does not fit in each group.

1. a. calculadora
   b. libro
   c. estudiante
   d. computadora

2. a. silla
   b. lección
   c. mesa
   d. pizarra

3. a. universidad
   b. estudiante
   c. profesora
   d. mujer

4. a. bolígrafo
   b. mochila
   c. lápiz
   d. papel

CD 1, Track 18

1-33 Mi clase de español. You will hear a conversation that takes place in a classroom. Select all the letters that complete the statements. You may need to listen more than once.

1. La profesora está…
   a. bien.
   b. muy bien.
   c. mal.

2. La mochila es…
   a. verde.
   b. roja.
   c. azul.

3. Es verde:
   a. el cuaderno.
   b. la silla.
   c. el bolígrafo.

4. Tomás tiene tres…
   a. cuadernos.
   b. relojes.
   c. lápices.

Nombre: ______________________________ Fecha: ______________________

5. En la clase, hay diecisiete…
   a. libros.
   b. sillas.
   c. mesas.
6. Los estudiantes son…
   a. aburridos.
   b. malos.
   c. inteligentes.
7. La profesora es…
   a. simpática.
   b. cara.
   c. grande.

¡Así lo decimos! Vocabulario (Textbook p. 19)

1-34 Los colores. Find and circle the names of ten colors in the puzzle.

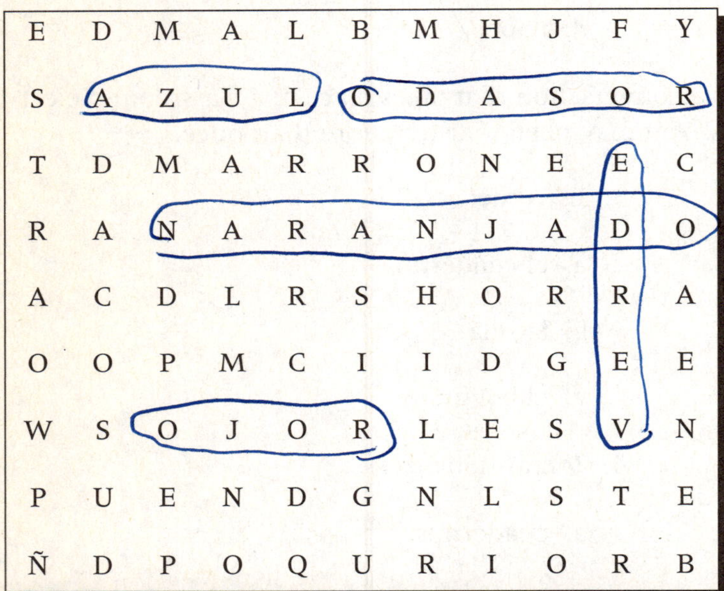

E	D	M	A	L	B	M	H	J	F	Y
S	A	Z	U	L	O	D	A	S	O	R
T	D	M	A	R	R	O	N	E	E	C
R	A	N	A	R	A	N	J	A	D	O
A	C	D	L	R	S	H	O	R	R	A
O	O	P	M	C	I	I	D	G	E	E
W	S	O	J	O	R	L	E	S	V	N
P	U	E	N	D	G	N	L	S	T	E
Ñ	D	P	O	Q	U	R	I	O	R	B

azul
verde
rosado
naranjado
rojo

1-35 Antónimos. Match the opposite adjectives from the following lists.

1. _____ interesante
2. _____ grande
3. _____ realista
4. _____ bueno
5. _____ tímido
6. _____ barato

a. idealista
b. caro
c. malo
d. pequeño
e. extrovertido
f. aburrido

CD 1, Track 19

1-36 Tu profesor. You will hear a teacher giving certain instructions in class. Write the letter of the statements you hear next to each corresponding picture.

1. _____

2. _____

3. _____

4. _____

5. _____

6. _____

Nombre: ________________________ Fecha: ________________________

1-37 ¿Qué hay en la clase? List seven items that you see in the classroom drawn below.

Modelo: *Hay una pizarra.*

1. ________________________
2. ________________________
3. ________________________
4. ________________________
5. ________________________
6. ________________________
7. ________________________

1-38 El profesor López. Professor López is a Spanish instructor who gives directions to his class in Spanish. Following the model, give the Spanish equivalent of his instructions in the third person plural (**ustedes**) form.

Modelo: Write in Spanish.
Escriban en español.

1. Answer in Spanish.

____

2. Listen.

____

3. Go to the board.

____

4. Study.

____

5. Read the dialogue.

____

6. Close the book.

____

1-39 Descripciones de la clase. Think of one of your classes this semester and the students in that class. In six sentences describe your class and/or the students. Be sure to watch for gender and number agreement.

MODELO: *La clase es grande.*

1. ____
2. ____
3. ____
4. ____
5. ____
6. ____

¡Así lo hacemos! Estructuras

4. Nouns and articles (TEXTBOOK P. 22)

1-40 El artículo definido. For each word, write the matching definite article in Spanish.

1. _____ estudiante
2. _____ mochila
3. _____ mapa
4. _____ silla
5. _____ cuaderno
6. _____ libros
7. _____ papeles
8. _____ pizarras

1-41 El artículo indefinido. Look at the words from the previous activity and for each, write the matching indefinite article.

1. _____ estudiante
2. _____ mochila
3. _____ mapa
4. _____ silla
5. _____ cuaderno
6. _____ libros
7. _____ papeles
8. _____ pizarras

Nombre: ______________________________ Fecha: ______________________

1-42 ¿Masculino o femenino? Indicate whether the following nouns are masculine or feminine by writing M or F.

1. _____ día
2. _____ papel
3. _____ calculadora
4. _____ mapa
5. _____ diccionario
6. _____ profesora
7. _____ lápiz
8. _____ cuaderno
9. _____ pizarra
10. _____ diálogo

CD 1, Track 20

1-43 ¿El, la, los, las? Based on the word you hear, write the corresponding definite article as well as the word. Then listen and repeat as the speaker gives the correct answer.

1. _____ ____________________
2. _____ ____________________
3. _____ ____________________
4. _____ ____________________
5. _____ ____________________
6. _____ ____________________
7. _____ ____________________
8. _____ ____________________

CD 1, Track 21

1-44 ¿Un, una, unos, unas? Based on the word you hear, write the corresponding indefinite article as well as the word. Then listen and repeat as the speaker gives the correct answer.

1. _____ ____________________
2. _____ ____________________
3. _____ ____________________
4. _____ ____________________
5. _____ ____________________
6. _____ ____________________
7. _____ ____________________
8. _____ ____________________

Nombre: ______________________ Fecha: ______________________

1-45 Del plural al singular. Change each phrase from plural to singular.

Modelo: los libros grandes
el libro grande

1. las clases interesantes la clase interesante
2. unos buenos días un bueno día
3. las mochilas blancas la mochila blanca
4. unos cuadernos anaranjados un cuaderno anaranjado
5. las estudiantes trabajadoras la estudiante trabajadora
6. los amigos extrovertidos ______________________
7. las computadoras caras ______________________
8. unos libros fascinantes ______________________

1-46 Tu compañero de piso. Your roommate wants to make sure that you have everything you need for your classes. Answer his questions following the model and the word in parentheses.

Modelo: ¿Necesitas un lápiz? (Sí) or (No)
Sí, necesito un lápiz. or *No, gracias. Tengo un lápiz.*

1. ¿Necesitas el libro de español? (No)

____

2. ¿Necesitas la computadora? (Sí)

____

3. ¿Necesitas la calculadora? (Sí)

____

4. ¿Necesitas un bolígrafo? (No)

____

5. ¿Necesitas un cuaderno? (No)

____

6. ¿Necesitas una mochila? (Sí)

____

Nombre: ______________________ Fecha: ______________________

5. Adjective form, position, and agreement (Textbook p. 24)

1-47 Cambio de número. The following sentences need to be changed from singular to plural. For each sentence given in the singular form, provide the plural form as in the model.

Modelo: El cuaderno es pequeño.
Los cuadernos son pequeños.

1. La mesa negra es grande.

   ____.

2. La mochila gris es cara.

   ____.

3. El reloj grande es barato.

   ____.

4. El cuaderno azul es bueno.

   ____.

5. El estudiante inteligente es trabajador.

   ____.

6. La profesora extrovertida es simpática.

   ____.

Nombre: ______________________________ Fecha: ______________________

1-48 Los artículos y los adjetivos. Fill in the blanks with the correct forms of the article and adjective in parentheses.

Modelo: ____ pizarra ________________ (el/negro)
la pizarra negra

1. ____ computadoras ________________ (un/caro)
2. ____ estudiantes ________________ (el/simpático)
3. ____ señora ________________ (el/trabajador)
4. ____ profesores ________________ (un/aburrido)
5. ____ profesora ________________ (un/interesante)
6. ____ clase ________________ (el/grande)
7. ____ sillas ________________ (el/amarillo)
8. ____ bolígrafos ________________ (el/azul)

1-49 Características opuestas. Change the gender and number in the following phrases to the opposite.

Modelo: una estudiante trabajadora
unos estudiantes trabajadores

1. unos señores extrovertidos

   ____

2. unas profesoras simpáticas

   ____

3. una estudiante tímida

   ____

4. un buen amigo

   ____

5. unos hombres aburridos

   ____

Nombre: ______________________ Fecha: ______________________

1-50 Tus descripciones. Complete the following descriptions of people and objects you know. Use colors, adjectives of nationality, or descriptive adjectives.

1. Mi amigo/a es ______________________
2. El hombre/mujer ideal es ______________________
3. El/La profesor/a de español es ______________________
4. Mi clase de español es ______________________
5. La universidad es ______________________

CD 1, Track 22

1-51 La clase y los estudiantes. Describe the class and the students in the class by using the cues provided. Then listen and repeat as the speaker gives the correct answer.

Modelo: You see: blanco
You hear: papeles
You write and say: *En la clase hay papeles blancos.*

1. negro ______________________
2. trabajador ______________________
3. caro ______________________
4. extrovertido ______________________
5. rojo y verde ______________________

CD 1, Track 23

1-52 La clase y las descripciones. Based on the cues provided, write the number of people and objects that there are in your class, as well as their descriptions. Then listen and repeat as the speaker gives the correct answer.

Modelo: You see: 2 / pequeño
You hear: mochilas
You write and say: *Hay dos mochilas pequeñas.*

1. 2 / grande ______________________
2. 1 / interesante ______________________
3. 8 / malo ______________________
4. 1 / simpático______________________
5. 3 / aburrido ______________________
6. 21 / gris ______________________

Nombre: ______________________ Fecha: ______________________

CD 1, Track 24

1-53 De uno a muchos. You will hear the description of a single object or person. Based on the cues provided, apply that same description in the plural and make all other necessary changes, including the articles and verbs.

Modelo: You hear: La mochila es roja.
You write: *Las mochilas son rojas.*

1. ______________________
2. ______________________
3. ______________________
4. ______________________
5. ______________________

6. Subject pronouns and the present tense of *ser* (Textbook p. 26)

1-54 Los sujetos. Choose the corresponding subject pronoun for each person or group of people.

1. María Luisa:

   a. Yo b. Usted c. Ella

2. Susana y yo:

   a. Ellos/as b. Nosotros/as c. Yo

3. Quique y Ramón:

   a. Ellos b. Nosotros c. Vosotros

4. Las profesoras:

   a. Ellas b. Ustedes c. Ellos

5. Tú y yo:

   a. Nosotros/as b. Ellos/as c. Vosotros/as

6. Eduardo:

   a. Él b. Ella c. Tú

7. Anita, Carmen y José:

   a. Ustedes b. Ellos c. Ellas

8. Lucía, Mercedes y Teresa:

   a. Ustedes b. Ellos c. Ellas

9. Ricardo y las estudiantes:

   a. Nosotros b. Ellos c. Ustedes

10. Raúl y ellas:

   a. Ellas b. Ellos c. Ustedes

1-55 Manuel Rivera. Complete Manuel's description with the correct form of *ser*.

¡Hola! Yo (1) ______________ Manuel Rivera y (2) ______________ de Sevilla. Mi papá (3) ______________ colombiano y mi mamá (4) ______________ española. Mis padres (5) ______________ muy trabajadores. Mis padres y yo (6) ______________ muy simpáticos. ¿De dónde (7) ______________ tú? ¿Cómo (8) ______________ tú? ¿Cómo (9) ______________ tu clase de español?

1-56 Ramón y Rosario. Complete the conversation between Ramón and Rosario with the correct form of *ser*.

— Hola, yo (1) ______________ Ramón Larrea Arias.

— Encantada, Ramón. (2) ______________ Rosario Vélez Cuadra.

— ¿De dónde (3) ______________ ?

— (4) ______________ de Puerto Rico, ¿y tú?

— (5) ______________ de Panamá, pero mis padres (6) ______________ de Colombia.

— ¿Cómo (7) ______________ tu clase de inglés?

— Mi clase (8) ______________ muy interesante y nosotros (9) ______________ muy trabajadores.

— Y, ¿cómo (10) ______________ la profesora?

— La profesora (11) ______________ muy simpática. Ella (12) ______________ de Canadá.

— ¡Ay! Tengo clase ahora. Hasta pronto, Ramón.

— Adiós, Rosario.

Nombre: ______________________ Fecha: ______________________

CD 1, Track 25

1-57 Personalidades. Write the answers to the questions according to the cues, using the correct subject pronoun and form of ***ser***.

Modelo: You hear: ¿Cómo es María?
You see: __________ __________ inteligente.
You write: *Ella es* inteligente.

1. __________ __________ bueno.
2. __________ __________ impaciente.
3. __________ __________ extrovertida.
4. __________ __________ interesantes.
5. __________ __________ simpáticos.
6. __________ __________ tímidas.
7. __________ __________ inteligentes.
8. __________ __________ trabajador/a.

CD 1, Track 26

1-58 Susana y sus amigos. Complete the following descriptions that Susana gives of herself and her friends. Write the subjects in the first blank space and the correct form of ***ser*** in the second blank space. Then listen and repeat as the speaker gives the correct answer.

Modelo: You hear: Ella
You see: __________ __________ Lorena.
You write: *Ella es* Lorena.

1. __________ __________ Susana.
2. __________ __________ Marcos, Viviana y Juan.
3. __________ __________ estudiantes excelentes.
4. __________ __________ trabajadores.
5. __________ __________ extrovertido.
6. __________ __________ una cantante (*singer*) muy buena.
7. __________ __________ muy tímido.
8. __________ __________ pacientes.
9. Todos __________ __________ simpáticos.
10. ¿Y __________ ? ¿ __________ simpático/a?

Nombre: ______________________ Fecha: ______________________

1-59 Identidades. Use the words provided and the correct form of the verb ***ser*** to form complete sentences or questions. Remember to change the forms of articles and adjectives as necessary.

Modelo: yo / ser / alumna / puertorriqueño
Yo soy una alumna puertorriqueña.

1. nosotros / ser / profesor / interesante

____

2. Ana y Felipe / ser / estudiante / inteligente

____

3. ¿ser / tú / muchacho / aburrido?

____

4. Marisol / ser / señora / fascinante

____

5. ¿ser / ustedes / estudiantes / trabajador?

____

6. ¿ser / usted / señor / simpático?

____

7. María Eugenia / ser / señorita / tímido

____

8. Guillermo y Rodrigo / ser / muchacho / extrovertido

____

Nombre: ______________________ Fecha: ______________________

1-60 Tu propia descripción. Write five sentences describing yourself. State your origin, occupation, and some of your inherent qualities.

____

____

____

____

____

¿Cuánto sabes tú?

1-61 ¿Sabes el verbo *ser*? Match each statement on the left column with the appropriate form of *ser.*

1. Los estudiantes ____ idealistas.	a. Eres
2. El profesor ____ impaciente.	b. somos
3. Yo ____ tímido.	c. es
4. Mis amigos y yo ____ estudiantes.	d. son
5. ¿____ tú estudiante?	e. soy

1-62 ¿Sabes usar los nombres, los artículos y los adjetivos? Fill in the blanks with one of the words from the word bank.

inteligente	la	un	aburridas	trabajadora	una	interesantes	las

Hola. Me llamo Carla. Soy (1) ______________ estudiante (2) ______________ en (3)______________ universidad. Mi amigo Luis es (4) ______________ estudiante (5) ______________. ¡Nosotros somos (6)______________, pero (7) ______________ clases son (8) ______________!

Nombre: ______________________ Fecha: ______________________

CD 1, Track 27

1-63 ¿Cómo se dice? How would you accomplish the following communication tasks in Spanish? After completing each item, listen and repeat as the speaker gives the correct answer.

1. ______________________
2. ______________________
3. ______________________
4. ______________________
5. ______________________
6. ______________________

CD 1, Track 28

1-64 El primer día de clases. Write an appropriate response to the following questions or statements.

1. ______________________
2. ______________________
3. ______________________
4. ______________________
5. ______________________

Nombre: ______________________ Fecha: ______________________

Observaciones (TEXTBOOK P. 29)

Antes de ver el video

1-65 ¿Qué pasa? Select the letter of the statement that best answers each question below.

1. As the people in doña María's home begin to introduce themselves, what would you expect Felipe to say when he meets the group?

   a. Buenos días. Me llamo Felipe. ¿Cómo están?

   b. Igualmente. ¡Adiós!

   c. Hasta pronto.

2. What does Patricio likely say to Felipe when they first meet?

   a. Buenas noches. ¿Cómo están ustedes?

   b. Igualmente. ¡Hasta luego, Felipe!

   c. Hola, Felipe. Mucho gusto. Soy Patricio Rodríguez.

3. What might be the next topic they talk about?

   a. las profesiones

   b. los colores

   c. las frutas exóticas

4. What is a likely description of Silvia?

   a. Es una mujer linda.

   b. Es una mala estudiante.

   c. Es argentina.

5. Considering that Silvia is a researcher, what might she say to describe her job?

   a. Hay mapas en la mochila.

   b. Estudio el clima.

   c. Soy la mujer ideal para Felipe.

Nombre: ______________________ Fecha: ______________________

A ver el video

1-66 Los personajes. Match the names of the characters with their descriptions by writing the correct letters on the lines provided.

1. ____ biológo y guía en el parque nacional	a. Silvia
2. ____ fotógrafo, argentino	b. Patricio
3. ____ investigadora del clima	c. Marcela
4. ____ uno de los amigos, Montero	d. Felipe
5. ____ buena y simpática	e. Doña María
6. ____ una amiga de Silvia	f. Hermés

1-67 La conversación. Fill in the blanks with the missing words, according to the dialogue in the selected video segments.

Patricio: Felipe, (1) ______________ uruguayo, ¿verdad?

Felipe: Uruguayo no, (2) ______________, de papá puertorriqueño. Criado en (3) ______________ y en Estados Unidos. Vivo en Buenos Aires.

Patricio: ¿Vienes de Buenos Aires? ¿Y en (4) ______________?

Felipe: No, en (5) ______________. ¡Pero no funciona!

Patricio: ¿Cuántos (6) ______________son?

...

Silvia: Yo tengo una camioneta en España.

Felipe: ¿De verdad? ¿(7) ______________es?

Silvia: Es una alemana, (8) ______________.

Después de ver el video

1-68 La acción. Determine whether the following statements are **cierto** (C) or **falso** (F) and write the correct letter on the lines provided.

1. Las conversaciones son por la noche. ____
2. Felipe tiene que trabajar. ____
3. Patricio estudia plantas y animales. ____

4. Silvia trabaja en la universidad. ____

5. Felipe estudia el clima. ____

6. La guayaba es una fruta. ____

7. Patricio vive en Buenos Aires. ____

8. La camioneta de Felipe es negra. ____

NUESTRO MUNDO

Panoramas

1-69 ¡A informarse! Based on the information from **Nuestro mundo,** decide if the following statements are **cierto** (C) or **falso** (F).

1. Hay muchos hispanos en el suroeste de EE.UU. ____

2. En las capitales sudamericanas no hay rascacielos (*skyscrapers*). ____

3. Las capitales sudamericanas son pequeñas. ____

4. En muchas capitales hay contaminación. ____

5. Santa Fe de Bogotá es la capital de Venezuela. ____

6. El nombre de Santa Fe de Bogotá es de origen indígena y español. ____

7. En la cordillera de los Andes no hace mucho frío. ____

8. Tulum está en México. ____

Ritmos

1-70 ¡Viva la salsa! In Chapter 1, you sampled some salsa music by the Cuban group *Típica Novel*. Now visit **http://www.prenhall.com/arriba** and make a list of five famous musicians who have shaped the history of salsa music.

____

____

____

____

____

Nombre: ______________________ Fecha: ______________________

Páginas

1-71 Tu poema. Read the poem from Chapter 1 again and substitute the words in bold (nouns and adjectives) for words that you know to create your own poem. Try to be as creative as possible using the vocabulary from Chapter 1.

Cultivo una rosa **blanca,** ______________________

En **julio** como en **enero,** ______________________

Para el **amigo** sincero ______________________

Que me da (*gives*) su mano (*hand*) franca. ______________________

Y para el cruel que me arranca (*yanks out*) ______________________

El corazón (*heart*) con que vivo, ______________________

Cardo (*thistle*) ni ortiga (*nettle; a prickly plant*) cultivo: ______________________

Cultivo una rosa **blanca.** ______________________

Taller

1-72 La comunidad. Identify a native Spanish speaker at your university whom you can interview. If no native speakers are available, choose a classmate or your professor. Write four or five things you might tell or ask him/her.

Here are some suggestions:

¿Cómo te llamas? / ¿Cómo se llama usted?

¿Cuántos años tienes? / ¿Cuántos años tiene usted?

¿Eres estudiante? / ¿Es usted profesor?

¿Cómo eres? / ¿Cómo es usted?

____

____

____

____

____

Nombre: ______________________________ Fecha: ______________________

1-73 Una entrevista. Interview the person you identified by using the expressions and questions from the previous activity.

1-74 El resumen. Summarize the information you learned about the person you interviewed and write a small paragraph including one or two sentences describing his/her personality.

____

____

____

____

____

____

____

____

Nombre: ______________________ Fecha: ______________________

2 ¿De dónde eres?

Primera parte

¡Así es la vida!

2-1 ¿Cierto o falso? Reread **¡Así es la vida!** on page 40 of your textbook and indicate whether each statement is **cierto** (C) or **falso** (F).

1. José es de Salamanca. ____
2. José es estudiante en Algeciras, un puerto en el mar Mediterráneo. ____
3. Isabel es de Sevilla. ____
4. Isabel es inteligente y trabajadora, pero no es simpática. ____
5. Daniel es rubio, alto y delgado. ____
6. Daniel es de la capital de España. ____
7. Paco es del sur de España. ____
8. María es de México. ____

CD 2, Track 1

2-2 Horacio y Natalia. Listen to the following conversation between Horacio and Natalia. Then select the correct answer based on what you hear.

1. Natalia es:

   a. chilena. b. peruana. c. española.

2. Horacio es:

   a. mexicano. b. argentino. c. español.

3. Maribel es:

   a. española. b. argentina. c. chilena.

Nombre: ______________________ Fecha: ______________________

4. Maribel es:

   a. estudiante. b. profesora. c. visitante.

5. Horacio es:

   a. guapo. b. simpático. c. inteligente.

6. Maribel es amiga de:

   a. Horacio. b. Natalia. c. los padres de Natalia.

¡Así lo decimos! Vocabulario (TEXTBOOK P. 41)

2-3 Gente que lleva la contraria. Some people seem to oppose everything you say. How would they respond to each of the following statements? Match each statement with the opposite adjective.

1. Los estudiantes son pobres.
   No, son c.
2. La muchacha es bonita.
   No, es f.
3. El muchacho es alto.
   No, es d.
4. Mi amigo es delgado.
   No, es a.
5. La mochila es nueva.
   No, es g.
6. Las clases son grandes.
   No, son e.
7. La profesora es rubia.
   No, es b.

a. gordo
b. morena
c. ricos
d. bajo
e. pequeñas
f. fea
g. vieja

Nombre: ______________________ Fecha: ______________________

CD 2, Track 2

2-4 Preguntas. Listen to the following questions and then select all letters corresponding to logical answers. There may be more than one logical answer for each question.

1. a. Es la capital.
   b. Se llama Josefina.
   c. Es alto y delgado.
2. a. Están muy bien, gracias.
   b. Altos y morenos.
   c. Son bajos.
3. a. No son españoles.
   b. Sí, somos de la capital.
   c. Sí, ustedes son viejos.
4. a. Emilia es chilena.
   b. Sí, son mexicanos.
   c. Son de Barcelona.
5. a. Es una muchacha morena muy simpática.
   b. Es una universidad grande.
   c. Es mi amiga cubana.
6. a. Es de Isabel.
   b. Es de Panamá, de la capital.
   c. Son mis padres.

2-5 Nacionalidades. José explains where some of his friends and acquaintances are from. Complete each of his explanations with the correct form of the corresponding adjective of nationality.

Modelo: Luisa y Ramón son de Puerto Rico.
Son *puertorriqueños*.

1. Ana es de Colombia. Es ______________________.
2. Federico es de La Habana, Cuba. Es ______________________.
3. Nosotras somos de Buenos Aires, Argentina. Somos ______________________.
4. Alicia es de la República Dominicana. Es ______________________.
5. Los profesores son de México. Son ______________________.
6. La señora Prieto es de Caracas, Venezuela. Es ______________________.
7. Eva y Claire son de Toronto, Canadá. Son ______________________.
8. Anita y Lucía son de Panamá. Son ______________________.

Nombre: ______________________ Fecha: ______________________

2-6 El crucigrama hispano. Complete the following crossword puzzle with the correct information below.

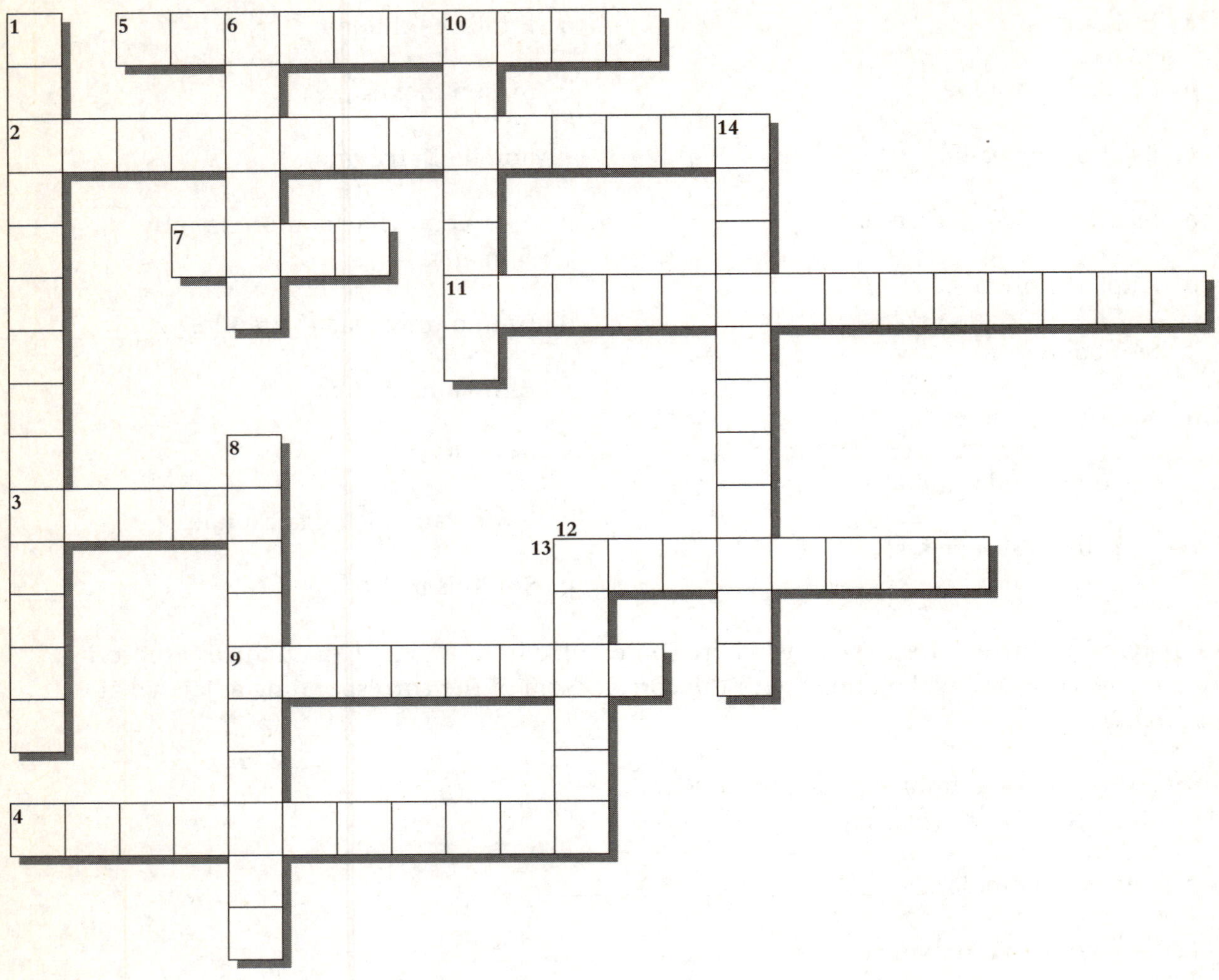

Across

2. Persona de los Estados Unidos
3. Capital de Ecuador
4. Mujer de El Salvador
5. Mujer de la República Dominicana
7. Capital de Perú
9. Hombre de México
11. Hombre de Norteamérica
13. Mujer de Panamá

Down

1. Mujer de Puerto Rico
6. Capital de España
8. Hombre de Colombia
10. Mujer de Chile
12. Capital de Panamá
14. Hombre de Ecuador

Nombre: ______________________ Fecha: ______________________

2-7 Los dos géneros. Change the gender of the words in italics and make all the necessary changes to each statement. Be sure to follow the model closely.

Modelo: El *señor* pelirrojo es mexicano.
La señorita pelirroja es mexicana.

1. El *profesor* argentino es delgado.

   ____

2. Los *amigos* morenos son norteamericanos.

   ____

3. Las *muchachas* inteligentes son panameñas.

   ____

4. La *señora* guapa es chilena.

   ____

5. El *estudiante* español es alto.

   ____

6. El *padre* es puertorriqueño y rubio.

   ____

7. Los *muchachos* son inteligentes y trabajadores.

   ____

8. La *amiga* es joven.

   ____

Nombre: ______________________ Fecha: ______________________

¡Así lo hacemos! Estructuras

1. Telling time (Textbook p. 44)

2-8 ¿Qué hora es? Match each time from the first column with the correct time from the second column. Write the correct letter on the lines provided.

1. _____ la una en punto de la tarde — a. 11:15 AM
2. _____ las diez y cuarto de la mañana — b. 9:05 AM
3. _____ las siete y media de la tarde — c. 1:00 PM
4. _____ las once y cuarto de la mañana — d. 7:30 PM
5. _____ las cinco menos cuarto de la tarde — e. 4:45 PM
6. _____ las nueve y cinco de la mañana — f. 10:15 AM

2-9 Los horarios de vuelo. Read the timetable of "AEROMEDiterráneo" and answer the following questions based on the model. Remember to spell out the times.

Modelo: ¿A qué hora es la salida del vuelo AZ1373?
La salida es a las ocho menos cinco de la mañana.

(Horarios sujetos a posibles variaciones)

AEROMEDiterráneo

España - Italia (IDA)

RUTA	VUELO	DÍAS	SALIDA	LLEGADA
MADRID-ROMA*	AZ1373	DIARIO	07:55	10:20
MADRID-ROMA*	AZ367	DIARIO	12:50	15:15
MADRID-ROMA*	AZ365	DIARIO	17:55	20:20
MADRID-MILÁN	AZ1377	DIARIO	08:15	10:20
MADRID-MILÁN	AZ1355	DIARIO	12:20	14:25
MADRID-MILÁN	AZ355	DIARIO	18:25	20:30

Teléfonos de Información y Reservas:
- Madrid-Ciudad: 559 95 00 (De lunes a viernes, de 9 a 19h.)
- Aeropuerto de Barajas: 305 43 35 (Todos los días, de 7 a 19h.)
- AEROMED Premium Program: 900 210 599 (De lunes a viernes, de 9 a 17h.)

***Más de 150 conexiones a 40 ciudades de todo el mundo.**

vuelo = *flight;* salida = *departure;* llegada = *arrival*

1. ¿A qué hora es la llegada del vuelo AZ355?

____

____

2. ¿A qué hora es la llegada del vuelo AZ1373?

____

____

3. ¿A qué hora es la llegada del vuelo AZ365?

____

____

4. ¿A qué hora es la llegada del vuelo AZ367?

____

____

5. ¿A qué hora es la salida del vuelo AZ367?

____

____

6. ¿A qué hora es la salida del vuelo AZ1377?

____

____

Nombre: ______________________________ Fecha: ____________________

CD 2, Track 3

2-10 ¿A qué hora...? You work at a travel agency and are filling in appointment slots for tomorrow's meetings. Write the name of the client you hear next to the time of the appointment.

11:00	
11:20	
12:00	
12:40	
2:30	
3:45	
4:15	

2-11 Los programas de televisión. Look at the timetable of television programs from Spain and answer the following questions following the model.

Modelo: ¿A qué hora es "Los desayunos de TVE"?
"Los desayunos de TVE" es a las nueve de la mañana.

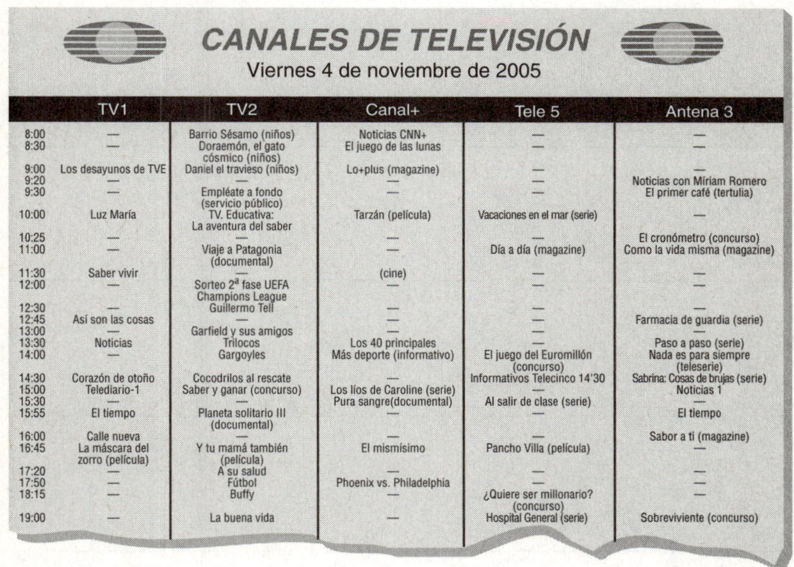

CANALES DE TELEVISIÓN
Viernes 4 de noviembre de 2005

	TV1	TV2	Canal+	Tele 5	Antena 3
8:00	—	Barrio Sésamo (niños)	Noticias CNN+	—	—
8:30	—	Doraemón, el gato cósmico (niños)	El juego de las lunas	—	—
9:00	Los desayunos de TVE	Daniel el travieso (niños)	Lo+plus (magazine)	—	—
9:20	—	—	—	—	Noticias con Míriam Romero
9:30	—	Empléate a fondo (servicio público)	—	—	El primer café (tertulia)
10:00	Luz María	TV. Educativa: La aventura del saber	Tarzán (película)	Vacaciones en el mar (serie)	—
10:25	—	—	—	—	El cronómetro (concurso)
11:00	—	Viaje a Patagonia (documental)	—	Día a día (magazine)	Como la vida misma (magazine)
11:30	Saber vivir	—	(cine)	—	—
12:00	—	Sorteo 2ª fase UEFA Champions League	—	—	—
12:30	—	Guillermo Tell	—	—	—
12:45	Así son las cosas	—	—	—	Farmacia de guardia (serie)
13:00	—	Garfield y sus amigos	—	—	—
13:30	Noticias	Trilocos	Los 40 principales	—	Paso a paso (serie)
14:00	—	Gargoyles	Más deporte (informativo)	El juego del Euromillón (concurso)	Nada es para siempre (teleserie)
14:30	Corazón de otoño	Cocodrilos al rescate	—	Informativos Telecinco 14'30	Sabrina: Cosas de brujas (serie)
15:00	Telediario-1	Saber y ganar (concurso)	Los líos de Caroline (serie)	—	Noticias 1
15:30	—	—	Pura sangre(documental)	Al salir de clase (serie)	—
15:55	El tiempo	Planeta solitario III (documental)	—	—	El tiempo
16:00	Calle nueva	—	—	—	Sabor a ti (magazine)
16:45	La máscara del zorro (película)	Y tu mamá también (película)	El mismísimo	Pancho Villa (película)	—
17:20	—	A su salud	—	—	—
17:50	—	Fútbol	Phoenix vs. Philadelphia	—	—
18:15	—	Buffy	—	¿Quiere ser millonario? (concurso)	—
19:00	—	La buena vida	—	Hospital General (serie)	Sobreviviente (concurso)

1. ¿A qué hora es *Tarzán*?

____

2. ¿A qué hora es "Saber vivir"?

____

3. ¿A qué hora es "Farmacia de guardia"?

____

4. ¿A qué hora es "El tiempo"?

____

5. ¿A qué hora es *Pancho Villa*?

____

6. ¿A qué hora es "A su salud"?

____

2. Formation of yes/no questions and negation (TEXTBOOK P. 48)

2-12 ¿No? Unscramble each group of words to form statements with tag questions.

MODELO: ¿verdad? / es / Charo / de Colombia
Charo es de Colombia, ¿verdad?

1. ¿no? / son / muy delgados / Memo y Quique

____

2. es / inteligente / la estudiante / ¿cierto?

____

3. Tere / ¿verdad? / se llama / la señora

____

4. ¿no? / es / Toño / bajo

____

5. es / ¿verdad? / Alex / panameño

____

Nombre: ______________________ Fecha: ______________________

2-13 Información equivocada. Give a negative answer to all the following questions. Then, state the correct information based on the information in parentheses.

MODELO: ¿Es Antonio Banderas mexicano?
No, Antonio Banderas no es mexicano. Antonio Banderas es español.

1. ¿Es Gloria Estefan panameña? (*Cuban*)

____

2. ¿Es Shakira argentina? (*Colombian*)

____

3. ¿Es Ricky Martin dominicano? (*Puerto Rican*)

____

4. ¿Es Penélope Cruz venezolana? (*Spanish*)

____

5. ¿Es Tiger Woods colombiano? (*American*)

____

2-14 Amigo en la Red. A new e-friend wants to get to know you better and has a list of questions for you. Answer his questions with complete statements.

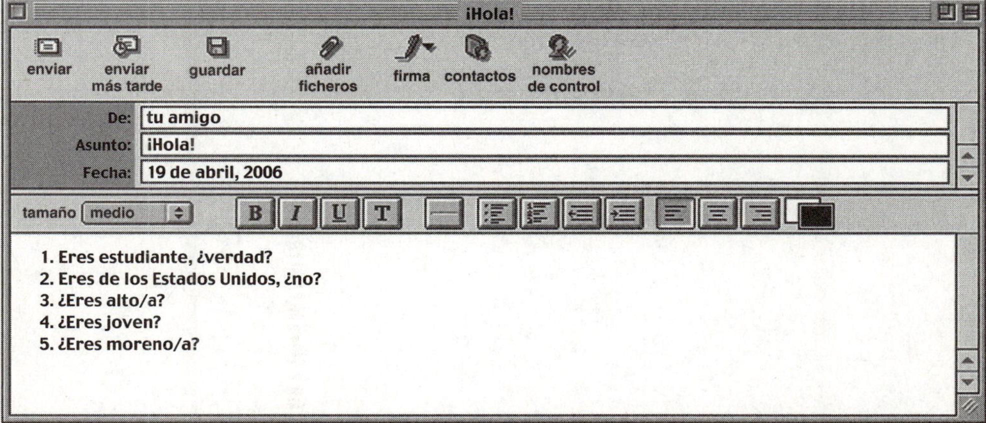

1. ______________________
2. ______________________
3. ______________________
4. ______________________
5. ______________________

Nombre: ________________________ Fecha: ________________________

CD 2, Track 4

2-15 ¿Sí o no? Create a question based on the descriptions of the following people you hear.

Modelo: You see: puertorriqueño
You hear: Usted
You write and say: *¿Es usted puertorriqueño?*

1. rubios ______________________________
2. colombiano/a ______________________________
3. ricos ______________________________
4. salvadoreñas ______________________________
5. bajo/a ______________________________
6. inteligentes ______________________________

CD 2, Track 5

2-16 No, no y no. Answer the following questions negatively. Then listen and repeat as the speaker gives the correct answer.

Modelo: You hear: Es usted ecuatoriana?
You write and say: *No, yo no soy ecuatoriana.*

1. ______________________________
2. ______________________________
3. ______________________________
4. ______________________________
5. ______________________________
6. ______________________________

Nombre: ______________________ Fecha: ______________________

3. Interrogative words (Textbook p. 50)

2-17 ¿Cuáles son las preguntas? You heard the answers in an interview but didn't catch the questions. Select the letter of the question that prompted each response.

Modelo: Soy Antonio Ramírez.
¿Quién es usted?

1. Soy de Santiago de Compostela.
   a. ¿Quién es usted?
   b. ¿De dónde es usted?
   c. ¿Cómo es usted?
   d. ¿Qué es usted?
2. El profesor es muy simpático.
   a. ¿Quién es el profesor?
   b. ¿De dónde es el profesor?
   c. ¿Cómo es el profesor?
   d. ¿Qué es el profesor?
3. Los estudiantes de la clase son inteligentes.
   a. ¿Cómo se llaman los estudiantes?
   b. ¿Quiénes son los estudiantes?
   c. ¿De dónde son los estudiantes?
   d. ¿Cómo son los estudiantes?
4. La mochila es de Raúl.
   a. ¿Cómo es la mochila?
   b. ¿De dónde es Raúl?
   c. ¿Cómo es Raúl?
   d. ¿De quién es la mochila?
5. Los estudiantes venezolanos son Carlos, Andrés y Rafael.
   a. ¿De dónde son los estudiantes?
   b. ¿Quiénes son los estudiantes venezolanos?
   c. ¿Cómo son los estudiantes venezolanos?
   d. ¿Qué son los estudiantes venezolanos?
6. La clase es a las dos de la tarde.
   a. ¿Cómo es la clase?
   b. ¿Cuándo es la clase?
   c. ¿Cuál es la clase?
   d. ¿Dónde es la clase?

CD 2, Track 6

2-18 Más preguntas. Match the letter of the statements you hear to the questions that would logically precede them.

1. ¿De dónde es María? _____
2. ¿Cómo es la profesora? _____
3. ¿Cómo son Víctor y Paco? _____
4. ¿Quién es Javier? _____
5. ¿Cuándo es la clase? _____
6. ¿Cuál es la capital de Colombia? _____

Nombre: ______________________ Fecha: ______________________

2-19 Muchas preguntas. Imagine that you have just met Susana at a party and are trying to get to know her. Taking into consideration her answers, complete each question with the most appropriate interrogative word/s from the word bank. You will have to use one of the words twice.

qué	cuál	de dónde	cómo	quién	dónde	quiénes

1. ¿______________ te llamas?

   Me llamo Susana.

2. ¿______________ eres?

   Soy de los Estados Unidos.

3. ¿______________ estudias?

   En la universidad.

4. ¿______________ estudias?

   Historia y matemáticas.

5. ¿ ______________ es tu ciudad ?

   Mi ciudad es Houston.

6. ¿______________ son estas (*these*) personas en la foto?

   Son mis padres y Antonio.

7. ¿ ______________ es Antonio?

   Es un amigo.

8. ¿ ______________ es?

   Es alto, delgado y muy simpático.

2-20 Decisiones. For each question, decide whether *qué* or *cuál(es)* is the most appropriate answer.

Modelo: ¿*Qué* hora es?

1. ¿ ______________ de los estudiantes es Cheo?
2. ¿ ______________ son tus clases interesantes?
3. ¿______________ hay en la clase de español?
4. ¿______________ hora es?
5. ¿______________ día es hoy?
6. ¿______________ es el libro de español?

Nombre: ______________________ Fecha: ______________

CD 2, Track 7

2-21 A contestar. Answer the questions you hear using the cues given below. Then listen and repeat as the speaker gives the correct answer.

Modelo: You hear: ¿Cuándo es la clase?
You see: mañana
You write and say: *La clase es mañana.*

1. inteligente ______________________
2. jueves ______________________
3. Pamplona ______________________
4. simpático ______________________
5. Madrid ______________________

2-22 En la cafetería. Imagine that you have just met someone in the cafeteria. He asks you the following questions. How would you answer? Use complete sentences.

1. ¿Cómo te llamas? ______________________
2. ¿De qué país eres? ______________________
3. ¿De qué ciudad eres? ______________________
4. ¿Cómo eres? ______________________
5. ¿Cómo es tu clase de español? ______________________
6. ¿De dónde es el/la profesor/a de español? ______________________

¿Cuánto sabes tú?

2-23 ¿Sabes qué hora es? On the lines provided, write the letter of the digital time that matches the time spelled out in words.

1. _____ mediodía — a. 7:40
2. _____ las tres y diez — b. 12:00 PM
3. _____ las ocho menos cuarto — c. 3:15
4. _____ las ocho y media — d. 7:45
5. _____ las tres y cuarto — e. 12:00 AM
6. _____ las ocho menos veinte — f. 8:30
7. _____ medianoche — g. 3:10

Nombre: ______________________ Fecha: ______________________

🔊 CD 2, Track 8

2-24 Ideas completas. Select the letter that best completes the statement.

1. a. a las diez.
   b. son las diez.
   c. diez.
2. a. panameña.
   b. jóvenes.
   c. peruanos.
3. a. un país.
   b. una ciudad pequeña.
   c. la capital de España.
4. a. son las tres.
   b. ahora.
   c. en punto.
5. a. morenos.
   b. viejo.
   c. simpáticas.

2-25 ¿Sabes preguntar? For each question, select the letter of the most logical interrogative word.

1. ¿__________ se llama tu amigo?
   a. Cuántos b. Cómo
2. ¿__________ años tiene él?
   a. Cuántos b. Por qué
3. ¿__________ es tu amigo?
   a. De dónde b. Dónde
4. ¿__________ estudia él?
   a. De quién b. Qué
5. ¿__________ es la novia de tu amigo?
   a. Cómo b. Cuántos
6. ¿__________ vive tu amigo?
   a. Dónde b. De dónde

🔊 CD 2, Track 9

2-26 Preguntas personales. Answer the following personal questions in Spanish using complete sentences.

1. ____.
2. ____.
3. ____.
4. ____.
5. ____.
6. ____.

Nombre: ______________________ Fecha: ______________________

Segunda parte

¡Así es la vida!

2-27 Nuevos amigos. Look again at page 54 of your textbook and reread the dialogue. Then select the letter of the correct answer to each question.

1. ¿Qué idiomas habla Celia?
   a. inglés
   b. inglés y español
   c. inglés, español y francés
   d. francés y español

2. ¿Qué estudia Celia?
   a. matemáticas
   b. biología
   c. ciencias
   d. idiomas

3. ¿Cuándo es el examen de alemán?
   a. hoy
   b. esta tarde
   c. mañana por la mañana
   d. mañana por la tarde

4. Para recibir ayuda, ¿con quién debe hablar Celia?
   a. la secretaria
   b. Rogelio
   c. el profesor
   d. una amiga

5. ¿Cuándo estudia Rogelio con los amigos?
   a. los lunes
   b. los lunes y miércoles
   c. mañana
   d. los lunes, miércoles y viernes

6. ¿Qué hace Rogelio esta noche?
   a. Va a la cafetería.
   b. Estudia con sus amigos.
   c. Asiste a clase.
   d. Asiste a un concierto.

Nombre: ______________________ Fecha: ______________________

CD 2, Track 10

2-28 La conversación. Listen to the following conversation among three students at the university cafeteria. Then select all letters corresponding to statements that are correct according to what you hear.

1. Ana está…
   a. mal.
   b. bien.
   c. más o menos.
2. Manuel está…
   a. más o menos.
   b. bien.
   c. muy mal.
3. Manuel…
   a. estudia y trabaja.
   b. practica fútbol.
   c. practica tenis.
4. Ana…
   a. tiene un examen mañana.
   b. camina.
   c. practica tenis.
5. Ana…
   a. baila en la fiesta.
   b. estudia alemán.
   c. trabaja con Pedro.
6. Manuel y Pedro son…
   a. portugueses.
   b. estudiantes.
   c. mexicanos.
7. Manuel, Pedro y Ana son…
   a. amigos.
   b. feos.
   c. profesores.
8. Pedro…
   a. estudia y trabaja.
   b. practica béisbol.
   c. no estudia.

Nombre: ______________________ Fecha: ______________________

¡Así lo decimos! Vocabulario (Textbook p. 55)

2-29 Actividades. Match each activity with the most logical expression.

1. _____ escuchar	a. en un apartamento
2. _____ hablar	b. deportes
3. _____ nadar	c. historia en la universidad
4. _____ vivir	d. español, italiano y francés
5. _____ ver	e. música clásica
6. _____ estudiar	f. la televisión
7. _____ practicar	g. en el mar
8. _____ preparar	h. una pizza

2-30 ¡A practicar deportes (1)! Match the following drawings with the name of the sport.

1. _____

2. _____

3. _____

4. _____

a. tenis

b. baloncesto

c. fútbol

d. natación

Nombre: ______________________ Fecha: ______________________

2-31 Fuera de lugar. Select the letter of the word that does not belong in each group.

1. a. baloncesto b. francés c. italiano d. ruso
2. a. tenis b. salvadoreño c. natación d. fútbol
3. a. estudiar b. leer c. viajar d. escribir
4. a. trabajar b. practicar c. estudiar d. fácil
5. a. bailar b. creer c. caminar d. nadar

CD 2, Track 11

2-32 Los amigos y las clases. Select the letter corresponding to the most logical answer to each question you hear. Then listen and repeat as the speaker gives the correct answer.

1. a. Sí, hablo francés.
   b. No, hablo francés.
   c. Sí, hablas alemán.
2. a. No, trabajamos por las tardes.
   b. Sí, practicas fútbol.
   c. Sí, nadamos por las tardes.
3. a. Sí, estudia todos los días.
   b. Sí, tiene un examen.
   c. Sí, estudia historia.
4. a. Esta noche camino con él.
   b. Converso con él en español.
   c. Miro los libros y converso un poco.
5. a. Estudio esta noche y mañana.
   b. Estudian con amigos.
   c. Estudiamos idiomas.
6. a. Leemos por la tarde.
   b. Leen en la cafetería.
   c. Leemos y practicamos tenis.
7. a. Aprendo mucho en la clase.
   b. No recibo muchos correos electrónicos.
   c. ¡Bailo con mis amigas!

Nombre: ______________________________ Fecha: ______________________

2-33 ¡A practicar deportes (2)! Answer the questions following the model. If you do not practice each of these sports, try to name someone who does!

Modelo: ¿Practicas baloncesto?
Sí, practico baloncesto. or
No, no practico baloncesto, pero Shaquille O'Neal practica baloncesto.

1. ¿Practicas tenis?

____

2. ¿Practicas fútbol americano?

____

3. ¿Practicas béisbol?

____

4. ¿Practicas natación?

____

5. ¿Practicas fútbol?

____

Letras y sonidos (Textbook p. 57)

CD 2, Track 12

2-34 Glides. Determine whether the word you hear contains a glide (a brief sound combined with a vowel to form one syllable) and identify the syllable where it falls in the word.

1. ____________________
2. ____________________
3. ____________________
4. ____________________
5. ____________________

CD 2, Track 13

2-35 Completamos la palabra. Complete the word with the corresponding vowel combination. Some vowels are accented.

1. est _____
2. h _____
3. l _____ n
4. Mar_____
5. natac_____n

Nombre: ______________________ Fecha: ______________________

¡Así lo hacemos! Estructuras

4. The present tense of regular *-ar* verbs (Textbook p. 57)

2-36 ¿Qué hacen? Complete each sentence with the correct form of the verb in parentheses.

1. Nosotros (caminar) ______________________ por las tardes.
2. Los estudiantes (preparar) ______________________ la lección.
3. ¿(Trabajar) ______________________ tú mucho?
4. Los muchachos (nadar) ______________________ bien.
5. Alejandro y yo (practicar) ______________________ fútbol.
6. ¿Qué (mirar) ______________________ ellos?
7. Ana y Federico (bailar) ______________________ muy mal.
8. Los amigos (conversar) ______________________ en la cafetería.
9. Amalia y Laura (estudiar) ______________________ español.
10. Yo (escuchar) ______________________ música popular.

CD 2, Track 14

2-37 ¿Cuándo y quién? Complete the sentences with subjects you hear and supply the corresponding form of the verb provided. Then listen and repeat as the speaker gives the correct answer.

Modelo: You see: ______________________ un e-milio. (escribir)
You hear: Yo
You write and say: *Yo escribo* un e-milio.

1. ________________ ________________ música peruana. (escuchar)
2. ________________ ________________ todos los días. (nadar)
3. ________________ ________________ a Bolivia en el verano. (viajar)
4. ________________ ________________ con la profesora. (conversar)
5. ¿Cuándo ________________ ________________? (regresar)
6. ________________ ________________ a las tres de la tarde. (trabajar)
7. ________________ ________________ básquetbol. (practicar)

Nombre: ______________________ Fecha: ______________________

CD 2, Track 15

2-38 Más actividades. Answer the following questions using the words provided. Then listen and repeat as the speaker gives the correct answer.

MODELO: You hear: ¿Practican ustedes fútbol?
You see: Sí, ______________ fútbol.
You write and say: Sí, *nosotros practicamos* fútbol.

1. No, ______________ no ______________ en la clase de español.
2. No, ______________ ______________ por la tarde.
3. Sí, ______________ ______________ japonés.
4. Sí, ______________ ______________ mañana.
5. Sí, ______________ ______________una universidad grande.
6. No, ______________ ______________ cuatro clases.
7. Sí, ______________ ______________ bien el español.
8. No, ______________ ______________ comprar una calculadora.
9. No, ______________ no ______________ ruso.
10. Sí, ______________ ______________ la lección.

2-39 ¡A combinar! Combine elements from the three columns below to form logical sentences.

Yo	viajamos	música
Tú	hablan	en el mar
Mi amigo	nado	a Hawaii
Mis padres y yo	escucha	en la universidad
Ustedes	estudias	inglés y español

1. ______________________________
2. ______________________________
3. ______________________________
4. ______________________________
5. ______________________________

Nombre: ______________________________ Fecha: ______________________

2-40 ¿Te gusta? Look at the following drawings and state whether you like or dislike each action. Then think of a friend or relative that might like or dislike each action. Follow the model.

MODELO:

A mí me gusta practicar tenis.
A mi amigo Luis no le gusta practicar tenis.

1. ______________________________
____
____
____

2. ______________________________
____
____
____

3. ______________________________
____
____
____

4. ______________________________
____
____
____

Nombre: ______________________ Fecha: ______________________

5. The present tense of regular *-er* and *-ir* verbs (Textbook p. 60)

2-41 Hacemos mucho. Everyone is busy today. Describe what each person is doing with the correct form of each verb in parentheses.

1. Adela (asistir) ____________________ a la clase de francés.
2. Yo (escribir) ____________________ una composición.
3. Mis padres (leer) ____________________ un libro.
4. Mi hermanita (aprender) ____________________ a bailar.
5. Ustedes (comer)____________________ en la cafetería.
6. Mi amigo (abrir) ____________________ la puerta de la biblioteca.
7. Nosotros (decidir) ____________________ estudiar español.
8. Pancho y yo (vivir) ____________________ en la universidad.

2-42 Mis amigas. Complete the description of three friends with the correct form of the verb in parentheses.

Mis amigas Bárbara, Isabel y Victoria (1) ____________________ (vivir) en la residencia estudiantil. Ellas (2) ____________________ (aprender) inglés en la universidad y (3) ____________________ (asistir) a clase por la mañana. Isabel y Bárbara (4) ____________________ (escribir) inglés muy bien, pero Victoria no (5) ____________________ (leer) inglés muy bien. Al mediodía, cuando la cafetería (6) ____________________ (abrir), ellas (7) ____________________ (comer) allí. Yo también (8) ____________________ (comer) con ellas en la cafeteria y todos los días nosotros hablamos sobre las clases. Ellas (9) ____________________ (creer) que es difícil aprender inglés, pero (ellas) practican todos los días. Y tú, (10) ____________________ (creer) que es difícil aprender español?

CD 2, Track 16

2-43 Muchas actividades. Complete each sentence with the correct form of the verb you hear. Then listen and repeat the sentence as the speaker gives the correct answer.

Modelo: You see: Nosotros ____________________ un examen mañana.
You hear: tener
You write and say: Nosotros *tenemos* un examen mañana.

1. Yo ____________________ que son las tres.
2. Los tutores ____________________ muy bien la lección.

3. Rafael ____________ muy bien.

4. ¿ ____________ tus libros al final del semestre?

5. Ellos ____________ el laboratorio a las ocho.

6. Victoria y yo ____________ beber café.

CD 2, Track 17

2-44 Nosotros... Answer the questions you hear using the **nosotros** form of the verb and the cues provided. Then listen and repeat as the speaker gives the correct answer.

1. Sí, ____________ bien.
2. ____________ mucho vocabulario en la clase.
3. ____________ en la computadora.
4. ____________ la Lección 2.
5. ____________ a clase los martes y jueves.
6. Sí, ____________ los libros en diciembre.
7. ____________ en Bilbao.

2-45 Preguntas y respuestas. Answer each question regarding your university and your Spanish class in complete sentences.

1. ¿A qué universidad asistes?

   ____

2. ¿A qué hora abren la biblioteca de tu universidad?

   ____

3. ¿Comes en la cafetería de la universidad todos los días?

   ____

4. ¿Aprenden los estudiantes a hablar en la clase de español?

   ____

5. ¿Escribes composiciones en tu clase de español?

   ____

6. ¿Crees que es importante aprender español?

   ____

6. The present tense of *tener* (TEXTBOOK P. 63)

2-46 Dibujos y obligaciones. Match the following drawings with the most appropriate statement.

1. ____ 

2. ____ 

3. ____ 

4. ____ 

5. ____ 

a. Tiene que preparar la comida (*food*).

b. Tiene que ayudar a su madre.

c. Tiene dinero.

d. Tiene que beber agua.

e. Tienen que comprar un carro nuevo.

2-47 Tener. Complete each statement by selecting the letter of the correct form of ***tener.***

1. Tú ______________ clase todos los días.

   a. tengo

   b. tienes

   c. tienen

2. Él y yo ______________ que estudiar esta noche.

   a. tienes

   b. tienen

   c. tenemos

3. Merche y Lola ______________ dos clases esta tarde.

   a. tienen

   b. tengo

   c. tiene

4. Usted ______________ novio/a, ¿no?

   a. tiene

   b. tenemos

   c. tengo

5. Nosotras ______________ que hablar con Quique.

   a. tienes

   b. tienen

   c. tenemos

6. Yo ______________ muchos amigos en la universidad.

   a. tiene

   b. tengo

   c. tener

Nombre: ______________________ Fecha: ______________________

CD 2, Track 18

2-48 ¿Qué tienen? Use the appropriate form of ***tener*** to tell what the following people have. Then listen and repeat as the speaker gives the correct answer.

MODELO: You see: __________ __________ padres liberales.
You hear: ustedes
You write and say: *Ustedes tienen* padres liberales.

1. __________ no __________ mi mochila hoy.
2. __________ __________ muchas ciudades bonitas.
3. __________ __________ muchos bolígrafos rojos.
4. __________ __________ cinco clases, ¿verdad?
5. __________ __________ una clase interesante.
6. __________ no __________ profesores jóvenes.
7. __________ __________ tres libros en la mochila.

2-49 Responsabilidades. List three things you have to do tomorrow and three things other people have to do.

MODELO: *Yo tengo que estudiar.*

1. Yo ______________________________.
2. Yo ______________________________.
3. Yo ______________________________.
4. Mis padres ______________________________.
5. Mi amigo ______________________________.
6. El/La profesor/a ______________________________.

CD 2, Track 19

2-50 ¿Qué tienen que hacer? Based on the drawings, tell what the people you hear have to do.

1. ______________________________

______________________________.

2. ______________________________

______________________________.

Nombre: ______________________ Fecha: ______________________

3. ____.

4. ____.

¿Cuánto sabes tú?

CD 2, Track 20

2-51 Acciones. Select the letter that best answers the question you hear.

1. a. Tengo que conversar con mi profesora de alemán.
   b. Debemos practicar tenis.
   c. Tienes que aprender idiomas.
2. a. Mis padres venden diccionarios.
   b. Vives en una ciudad estupenda.
   c. Viven en la capital.
3. a. Debo estudiar francés y español.
   b. Debo estudiar natación y básquetbol.
   c. Debo estudiar italiano y tenis.
4. a. Es mediodía.
   b. Por la mañana.
   c. Son las cinco de la tarde.
5. a. Sí, trabajo todos los días.
   b. No, no trabajamos.
   c. Trabajas mucho en la clase.

Nombre: ________________________________ Fecha: ______________________

2-52 Mi vida en la universidad. Fill in the blank with the appropriate form of the verbs from the word bank. You will have to use one of them twice.

estudiar asistir aprender enseñar comer practicar nadar regresar vivir

Yo (1) ________________ en la universidad. Todos los días yo (2) ________________ a mis clases. (Yo) (3) ________________ mucho en mis clases porque los profesores (4) ________________ muy bien. Mis amigos y yo (5) ________________ en la cafetería al mediodía. Después, nosotros (6) ________________ tenis y (7) ________________ en la piscina *(pool)* de la universidad. A las cinco de la tarde nosotros (8) ________________ a casa. Yo (9) ________________ con mis padres pero ellos (10) ________________ en un apartamento cerca del campus universitario.

2-53 Obligaciones y posesiones. Fill in the blank with the appropriate form of ***tener.***

1. Anita y Lupe ________________ que trabajar esta tarde.
2. Anita ________________ muchas clases en la universidad.
3. Lupe________________ mucha tarea.
4. Yo ________________ que ayudar a Anita con su tarea.
5. Nosotros________________ un examen mañana.

CD 2, Track 21

2-54 Otras preguntas personales. Answer the following personal questions in Spanish using complete sentences.

1. ____.
2. ____.
3. ____.
4. ____.
5. ____.
6. ____.

Observaciones

Antes de ver el video

2-55 ¿Qué pasa? Select the letter of the statement that best answers each question below.

1. What do you think Marcela likes about Costa Rica?
   a. las ciudades rusas
   b. la gente y sus costumbres
   c. el béisbol y el fútbol

2. Hermes is Cuban. What is a possible statement about his family?
   a. Soy de Costa Rica, un país de Centroamérica.
   b. Mi familia es de los Estados Unidos.
   c. Tengo una hermana en La Habana.

3. Why is he at the hostel?
   a. Prefiere Costa Rica y le gusta la gente costarricense.
   b. El béisbol es su deporte favorito.
   c. Es un hombre inteligente.

4. What does Felipe have to do before he can go to México D.F.?
   a. jugar al fútbol
   b. tomar unas fotos
   c. arreglar su camioneta

Nombre: ______________________ Fecha: ______________________

A ver el video

2-56 Los personajes. Write the letter of each character on the line next to his/her country of origin.

1. _____ Costa Rica	a. Silvia
2. _____ España	b. Patricio
3. _____ México	c. Marcela
4. _____ Colombia	d. Felipe
5. _____ Cuba	e. Doña María
6. _____ Argentina	f. Hermés

2-57 La conversación. Fill in the blanks with the missing words according to the dialogue in the selected segments.

Marcela: Estudio (1) ______________________ en México D.F., la capital. México es un país grande, con muchas ruinas (2) ______________________ y aztecas.

...

Silvia: Patricio y Felipe son muy (3) ______________________, pero Hermés es mi favorito... Es muy (4) ______________________.

...

Marcela: Felipe es de todas partes. ¡Ay Felipe! ¡Felipito! ¡Es mi príncipe azul! ¡Tan (5) ______________________!

...

Patricio: Silvia es española... Además, Silvia habla cinco (6) ______________________: francés, inglés, alemán, español... y (7) ______________________.

...

Felipe: Patricio es un buen (8) ______________________. Trabaja en el Parque Nacional Braulio Carrillo.

2-58 Preferencias. Throughout the video you will hear the characters talking about what they and their friends like or like to do. Listen for expressions such as **me gusta, me encanta, me fascina, me interesa** and write the name of the person next to his/her preference.

1. ______________ tener jóvenes alegres en casa
2. ______________ estar en el hostal
3. ______________ la gente y las costumbres de Costa Rica; la historia
4. ______________ el fútbol
5. ______________ la música y el béisbol
6. ______________ hablar con Patricio

Después de ver el video

2-59 Más información. Next to each country, write the name of the city or cities that are mentioned in the video.

PAÍSES	CIUDADES
1. Costa Rica	______________
2. Colombia	______________
3. México	______________
4. Cuba	______________ y ______________

Nombre: ______________________ Fecha: ______________________

Nuestro mundo

Panoramas

2-60 ¡A informarse! Based on the information from **Nuestro mundo,** decide if the following statements are **cierto** (C) or **falso** (F).

1. La pesca *(fishing)* en España es muy mala. ____
2. Andalucía es importante por el cultivo de aceitunas. ____
3. SEAT es un coche *(car)* grande. ____
4. Santiago Calatrava es un pintor. ____
5. L'Hemisfèric está en Valencia. ____
6. La Costa del Sol está en el norte de España. ____
7. El turismo es muy importante para la economía española. ____
8. Pedro Almodóvar es un director de cine. ____

2-61 Más información sobre España. Look at the map of Spain and write the letter of the different regions described below.

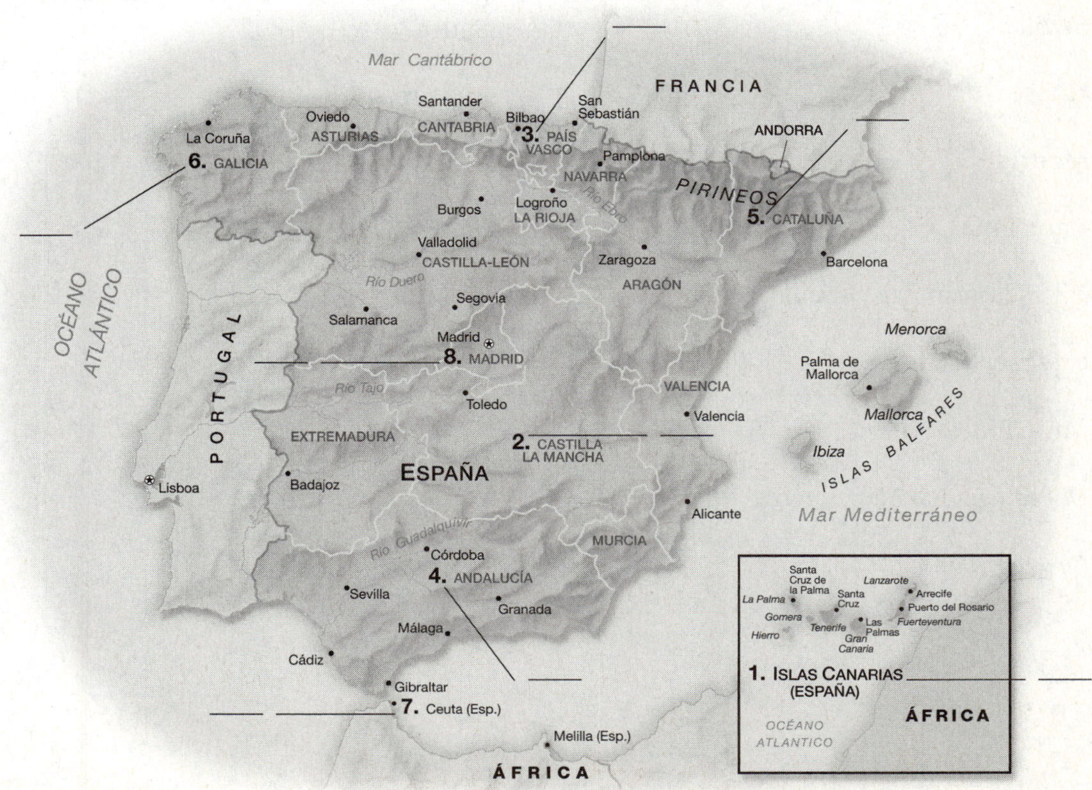

a. Región famosa por el cultivo de aceitunas

b. Región famosa por Don Quijote

c. Región donde la gente habla gallego

d. Región donde la gente habla euskera

e. Región donde la gente habla catalán

f. Islas en la costa de África

g. Capital de España

h. Ciudad española en el norte de África

Ritmos

2-62 El flamenco y el cine. You have already learned some information about flamenco and the musical group *Tachú*. Now visit **www.prenhall.com/arriba** and answer the following questions about Carlos Saura and flamenco in the movies.

1. ¿Quién es Carlos Saura?
   a. un cantante de flamenco
   b. un pintor
   c. un director de cine
   d. un actor

2. ¿De dónde es Carlos Saura?
   a. Sevilla
   b. Huesca
   c. Madrid
   d. Barcelona

3. ¿Cuál es la primera película de Saura?
   a. *Cría cuervos,* 1975
   b. *¡Ay, Carmela!,* 1990
   c. *El Pequeño Río Manzanares,* 1956
   d. *Carmen,* 1983

4. ¿Qué película de Saura recibió (*received*) el Premio Goya en 1990?
   a. *Cría cuervos*
   b. *¡Ay, Carmela!*
   c. *Bodas de sangre*
   d. *Carmen*

5. ¿Cómo se llama el primer documental de Saura?
   a. *Carmen*
   b. *El amor brujo*
   c. *Cuenca*
   d. *¡Ay, Carmela!*

Páginas

2-63 Los "e-milios". Based on the information from the **Páginas** section of the text, decide if the following statements are **cierto** (C) or **falso** (F).

1. En España no hay carteros (*mail carriers*). ____
2. Un "e-milio" es un correo electrónico. ____
3. Las oficinas del Departamento de Correos están abiertas veinticuatro horas al día. ____
4. Mandar una carta en España cuesta 28 céntimos. ____
5. Mandar una carta electrónica es gratis. ____
6. El príncipe Felipe de España es muy cibernético. ____

Taller

2-64 La vida de Maribel. Read the description of Maribel, and then answer the questions.

Maribel es una estudiante muy buena en la Universidad de Navarra. Es de Bilbao. Tiene veinte años y es inteligente y muy trabajadora. Habla tres idiomas: español, inglés y francés. Estudia derecho en la universidad y participa en muchas otras actividades. Nada por las tardes y también practica fútbol. Hoy tiene que estudiar mucho porque tiene un examen de derecho mañana. Ella también tiene una clase de francés. No hay muchos estudiantes en la clase, solamente nueve: tres españoles, dos chilenos, un italiano, dos portugueses y ella. La profesora es muy simpática. Siempre prepara bien la lección para la clase.

1. ¿Quién es Maribel? ______________________

   ____

2. ¿Dónde estudia? ¿Qué estudia? ______________________

   ____

3. ¿En qué actividades participa Maribel? ______________________

   ____

4. ¿Cuántos estudiantes hay en la clase de francés? ______________________

   ____

5. ¿Cuáles son las nacionalidades de los estudiantes y de Maribel? ______________________

   ____

6. ¿Cómo es la profesora de francés? ____________________

____

7. ¿Cuántos años tiene Maribel? ____________________

____

8. ¿Qué tiene que hacer Maribel hoy? ____________________

____

2-65 La entrevista. Now use the questions about Maribel as models for questions to interview a classmate. Write at least five questions that you can ask. Try to complete a student information card for him/her with the information you obtain.

1. ____________________
2. ____________________
3. ____________________
4. ____________________
5. ____________________

2-66 Tu vida universitaria. Using the description about Maribel as a model, write a brief paragraph about yourself and your life in school. Be sure to include your age, description, activities, and responsibilities. First, fill in the necessary information for your student identification card.

Nombre: ____________ Apellido: ____________

Nacionalidad: ____________ Edad (*age*): ____________

Ciudad: ____________ País: ____________

Descripción física: ____________________

____

____

____

____

____

____

Nombre: ______________________ Fecha: ______________________

3 ¿Qué estudias?

Primera parte

¡Así es la vida!

CD 3, Track 1

3-1 Después de la clase de física. Listen to the following conversation. Then select the letters for all statements that are correct according to the dialogue.

1. Ricardo y Teresa hablan...
   a. de las clases.
   b. en la universidad.
   c. con un amigo.
2. Teresa toma... este semestre.
   a. cuatro materias
   b. tres materias
   c. psicología
3. Ricardo toma... este semestre.
   a. cinco materias
   b. tres materias por la mañana
   c. tres materias por la noche
4. La profesora Corrales es...
   a. profesora de música.
   b. simpática.
   c. aburrida.
5. Ricardo tiene que...
   a. estudiar en la biblioteca.
   b. trabajar en la cafetería.
   c. conversar con la profesora.

Nombre: ______________________________ Fecha: ______________________

3-2 ¿Recuerdas? Reread the conversation in **¡Así es la vida!** on page 76 of your textbook and answer the questions with complete sentences in Spanish.

1. ¿Qué miran Carmen y Pedro?

   ____

2. ¿Qué materias tiene Carmen?

   ____

3. ¿Cómo es el horario de Carmen?

   ____

4. ¿Cuántas materias tiene que tomar Pedro?

   ____

5. ¿Quién tiene hambre?

   ____

6. ¿Por qué no tienen tiempo para comer?

   ____

7. ¿A qué hora es la clase de biología?

   ____

8. ¿Qué tiene que comprar Carmen?

   ____

Nombre: ______________________ Fecha: ______________________

¡Así lo decimos! Vocabulario (TEXTBOOK P. 77)

3-3 Emparejamientos (*Matching*). Make the most logical associations between the two columns of words below.

1. _____ el cálculo
2. _____ la química
3. _____ la veterinaria
4. _____ las finanzas
5. _____ la historia
6. _____ los idiomas
7. _____ el arte
8. _____ el inglés

a. los animales
b. el diccionario
c. el dinero
d. Shakespeare
e. la calculadora
f. 1776
g. Picasso
h. H_2O

3-4 Gustos e intereses. Look at the list of classes below and place them in the right column based on your likes and dislikes.

las ciencias políticas	la contabilidad	la educación física	la física
la geografía	la geología	las lenguas	la literatura
las matemáticas	la psicología		

ME GUSTA(N)	NO ME GUSTA(N)
la psicolgía	______________
las matemáticas	______________
las lenguas	______________
______________	______________
______________	______________

Nombre: ______________________________ Fecha: ______________________

3-5 En la universidad. Listen to the questions and select the letter that corresponds to the most logical answer. Then listen and repeat as the speaker gives the correct answer.

1. a. En la biblioteca yo estudio álgebra.
   b. Contabilidad, cálculo, finanzas e inglés.
   c. Las clases de álgebra y química son exigentes.
2. a. Sí, es una materia complicada.
   b. No chico, no estudio los domingos.
   c. Sí, hablo con la profesora.
3. a. Es a las nueve en punto.
   b. Son a las nueve de la mañana.
   c. Mi reloj tiene las nueve en punto.
4. a. Alemán y diseño.
   b. Portugués y coreano.
   c. Cálculo y ruso.
5. a. Estudio todos los días.
   b. Sí, tengo una clase a las nueve.
   c. Estudiamos en el centro estudiantil.
6. a. Necesito un libro de la biblioteca.
   b. Hablo con mi profesora de literatura después de la clase.
   c. Tengo que comprar una novela para mi clase de literatura.

Nombre: ______________________ Fecha: ______________________

3-6 Las carreras. Based on each statement, fill in the blank with the major of each student. Choose from the word bank provided.

medicina	administración de empresas	ciencias sociales	lenguas
matemáticas	pedagogía	arquitectura	

1. Pedro tiene clase de contabilidad y clase de finanzas.

   La carrera de Pedro es ____________________.

2. Ana tiene clase de álgebra y clase de cálculo.

   La carrera de Ana es ____________________.

3. Roberto tiene clase de arte y clase de diseño.

   La carrera de Roberto es ____________________.

4. Carmen tiene clase de biología y clase de química.

   La carrera de Carmen es ____________________.

5. Luisa tiene clase de historia y clase de sociología.

   La carrera de Luisa es ____________________.

6. Eduardo tiene clase de ruso y clase de francés.

   La carrera de Eduardo es ____________________.

7. Manuel tiene clase de psicología y clase de inglés.

   La carrera de Manuel es ____________________.

3-7 Tu horario de clases. Complete the chart to show your class schedule for this semester.

NOMBRE: ______________________ FECHA: ______________

	9 A.M.	10 A.M.	11 A.M.	12 A.M.	1 P.M.	2 P.M.	3 P.M.	4 P.M.	5 P.M.	6 P.M.
lun.										
mar.										
miér.										
jue.										
vier.										

¡Así lo hacemos! Estructuras

1. The numbers 101–3,000,000 (TEXTBOOK P. 81)

CD 3, Track 3

3-8 La puntuación máxima. Listen to the following dialogue about the high score (*la puntuación máxima*) that different friends have on a video game. Write the number that corresponds to the person's name. Then listen and repeat the numbers in the correct order.

1. Juan Rafael ______________________
2. María Luisa ______________________
3. José Antonio ______________________
4. Ana María ______________________
5. Diego ______________________

3-9 El recuento. The state has asked all higher-education institutions to make a joint inventory of several items. Spell out the numbers for each item in Spanish. Remember to watch for agreement.

1. 1.623 mil seiscientas veintitrés calculadoras f
2. 5.566 Cinco mil quinientos el → sesenta y seis escritorios m
3. 12.397 ______________________ computadoras f
4. 799 ______________________ microscopios m
5. 581 ______________________ fotocopiadoras f
6. 1.500.000 ______________________ libros m
7. 2.740 ______________________ clases f
8. 4.388 ______________________ relojes m

3 doce mil trescientas noventa y siete
4. setecientos noventa y nueve
5. quinientas ochenta y uno
6 un millón de quinientos mil
7 dos mil setecientas cuarenta
8 cuatro mil trescientos ochenta y ocho

Nombre: ______________________ Fecha: ______________

3-10 La Loto. Look at the following lottery information (picture A). Then, fill in the blanks corresponding to the letters on picture B with the numbers spelled out.

LA LOTO		Escrutinio	
28 de mayo		Acertantes	Pesos
Combinación ganadora:	6	1	4.256.090
2 17 25 35 37 48	5+c	4	447.056
	5	101	7.082
Complementario: 31 Reintegro 7	4	6.775	167
	3	123.439	22

A

LA LOTO		Escrutinio	
28 de mayo		Acertantes	Pesos
Combinación ganadora:	6	1	4.256.090
2 (a) 25 35 37 (b)	5+c	4	(d)
	5	(e)	(f)
Complementario: (c) Reintegro 7	4	6.775	(g)
	3	(h)	22

B

a. dieciséis
b. Cuarenta y ocho
c. triento y uno
d. Cuatrocientos cuarenta y siete cero cincuenta y seis
e. Ciento uno
f. siete. cero ochenta y dos
g. Ciento
h. ______________________

3-11 En clase de matemáticas. Select the most appropriate answer for each of the following math problems.

225×2=

1. (525 – 300) × 2 =

(a.) doscientos veinticinco
c. cuatrocientos cincuenta

b. ochocientos veinticinco
d. setenta y cinco

2. (21 ÷ 3) × 100 =

   a. setecientos
   b. doscientos diez
   c. trescientos treinta
   d. setenta

3. 111 + 222 + 333 =

   a. quinientos sesenta y cinco
   b. seiscientos sesenta y seis
   c. setecientos cincuenta y seis
   d. cuatrocientos treinta y tres

4. 1.350 × 3 =

   a. cuatrocientos cincuenta
   b. cuatro mil cincuenta
   c. cuarenta mil quinientos
   d. cuarenta mil cincuenta

5. 7.700 ÷ 7 =

   a. ciento uno
   b. mil uno
   c. mil ciento uno
   d. mil cien

6. 8.600.000 – 7.399.999 =

   a. mil doscientos uno
   b. cien mil doscientos diez
   c. doce mil cien
   d. un millón doscientos mil uno

7. 110 × 5 =

   a. quinientos cinco
   b. quinientos cincuenta
   c. cincuenta y cinco
   d. cinco mil quinientos

8. (3.500 × 10) ÷ 2 =

   a. ciento setenta mil
   b. mil setecientos cincuenta
   c. diecisiete mil quinientos
   d. ciento setenta y cinco

Nombre: ______________________________ Fecha: ______________________

3-12 Matemáticas. Solve the following addition problems out loud in Spanish. Then listen and repeat as the speaker gives the correct answer.

CD 3, Track 4

1. 100 + 21 = ciento viente y uno
2. 233 + 117 = trescientos cincuenta 350
3. 3.104 + 436 =
4. 180.000 + 1.000.000 =
5. 2.465.114 + 513.765 =
6. 2.000 + 3.984 =

2. Possessive adjectives (TEXTBOOK P. 83)

3-13 Mis amigos. Complete David's description of his friends with the correct form of the possessive adjective in parentheses.

(1) ________________ (*Our*) amigos Alfonso y Sonia asisten a (2) ________________(*our*) universidad. (3) ________________ (*Their*) horarios son diferentes. Sonia tiene cuatro clases. (4) ________________ (*Her*) clases son matemáticas, informática, biología y química. (5) ________________ (*Her*) clases favoritas son química y biología porque (6) ________________ (*her*) profesores no son muy exigentes. Alfonso tiene cuatro materias también. (7) ________________ (*His*) materias son literatura, francés, música y psicología. Música es (8) ________________ (*his*) materia favorita. Alfonso y Sonia tienen muchos amigos. (9) ________________ (*Their*) amigos son (10) ________________(*my*) amigos también. ¿Cómo son (11) ________________ (*your*) amigos? Vas a ser (12) ________________(*my*) amigo/a, ¿verdad?

3-14 La vida estudiantil. Read the following paragraphs and fill in the blanks with the appropriate possessive adjective based on the subject of the sentences.

1. Soy Raúl Ramos, estudiante de la UNAM. ________________ carrera es historia, y ________________ clases son solamente por la mañana. ________________ apartamento está cerca de la universidad y vivo con ________________ amigos.
2. Somos Margarita y Sara. Somos hermanas y estudiamos administración de empresas. ________________ clases son muy difíciles, pero siempre estudiamos con ________________ amigos. Vivimos en ________________ apartamento, pero vamos a ________________ casa los fines de semana.

3. Él se llama Ramón Espinosa. Estudia informática. ______________ clases son complicadas y ______________ profesores son exigentes. Él siempre trabaja con ______________ computadora. Por la tarde le gusta hablar con ______________ novia.

3-15 Objetos y posesiones. Rewrite the following sentences using the appropriate possessive adjective.

Modelo: La computadora es de Sara.
Es su computadora.

1. La novela es del profesor.

____

2. Los libros son de Ana y Sofía.

____

3. El escritorio es de Ud.

____

4. El apartamento es de Ud. y de su amigo.

____

5. El horario de clases es de Alberto.

____

6. Los microscopios son de los estudiantes de biología.

____

7. Las computadoras son de la universidad.

____

8. La calculadora es de Ud. y de su amigo.

____

CD 3, Track 5

3-16 ¿De quién? Listen for the subject of each sentence. Conjugate the verb accordingly and complete each sentence with the appropriate possessive adjective. Then listen and repeat as the speaker gives the correct answer.

Modelo: You see: mirar / libros
You hear: yo
You write and say: *Yo miro mis libros.*

1. estudiar mucho en / clase ______________________
2. escuchar a / profesora ______________________
3. ¿tener / papeles? ______________________
4. hablar con / amigos ______________________
5. escribir / cuaderno ______________________
6. ¿estar en / casa por la noche? ______________________

CD 3, Track 6

3-17 Preguntas en la clase. You will hear several questions related to school and classes. Based on the subject in each question, complete the sentences with the appropriate possessive adjective. Then listen and repeat as the speaker gives the correct answer.

Modelo: You hear: ¿Ana tiene dos exámenes?
You see: _____ exámenes son mañana.
You write and say: *Sus* exámenes son mañana.

1. ________ microscopio está en el laboratorio.
2. ________ libro está en la mochila.
3. ________ cuadernos están en la mesa.
4. ________ dinero está en casa.
5. ________ papeles están en el escritorio de la profesora.
6. ________ amigos están en el gimnasio.

3. Other expressions with *tener* (Textbook p. 85)

3-18 Sensaciones. Make the most logical associations between the elements of both columns.

1. ____ En el invierno
2. ____ En el verano
3. ____ Cuando no como
4. ____ Cuando no tomo
5. ____ Cuando veo una película de terror
6. ____ A las tres de la mañana
7. ____ Cuando llego tarde
8. ____ Cuando estoy en el carro

a. tengo hambre.
b. tengo cuidado.
c. tengo miedo.
d. tengo frío.
e. tengo sed.
f. tengo calor.
g. tengo sueño.
h. tengo prisa.

CD 3, Track 7

3-19 En situaciones diferentes. Listen to what the following people are experiencing in each situation and write the most logical response using expressions with *tener*. Then listen and repeat as the speaker gives the correct answer.

1. Yo ______________________.
2. Nosotros ______________________.
3. Usted ______________________.
4. Tú ______________________.
5. Julia y Tomás ______________________.

3-20 Tus respuestas. Answer the following questions in complete sentences in Spanish.

1. ¿Cuántos años tienes?

   ____

2. ¿Cuántos años tiene tu mejor amigo/a?

   ____

3. ¿A qué hora tienes hambre generalmente?

   ____

4. ¿Tienes frío en el verano?

   ____

5. ¿Con qué películas tienes miedo?

   ____

6. ¿A qué hora generalmente tienes sueño?

   ____

¿Cuánto sabes tú?

3-21 ¿Cuánto sabes de números y posesiones? Answer each question with the appropriate possessive adjective and spell out the number in parentheses.

1. ¿Cuánto cuesta tu carro?

   ____________ carro cuesta (*160.830*) ________________ pesos.

2. ¿Cuánto cuesta el apartamento de Uds.?

   ____________ apartamento cuesta (*7.450*) ________________ pesos al mes.

3. ¿Cuánto cuesta su computadora?

   ____________ computadora cuesta (*12.175*) ________________ pesos.

4. ¿Cuánto cuesta mi calculadora?

   ____________ calculadora cuesta (*225*) ________________ pesos.

5. ¿Cuánto cuesta el piano de tus padres?

   ____________ piano cuesta (*54.620*) ________________ pesos.

Nombre: ______________________________ Fecha: ______________________

CD 3, Track 8

3-22 En la clase de español. Select the word or phrase that best completes each answer to the following questions that your Spanish professor might ask you. Listen and repeat as the speaker gives the correct answer.

diecinueve años	Frida Kahlo	su	
informática	veintiséis mil dólares	mi	un examen

1. ______________ artista favorita mexicana es ____________________.
2. ______________ carro cuesta ____________________.
3. Estudia____________________.
4. Tiene ____________________.
5. Tengo ____________________ mañana.

3-23 ¿Sabes usar el verbo *tener*? Match each expression using ***tener*** with the most logical statement.

1. _____ Cuando la temperatura exterior es 110° F… a. tengo miedo.
2. _____ Cuando veo una película de horror… b. tengo sed.
3. _____ Cuando la temperatura exterior es -10 F… c. tengo frío.
4. _____ Cuando hago ejercicio por dos horas… d. tengo calor.
5. _____ Cuando voy en coche… e. tengo cuidado.

CD 3, Track 9

3-24 La vida en la universidad. Listen to the questions. Then write, as well as say, your answers.

1. ____.
2. ____.
3. ____.
4. ____.
5. ____.

Segunda parte

¡Así es la vida!

3-25 ¿Cierto o falso? Reread the conversations in **¡Así es la vida!** on page 90 of your textbook, and indicate if each statement is **cierto** (C) or **falso** (F).

1. Carmen tiene que ir a la librería.  ____
2. Carmen va a comprar un diccionario.  ____
3. Pedro tiene que ir a la librería.  ____
4. La librería está detrás de la Facultad de Medicina. 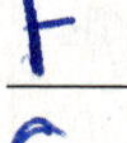 ____
5. Pedro tiene que escribir una biografía sobre Frida Kahlo.  ____
6. Frida Kahlo es una artista mexicana.  ____
7. La especialidad de Carmen es el arte mexicano.  ____
8. Marisa vive lejos.  ____
9. Los padres de Marisa viven en Coyoacán.  ____
10. Marisa asiste a clase todos los días. ____

CD 3, Track 10

3-26 En la clase de biología. Listen to the following conversation among three students. Then read the statements that follow and select all items that apply to each statement.

1. Estudia(n) biología:

   a. Pablo b. Inés c. Elena

2. Necesita(n) ir a la biblioteca hoy:

   a. Inés b. Pablo c. Elena

3. Está enfrente del laboratorio de lenguas:

   a. la librería b. la biblioteca c. la cafetería

4. Está al lado de la biblioteca:

   a. el centro estudiantil b. la cafetería c. el auditorio

Nombre: ______________________________ Fecha: ______________________

¡Así lo decimos! Vocabulario (Textbook p. 91)

3-27 La universidad y sus facultades. In the following word search puzzle, find nine words related to colleges and places on campus.

D	V	I	P	J	H	A	Z	R	C	O	U	T	Q	I	R
I	B	H	O	P	G	V	Y	A	Q	U	F	O	T	E	O
N	A	T	L	L	A	O	Y	M	T	N	J	R	C	S	G
G	I	M	N	A	S	I	O	C	A	F	T	T	I	C	H
E	S	R	E	J	U	R	F	I	N	Z	O	A	E	A	B
N	V	O	D	U	T	O	R	C	U	R	F	E	N	T	I
I	A	N	E	Z	I	T	Z	G	I	B	A	T	C	N	D
E	C	E	R	L	L	I	A	A	Y	R	D	E	I	S	O
R	A	L	E	O	T	D	S	I	U	J	E	F	A	P	R
I	G	E	C	M	Y	U	Q	T	R	P	B	Z	S	O	S
A	C	A	H	P	J	A	T	U	B	E	B	E	N	D	A
M	R	G	O	E	F	D	Z	I	B	A	T	R	O	N	G
L	I	T	R	V	A	M	O	Y	E	Z	P	E	L	M	U
O	B	T	E	N	E	S	T	A	D	I	O	L	F	I	D
S	I	M	T	A	V	L	A	S	F	J	U	P	O	A	I
E	B	L	A	N	D	I	G	T	E	S	A	M	S	A	C

3-28 ¡A emparejar! Match each word of the first column with the most logical option from the second column.

1. _____ el gimnasio
2. _____ el auditorio
3. _____ el teatro
4. _____ la cafetería
5. _____ la rectoría
6. _____ la Facultad de Ingeniería
7. _____ el museo

a. la tecnología
b. el ejercicio
c. la comida
d. la obra de teatro
e. el concierto
f. el arte
g. la oficina

CD 3, Track 11

3-29 Completamos las ideas. Complete the following sentences with the most logical choice. Then listen and repeat as the speaker gives the correct answer.

1. a. está cerca de la biblioteca.
   b. está en mi casa.
   c. vende libros.
2. a. la cancha de tenis.
   b. el museo.
   c. el estadio.
3. a. está a la izquierda.
   b. es la rectoría.
   c. es la hora del almuerzo.
4. a. enferma.
   b. al lado del centro estudiantil.
   c. después de la clase.
5. a. el examen de estadística.
   b. el horario de clases.
   c. el laboratorio de biología.

Nombre: ______________________ Fecha: ______________________

3-30 La universidad. Some new students on campus need help finding their classes. Answer their questions based on the campus map and following the model.

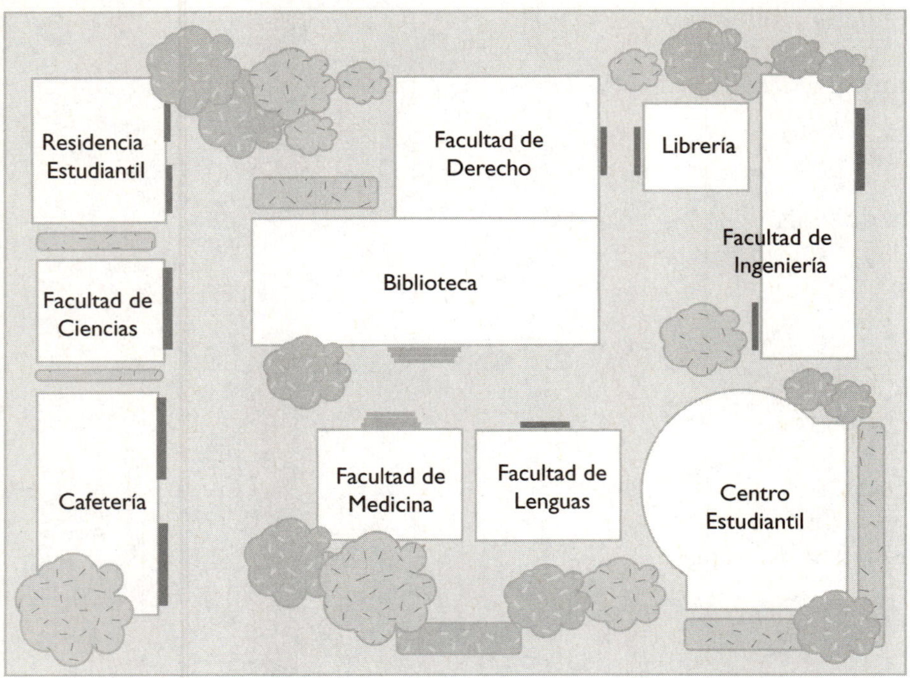

MODELO: ¿Dónde está la Facultad de Medicina?
Está al lado de la Facultad de Lenguas.

1. ¿Dónde está la Facultad de Ciencias?

   ____

2. ¿Dónde está el centro estudiantil?

   ____

3. ¿Dónde está la cafetería?

   ____

4. ¿Dónde está la residencia estudiantil?

   ____

5. ¿Dónde está la biblioteca?

   ____

Nombre: ______________________ Fecha: ______________________

Letras y sonidos (TEXTBOOK P. 92)

CD 3, Track 12

3-31 Muchas sílabas. You will hear a series of Spanish words. Write the number that corresponds to the number of syllables in each word. You will hear the correct answer on the recording.

a. ____ f. ____

b. ____ g. ____

c. ____ h. ____

d. ____ i. ____

e. ____ j. ____

CD 3, Track 13

3-32 La primera sílaba. For each word, write only the letters that correspond to the first syllable on the lines provided. Then listen and repeat as the speaker pronounces each word.

1. educación ____
2. Enrique ____
3. horario ____
4. izquierda ____
5. marrón ____
6. Pedro ____
7. perfecto ____
8. piano ____
9. pintura ____
10. trabajo ____

Nombre: ______________________ Fecha: ______________________

¡Así lo hacemos! Estructuras

4. The present indicative tense of *ir* (to go) and *hacer* (to do; to make)

(Textbook p. 95)

3-33 ¿Qué va a hacer? Match each of the following sentences with a logical related statement.

1. _____ Ramón tiene mucha sed.
2. _____ Juanjo tiene hambre.
3. _____ Yo tengo un examen mañana.
4. _____ Tú tienes que hacer ejercicio.
5. _____ Nosotros necesitamos libros para las clases.

a. Va a comer en la cafetería.
b. Vamos a comprar unos (*some*) en la librería.
c. Voy a estudiar toda la noche.
d. Va a tomar agua mineral.
e. Vas a ir al gimnasio.

CD 3, Track 14

3-34 El mapa del campus. Refer to the map to say where the following people are going to accomplish the activities listed. Then listen and repeat as the speaker gives the correct answer.

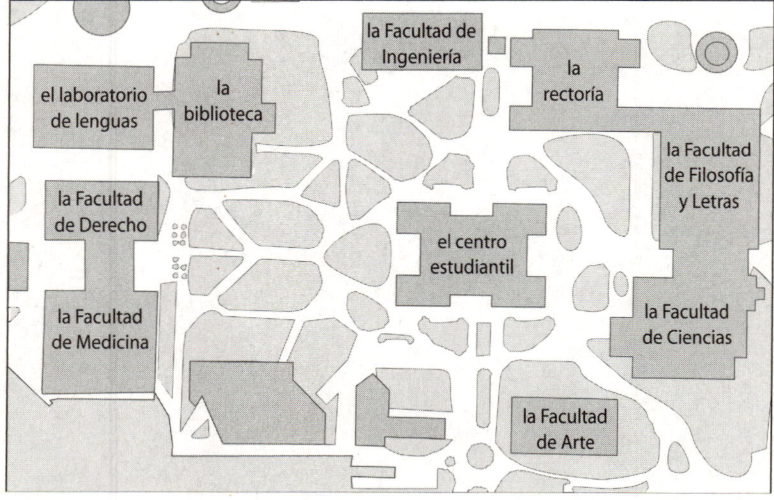

Modelo: Tengo la clase de literatura.
Voy a la Facultad de Filosofía y Letras.

1. ____.
2. ____.
3. ____.
4. ____.
5. ____.

Nombre: ______________________ Fecha: ______________________

3-35 En la residencia estudiantil. Complete the description of what the students do at their dorm with the correct forms of ***hacer.***

Mis amigas y yo vivimos en la residencia estudiantil de nuestra universidad y nosotras (1) hacemos muchas cosas todo el día. Por la mañana, yo (2) hago ejercicio en el gimnasio y mi amiga Elisa (3) hace su tarea. Por la tarde, mis otras amigas Marta y Luisa (4) hacen su trabajo. Por la noche, ellas (5) hacen la comida y siempre (6) hacen pizza. ¿Qué (7) haces tú en la residencia estudiantil? ¿Qué vas a (8) ______ este fin de semana?

CD 3, Track 15

3-36 ¿Qué vamos a hacer? Listen for the subject of each sentence. Say and write the correct form of the verb ***ir*** to say what the people are going to do. Listen and repeat as the speaker gives the correct answer.

Modelo: You see: _____ a asistir a clase.
You hear: David y tú
You write and say: *David y tú van* a asistir a clase.

1. ______________________ a trabajar esta noche.
2. ______________________ a regresar por la mañana.
3. ______________________ a practicar béisbol.
4. ______________________ a hacer la tarea.
5. ______________________ a vivir en un apartamento.
6. ______________________ a estar en la cancha de tenis.
7. ______________________ a practicar en el estadio.

CD 3, Track 16

3-37 ¡Vamos! Respond to the following statements by using the construction ***ir a*** and the place to which each person is going. Then listen and repeat as the speaker gives the correct answer.

el auditorio	la cafetería	la clase
la Facultad de Ingeniería	el gimnasio	el museo

MODELO: You hear: Valeria va a dormir.
You write and say: *Va a la residencia estudiantil.*

1. ______________________________.
2. ______________________________.
3. ______________________________.
4. ______________________________.
5. ______________________________.
6. ______________________________.

3-38 Mañana. Rewrite the following sentences so the actions will take place tomorrow instead of today. Use the appropriate form of ***ir a*** and the infinitive.

MODELO: Carmen estudia hoy.
Carmen va a estudiar mañana.

1. Roberto practica vólibol hoy.

____

2. Yo como en la cafetería hoy.

____

3. Tú compras una calculadora hoy.

____

4. Ana habla con el profesor hoy.

____

5. Los estudiantes toman el examen hoy.

____

6. Mis amigos y yo asistimos a la obra de teatro hoy.

____

CD 3, Track 17

3-39 ¿Qué hacen en la clase de ingeniería? Complete the dialogue with the correct forms of ***hacer***. Then, listen and repeat as the speaker gives the correct answer.

1. Hola, Margarita, ¿qué ______________ tú?
2. ¿Yo? ______________ mi tarea para la clase de ingeniería.
3. ¿Qué ______________ Uds. en la clase de ingeniería?
4. Nosotros ______________ diseños de carros este semestre. Es muy interesante.
5. ¿Los estudiantes ______________ los diseños en la computadora?
6. Pues sí. Y mi amigo, Rafael, ______________ unos diseños excelentes.

CD 3, Track 18

3-40 ¡Hacemos muchas cosas! You will see a series of two sentences. Complete the first sentence with the correct form of the verb ***hacer*** according to the subject you hear. Next, answer the question with the correct subject and with the correct form of the verb in parentheses. Finally, listen and repeat as the speaker gives the correct answer.

MODELO: You see: ¿Qué ______________ ______________ en la clase de música?

______________ ______________ el piano. (tocar)

You hear: Óscar
You write and say: ¿Qué *hace Óscar* en la clase de música?
Óscar toca el piano.

1. ¿Qué ______________ ______________ en el laboratorio?

   ______________ ______________ la lección. (escuchar)

2. ¿Qué ______________ ______________ en el gimnasio?

   ______________ ______________. (nadar)

3. ¿Qué ______________ ______________ en el examen?

   ______________ ______________ oraciones completas. (escribir)

4. ¿Qué ______________ ______________ en la clase de literatura?

   ______________ ______________ muchas novelas. (leer)

5. ¿Qué ______________ ______________ en clase hoy?

   ______________ ______________ el vocabulario. (practicar)

3-41 ¿Qué vas a hacer mañana? Write a paragraph explaining what you are going to do tomorrow. Include places that you are going to go (***ir***) and activities that you are going to do (***hacer***).

____

____

____

____

____

____

5. The present tense of *estar* (to be) (Textbook p. 97)

3-42 Nuestro amigo Antonio. Antonio is the opposite of how his friends generally are. For each sentence, select the statement that describes Antonio's contrary mood or lifestyle.

1. _____ Elisa está contenta, pero…
2. _____ Miguel está casado, pero…
3. _____ Isabel está sana (*healthy*), pero…
4. _____ Luz está aburrida, pero…
5. _____ Sebastián está tranquilo (*calm*), pero…

a. Antonio está ocupado.
b. Antonio está triste.
c. Antonio está divorciado.
d. Antonio está nervioso.
e. Antonio está enfermo.

Nombre: ____________________ Fecha: ____________________

3-43 En el teléfono. Complete the phone conversation between Alfredo and Teresa with the correct form of ***estar.***

Alfredo: ¡Hola, Teresa! ¿Cómo (1) estas ____________________?

Teresa: (2) ____________________ bien, gracias, ¿y tú?

Alfredo: (3) ____________________ bien también. ¿Dónde (4) ____________________ Ramón?

Teresa: Él (5) ____________________ en su casa porque (6) ____________________ muy ocupado.

Alfredo: Y, ¿cómo (7) ____________________ Luisa y Sandra?

Teresa: Ellas (8) ____________________ ocupadas también, y ahora yo (9) ____________________ preocupada. Tenemos un examen de física mañana y no tengo mi libro.

Alfredo: ¿Tu libro? Ay, Teresa... Tu libro (10) ____________________ en mi escritorio.

Teresa: ¿En tu escritorio?

Alfredo: Pues sí. ¿(11)____________________ contenta ahora?

Teresa: Sí, (12) ____________________ contenta. Hasta mañana, Alfredo.

Alfredo: Adiós.

3-44 ¿Cómo están? Describe the probable feelings or conditions of each person using ***estar*** and one of the given adjectives. Remember to watch for correct agreement.

aburrido/a	enamorado/a	cansado/a	enojado/a
enfermo/a	ocupado/a	preocupado/a	contento/a

MODELO: Laura tiene un examen de cálculo por la mañana.
Ella *está nerviosa.*

1. ¡Qué bonita e inteligente es Rosa!

   Yo ____________________ ____________________.

2. Tienen que leer una novela, escribir una composición y estudiar para un examen.

   Ellos ____________________ ____________________.

3. No estudiamos más. Es medianoche.

   Nosotros ______________ ______________.

4. El profesor de historia habla y habla. No es interesante.

   Nosotros ______________ ______________.

5. Roberto no habla con sus amigos.

   Roberto ______________ ______________.

6. Es medianoche. Roberto no está en casa.

   Sus padres ______________ ______________.

7. Mi novia no está bien. Va al hospital.

   Ella ______________ ______________.

8. ¡Mañana voy a ir a México!

   Yo ______________ ______________.

CD 3, Track 19

3-45 ¿Cómo estás? Listen to the following statements. For each one you hear, write an appropriate response using ***estar*** and an adjective.

Modelo: You hear: Es medianoche y los hijos del Sr. Pérez no están en casa.
You write: *Sr. Pérez está preocupado.*

1. ____
2. ____
3. ____
4. ____
5. ____

Nombre: ________________________ Fecha: ________________________

3-46 En la taquilla. Refer to the drawing to say where the following people are located in reference to the other people whose names you hear. Then listen and repeat as the speaker gives the correct answer.

1. Paula ________________________
2. Adrián ________________________
3. Paula y Pepe ________________________
4. Marcela ________________________
5. Adrián ________________________

6. Summary of uses of *ser* and *estar* (Textbook p. 100)

3-47 Vicente. Read the following statements about Vicente and decide in each case if the description that fits him uses ***ser*** or ***estar.***

1. Vicente siempre habla de cosas (*things*) interesantes.

   a. No es aburrido. b. No está aburrido.

2. Él habla muchos idiomas.

   a. Es listo. b. Está listo.

3. Hoy Vicente no tiene que hacer nada.

   a. Es aburrido. b. Está aburrido.

4. Son las seis. Va a comer con su novia.

   a. Es listo. b. Está listo.

5. La novia de Vicente es como Salma Hayek.

   a. Es bonita. b. Está bonita.

3-48 Mi pequeño mundo. Complete the descriptions of the following people with the correct forms of the verbs ***ser*** and ***estar.***

A. Mi familia (1) ________________ mexicana. Nosotros (2) ________________ de Guadalajara. Guadalajara (3) ________________ en el estado de Jalisco. Mi papá y mi mamá (4) ________________ muy trabajadores y (5) ________________ muy simpáticos.

B. Mis padres (6) ________________ profesores. Ellos trabajan en la universidad. La universidad (7) ________________ cerca de casa. Mi madre (8) ________________ profesora de literatura y mi padre (9) ________________ profesor de matemáticas. ¡Ellos (10) ________________ muy listos!

C. Pedro (11) ________________ mi amigo. Él (12) ________________ listo y siempre (13) ________________ contento, pero hoy él (14) ________________ preocupado. Nosotros (15) ________________ en la biblioteca hoy porque tenemos que estudiar y los exámenes siempre (16) ________________ difíciles.

3-49 La fiesta de esta noche. Complete the following paragraph with the correct form of ***ser, estar,*** or ***hay.***

Esta noche (1) ________________ una fiesta en casa de Luisa. Su casa (2) ________________ cerca de mi casa. La fiesta (3) ________________ a las nueve de la noche. Los padres de Luisa no (4) ________________ en casa; ellos (5) ________________ en Cancún. Luisa (6) ________________ preocupada porque su novio Raúl (7) ________________ enfermo y no va a (8) ________________ en la fiesta. Las fiestas en casa de Luisa siempre (9) ________________ muy divertidas y Raúl (10) ________________ enojado porque no puede ir.

Nombre: ______________________ Fecha: ______________________

CD 3, Track 21 **3-50 Descripciones.** Complete each description with the correct form of ***ser*** or ***estar*** and the appropriate adjective. Then listen and repeat as the speaker gives the correct answer.

MODELO: You see: Los estudiantes (*are bored*).
You write and and say: *Los estudiantes están aburridos.*

1. Jaime (*is handsome*)____________________.
2. José y María (*are ill*) ____________________.
3. Josefina (*looks pretty*) ____________________ esta noche.
4. Tus amigos (*are clever*) ____________________.
5. Mis padres (*are ready*) ____________________.
6. Tu profesora (*is boring*) ____________________.

CD 3, Track 22 **3-51 ¿Ser o no ser?** Complete the sentences with the appropriate form of ***ser*** or ***estar,*** based on the cues you hear. Then listen and repeat as the speaker gives the correct answer.

MODELO: You see: mis padres / de Guadalajara
You hear: ser
You say: *Mis padres son de Guadalajara.*

1. la madre de Felicia / mexicana

   ____

2. hoy / el 20 de marzo

   ____

3. yo / preocupado(a) porque mi amiga / enferma

   ____

4. la biblioteca / detrás de la Facultad de Medicina

   ____

5. tú / en el gimnasio

   ____

6. el concierto / en el Teatro Cervantes

   ____

Nombre: ______________________________ Fecha: ______________________

3-52 Tu mejor amigo/a. Write a brief description of your best friend using the correct forms of ***ser*** and ***estar.***

____

____

____

____

____

____

¿Cuánto sabes tú?

3-53 ¿Sabes hacer planes? Fill in the blanks with the appropriate form of ***ir*** or ***hacer.***

Yo (1) ____________________ todos los días a la biblioteca y (2) ____________________ mi tarea. Mis amigos también (3) ____________________ a la biblioteca para estudiar. Después de estudiar, nosotros (4) ____________________ al gimnasio. Todos los viernes, nosotros (5) ____________________ al laboratorio de lenguas para hablar en español. Los sábados, nosotros (6) ____________________ nuestra tarea del fin de semana y por la noche (7) ____________________ a ver una película a casa de un amigo. Los domingos, yo (8) ____________________ a comer a la casa de mis padres y ellos (9) ____________________ a tomar café a la cafetería de la universidad. ¿Qué (10) ____________________ tú en la universidad?

Nombre: ______________________ Fecha: ______________________

3-54 ¿Sabes la diferencia entre *ser* y *estar*? Fill in the blanks with the appropriate form of ***ser*** or ***estar***.

Toño (1) __________ un estudiante mexicano. Él (2) __________ en Los Ángeles. Él estudia en los Estados Unidos para (3) __________ ingeniero. Toño (4) __________ un buen estudiante, pero hoy (5)__________ preocupado porque tiene un examen de matemáticas. Los exámenes de matemáticas (6) __________ difíciles, pero Toño (7) __________ listo para el examen. La profesora de matemáticas (8)__________ muy amable y ella (9) __________ muy contenta con los estudiantes. (10) __________ importante estudiar para tener buenas notas.

CD 3, Track 23

3-55 ¿Qué pasa? Tell what you and your friends are doing, based on the verbs you hear. Then listen and repeat as the speaker gives the correct answer.

1. Yo __________ a la Facultad de Medicina.
2. Luego, Susana y yo __________ a la cafetería.
3. Hoy Ramón y Pedro __________ a casa a estudiar.
4. Tú __________ en la biblioteca, ¿verdad?
5. Perdón, ¿qué __________ Pablo y tú esta noche?
6. Yo __________ cansado.

CD 3, Track 24

3-56 Unas preguntas personales. Listen to the questions. Then write, as well as say, your answers.

1. ______________________________
2. ______________________________
3. ______________________________
4. ______________________________
5. ______________________________

Nombre: ______________________ Fecha: ______________________

Observaciones

Antes de ver el video

3-57 ¿Qué pasa? Select the letter of the question or statement that best answers each of the following questions.

1. What would Patricio ask Silvia as they make plans to meet?

   a. ¿Vamos a almorzar?

   b. Estoy aburrido. ¿Qué tal tú?

   c. ¿Estás loca?

2. What would be a likely response that Silvia gives to Patricio?

   a. Hoy tengo que trabajar.

   b. ¿Cómo llego desde aquí?

   c. ¿Por qué no vamos al Restaurante Manolo?

3. What does Silvia likely ask Patricio about his future plans to attend a university in the United States?

   a. ¿Son muy caras?

   b. ¿Por qué quieres estudiar?

   c. ¿Cuántos años tienes?

4. As the friends discuss Patricio's scholarship application, how does Silvia show her encouragement?

   a. El examen no es muy exigente… Tienes tiempo para prepararte.

   b. Es un examen de inglés para extranjeros.

   c. Es un programa de intercambio cultural. ¿Qué tal tu inglés?

5. How might Silvia indicate that she has to leave?

   a. Patricio, tienes razón. El restaurante está lleno de turistas.

   b. Patricio, es muy tarde. ¿Puedes llamar al camarero?

   c. Patricio, ¿cuáles son los requisitos para la beca?

A ver el video

 **3-58 La conversación.** Fill in the blanks in the dialogue about Patricio's application for a Fulbright grant according to the conversation in the video.

Patricio: También, hay que tener estudios universitarios de, al menos, (1) ____________________ años.

Silvia: ¿Solamente eso?

Patricio: Hay otros (2) ____________________ académicos. Por ejemplo, tienes que aprobar unos (3) ____________________ de algunas materias.

Silvia: ¿Qué materias?

Patricio: Creo que son álgebra, (4) ____________________, química… y algo más. ¡Ah sí!, (5) ____________________.

Silvia: Claro, tienes que tomar el TOEFL.

Patricio: ¿El qué?

Silvia: Sí, el TOEFL. Es un (6) ____________________ de inglés para extranjeros. ¿Qué tal tu inglés?

Patricio: Pues, *so, so*…

Silvia: No es un examen muy (7) ____________________, ¿sabes?

Patricio: ¿Tú (8) ____________________?

3-59 Más información. Fill in the blanks with the correct information based on the video segment.

1. El Restaurante ____________________ está lleno de turistas.
2. La moneda (*currency*) de Costa Rica se llama el ____________________.
3. El restaurante en la Avenida 2 y la Calle 15 se llama ____________________.
4. La beca Fulbright es parte de un programa de ____________________ cultural.

Después de ver el video

3-60 La acción y los personajes. Determine whether the following statements are **cierto** (C) or **falso** (F) and write the correct letter on the lines provided.

1. Patricio y Silvia van al Restaurante Bakea. ____
2. El restaurante Nuestra Tierra está en la Calle 15. ____
3. Silvia toma un taxi porque el restaurante está lejos. ____
4. Silvia va a solicitar una beca Fulbright. ____
5. Uno de los requisitos para la beca es ser colombiano. ____
6. Patricio tiene que aprobar exámenes de cálculo e inglés. ____

Nombre: ______________________________ Fecha: ______________________

NUESTRO MUNDO

3-61 ¡A informarse! Based on the information from **Nuestro mundo,** decide if the following statements are **cierto** (C) or **falso** (F).

1. Taxco es famoso por la artesanía de plata. ____
2. En Oaxaca se puede encontrar artesanía de madera. ____
3. Las maquiladoras no son importantes para la economía de los EE.UU. ____
4. Los trabajadores de las maquiladoras ganan (*earn*) mucho dinero. ____
5. En las maquiladoras se produce principalmente aparatos electrónicos. ____
6. Los mariachis tienen su origen en el siglo XVII. ____
7. "Las mañanitas" es una canción (*song*) de serenata para celebrar la Navidad. ____
8. Los estudiantes del Tec de Monterrey no van a estudiar a otros países. ____
9. Los estudiantes principiantes toman clases de ingeniería. ____
10. La isla de Cozumel es un lugar muy turístico. ____

3-62 El mapa de México. Look at the following map of México and write the name of the city that corresponds to each number on the map.

1. ____________________

2. ____________________

3. ____________________

4. ____________________

5. ____________________

6. ____________________

7. ____________________

8. ____________________

3-63 Tu propia experiencia. The UNAM (*Universidad Nacional Autónoma de México*) offers a wide variety of college degrees as well as specialized high school programs. Go to **http://www.prenhall.com/arriba** and review the courses that students have to take in order to obtain the equivalent to high school diploma at UNAM. Then, mark with an X in the first column the courses that students have to take at UNAM and mark with an X in the second column the courses that you took in school.

	UNAM	TU PROPIA EXPERIENCIA
1. matemáticas		
2. arte		
3. biología		
4. cálculo		
5. inglés		
6. historia		
7. física		
8. filosofía		
9. química		
10. educación física		

Ritmos

3-64 La Bamba. In the text you heard one of the versions of the well-known song "La Bamba." Now, visit **www.prenhall.com/arriba** to answer the following questions about some famous singers who also made this song a popular hit.

1. ¿Quién es Ritchie Valens?

   a. un pintor   b. un actor   c. un cantante

2. ¿Cuál es su verdadero nombre?

   a. Richard Valenzuela   b. Ricardo Valencia   c. Rodolfo Valentino

3. ¿De dónde es Ritchie Valens?

   a. México   b. Los Ángeles   c. Cuba

4. ¿Cómo se llama la banda de Ritchie Valens?

   a. Los Lobos   b. La Bamba   c. The Silhouettes

5. ¿Quién canta "La Bamba" en la película (*movie*) (1987)?

   a. Enrique Iglesias   b. Alejandro Sanz   c. Los Lobos

6. ¿De dónde son Los Lobos?

   a. Cuba   b. México   c. Estados Unidos

Páginas

3-65 El Museo de Antropología de México. Based on the information from **Páginas** on page 108 of your textbook, decide if the following statements are **cierto** (C) or **falso** (F).

1. En el museo hay lo más representativo del mundo prehispánico. ____
2. Los mayas son una civilización moderna. ____
3. Los mayas construyeron pirámides. ____
4. El museo está cerrado los lunes. ____
5. El museo está abierto de 9:00 a 19:00 hrs. ____

Taller

3-66 Una carta de un amigo mexicano. Read the following letter and answer the questions below.

México D.F., 7 de febrero de 2006

Estimado Carlos:

Hoy es martes, 7 de febrero. Estoy en la universidad porque hoy tengo muchas clases. A las nueve y media tengo clase de matemáticas. ¡Es muy difícil! Afortunadamente (*Fortunately*), la profesora es muy buena. A las diez y media tengo clase de psicología. La clase es un poco complicada y el profesor es exigente, pero como estudio mucho recibo buenas notas en la clase. A las once y media tengo clase de informática. La clase es bastante fácil porque a mí me gustan las computadoras. A la una como con mis amigos en la cafetería de la universidad. Después de comer, estudio en la biblioteca y a las tres tengo clase de inglés. Es mi clase favorita porque me gustan los idiomas, aunque (*even though*) todavía no hablo inglés muy bien. A las cuatro tengo clase de historia con mi profesora favorita. Ella habla de muchos temas fascinantes; su clase es muy interesante. Este semestre tengo clases todos los días, pero como (*since*) las clases son muy buenas, me gusta la universidad.

Un abrazo de tu amigo,

Roberto

1. ¿Dónde está Roberto?

____

2. ¿Qué clases tiene Roberto hoy?

____

3. ¿A qué hora tiene clase de psicología?

____

4. ¿Qué hace Roberto a la una?

____

5. ¿Qué clase es difícil?

____

6. ¿Qué clase es fácil?

____

7. ¿Cuál es la clase favorita de Roberto?

____

8. ¿Cuál es la profesora favorita de Roberto?

____

3-67 Tu propia carta. Write a similar letter to one of your friends explaining what your day at the university is like. List the classes you take, the times, and a brief description of each class. Don't forget to include place, date, greeting, and farewell.

____

____

____

____

____

____

____

____

____

____

____

____

4 ¿Cómo es tu familia?

PRIMERA PARTE

¡Así es la vida!

4-1 ¿Recuerdas? Answer the questions by choosing the letter of the correct option according to the e-mail from **¡Así es la vida!**

1. ¿Quién escribe el correo electrónico?

   a. Hilda
   b. Eduardo
   c. Juan Antonio
   d. Ana María

2. ¿Quién recibe el correo electrónico?

   a. Hilda
   b. Eduardo
   c. Juan Antonio
   d. Ana María

3. ¿Quiénes son los viejos?

   a. los padres de Juan Antonio
   b. Hilda y Eduardo
   c. Juan Antonio y Ana María
   d. los padres de Ana María

4. ¿Qué celebran esta noche?

   a. el aniversario de Juan Antonio y Ana María
   b. el cumpleaños de Juan Antonio
   c. el aniversario de los viejos
   d. el aniversario de Hilda y Eduardo

5. ¿Quién asiste a la celebración?

   a. los padres de Ana María
   b. la familia de Juan Antonio
   c. los hermanos de Ana María
   d. Ana María

6. Juan Antonio invita a Ana María a…

 a. el aniversario de Hilda y Eduardo.
 b. la boda de su hermano.
 c. el cumpleaños de su hermana.
 d. pasar un fin de semana con él.

CD 4, Track 1

4-2 La familia de Luisa. Listen to the following description. Then select all the letters corresponding to statements that are correct according to what you hear.

1. ... de Luisa celebran el aniversario.
 a. Los tíos
 b. Los padres
 c. Los abuelos
2. Federico es...
 a. el esposo de Catalina.
 b. el padre de Luisa.
 c. salvadoreño.
3. La familia de Luisa...
 a. es unida.
 b. vive en Quetzaltenango.
 c. es pequeña.
4. Griselda es...
 a. la hermana de Samuel.
 b. la hija de Catalina.
 c. la tía de Luisa.
5. Luisa visita a la familia en…
 a. la capital.
 b. Antigua.
 c. Quetzaltenango.
6. Samuel...
 a. es gracioso.
 b. tiene muchos hermanos.
 c. está ahora en Antigua.
7. ... de Luisa va a vivir en Quetzaltenango con su familia.
 a. El abuelo
 b. El tío
 c. El hermano
8. Luisa tiene...
 a. un hermano menor.
 b. dos hermanos.
 c. una hermana mayor.

Nombre: ______________________ Fecha: ______________________

¡Así lo decimos! Vocabulario (TEXTBOOK P. 117)

4-3 Los parentescos. Circle the names of the nine family members in the puzzle.

H	H	U	C	L	S	O	F	H	I	P	A
E	I	R	U	A	O	O	U	L	F	R	L
R	J	J	Ñ	P	B	E	B	E	N	A	H
M	T	F	A	H	N	P	B	R	O	S	R
A	A	O	D	U	A	L	D	D	I	J	T
N	L	D	A	D	L	E	A	A	V	N	I
O	G	I	R	C	O	S	L	M	F	A	O
R	O	E	J	I	G	M	E	P	Ñ	S	L
F	M	P	O	S	T	A	U	O	E	R	P
I	P	O	M	I	R	P	B	L	L	O	F
V	A	Y	T	O	S	R	A	U	C	S	E
E	S	P	O	S	A	C	L	S	Ñ	A	M

4-4 Tu familia. Describe your family relationships by completing each sentence with a word from **¡Así lo decimos!**

1. El padre de mi padre es mi ______________________.
2. La hermana de mi madre es mi ______________________.
3. El esposo de mi hermana es mi ______________________.
4. Los hijos de mi hermana son mis ______________________.
5. La madre de mi esposo es mi ______________________.
6. Las hijas de mi tío son mis ______________________.
7. La esposa de mi hijo es mi ______________________.
8. El hijo de mis padres es mi ______________________.
9. Los padres de mi madre son mis ______________________.
10. El esposo de mi hija es mi ______________________.

Nombre: ______________________ Fecha: ______________________

CD 4, Track 2

4-5 El árbol genealógico. Looking at the family tree, answer the questions about the family relationships.

abuelo (Pablo)
abuela (Manuela)
tío Gustavo
esposa de Gustavo (Elena)
tío José
madre (Juana)
padre (Paco)
tía Teresa
hermano (Ernesto)
Yo (Ana María)
hermana (Carmen)
primo (Pablo)
prima (Cristina)

1. ______________________.
2. ______________________.
3. ______________________.
4. ______________________.
5. ______________________.
6. ______________________.
7. ______________________.

4-6 Preguntas personales. Your roommate wants to know more about your family. Answer his/her questions in Spanish.

1. ¿De dónde son tus abuelos?

____

2. ¿Tienes hermanos o hermanas? ¿Son mayores o menores?

____

3. ¿Tienes cuñados o cuñadas? ¿Cómo se llaman?

____

4. ¿Tienes muchos primos? ¿Están casados, divorciados o son solteros?

____

5. ¿Cuántos tíos y tías tienes? ¿Dónde viven?

____

Nombre: ______________________ Fecha: ______________________

¡Así lo hacemos! Estructuras

1. The present tense of stem-changing verbs: *e→ie, e→i, o→ue*
(TEXTBOOK P. 119)

4-7 La clase de matemáticas (1). Fill in the blanks with the correct form of the verb in parentheses.

1. La clase de matemáticas ____________________ (empezar) al mediodía.
2. La clase es difícil y los estudiantes no ____________________ (entender) al profesor.
3. Por eso, en la clase algunos estudiantes ____________________ (soñar) con las vacaciones.
4. Pero los estudiantes buenos ____________________ (preferir) estudiar en la biblioteca.
5. Después de la clase, los estudiantes ____________________ (almorzar) en la cafetería.
6. En la cafetería ____________________ (servir) pizza.

4-8 La clase de matemáticas (2). Now match the letters of each of the drawings below to one of the statements from the previous activity. Write the number of the statement next to the drawing on the line provided.

a. _____

d. _____

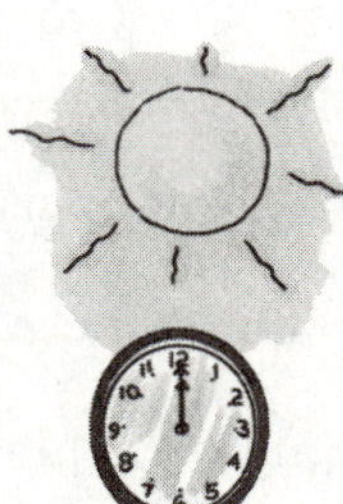

b. _____

e. _____

c. _____

f. _____

4-9 Nuestra familia. Fill in the blanks with the correct form of the verb in parentheses.

1. Cuando yo ________________ (almorzar) en la cafetería, yo ________________ (querer) comer pizza.
2. Mi hermana ________________ (poder) jugar bien al tenis, pero mi hermano no ________________ (jugar) bien.
3. Mi tío siempre ________________ (dormir) por la tarde y él ________________ (soñar) con ser rico.
4. Mis primas ________________ (servir) el almuerzo cuando mis abuelos ________________ (venir) a casa.
5. Yo ________________ (preferir) a mi tía porque ella ________________ (entender) mis problemas.

4-10 Un lunes en la vida de Tomás. What does your cousin Tomás do on a typical day? Complete the description with the correct form of each verb in parentheses.

Todos los lunes Tomás (1) ________________ (tener) que asistir a tres clases, y la primera clase (2) ________________(empezar) a las ocho de la mañana. Él (3) ________________ (preferir) dormir toda la mañana, pero no (4) ________________ (poder). A las once y media (5) ________________(almorzar) en la cafetería y casi siempre (6) ________________ (pedir) pizza. A las dos de la tarde (7) ________________ (volver) a su apartamento para estudiar. A las cuatro (8) ________________ (jugar) al baloncesto con unos amigos. Él (9) ________________ (pensar) que juega bien porque él nunca (10) ________________ (perder).

CD 4, Track 3

4-11 ¿Qué piensas tú? Complete the sentences with the correct form of the verb you hear, according to the subject provided. Then listen and repeat as the speaker gives the correct answer.

1. Yo ________________ las películas cómicas pero Juanita ________________ las de misterio.
2. Tú ________________ todos los días con la familia, pero nosotros ________________ con nuestros amigos.
3. Nosotros ________________ ir a la casa de Marcos este fin de semana, pero ¿qué ________________ tú?
4. ¿Cuántas horas ________________ tu hermana?

   Generalmente, ella ________________ ocho horas.
5. ¿Tú ________________ con Rodrigo al laboratorio?

   Sí, yo ________________ con él.

CD 4, Track 4

4-12 Cosas de la vida. Answer the questions using the cues provided. Then listen and repeat as the speaker gives the correct answer.

1. ________________ con visitar Guatemala.
2. ________________ mañana.
3. Siempre ________________ chocolate.
4. Mis yernos no ________________ su nombre.
5. Yo ________________ servir el almuerzo.
6. Sí, ________________ con Uds.
7. ________________ pronto a Guatemala.
8. ________________ mucho dinero.

CD 4, Track 5

4-13 ¡El preguntón! Answer the following questions in complete sentences. Then listen and repeat as the speaker gives the correct answer.

Modelo: You hear: ¿Ángela tiene muchos hermanos?
You see: Sí,...
You write and say: Sí, *Ángela tiene muchos hermanos.*

1. No, ________________________.
2. Sí, ________________________.
3. No, ________________________.
4. Sí, ________________________.
5. No, ________________________.
6. Sí, ________________________.

Nombre: ______________________ Fecha: ______________________

CD 4, Track 6

4-14 No. Write the answer to the question you hear by responding negatively. Then using the cues provided below, give additional information in complete sentences. Follow the model. Finally, listen and repeat as the speaker gives the correct answer.

MODELO: You hear: ¿Quieres jugar al tenis?
You see: mis primos
You write and say: *No, no quiero jugar al tenis. Mis primos quieren jugar al tenis.*

1. tarde ______________________
2. jugar al básquetbol ______________________
3. mañana ______________________
4. yo ______________________
5. tú ______________________
6. mi sobrina ______________________

4-15 En la cafetería. Look at the following drawing and make six complete sentences using six of the verbs in the word bank. Use the model as an example.

pensar	soñar	querer	tener
servir	pedir	encontrar	almorzar

MODELO: *Los estudiantes comen en la cafetería.*

1. ______________________
2. ______________________
3. ______________________
4. ______________________
5. ______________________
6. ______________________

2. Direct objects, the personal *a,* and direct object pronouns

(TEXTBOOK P. 125)

4-16 Reunión familiar. Complete the descriptions of a family reunion with the personal **a** when needed.

1. Esteban visita __________ su primo Jorge y __________ su primo Gustavo.
2. Llevo __________ mis hermanos a dar un paseo.
3. Mis hermanos y yo vemos __________ la película en el cine.
4. Invito __________ mi cuñado a almorzar en un restaurante.
5. Esteban tiene __________ muchos primos y los visita.
6. Mis abuelos quieren __________ sus nietos.
7. Mis tíos no entienden __________ mis padres.
8. Mis padres quieren __________ un yerno simpático.
9. El tío Eduardo y la tía Teresa llaman por teléfono __________ sus sobrinos.
10. Mi madrastra va a visitar __________ un museo.

4-17 ¡A completar! Complete each sentence with the direct object pronoun that corresponds to the subject in italics.

MODELO: *Nosotros* debemos esperar aquí porque tu madre *nos* busca.

1. *Yo* estoy feliz porque Mercedes __________ recuerda.
2. *Tú* llamas a María pero ella no __________ llama.
3. *Marta y Gisela* viven en Tegucigalpa, pero yo siempre __________ visito.
4. *Yo* hablo con mi hermano, pero él no __________ entiende.
5. *Nosotros* vemos a las muchachas, pero ellas no __________ ven.
6. *Ella* te quiere mucho, pero tú no __________ quieres.
7. *Carlos y Adrián* buscan a Marisa para conversar en un café, pero ella no __________ busca.
8. *Él* espera a su novia, pero ella no __________ espera a él.

Nombre: ______________________ Fecha: ______________________

4-18 Las repeticiones. Fill in the blanks with the appropriate direct object pronoun from the word bank to avoid repeating the words in italics.

me	te	lo	la	los	las	nos

1. Yo tengo *tres primos* y ______________ llamo todos los días.
2. Tenemos *muchas novelas* en casa porque mi madrastra ______________ compra.
3. *Nosotros* vivimos en San Salvador; por eso mi tío ______________ invita a comer todos los viernes.
4. *Tu coche* es muy grande; tu cuñado ______________ necesita el lunes.
5. *Tú* visitas a tus abuelos todos los domingos y por eso ellos ______________ quieren mucho.
6. *Yo* llego mañana y mis suegros ______________ invitan a la fiesta.
7. *Mi prima* estudia en Nueva York y yo ______________ quiero visitar.

CD 4, Track 7

4-19 *A* personal. Complete the sentences with the cues you hear and then with the personal *a* when necessary. Then listen and repeat as the speaker gives the correct answer.

MODELO: You see: Veo ______________ en la fiesta.
You hear: mi primo
You write and say: *Veo a mi primo en la fiesta.*

1. Llaman ______________ todos los días.
2. Llaman ______________ por la mañana.
3. Ven ______________ en el museo.
4. Ven ______________.
5. Invito ______________, ______________ y ______________ a la fiesta.
6. Quiero ______________.
7. Quiero mucho ______________.
8. Compro ______________.
9. ¿ ______________ tienes?
10. ¿ ______________ visitas frecuentemente?

Nombre: ______________________ Fecha: ______________________

CD 4, Track 8

4-20 ¿Cuál es el complemento? Identify the direct object in the sentences you hear. Then listen and repeat as the speaker gives the correct answer.

Modelo: You hear: Aurelia tiene dos hermanas.
You write and say: *dos hermanas*

1. ______________
2. ______________
3. ______________
4. ______________
5. ______________

CD 4, Track 9

4-21 ¿Quién hace qué? Answer the following questions, replacing the direct objects with the appropriate pronouns. Then listen and repeat as the speaker gives the correct answer.

Modelo: You hear: ¿Quién llama a Susana?
You see: Yo
You write and say: *Yo la llamo.*

1. Nosotros ______________.
2. Ustedes ______________.
3. Yo ______________.
4. Ella ______________.
5. Rodrigo y yo ______________.
6. Tú ______________.
7. Yo ______________.
8. Mi tía ______________.

CD 4, Track 10

4-22 ¿Sí o no? Answer the following questions affirmatively or negatively according to the cues provided. Then listen and repeat as the speaker gives the correct answer.

Modelo: You hear: ¿Ves a los García allí?
You write and say: No, *no los veo.*

1. No, ______________.
2. No, ______________.
3. Sí, ______________.
4. No, ______________.
5. Sí, ______________.
6. Sí, ______________.

Nombre: ______________________________ Fecha: ______________________

CD 4, Track 11

4-23 ¿Quién va a hacerlo? Answer the questions you hear using direct object pronouns. Then listen and repeat as the speaker gives the correct answer.

MODELO: You hear: ¿Quién va a comprar los refrescos?
You see: yo
You write and say: Yo *voy a comprarlos.*

1. Nosotros ______________________________.
2. Yo ______________________________.
3. Tú ______________________________.
4. Santiago ______________________________.
5. Olivia y Juan ______________________________.

4-24 Preguntas sobre tu familia. Answer the following questions using direct object pronouns to avoid repetitions.

MODELO: ¿Llamas a tus padres todos los días?
No, no los llamo todos los días.

1. ¿Tienes los números de teléfono de tu familia?

____

2. ¿Visitas a tus abuelos los fines de semana?

____

3. ¿Ves películas con tu esposo/a o tu novio/a?

____

4. ¿Invitas a tus hermanos a almorzar?

____

5. ¿Practicas deportes con tu familia?

____

6. ¿Quieres a tu familia?

____

Nombre: ______________________ Fecha: ______________________

3. The present tense of *poner, salir,* and *traer* (TEXTBOOK P. 128)

4-25 Varias situaciones. What do people do on different occasions? Fill in the blanks with the correct form of the indicated verb.

1. poner

Ana y Pepe siempre (1) ______________ los libros en la mochila. Yo (2) ______________ los libros en una bolsa grande. Y tú, ¿dónde (3) ______________ los libros? Mi amigo Raúl no (4) ______________ los libros en una mochila. ¡Los tiene en el coche!

2. salir

Sandra (5) ______________ con Teodoro. Ellos (6) ______________ a nadar todas las tardes y por la noche (7) ______________ a comer en un restaurante. Mi vida es más difícil. Yo (8) ______________ de la casa a las ocho de la mañana y (9) ______________ del trabajo a las cinco. Mis amigos y yo sólo (10) ______________ a cenar los viernes porque los restaurantes son muy caros. Los sábados (11) ______________ para las montañas para pasar el fin de semana.

3. traer

¿Qué (12) ______________ tú a la clase? Yo (13)______________ el libro y Teresa (14) ______________ el cuaderno de actividades. Quique y Eduardo (15) ______________ el diccionario.

4-26 Los planes. These friends have plans for the weekend. Fill in each blank with the forms listed in the word bank. You will have to use one of them twice.

salir	traigo	pone	salen	poner	salimos	trae	salgo

Alejandro y Eduardo (1) ______________ hoy para la playa. Alejandro (2) ______________ todas las cosas en su coche. Quieren (3) ______________ a las tres de la tarde. A las dos y media Eduardo llama a Alejandro.

Eduardo: ¡Hola, Alex! ¿A qué hora (4) ______________ (nosotros)?

Alejandro: En treinta minutos. Yo tengo que (5) ______________ mis cosas en el coche ahora.

Eduardo: Alex, ¿no es posible (6) ______________ a las cuatro? Necesito visitar a mi hermano.

Alejandro: ¿A qué hora tienes que visitar a tu hermano?

Eduardo: A las tres y cuarto. (7) ______________ (yo) de mi casa ahora.

Alejandro: Chico, no hay problema. ¿Quién (8) ______________ la música?

Eduardo: No te preocupes, yo (9) ______________ la música. Hasta pronto.

Alejandro: Adiós.

CD 4, Track 12

4-27 Planes para la noche. Fill in the blanks with the correct form of the verb in parentheses. Then listen and repeat as the speaker gives the correct answer.

Modelo: You see: ______________ para la fiesta a las nueve de la noche. (salir)
You hear: yo
You write and say: *Salgo* para la fiesta a las nueve de la noche.

1. ______________ los nombres de nuestros amigos en la mesa. (poner)
2. ______________ música. (traer)
3. ______________ mi guitarra. (traer)
4. ¡Fantástico! Podemos escuchar mucha música. ______________ mi guitarra en el carro ahora. (poner)
5. ¿Qué piensas si ______________ con nosotros también? (salir)
6. Buena idea. Oye, ¿dónde ______________ los números de teléfono de todas las primas? (poner)
7. Los ______________ en mi librito (*little book*). (poner)

Nombre: ______________________________ Fecha: ______________________

CD 4, Track 13

4-28 Preferencias. Answer each question with a complete sentence using the cues provided. Then listen and repeat as the speaker gives the correct answer.

MODELO: You hear: ¿A dónde salimos esta noche?
You see: un restaurante
You write and say: *Salimos a un restaurante.*

1. dos libros de biología ______________________________
2. la mochila ______________________________
3. los cuadernos ______________________________
4. a las ocho y media ______________________________
5. en la mesa ______________________________

CD 4, Track 14

4-29 ¡Salgo! Complete the sentences with **"Salgo"** followed by the correct preposition, according to the cues you hear. Then listen and repeat as the speaker gives the correct answer.

MODELO: You see: a. a b. con c. de d. para
You hear: salgo, correr
You select and say: *a. Salgo a correr.*

1. a. a b. con c. de d. para
2. a. a b. con c. de d. para
3. a. a b. con c. de d. para
4. a. a b. con c. de d. para

¿Cuánto sabes tú?

4-30 ¿Sabes usar pronombres de objeto directo? Match the following sentences with the direct object pronoun needed. Write the correct letter on each line.

1. Quiero mucho a mis abuelos y ____ visito todas las semanas. a. me
2. Mi hermana ayuda mucho a mi madre; ____ quiere mucho. b. la
3. Mi primo me pide ayuda y yo ____ ayudo. c. los
4. Yo pido ayuda a mi primo y él ____ ayuda. d. nos
5. Mis abuelos viven cerca de nuestra casa; ____ visitan todos los viernes. e. lo

Nombre: ______________________ Fecha: ______________________

4-31 ¿Sabes usar los verbos irregulares? Complete the following sentences with the appropriate form of the verb in parentheses.

1. Mi madre me ______________ (querer) mucho.
2. Yo no ______________ (entender) a mis amigos.
3. Mi hermano ______________ (pensar) mucho en su novia.
4. Mis tíos ______________ (preferir) salir para las montañas mañana.
5. Normalmente yo ______________ (volver) a casa tarde.
6. Mis primos no ______________ (poder) ir al cine con nosotros.

CD 4, Track 15

4-32 ¿Sabes contestar? Answer the questions you hear using direct object pronouns when possible.

1. ____.
2. ____.
3. ____.
4. ____.
5. ____.

CD 4, Track 16

4-33 Preguntas personales. Answer the questions you hear based on your personal experience.

1. ____.
2. ____.
3. ____.
4. ____.
5. ____.
6. ____.

Nombre: ______________________________ Fecha: ______________________

Segunda parte

¡Así es la vida!

CD 4, Track 17

4-34 ¿Al cine? Listen to the following conversation. Then indicate whether the statements that follow are **cierto** (C) or **falso** (F).

1. Jorge invita a Ana al cine. ____
2. Jorge quiere ver una película dramática. ____
3. La película empieza a las siete y media. ____
4. Ana quiere invitar a Santiago. ____
5. Jorge está en el cine. ____

4-35 Una invitación. Complete the sentences according to the dialogue from **¡Así es la vida!**

1. Raúl llama a Laura para ver si...

   a. está bien. b. quiere ir al cine. c. quiere ir a cenar.

2. Laura le pregunta a Raúl...

   a. quiénes son los actores. b. qué película ponen. c. a qué hora es la película.

3. El cine se llama...

   a. John Leguizamo. b. Rialto. c. Tlatelolco.

4. En el cine ponen…

   a. *Tlatelolco: México 68.* b. Rialto. c. John Leguizamo.

5. La película empieza...

   a. a las siete. b. a las seis y media. c. esta noche.

Nombre: ______________________ Fecha: ______________________

¡Así lo decimos! Vocabulario (Textbook p. 133)

4-36 Respuestas a una invitación. Based on the statements below, decide if each statement is used to accept (***aceptar***) or decline (***rechazar***) the invitation. Circle the correct answer.

1. Sí, claro.	Aceptar	Rechazar
2. Me encantaría.	Aceptar	Rechazar
3. Me encantaría, pero tengo que trabajar.	Aceptar	Rechazar
4. De acuerdo.	Aceptar	Rechazar
5. No, lo siento.	Aceptar	Rechazar
6. ¡Vamos!	Aceptar	Rechazar
7. Gracias, pero no puedo.	Aceptar	Rechazar
8. Estoy muy ocupado/a.	Aceptar	Rechazar

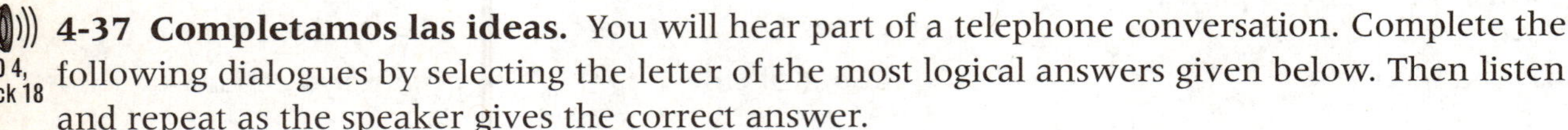

CD 4, Track 18

4-37 Completamos las ideas. You will hear part of a telephone conversation. Complete the following dialogues by selecting the letter of the most logical answers given below. Then listen and repeat as the speaker gives the correct answer.

1. a. Sí, con Juan, por favor.
   b. Bueno.
   c. Aló.
2. a. Te llamo para invitarte a bailar esta noche.
   b. Lo siento, pero estoy ocupada.
   c. Quiero ir al cine.
3. a. Lo siento, no puedo.
   b. A las nueve y media.
   c. Claro, ¿quieres pasear por el centro?
4. a. No, gracias. No puedo.
   b. Me gusta la orquesta.
   c. Es un café al aire libre.
5. a. De acuerdo. Vamos al teatro el sábado.
   b. Sí, claro. ¡Me encantaría ver el partido!
   c. El parque es muy popular.
6. a. ¡Vamos!
   b. No, gracias, estoy ocupado.
   c. De acuerdo, ¿qué van a presentar?
7. a. ¡De acuerdo! ¿A qué hora es la función?
   b. La orquesta es fabulosa.
   c. ¿Puedes ir al cine?

Nombre: ______________________ Fecha: ______________________

4-38 Más invitaciones. Laura and Raúl had a wonderful time at the movies and have decided to see each other again. Using the dialogue on page 132 of your textbook as a model and the vocabulary in **¡Así lo decimos!,** arrange the conversation in logical order.

a. ¡Me encantaría! ¿Quién canta?

b. De acuerdo. ¡Vamos!

c. Sí, soy Raúl.

d. ¿Aló?

e. Alejandro Sanz. El concierto es a las ocho. Paso por ti a las siete, ¿de acuerdo?

f. ¿Está Raúl, por favor?

g. Raúl, soy Laura. ¿Te gustaría ir a un concierto esta noche?

1. ______________________

2. ______________________

3. ______________________

4. ______________________

5. ______________________

6. ______________________

7. ______________________

Letras y sonidos (Textbook p. 136)

CD 4, Track 19

4-39 El énfasis. Select the stressed syllable in each word according to what you hear.

Modelo: You hear: invierno
You select: in<u>vier</u>no

1. abril
2. aire
3. diccionario
4. Eduardo
5. estudiante
6. papel
7. practico
8. profesor
9. reloj
10. suegro
11. universidad
12. visito

Nombre: ______________________ Fecha: ______________________

CD 4, Track 20

4-40 ¿Dónde hay acento? Write the word or word groups you hear, including the written accent if it is necessary.

1. ______________________
2. ______________________
3. ______________________
4. ______________________
5. ______________________
6. ______________________
7. ______________________
8. ______________________
9. ______________________
10. ______________________

¡Así lo hacemos! Estructuras

4. Demonstrative adjectives and pronouns (TEXTBOOK P. 137)

4-41 De compras. You are shopping at the university store. Indicate your preferences by completing each statement below with the correct demonstrative adjective.

1. Quiero (*these*) ______________ mochilas.
2. Prefiero (*those*) ______________ mochilas.
3. No me gustan (*those over there*) ______________ libros.
4. Voy a comprar (*that*) ______________ libro.
5. Deseo (*these*) ______________ cuadernos.

Nombre: ______________________ Fecha: ______________________

4-42 En la fiesta. Your family is attending a party at your friend's house. He approaches you and wants to know who, among the crowd, each member of your family is. Fill in the blank with the appropriate demonstrative adjective or pronoun.

Amigo: ¡Hola! ¿Está toda tu familia aquí?

Tú: Sí, gracias por invitarnos.

Amigo: ¿Quiénes son tus padres?

Tú: Mi padre es (1) ______________ señor alto y moreno que está allá lejos hablando con tu padre.

Amigo: ¿Es tu madre (2) ______________ señora que está aquí?

Tú: No, (3) ______________ es mi tía. Mi madre es (4) ______________ señora que está cerca de mi padre.

Amigo: ¿Están tus hermanos en la fiesta?

Tú: ¡Por supuesto! Mi hermano es (5) ______________ chico de allí, (6) ______________ que está cerca de la puerta.

Amigo: ¿Y tus hermanas?

Tú: Son (7) ______________ chicas con las que hablo. Te las presento. (8) ______________ es Ángela y (9) ______________ es Carmen.

Amigo: Encantado. Mucho gusto en conocerlas.

Tú: Muchas gracias por invitarnos. (10) ¡______________ fiesta es maravillosa!

Amigo: Sí, hay mucha gente. ¡(11) ______________ me gusta!

CD 4, Track 21

4-43 Identificaciones. Complete the sentences with the correct form of the demonstrative adjective you hear. Then listen and repeat as the speaker gives the correct answer.

1. ¡Qué interesante son ______________ partidos de fútbol!
2. ¿Cuánto cuestan ______________ refrescos?
3. Escucho mi música favorita cuando toca ______________ orquesta.
4. Marcos va a comprar ______________ entradas.
5. ______________ biblioteca es grande.
6. Vengo frecuentemente a ______________ cine.

7. Me gusta correr en ____________ parque.

8. Me gustan ____________ películas.

9. ¿Quieres hacer ejercicio en ____________ gimnasio?

10. Siempre hay muchos turistas en ____________ cafés al aire libre.

4-44 ¿Qué prefieres? At the store, a clerk asks you which of the following items you would like to buy. Reply using the appropriate demonstrative adjective based on the three columns below, and use the model as an example.

AQUÍ	ALLÍ	ALLÁ
escritorio	computadora	microscopio
novela	libros	lápices
cuadernos	diccionario	bolígrafo
calculadoras	mapas	mochilas

Modelo: ¿Qué escritorio quiere?
Quiero este escritorio.

1. ¿Qué cuadernos prefiere?

____

2. ¿Qué computadora quiere?

____

3. ¿Qué microscopio le gusta?

____

4. ¿Qué lápices prefiere?

____

5. ¿Qué libros quiere?

____

6. ¿Qué diccionario le gusta?

____

7. ¿Qué calculadoras le gustan?

____

8. ¿Qué mochilas prefiere?

____

4-45 ¿Cómo se llaman los estudiantes? Based on the drawing and the given name of each student, answer the following questions using demonstrative pronouns. Follow the model.

1. Eugenio	5. Gonzalo
2. María Eugenia	6. Virginia
3. Antonio	7. Alicia
4. María Antonia	8. Juan Manuel

Modelo: ¿Cómo se llaman estos estudiantes *(5 y 3)*?
Éstos se llaman Gonzalo y Antonio.

1. ¿Cómo se llama esta estudiante *(4)*?

   ____

2. ¿Cómo se llama este estudiante *(1)*?

   ____

3. ¿Cómo se llaman esas estudiantes *(2 y 6)*?

   ____

4. ¿Cómo se llama aquella estudiante *(7)*?

   ____

5. ¿Cómo se llama aquel estudiante *(8)*?

   ____

Nombre: ______________________ Fecha: ______________________

CD 4, Track 22

4-46 ¿Éste, ése o aquél? Answer the following questions using the cues provided. Then listen and repeat as the speaker gives the correct answer.

MODELO: ¿Vas a comer en esta cafetería?
You see: aquél
You write and say: *No, voy a comer en aquélla.*

1. éste ______________________
2. aquél ______________________
3. ése ______________________
4. éste ______________________
5. ése ______________________
6. aquél ______________________

5. *Saber* and *conocer* (TEXTBOOK P. 139)

4-47 Más información. Your friend wants to know more about your cousins. Complete each question with the correct form of ***saber*** or ***conocer.***

1. ¿ ______________ ellas jugar al vólibol?
2. ¿ ______________ ellas a toda tu familia también?
3. ¿ ______________ bailar bien Charo?
4. ¿ ______________ (ellas) a tus padres también?
5. ¿ ______________ (tú) si ellas visitan a sus padres en diciembre?
6. ¿ ______________ (ellas) que yo estudio español?
7. ¿ ______________ Anita que tú vives en la residencia estudiantil?
8. ¿ ______________ (tú) al novio de Anita?
9. ¿ ______________ Carmen hablar francés?
10. ¿ ______________ (ellas) a mis tíos?

4-48 Una conversación. Complete the following conversation two friends are having about a new student with the correct form of ***saber*** or ***conocer.***

— ¿ (1) ____________________ al estudiante nuevo? ¿(2) ____________________ cómo se llama?

— No (3) ____________________ cómo se llama, pero (4) ____________________ que su apodo es Beto.

— ¿ (5) ____________________ si Beto habla español?

— Sí, (6) ____________________ que habla español.

— ¿ (7) ____________________ dónde vive?

— Yo no (8) ____________________ dónde vive, pero mi hermano (9) ____________________ que Beto vive cerca de la universidad.

— ¿ (10) ____________________ tú a Maribel, la novia de Beto?

— No, yo no (11) ____________________ a Maribel.

— ¡Vamos a conocerlos!

— ¡Vamos!

CD 4, Track 23

4-49 ¿Saber o conocer? Complete the sentences with the subject you hear followed by the correct form of ***saber*** or ***conocer.***

Modelo: You hear: yo
You see: ________ ____________________ a muchas personas en la orquesta.
You say and write: *Yo conozco* a muchas personas en la orquesta.

1. ________ ____________________ que ellos quieren ir al cine.
2. ________ no ____________________ a mi suegra, ¿verdad?
3. ________ ____________________ hablar francés.
4. ________ ____________________ Barcelona.
5. ________ no ____________________ dónde es el concierto.
6. ________ ____________________ bien a la familia de mi novio.

Nombre: ______________________ Fecha: ______________________

4-50 Unas preguntas. Based on the drawings, formulate questions using the **tú** form of ***saber*** or ***conocer***. Follow the model.

MODELO: 

¿Conoces a este chico?

1. 

____

3. 

____

2. 

____

4. 

____

Nombre: ______________________________ Fecha: ______________________

CD 4, Track 24

4-51 ¿Conozco o sé? Complete the sentences by selecting the letter of ***conozco*** or ***sé,*** according to what you hear. Then listen and repeat as the speaker gives the correct answer.

Modelo: You see: a. conozco b. sé
You hear: hablar ruso
You select the letter and say: *b. Sé hablar ruso.*

1. a. conozco b. sé
2. a. conozco b. sé
3. a. conozco b. sé
4. a. conozco b. sé
5. a. conozco b. sé

¿Cuánto sabes tú?

4-52 ¿Sabes usar los demostrativos? Complete each sentence with the most appropriate demonstrative adjective or pronoun.

1. Esta casa es de mis abuelos, pero ______________ es de mis tíos.

   a. este b. aquella c. aquélla d. esos

2. Mi primo es ______________ chico que está aquí.

   a. aquel b. este c. aquél d. éste

3. Mi hermana no quiere esta silla, pero quiere ______________ que está allí.

   a. ésa b. ese c. esa d. ése

4. Mis padres trabajan en ______________ edificio (*building*) allá lejos.

   a. esta b. ésta c. aquellos d. aquel

5. ______________ chico es mi amigo Ramón.

   a. estos b. este c. esos d. aquellas

6. ¿Qué es ______________ ?

   a. estos b. este c. éste d. esto

Nombre: ______________________________ Fecha: ______________________

4-53 **Federico y Elena.** Listen to the dialogue and answer the questions below to complete the sentence.

CD 4, Track 25

1. Esta noche Federico y Elena van …
   a. a un partido de béisbol.
   b. al cine.
   c. a una función de teatro.
2. Son las …
   a. diez.
   b. dos.
   c. doce.
3. …piensa que van a llegar tarde.
   a. Federico
   b. Amalia
   c. Elena
4. …piensa que tienen tiempo.
   a. El papá de Elena
   b. El hermano de Amalia
   c. Federico
5. …de Federico están en el café "La Paz".
   a. Los hermanos
   b. Los primos
   c. Las tías
6. Federico y Elena ...
   a. no pasean por el centro.
   b. van al café.
   c. llaman a los primos.
7. No van a llegar tarde porque …
   a. Elena está nerviosa.
   b. Federico compra las entradas temprano.
   c. la película comienza en dos horas.

4-54 ¿Sabes la diferencia entre *saber* y *conocer*? Fill in the blanks with the appropriate forms of ***saber*** or ***conocer.***

1. Yo no ____________________ Nueva York.
2. Mi madre ____________________ jugar al tenis muy bien.
3. Nosotros ____________________ quién es Rigoberta Menchú.
4. Mis padres ____________________ a mis amigos.
5. Los estudiantes de español ____________________ la diferencia entre ***saber*** y ***conocer.***

Nombre: ______________________ Fecha: ______________________

CD 4, Track 26

4-55 Otras preguntas personales. Answer the following personal questions using complete sentences in Spanish.

1. ____.
2. ____.
3. ____.
4. ____.
5. ____.
6. ____.

Observaciones

Antes de ver el video

4-56 ¿Qué pasa? Select the letter of the question or statement that best answers each question.

1. What might Felipe say to Marcela?

   a. El jueves es el gran día.

   b. ¿Conoces a Claudia?

   c. Estas flores son para doña María.

2. Regarding the tuxedo, what might Felipe say to explain his plans to Marcela?

   a. Claudia es mi hermana. Se casa aquí en San José, el jueves.

   b. ¿Qué es esto? Oh, sí. ¡Casi lo olvido!

   c. Todavía soy muy joven para casarme.

3. What might Marcela say to Felipe as she describes weddings in Mexico?

   a. Vengo de una familia grande.

   b. En México son espectaculares.

   c. Mi vida puede estar en México.

Nombre: ______________________ Fecha: ______________________

4. After Felipe says that he may want to live in Mexico, how might Marcela hint to Felipe that she's interested in him?

   a. ¿Y por qué en México? ¿Conoces a alguien de México?

   b. Claro. ¿Y tú? ¿Vuelves a Argentina?

   c. Y no es una de tus tías internacionales, ¿verdad?

5. What might Felipe say to Marcela that would make her drop the flowers?

   a. Voy a ver a una chica mexicana que conocí por Internet.

   b. Tengo muchos primos en España pero sólo conozco a uno.

   c. No sé si vuelvo a Argentina o no.

A ver el video

4-57 La conversación. Complete the following dialogue about the families of Felipe and Marcela with the missing words from the video segment.

Felipe: ¿Te gusta la vida de (1) ______________?

Marcela: Sí, vengo de una familia grande. Tengo dos hermanas, tres (2) ______________ y muchísimos primos y sobrinos. Mi hermana menor es hija de la segunda esposa de mi papá.

....

Felipe: Su (3) ______________ es canadiense, y viene con su mamá y sus hermanos. Mi familia viene del sur. Se casan en (4) ______________ porque es más conveniente para todos.

Marcela: Ah, ¡qué interesante!

Felipe: Sí, somos una familia muy internacional. La familia de mi mamá está toda en Italia, y en España tenemos muchos (5) ______________ y primos. Sólo en Madrid tenemos más de veinte (6) ______________.

Marcela: ¿Y se reúnen?

Felipe: Ahora con el correo electrónico es más fácil contactarnos, pero vernos es muy difícil. Sólo (7) ______________ a uno.

Nombre: ______________________ Fecha: ______________________

4-58 La acción y los personajes. Determine whether the following statements are **cierto** (C) or **falso** (F) and write the correct letter on the lines provided.

1. Hay un traje para Felipe. ____
2. Las flores son para Marcela. ____
3. La boda es el sábado. ____
4. Claudia, la hermana de Felipe, se casa. ____
5. Marisol y Laura son las hermanas de Marcela. ____
6. Felipe no se casa porque dice que es muy joven. ____
7. Marcela quiere formar una familia y tener hijos. ____
8. Felipe va a México para ver a Elvira, una mujer que él conoció (*met*) por Internet. ____

Después de ver el video

4-59 Más información. Select the letter of the answer that best completes each sentence.

1. El traje es para...
   a. el novio de Claudia.
   b. Hermés, de su padre.
   c. Felipe, de su hermana Claudia.
2. Marcela piensa que...
   a. Felipe se casa.
   b. Claudia es bonita.
   c. las flores son para Silvia.
3. Felipe necesita el traje para...
   a. su boda.
   b. la boda de su hermana.
   c. la boda de Marcela.
4. Marcela dice que...
   a. no tiene prisa por casarse.
   b. no quiere casarse.
   c. su boda es en un mes.
5. Según Marcela, las bodas en México son...
   a. aburridas.
   b. secretas.
   c. espectaculares.
6. Felipe tiene familia en...
   a. Costa Rica, México y Canadá.
   b. Argentina, Italia y España.
   c. México, Canadá y España.

Nombre: ______________________________ Fecha: ______________________

NUESTRO MUNDO

Panoramas

4-60 ¡A informarse! Based on the information from **Nuestro mundo,** decide if the following statements are **cierto** (C) or **falso** (F).

1. Hay muchas montañas y selvas en Centroamérica. ____
2. En Centroamérica es fácil hacer llegar al pueblo los avances de la medicina. ____
3. La paz llegó (*arrived*) a El Salvador en 1992. ____
4. El Izalco es un volcán en El Salvador. ____
5. El ecoturismo es una buena forma de viajar en El Savador. ____
6. Tikal es una ciudad de ruinas aztecas en Honduras. ____
7. La industria es muy importante para la economía centroamericana. ____
8. El café es un producto muy importante para la economía de Centroamérica. ____

4-61 De viaje a Centroamérica. Match each geographical place with the country it belongs to. Visit **www.prenhall.com/arriba** for additional help.

1. San Miguel:

   a. El Salvador b. Guatemala c. Honduras

2. Chichicastenango:

   a. El Salvador b. Guatemala c. Honduras

3. La Ceiba:

   a. El Salvador b. Guatemala c. Honduras

4. Tegucigalpa:

   a. El Salvador b. Guatemala c. Honduras

5. Antigua:

   a. El Salvador b. Guatemala c. Honduras

6. Joya de Cerén:

   a. El Salvador b. Guatemala c. Honduras

4-62 La artesanía. In Chapter 4 of your text, you saw photos of some of the woven goods from Guatemala. Now, visit **www.prenhall.com/arriba** for more information about the folklore and handmade items from this region, and make a list of five examples of Central American crafts.

1. ____________ 3. ____________ 5. ____________

2. ____________ 4. ____________

Ritmos

4-63 Ritmos centroamericanos. You have already heard the sounds of *Los profesionales* from Honduras. Now visit **www.prenhall.com/arriba** to answer the questions about Ricardo Arjona, another great artist from Central America.

1. Ricardo Arjona es…

   a. pintor. b. cantante. c. actor.

2. Ricardo Arjona es de…

   a. Guatemala. b. El Salvador. c. Honduras.

3. Ricardo Arjona vive en…

   a. Miami. b. Guatemala. c. México.

4. Su primer disco se llama…

   a. *Déjame decir que te amo.* b. *Santo pecado.* c. *Historias.*

Páginas

4-64 Una carta. Using the letters to Dolores from the **Páginas** section of Chapter 4 as a model, write a letter to Dolores describing your relationship with one of your family members.

____

____

____

____

____

Taller

4-65 Sus familias. Write eight questions in Spanish that you can use to find out about someone's family.

MODELO: *¿Estás casado/a?*
¿Cuántos hijos/hermanos tienes?

1. ______________________
2. ______________________
3. ______________________
4. ______________________
5. ______________________
6. ______________________
7. ______________________
8. ______________________

4-66 Entrevista. Interview a Spanish-speaking friend, fellow student, or your professor about his/her family. Use the questions you wrote in the previous activity.

4-67 Tus ideas. Use the information from the last activity to write a brief paragraph about the family of the person you interviewed.

MODELO: *Eduardo tiene una familia muy interesante...*

____

____

____

____

____

Nombre: ______________________________ Fecha: ______________________

5 ¿Cómo pasas el día?

PRIMERA PARTE

¡Así es la vida!

5-1 ¿Recuerdas? Reread the excerpt about "Los vecinos de la Calle Ricardo Arias en la Ciudad de Panamá" on page 156 of the textbook, and decide if the following statements are **cierto** (C) or **falso** (F).

1. Son las siete y cada vecino tiene que prepararse. ____
2. Antonio tiene que afeitarse. ____
3. Janet es la vecina del cuarto piso. ____
4. Janet tiene que acostarse. ____
5. Cristina y Eduardo son los vecinos del primero. ____
6. Cristina tiene que ver la televisión. ____
7. Cristina tiene que vestirse. ____
8. Eduardo tiene que salir inmediatamente. ____

CD 5, Track 1

5-2 La mañana de Manuel y Teresa. Listen to the following conversation and then select the letter that best completes each sentence.

1. Manuel no está bien porque...
   a. trabaja mucho.
   b. se acuesta tarde.
   c. se baña por la mañana.

2. Por la mañana, Teresa...
   a. despierta a Manuel.
   b. se pone furiosa con Manuel.
   c. hace la tarea con Manuel.

3. Teresa piensa que Manuel debe…

   a. mirarse en el espejo.

   b. cepillarse los dientes.

   c. acostarse más temprano.

4. Manuel se baña y luego…

   a. se afeita.

   b. se seca el pelo.

   c. se maquilla.

5. Después de cepillarse los dientes, Manuel…

   a. lee o hace la tarea.

   b. se divierte.

   c. se viste.

6. Manuel se acuesta…

   a. a las diez.

   b. a las dos.

   c. a las doce.

7. Teresa va a comprar…

   a. jabón y crema.

   b. champú y desodorante.

   c. un espejo nuevo y una navaja de afeitar.

Nombre: ______________________________ Fecha: ______________________

¡Así lo decimos! Vocabulario (TEXTBOOK P. 157)

5-3 ¡Fuera de lugar! In each set of words, choose the word or expression that is out of place.

1. a. acostarse
   b. bañarse
   c. dormirse
   d. despertarse
2. a. el secador
   b. el peine
   c. los ojos
   d. la máquina de afeitar
3. a. el maquillaje
   b. el desodorante
   c. la mano
   d. la loción
4. a. afeitarse
   b. vestirse
   c. ponerse contento
   d. peinarse
5. a. la navaja de afeitar
   b. la máquina de afeitar
   c. el desodorante
   d. la loción de afeitar
6. a. el champú
   b. la nariz
   c. la mano
   d. los ojos

5-4 Un poco de lógica. For each group of sentences, number them in logical order.

1. a. _____ Me seco.
   b. _____ Me levanto.
   c. _____ Me baño.
2. a. _____ Se viste.
   b. _____ Raúl se baña.
   c. _____ Sale de la casa.
3. a. _____ Se acuestan.
   b. _____ Se cepillan los dientes.
   c. _____ Se duermen.
4. a. _____ Nos despertamos.
   b. _____ Nos ponemos la crema de afeitar.
   c. _____ Nos afeitamos.

CD 5, Track 2

5-5 ¡Una casa ocupada! Match the letter of each description you hear with the scenes depicted in the illustration below.

CD 5, Track 3

5-6 Por la mañana. Select the letter that best answers the question you hear.

1. a. un cepillo
   b. maquillaje
   c. una navaja de afeitar
2. a. un espejo
   b. una loción
   c. una nariz
3. a. los dientes
   b. los ojos
   c. las manos
4. a. una máquina de afeitar
   b. un cepillo de dientes
   c. jabón
5. a. un ojo
   b. champú
   c. loción de afeitar
6. a. un lápiz labial
   b. un peine
   c. crema de afeitar

Nombre: ______________________ Fecha: ______________________

5-7 El crucigrama de las actividades diarias. Fill in the crossword puzzle with the answers to the questions below.

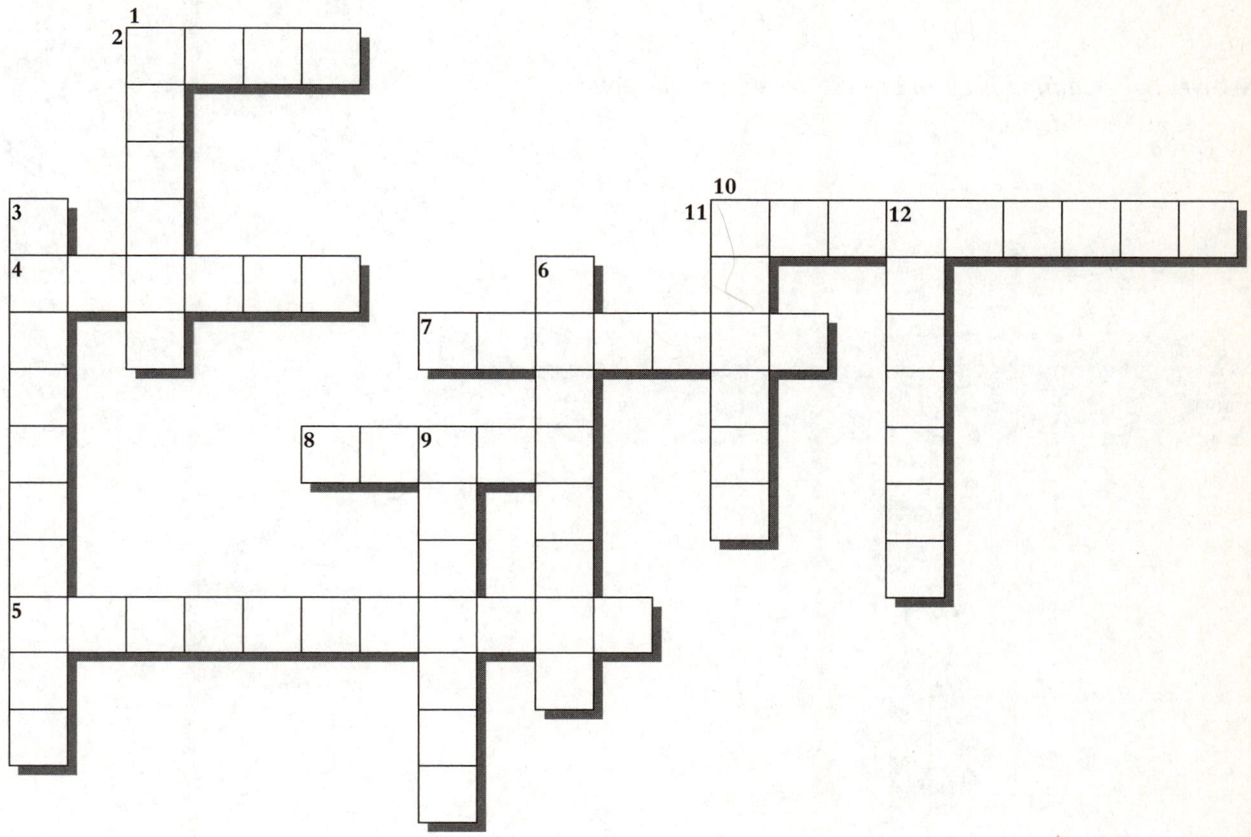

Across

2. Muchos hombres se afeitan la _____.
4. Para mirarnos cuando nos peinamos, usamos el _____.
5. Ella quiere el lápiz de labios; tiene que _____.
7. Todas las mañanas nos cepillamos los _____.
8. Cuando nos bañamos, usamos el _____.
11. Es la medianoche. Quiero _____.

Down

1. Para lavarse el pelo ella usa el _____.
3. Todas las mañanas nos _____ de la cama a las siete.
6. Él no tiene peine, pero tiene que _____.
9. Antes de vestirlos, nosotros _____ a los niños.
10. Yo me _____ con navaja todas las mañanas.
12. Nos secamos el pelo con el _____.

Nombre: ______________________ Fecha: ______________________

5-8 ¿Cómo te pones? Look at the following drawings and form sentences explaining how you feel in each situation. Choose an expression from the word bank and follow the model.

Modelo: *Cuando estoy en la clase de español, me pongo contento/a.*

ponerse contento/a	ponerse furioso/a	ponerse impaciente	ponerse nervioso/a
ponerse triste			

1. ______________________

____

3. ______________________

____

2. ______________________

____

4. ______________________

____

¡Así lo hacemos! Estructuras

1. Reflexive constructions: pronouns and verbs (TEXTBOOK P. 159)

5-9 Mis vecinos y sus actividades diarias. Based on the following drawing, state what each person is doing.

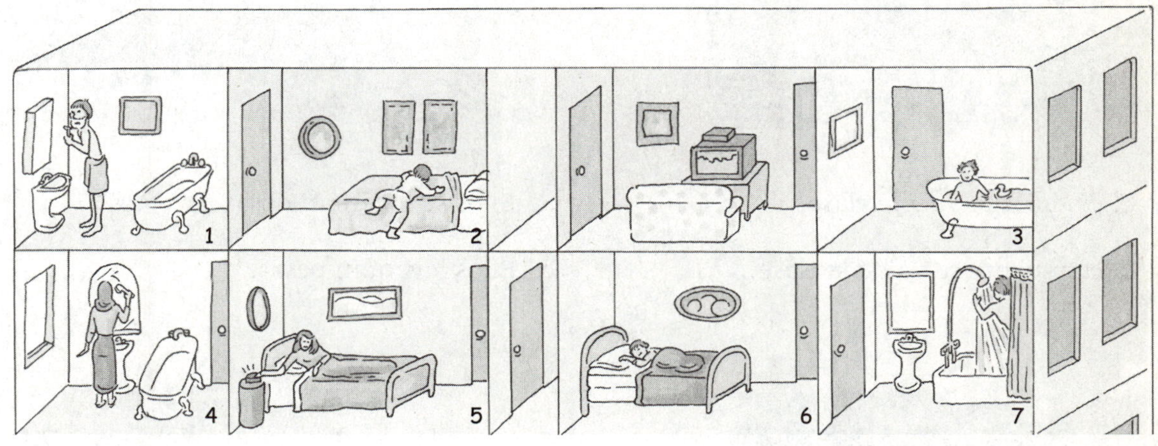

1. ______________________
2. ______________________
3. ______________________
4. ______________________
5. ______________________
6. ______________________
7. ______________________

5-10 ¿Reflexivo o no? Look at the following drawings and choose the sentence that best describes each one.

1.

a. Sonia llama a su amiga.

b. Sonia se llama su amiga.

2.

a. El estudiante va a la clase.

b. El estudiante se va de la clase.

3.

a. Él va al concierto.

b. Él se va del concierto.

4.

a. Ellos se levantan pesas (*weights*).

b. Ellos levantan pesas.

5.

a. Él se levanta a las nueve.

b. Él levanta a las nueve.

Nombre: ______________________ Fecha: ______________________

5-11 ¿Qué hacen estas personas por la mañana? Complete the sentences with the appropriate present tense form of the reflexive verbs in parentheses.

1. Ana María ______________________ (mirarse) en el espejo.
2. Nosotros ______________________ (levantarse) a las siete.
3. Carlos ______________________ (secarse) el pelo con un secador.
4. ¿Tú ______________________ (lavarse) la cara?
5. Mamá ______________________ (maquillarse).
6. Los niños ______________________ (cepillarse) los dientes.
7. Yo ______________________ (bañarse) después de levantarme.
8. Papá ______________________ (afeitarse) con una máquina de afeitar.

5-12 Por la mañana. Complete the following paragraph with the correct present tense form of the verbs from the list. You will have to use some verbs twice.

lavarse	afeitarse	maquillarse	levantarse	cepillarse	bañarse	peinarse

Yo (1) ______________________ a las siete de la mañana. Primero, (2) ______________________ la cara con jabón. Después, (3) ______________________ los dientes y (4) ______________________ con la máquina de afeitar. Yo no (5) ______________________ por la mañana porque siempre me ducho por la noche. A las siete y media mis hermanas (6) ______________________. Mientras Charo (7) ______________________ el pelo, Anita (8) ______________________ los dientes y (9) ______________________ con el lápiz labial. A las ocho y media nosotros desayunamos y después vamos a la escuela.

5-13 Maribel y Nacho. Maribel and Nacho just started dating and spend every day together. Complete the sentences to state what they do.

Modelo: llamarse
Ellos *se llaman* por teléfono todos los días.

1. quererse

   Ellos ______________________ mucho.

Nombre: ______________________________ Fecha: ______________________

2. escribirse

   Ellos ____________________ todos los días.

3. verse

   Ellos ____________________ por la mañana, por la tarde y por la noche.

4. despedirse

   Ellos ____________________ por la noche.

5. encontrarse

   Ellos ____________________ en la biblioteca después de clase.

CD 5, Track 4

5-14 ¿Cuándo lo haces? Complete the sentences using the cues provided. Then listen and repeat as the speaker gives the correct answer.

Modelo: You see: Yo ____________________ temprano.
You hear: levantarse
You say and write: Yo *me levanto* temprano.

1. Yo ____________________ a las diez.
2. Tú ____________________ a la medianoche.
3. Ella ____________________ el maquillaje.
4. Nosotros ____________________ todas las mañanas.
5. Los niños ____________________ por la tarde.
6. ¿Arturo ____________________ los dientes?
7. Tú ____________________ el pelo en cinco minutos.
8. Nosotros ____________________ a las siete.
9. Yo ____________________ el pelo todos los días.
10. Nuestras tías ____________________ mucho.

CD 5, Track 5

5-15 ¿Qué van a hacer? Using the cues provided, tell what the people below are going to do. Then listen and repeat as the speaker gives the correct answer.

MODELO: You see: Carlos ______________________
You hear: afeitarse
You say and write: Carlos *va a afeitarse.*

1. Margarita y Soledad ______________________ en el sofá.
2. Gabriel ______________________ nervioso.
3. Tú ______________________.
4. Manuel ______________________ en el espejo.
5. Nosotros ______________________ para la fiesta.

CD 5, Track 6

5-16 Mis amigos de la clase de español. You meet some new friends in your class and decide to form a study group. Describe what you do together, as in the model.

MODELO: You see: ______________________ para practicar el vocabulario.
You hear: escucharse
You say and write: *Nos escuchamos* para practicar el vocabulario.

1. ______________________ en la clase de español.
2. Siempre ______________________ con las tareas.
3. ______________________ si necesitamos algo.
4. ______________________ correos electrónicos de vez en cuando.
5. ______________________ antes de los exámenes para estudiar en grupo.

5-17 El verano. It's summer and you are no longer on campus. Answer these questions about your relationship with your friends.

1. ¿Qué hacen para mantenerse en contacto (*keep in touch*)?

____

2. ¿Se hablan por teléfono o por Internet?

____

3. ¿Cuándo se ven durante el verano?

____

4. ¿Dónde se encuentran?

____

5. ¿Con qué frecuencia se encuentran?

____

CD 5, Track 7

5-18 Actividades diarias. Answer the following questions positively or negatively, according to the cues. Then listen and repeat as the speaker gives the correct answer.

Modelo: You see: Sí, ______________________
You hear: ¿Te despiertas a las siete?
You say and write: Sí, *me despierto a las siete.*

1. Sí, ______________________
2. No, ______________________
3. Sí, ______________________
4. Sí, ______________________
5. No, ______________________
6. Sí, ______________________

5-19 Preguntas personales. Answer the questions with complete sentences in Spanish.

1. ¿A qué hora te despiertas?

____

2. ¿Te bañas por la mañana o por la noche?

____

3. ¿Con qué te afeitas, con máquina o con navaja?

____

4. ¿Cuál te pones con más frecuencia, perfume o loción?

____

5. ¿Cuándo te cepillas los dientes?

____

6. ¿Cuándo te lavas el pelo?

____

7. Generalmente, ¿a qué hora te acuestas?

____

Nombre: ______________________ Fecha: ______________________

2. Comparisons of equality and inequality (TEXTBOOK P. 163)

5-20 El ego de Roberto. Roberto is always comparing himself to his brother Jorge, because he thinks he is better than Jorge at everything. For each set of comparisons, select the one Roberto would most likely say.

1. a. Jorge es tan responsable como yo.

   b. Yo soy menos responsable que Jorge.

   c. Jorge es menos responsable que yo.

2. a. Yo me levanto más temprano que Jorge.

   b. Jorge se levanta tan temprano como yo.

   c. Yo me levanto menos temprano que Jorge.

3. a. Por la mañana, yo me baño y me visto menos rápidamente que Jorge.

   b. Por la mañana, yo me baño y me visto más rápidamente que Jorge.

   c. Por la mañana, Jorge se baña y se viste tan rápidamente como yo.

4. a. Jorge estudia más que yo.

   b. Jorge estudia tanto como yo.

   c. Jorge estudia menos que yo.

5. a. Yo tengo tantas clases como Jorge.

   b. Jorge tiene más clases que yo.

   c. Jorge tiene menos clases que yo.

6. a. Yo soy más inteligente que Jorge.

   b. Yo soy menos inteligente que Jorge.

   c. Jorge es tan inteligente como yo.

Nombre: ______________________ Fecha: ______________________

5-21 Más comparaciones. Look at the drawings and answer the question listed for each one of them.

Modelo: ¿Quién es más bonita, Penélope Cruz o Salma Hayek?
Penélope Cruz es más bonita que Salma Hayek. or
Salma Hayek es más bonita que Penélope Cruz.

1. ¿Quién tiene más dinero?

____

____

2. ¿Quién está más triste?

____

____

3. ¿Quién es más elegante?

____

____

4. ¿Quién está más gordo/a?

____

____

Nombre: ______________________ Fecha: ______________________

🔊 CD 5, Track 8

5-22 Comparaciones en la casa. Make comparisons of equality based on the cues provided. Then listen and repeat as the speaker gives the correct answer.

MODELO: You see: Tú ______________________ yo.
You hear: Yo tengo mucha loción.
You say and write: Tú *tienes tanta loción como* yo.

1. Nosotros ______________________ Uds.
2. Yo ______________________ mi prima.
3. Tú ______________________ nosotros.
4. Nuestro apartamento ______________________ el apartamento de ustedes.
5. Catalina y Clara ______________________ tú.
6. Mi abuelo ______________________ Joaquín.

🔊 CD 5, Track 9

5-23 ¡No hay diferencia! Use the descriptions you hear to talk about what is the same in the people and objects listed below. Then listen and repeat as the speaker gives the correct answer.

MODELO: You see: Uds. / ponerse / yo
You hear: impaciente
You say and write: *Uds. se ponen tan impacientes como yo.*

1. mis abuelos / ser / mis padres ______________________

____

2. yo / despertarse / mi mamá ______________________

____

3. mi profesora de español / ser / mi profesora de francés ______________________

____

4. lavarse las manos / ser / lavarse la cara ______________________

____

5. Teresa / no acostarse / Manuel ______________________

____

Nombre: ______________________ Fecha: ______________________

5-24 Cristina y Rosa. Cristina and Rosa are identical twins. Compare them by turning each sentence into a comparative statement using *tan... como, tanto/a/os/as... como,* or *tanto como.*

Modelo: Cristina y Rosa son altas.
Cristina es tan alta como Rosa.

1. Cristina y Rosa tienen muchos amigos.

   ____

2. Cristina y Rosa estudian mucho.

   ____

3. Cristina y Rosa se ponen nerviosas en los exámenes.

   ____

4. Cristina y Rosa son muy bonitas.

   ____

5. Cristina y Rosa son muy simpáticas.

   ____

6. Cristina y Rosa visten bien.

   ____

7. Cristina y Rosa se despiertan temprano.

   ____

8. Cristina y Rosa se maquillan.

   ____

Nombre: ______________________ Fecha: ______________________

CD 5, Track 10

5-25 ¿Elena o Mariana? First, listen to the quantities of different items relating to Elena and Mariana. Next, answer the questions based on the numbers you hear. Then, listen and repeat as the speaker gives the correct answer.

MODELO: You hear: Elena tiene nueve espejos. Mariana tiene siete espejos. ¿Quién tiene más espejos?
You say and write: *Elena tiene más espejos que Mariana.*

1. ______________________
2. ______________________
3. ______________________
4. ______________________
5. ______________________

5-26 Tus propias comparaciones. Think of a person close to you (family member, friend, roommate, etc.) who you can compare yourself to. Write a total of six comparisons combining comparisons of equality (*tan… como, tanto como*) and inequality (*más… que, menos… que*).

1. ______________________
2. ______________________
3. ______________________
4. ______________________
5. ______________________
6. ______________________

¿Cuánto sabes tú?

CD 5, Track 11

5-27 Las rutinas de mi familia. Select the letter that best completes the sentence. Then listen and repeat as the speaker gives the correct answer.

1. a. con el maquillaje.
   b. a las siete.
   c. en el espejo.

2. a. champú que Inés.
   b. crema de afeitar que mi papá.
   c. maquillaje como Rosario.

3. a. me siento.
   b. me duermo.
   c. me seco.
4. a. el maquillaje.
   b. la máquina de afeitar.
   c. el secador.
5. a. con loción.
   b. con la secadora.
   c. con champú.
6. a. ponerme impaciente.
   b. vestirme.
   c. bañarme por la mañana.
7. a. crema de afeitar que mi mamá.
   b. jabón como yo.
   c. lápiz labial como mi mamá.
8. a. el cepillo de dientes.
   b. el peine.
   c. el desodorante.

5-28 ¿Sabes las construcciones reflexivas? Fill in the blanks with the appropriate form of the verbs from the word bank.

cepillarse	maquillarse	peinarse	afeitarse	lavarse	secarse

1. Marcos ____________________ con navaja todas las mañanas.
2. Nosotras ____________________ con un lápiz labial especial.
3. ¿____________________ tú el pelo con secador?
4. Yo____________________ con el peine por la mañana.
5. Tenemos que ____________________ los dientes por la mañana y por la noche.
6. Menchu y Mabel ____________________ el pelo con un champú muy bueno.

Nombre: ____________________ Fecha: ____________________

5-29 ¿Sabes comparar? Form comparative sentences with the elements and instructions given in each case.

Modelo: Mi maquillaje / elegante / tu maquillaje (*inequality*)
Mi maquillaje es más elegante que tu maquillaje.

1. Mi champú / barato / tu champú (*equality*)

 ____

2. Eduardo / dormir / yo (*equality*)

 ____

3. La navaja / afeitar / bien / la máquina de afeitar (*equality*)

 ____

4. Mi loción de afeitar / mejor / tu loción de afeitar (*inequality*)

 ____

5. Yo / cepillarse los dientes / tú (*inequality*)

 ____

5-30 Otras preguntas personales. Listen to the questions and then write as well as say your answers.

CD 5, Track 12

1. ____________________
2. ____________________
3. ____________________
4. ____________________
5. ____________________
6. ____________________

Nombre: ______________________________ Fecha: ______________________

SEGUNDA PARTE

¡Así es la vida!

5-31 Las hijas de Cristina. After rereading **¡Así es la vida!** on page 168 decide who has to do the following chores around the house.

1. Lavar los platos:

   a. Rosa b. Paloma

2. Barrer el piso:

   a. Rosa b. Paloma

3. Pasar la aspiradora:

   a. Rosa b. Paloma

4. Sacar la basura:

   a. Rosa b. Paloma

5. Sacudir el polvo:

   a. Rosa b. Paloma

6. Ordenar la sala:

   a. Rosa b. Paloma

7. Lavar la ropa:

   a. Rosa b. Paloma

CD 5, Track 13

5-32 ¡Los quehaceres! Marcos, Verónica, and Diego are students sharing a house. Listen to the following descriptions of the household chores for which each of them is responsible. Then decide whether each statement below is **cierto** (C) or **falso** (F).

1. Dos veces por semana Marcos sacude los muebles. ____
2. Marcos se pone furioso cuando Verónica y Diego no limpian. ____
3. Verónica saca la basura. ____
4. Verónica pasa la aspiradora y lava los platos. ____
5. Diego pasa la aspiradora. ____
6. Los lunes y miércoles Marcos prepara la comida. ____
7. Verónica no come en casa los martes y jueves. ____
8. Diego, Marcos y Verónica limpian los dormitorios los fines de semana. ____

Nombre: ______________________ Fecha: ______________________

¡Así lo decimos! Vocabulario (TEXTBOOK P. 169)

5-33 Los quehaceres y los utensilios. Match each drawing with the most appropriate chore that each one represents. Write the correct letter on the lines provided.

1. ____ 
2. ____ 
3. ____ 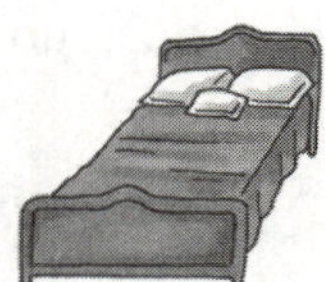
4. ____ 
5. ____ 
6. ____ 

a. planchar
b. poner la mesa
c. lavar la ropa
d. hacer la cama
e. sacar la basura
f. pasar la aspiradora

Nombre: ______________________________ Fecha: ______________________

CD 5, Track 14

5-34 ¿Cómo es mi casa? Listen as Magdalena describes her house. Select all the letters corresponding to statements that are correct according to what you hear.

1. ¿Quién no tiene mucho tiempo para limpiar la casa?

   a. Magdalena b. Rosario c. Diego

2. ¿Quién pasa la aspiradora?

   a. Magdalena b. Rosario c. Diego

3. ¿Quién prefiere sacudir el polvo de los muebles?

   a. Magdalena b. Rosario c. Diego

4. ¿Quién plancha mejor que Magdalena?

   a. su abuela b. Rosario c. Diego

5. ¿En qué parte de la casa trabaja Diego?

   a. la cocina o el comedor b. el patio o el garaje c. la terraza o el baño

6. ¿Dónde se sientan después de un día ocupado?

   a. en el patio b. en el comedor c. en la terraza

Nombre: ______________________________ Fecha: ______________________

5-35 Casas y apartamentos. Read the advertisement and answer the following questions.

1. ¿Cuántos dormitorios tiene la casa que está en Palo Seco?

   a. 3 b. 5 c. 1

2. ¿Cuál de las casas tiene terraza?

   a. Los Arcos b. Santo Domingo de Heredia c. Palo Seco

3. ¿Cuál es la casa más grande?

   a. Los Arcos b. Santo Domingo de Heredia c. Parritta

4. ¿Cuál es la casa con más baños?

   a. Los Arcos b. Parritta c. Palo Seco

5. ¿Cuál de las casas tiene garaje?

   a. Los Arcos b. Santo Domingo de Heredia c. Parritta

6. ¿Cuál es la casa más cara?

   a. a. Los Arcos b. Santo Domingo de Heredia c. Palo Seco

Nombre: ______________________________ Fecha: ______________________

7. ¿Cuánto cuesta la casa más cara?

   a. 39.265.000 colones b. 144.999.900 colones c. 15.000 m

8. ¿Cuánto cuesta la casa que está en Parritta?

   a. 820 colones b. 45.000.980 colones c. 39.700.000 colones

5-36 ¡A completar! Fill in each blank with the appropriate vocabulary word from the list.

basura	lavaplatos	estantes	mesa	secadora
cuadro	aspiradora	refrigerador	cama	sillón

1. Todos prefieren sentarse en el ________________ porque es más cómodo.
2. Hay un ________________ de Picasso en la pared.
3. ¡Tengo sed y no hay agua en el ________________!
4. Tengo que poner los platos en el ________________; están sucios.
5. Las novelas están en esos ________________.
6. En mi casa yo saco la ________________ los jueves.
7. Hago la ________________ todas las mañanas cuando me levanto.
8. La ropa está en la ________________. Tienes que doblarla.
9. Paso la ________________ por la sala.
10. Hoy vienen Pepe y Clara a cenar; tengo que poner la ________________.

Nombre: ______________________ Fecha: ______________________

5-37 Las partes de la casa de Leticia. Look at the drawing and select from the word bank the parts of Leticia's new house that appear on the drawing. Then, write the appropriate name of each room on the drawing. Keep in mind that only some of the rooms from the word bank appear on the drawing.

el baño	la terraza	el comedor	la sala	el garaje
el patio	el dormitorio	la cocina		

CD 5, Track 15

5-38 Mi casa nueva. Leticia is describing her new house to her mother. Looking at the picture from the previous activity, answer the mother's questions.

Modelo: You hear: ¿Qué hay sobre la cómoda?
You write: *Sobre la cómoda hay una lámpara.*

1. ______________________
2. ______________________
3. ______________________
4. ______________________
5. ______________________

Nombre: ______________________ Fecha: ______________________

5-39 ¿Con qué frecuencia? Answer the questions using time words or expressions.

Modelo: ¿Con qué frecuencia planchas la ropa?
Plancho la ropa de vez en cuando.

1. ¿Con qué frecuencia limpias tu cuarto?

____

2. ¿Cuándo haces la cama?

____

3. ¿Con qué frecuencia lavas la ropa?

____

4. ¿Con qué frecuencia pasas la aspiradora?

____

5. ¿Con qué frecuencia sacas la basura?

____

Letras y sonidos (Textbook p. 170)

CD 5, Track 16

5-40 La 'h'. Listen to the following phrases and write the word that begins with the letter 'h'.

1. ______________________
2. ______________________
3. ______________________
4. ______________________
5. ______________________

CD 5, Track 17

5-41 La 'ch'. Complete the sentence with a word containing 'ch'.

1. ______________________
2. ______________________
3. ______________________
4. ______________________
5. ______________________

Nombre: ________________________ Fecha: ________________________

¡Así lo hacemos! Estructuras

3. The superlative (Textbook p. 172)

CD 5, Track 18

5-42 Los mejores. Describe the following things using the cues provided. Then listen and repeat as the speaker gives the correct answer.

Modelo: You see: Estos sillones son ________________________ la casa.
You hear: más moderno
You say and write: Estos sillones son *los más modernos de* la casa.

1. Esta casa es ________________________ la ciudad.
2. Estos cuartos son ________________________ toda la casa.
3. Esta lavadora es ________________________ todas.
4. Esta mesa es ________________________ toda la sala.
5. Estos muebles son ________________________ este restaurante.

5-43 Tu casa. Choose an adjective from one word bank and a word for a part of the house from the other word bank and make five superlative statements. Follow the model.

sala	comedor	dormitorio	garaje
terraza	cocina	baño	

bonito/a	grande	limpio/a	pequeño/a
ordenado/a			

Modelo: *El garaje es la parte menos ordenada de mi casa.*

1. ________________________
2. ________________________
3. ________________________
4. ________________________
5. ________________________

CD 5, Track 19

5-44 Lo mejor de lo mejor. Using the adjectives that you hear, complete each sentence with the correct superlative form (***más***). Be sure to follow the model.

Modelo: You hear: difícil
You see: Hago los quehaceres ______________________ antes de comer.
You write: Hago los quehaceres *más difíciles* antes de comer.

1. Encuentro los libros ______________________ en la librería.
2. El estudiante ______________________ de esta clase se llama Carlos Vargas.
3. Vamos a ver la película ______________________ del cine porque Jorge quiere.
4. Los cuadros ______________________ del museo son los de Picasso.

4. The present progressive (Textbook p. 176)

5-45 ¡Estamos haciendo los quehaceres de la casa! Fill in the blank with the correct form of the present progressive of the verb in parentheses to express what each member of the Pérez family is doing.

1. La Sra. Pérez ______________________ (planchar) la ropa.
2. El Sr. Pérez ______________________ (sacudir) el polvo de los muebles.
3. Antonio ______________________ (lavar) los platos.
4. Rosa ______________________ (hacer) las camas.
5. Cristina ______________________ (pasar) la aspiradora.
6. Los muchachos ______________________ (ayudar) a su madre.
7. Yo no ______________________ (ordenar) mi casa.
8. Y tú, ¿______________________ (limpiar) tu casa?

5-46 Luces, cámara, acción. Look at the pictures below. Say what the following people are doing using the subjects you hear. Then listen and repeat as the speaker gives the correct answer.

CD 5, Track 20

1. (dormir)

____

2. (hablar)

____

3. (pedir un sándwich)

____

4. (comer)

____

5. (escribir)

____

6. (correr)

____

7. (leer un libro)

____

8. (cantar)

____

5-47 Cada uno a lo suyo. Based on the drawings, answer the questions that follow.

1. ¿Qué están haciendo la abuela y Arturo?

____

____

3. ¿Qué está haciendo Pedro?

____

____

2. ¿Qué está haciendo Eugenia?

____

____

4. ¿Qué están haciendo Víctor y Catalina?

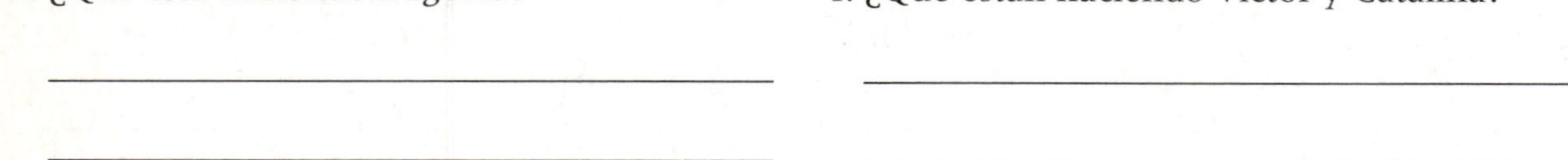

____

____

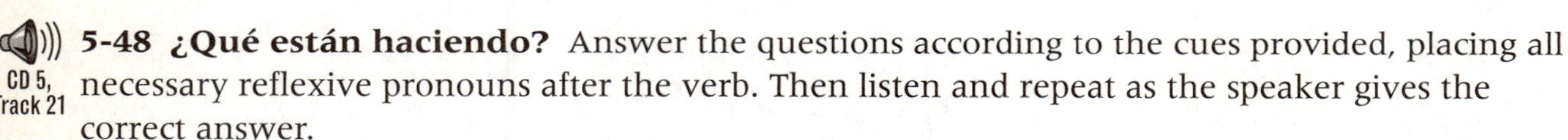

CD 5, Track 21

5-48 ¿Qué están haciendo? Answer the questions according to the cues provided, placing all necessary reflexive pronouns after the verb. Then listen and repeat as the speaker gives the correct answer.

Modelo: You hear: ¿Qué está haciendo Susana? / comprar cuadros
You say and write: *Susana está comprando cuadros.*

1. _______________________________________
2. _______________________________________
3. _______________________________________
4. _______________________________________
5. _______________________________________
6. _______________________________________

Nombre: ______________________________ Fecha: ______________________

¿Cuánto sabes tú?

CD 5, Track 22

5-49 Mi casa. As you listen to the description of the speaker's house, check each room and items in that room that are mentioned.

____ aspiradora	____ baño	____ cama	____ cocina
____ comedor	____ cómoda	____ cuadro	____ estantes
____ garaje	____ dormitorio	____ jardín	____ lámpara
____ mesa	____ patio	____ sala	____ secadora
____ sillas	____ sillón	____ sofá	____ terraza

5-50 ¿Sabes usar el superlativo? Ernesto likes to use the superlative when talking about himself. Form superlative statements with the elements given. Follow the model.

Modelo: Yo / simpático / la familia
Yo soy el más simpático de la familia.

1. Mi casa / bonita / la ciudad

   ____

2. Mi coche / caro / todos

   ____

3. Yo / inteligente / la clase

   ____

4. Mis amigos / populares / la escuela

   ____

5. Yo / mayor / mis hermanos

   ____

Nombre: ______________________ Fecha: ______________________

5-51 ¿Sabes usar el presente progresivo? Based on the information given, explain what chore each person is doing at the moment. Follow the model.

MODELO: Pedro usa la secadora.
Pedro está secando la ropa.

1. Elena tiene la aspiradora.

____

2. Ricardo tiene la plancha.

____

3. Sonia usa la lavadora.

____

4. Víctor pone los platos en la mesa.

____

5. Adriana tiene el basurero en la mano.

____

CD 5, Track 23

5-52 Más preguntas personales. Listen to the questions and then write as well as say your answers.

1. ____
2. ____
3. ____
4. ____
5. ____
6. ____

Nombre: ______________________ Fecha: ______________________

Observaciones

Antes de ver el video

5-53 ¿Qué pasa? Select the letter of the response that best answers each question.

1. As Hermés quits his job, what does he say to his boss?

   a. Sí, claro. Nos vemos en media hora.

   b. ¡Vuelve ahora mismo!

   c. ¡No quiero su dinero y no quiero esto!

2. How would Marcela indicate that she does too much housework?

   a. ¿Y quién limpia el baño? ¿Y quién pasa la aspiradora? ¡La a-mi-gui-ta Mar-ce-li-ta!

   b. ¿Y esta chaqueta encima de la mesa? ¿Es tuya?

   c. ¡No Hermés! ¡No me molesta todo! Me molesta la suciedad, eso sí.

3. What does Silvia say that would solve the problem?

   a. Aquí están las seis tareas principales de la casa: lavar los platos, sacudir el polvo, pasar la aspiradora, sacar la basura y lavar la ropa, y limpiar el baño.

   b. Todos los problemas tienen una solución.

   c. Es la lista con los quehaceres de la casa de doña María.

4. What would Silvia recommend as a fair way of taking care of ironing and making the bed?

   a. Cada uno plancha su ropa y hace su cama.

   b. Doña María hace todos los quehaceres.

   c. Patricio plancha toda la ropa y hace todas las camas.

A ver el video

5-54 Los personajes. Next to each household chore, write the letter of the character who has that responsibility.

1. _____ organizar y dividir los quehaceres	a. Hermés
2. _____ limpiar el baño	b. Felipe
3. _____ sacar la basura	c. Silvia
4. _____ pasar la aspiradora	d. Patricio
5. _____ lavar la ropa	e. Marcela
6. _____ lavar los platos	f. Doña María

Nombre: ________________________ Fecha: ________________________

5-55 La conversación. Complete the following dialogue between Marcela and Hermés with the missing words from the video segment.

Marcela: Siempre hago tus (1) ________________.

Hermés: ¿Ah sí? ¿Y quién saca siempre (2) ________________? ¿Y quién lava (3) ________________? ¡El amigo Hermés!

Marcela: ¿Y quién limpia (4) ________________? ¿Y quién pasa (5) ________________? ¡La a-mi-gui-ta Mar-ce-li-ta! Mira estos zapatos.

Hermés: ¿Qué (6) ________________?

Marcela: ¡Estos!

Hermés: ¿Esos? Sssí, son míos. ¿Los puedes (7) ________________ dentro del armario, por favor?

Marcela: ¿Yo? ¿Por qué? ¡Son tuyos!

Marcela: ¿Y esta chaqueta encima de (8) ________________? ¿Es tuya?

Después de ver el video

5-56 ¿En qué orden? Put the following events in chronological order, labeling them from 1–8 on the lines provided.

_____ A Marcela le gusta la lista, pero a Hermés no le gusta.

_____ Hermés dice que saca la basura.

_____ Silvia entra y les da una lista a sus compañeros.

_____ Hermés habla por teléfono en su trabajo.

_____ Marcela dice que pasa la aspiradora.

_____ Hermés sale del trabajo, furioso y no va a regresar.

_____ Marcela dice que siempre hace los quehaceres de Hermés.

_____ Silvia dice que cada uno (*each one*) plancha su ropa y hace su cama.

Nombre: ______________________________ Fecha: ______________________

Nuestro mundo

Panoramas

5-57 Tres países. Review the information from **Nuestro mundo** on page 180 of the textbook and select the letter of the country that best relates to each person, place, or thing.

1. El guacamayo escarlata:

   a. Nicaragua b. Costa Rica c. Panamá

2. Las islas de San Blas:

   a. Nicaragua b. Costa Rica c. Panamá

3. Las ranas:

   a. Nicaragua b. Costa Rica c. Panamá

4. Los indios Kuna:

   a. Nicaragua b. Costa Rica c. Panamá

5. Violeta Chamorro:

   a. Nicaragua b. Costa Rica c. Panamá

6. La iguana verde:

   a. Nicaragua b. Costa Rica c. Panamá

5-58 ¿De qué país estamos hablando? Read the following statements and choose the most appropriate country. You may need to look back in your text or research your answers.

1. La capital es San José:

   a. Nicaragua b. Costa Rica c. Panamá

2. País al sur de Honduras:

   a. Nicaragua b. Costa Rica c. Panamá

3. La capital es Managua:

   a. Nicaragua b. Costa Rica c. Panamá

4. La moneda es el colón:

   a. Nicaragua b. Costa Rica c. Panamá

5. El dólar estadounidense es la moneda oficial:

   a. Nicaragua b. Costa Rica c. Panamá

6. Conecta el Mar Caribe con el Océano Pacífico:

   a. Nicaragua b. Costa Rica c. Panamá

7. La moneda es la balboa:

   a. Nicaragua b. Costa Rica c. Panamá

8. No tiene ejército:

   a. Nicaragua b. Costa Rica c. Panamá

Nombre: ______________________ Fecha: ______________________

Ritmos

5-59 Cantantes. You have already sampled the sounds of Rubén Blades in your text. Willie Colón is another Hispanic singer/songwriter whose music often includes sociopolitical commentary. Visit **www.prenhall.com/arriba** to look up more information about these artists, their music, and their socio-political concerns. Find and write the following information on each singer.

- country of origin
- type of music
- names of popular songs and albums
- activism

Rubén Blades: ______________________

____

____

____

Willie Colón: ______________________

____

____

____

Páginas

5-60 Tu casa en Costa Rica. Go to **http://www.prenhall.com/arriba** and imagine you are house-hunting; choose one of the homes you like best, describe it, and explain why it appeals to you.

____

____

____

____

____

____

____

Taller

5-61 Las rutinas diarias. Make a list of your typical weekday morning or evening routine. Try to order the activities numerically and in sequence.

Modelo:

orden	actividad	la hora
1.	*Me despierto*	*las seis.*
2.	*Me levanto*	*las seis y cuarto.*

ORDEN	ACTIVIDAD	LA HORA
______	______	______
______	______	______
______	______	______
______	______	______
______	______	______

5-62 Tus actividades. Use the information you provided in the previous activity to write a description of your typical morning or evening. Add other details whenever possible.

Modelo: *En general, me despierto a las seis de la mañana porque mi primera clase es a las siete y media, pero muchos días no me levanto inmediatamente. Me levanto a las seis y cuarto. Después…*

Nombre: ______________________________ Fecha: ______________________

6 ¡Buen provecho!

Primera parte

¡Así es la vida!

6-1 ¡Buen provecho! Reread the conversation on page 190 of your textbook and indicate if each statement is **cierto** (C) or **falso** (F).

1. Arturo dice que el bufé es fantástico. ____
2. El restaurante sirve camarones a la parrilla. ____
3. A Arturo le gustan mucho los camarones. ____
4. La especialidad de la casa son los camarones. ____
5. Marta va a tomar una limonada. ____
6. Arturo quiere beber vino. ____
7. Marta quiere saber si tienen alguna especialidad de la casa. ____

CD 6, Track 1

6-2 Graciela y Adriana van a comer. Listen to the following conversation and select the letters corresponding to all statements that are correct according to what you hear.

1. Graciela y Adriana van a...
   a. desayunar.
   b. almorzar.
   c. cenar.
2. Graciela...
   a. tiene mucha hambre.
   b. quiere un té.
   c. quiere un café con azúcar.
3. Graciela quiere...
   a. una limonada.
   b. un café con leche.
   c. un té.
4. Adriana pide...
   a. pan tostado.
   b. jugo de naranja.
   c. huevos fritos.

Nombre: ______________________ Fecha: ______________________

5. Graciela prefiere...
   a. jugo de naranja.
   b. jugo de tomate.
   c. el bufé.
6. Graciela quiere...
   a. un yogur.
   b. huevos con jamón.
   c. cereal.
7. Graciela dice...
   a. "Los huevos están deliciosos".
   b. "El desayuno de Adriana está frío".
   c. "Me encantan las papas fritas".
8. El camarero...
   a. le trae más café a Adriana.
   b. es muy impaciente.
   c. dice que no hay más café.

¡Así lo decimos! Vocabulario (Textbook p. 191)

6-3 En el restaurante. How would you respond to each question or statement below in a restaurant? Next to each question, write the letter of the best response.

1. _____ ¿Desean algo de beber?
2. _____ ¿Me trae la cuenta, por favor?
3. _____ ¿Cuál es la especialidad de la casa?
4. _____ ¿Cómo está la comida?
5. _____ ¡Buen provecho!
6. _____ ¿Cuánto es la propina?

a. Enseguida.
b. Gracias.
c. La especialidad de la casa son los camarones.
d. ¡Exquisita!
e. El quince por ciento.
f. Agua mineral, por favor.

Nombre: ______________________ Fecha: ______________________

6-4 Fuera de lugar. For each group of words, select the letter of the one that does not belong.

1. a. el agua mineral
   b. el café
   c. el bistec
   d. la limonada
2. a. el bocadillo
   b. el helado
   c. el pastel
   d. la torta de chocolate
3. a. la banana
   b. el maíz
   c. la manzana
   d. la naranja
4. a. el bistec
   b. el azúcar
   c. el jamón
   d. el pavo
5. a. la lechuga
   b. el maíz
   c. las papas
   d. la cerveza
6. a. la leche
   b. los camarones
   c. los mariscos
   d. el pescado

6-5 Los alimentos. Locate and select 12 items related to food vocabulary.

A	Z	U	C	A	R	E	F	C	O	M	F	P	L
P	R	L	O	Z	E	M	A	P	L	A	E	O	E
H	X	R	B	C	F	J	L	O	M	S	H	D	C
L	U	H	O	A	R	I	D	J	C	O	A	V	H
O	E	B	Y	Z	E	F	U	A	I	B	Z	U	E
S	M	O	S	U	S	O	D	Z	Q	L	A	M	I
G	V	J	I	B	C	O	S	X	H	A	N	A	T
Y	H	U	E	V	O	S	E	B	A	N	A	N	A
Q	O	D	P	N	F	H	O	I	G	I	H	A	B
A	T	A	O	I	S	R	S	A	R	L	O	Z	R
O	Z	M	V	A	R	Q	E	T	V	Z	R	N	O
P	A	F	U	L	O	P	U	Y	U	E	I	A	L
J	I	R	A	L	L	I	Q	E	T	N	A	M	S

Nombre: ______________________ Fecha: ______________________

6-6 Las comidas del día. Choose six different items from the menu below and form full sentences combining them with the words for the meals of the day (***el desayuno, el almuerzo, la merienda, la cena***). Follow the model.

Modelo: *Yo bebo café con leche para el desayuno.*

1. ____

2. ____

3. ____

4. ____

5. ____

6. ____

Nombre: ______________________ Fecha: ______________________

CD 6, Track 2

6-7 ¿Cuál es la comida? Look at the following pictures and answer the questions you hear about them, using expressions and vocabulary from your textbook.

1. ______________________.
2. ______________________.
3. ______________________.

4. ______________________.
5. ______________________.
6. ______________________.

7. ______________________.
8. ______________________.
9. ______________________.

6-8 Cuestionario. Your new friend is curious about your eating habits. Answer her questions with complete sentences in Spanish.

1. ¿A qué hora almuerzas?

____

2. ¿Qué comes para el almuerzo normalmente?

____

3. ¿Dónde cenas?

____

4. ¿Qué comes para el desayuno generalmente?

____

5. ¿Cuál es tu comida favorita? ¿Y tu restaurante favorito?

____

¡Así lo hacemos! Estructuras

1. The verbs *decir* and *dar*, indirect objects, and indirect object pronouns
(TEXTBOOK P. 195)

6-9 ¡A completar! Fill in each blank with the appropriate indirect object pronoun to match the indirect object in italics.

MODELO: Victoria ____________________ prepara un bocadillo *a su hijo.*
Victoria *le* prepara un bocadillo.

1. Mi hermana ____________________ compra el desayuno *a mí.*
2. Ella ____________________ dice la verdad *a sus hermanos.*
3. Tú ____________________ cocinas la cena *a tu familia* todos los días.
4. Ella ____________________ da la merienda *a ti.*
5. Mis amigos ____________________ preparan el almuerzo *a ustedes.*
6. Yo ____________________ preparo la cena *a mi novia.*
7. Él ____________________ pide el jugo de naranja *a nosotros.*
8. ¿ ____________________ compras un refresco *a mí,* por favor?
9. Yo ____________________ pido la cerveza *a ti.*
10. Tú y tu hermano ____________________ cocinan el pavo *a los Pérez* todos los años.

Nombre: ______________________ Fecha: ______________________

6-10 Mi restaurante favorito. Fill in the blank with the correct indirect object pronoun and the appropriate form of the verb in parentheses.

MODELO: El camarero __________ __________ (dar) la comida a *nosotros.*
El camarero *nos da* la comida.

1. El camarero __________ __________ (dar) el menú a *nosotros.*
2. El camarero __________ __________ (decir) la especialidad de la casa a *mis padres.*
3. Mis hermanas __________ __________ (decir) al *camarero* que son vegetarianas.
4. El camarero __________ __________ (dar) vino a *mi hermana.*
5. Él __________ __________ (dar) la cuenta a *mí.*
6. Nosotros __________ __________ (dar) propina a *los camareros.*

CD 6, Track 3

6-11 ¿Qué decimos? Write the subjects you hear and provide the correct form of the verb *decir*. Then listen and repeat as the speaker gives the correct answer.

MODELO: You see: __________ __________ "adiós" pero

__________ __________ "hasta luego".

You hear: tú, Elena

You write and say: *Tú dices* "adiós" pero *Elena dice* "hasta luego".

1. Cuando hablamos con el camarero, __________ le __________ "usted" pero __________ le __________ "tú".
2. __________ __________ "coche" pero __________ __________ "carro".
3. __________ __________ "muchachos" pero __________ __________ "chicos".
4. __________ __________ "mucho gusto", pero __________ __________ "encantada".
5. __________ __________ "patatas" pero __________ __________ "papas".
6. __________ __________ "sándwich" pero __________ __________ "bocadillo".

Nombre: ______________________ Fecha: ______________________

CD 6, Track 4

6-12 ¿Qué le damos de comer? Arturo is on a strict diet and his friends give him different things to eat to help him. Based on the subjects provided, tell what the following people are going to give to him using the verb ***dar.*** Then listen and repeat as the speaker gives the correct answer.

MODELO: You see: ______________ le ______________ unas bananas.
You hear: Silvia y tú
You write and say: *Silvia y tú* le *dan* unas bananas.

1. ______________ le ______________ toronjas.
2. ______________ le ______________ un plato vegetariano.
3. ______________ le ______________ agua mineral.
4. ______________ le ______________ una sopa de pollo muy rica.
5. ______________ le ______________ un té caliente.
6. ______________ le ______________ una merienda.

6-13 Repartición de comida. You are sharing food. Explain whom each item is for, using the model as an example.

MODELO: a mi tío / una manzana
Le doy una manzana a mi tío.

1. a mis primos / unas naranjas

____

2. a ti / una sopa

____

3. a mi papá / una torta de chocolate

____

4. a mi primo y su esposa / unos bocadillos

____

5. a ti / unos yogures

____

6. a mi esposo(a) / un refresco

____

Nombre: ______________________ Fecha: ______________________

CD 6, Track 5

6-14 Somos muy generosos. To begin, fill in the first blank of each sentence with the subjects you hear. Next, add the indirect object pronoun that corresponds to the subject of the opposite sentence. Finally, include the correct form of ***dar*** to say what each person gives to the other. Then listen and repeat as the speaker gives the correct answer.

Modelo: You see: __________ __________ __________ helado.

__________ __________ __________ un flan.

You hear: tú, nosotros

You write and say: *Tú nos das* helado.

Nosotros te damos un flan.

1. __________ una manzana.

   __________ una toronja.

2. __________ un poquito de sopa.

   __________ un bocadillo.

3. __________ la cuenta.

   __________ la propina.

4. __________ un refresco.

   __________ agua mineral.

5. __________ unos frijoles.

   __________ arroz con pollo.

6. __________ la sal.

   __________ la mantequilla.

CD 6, Track 6

6-15 El camarero ocupado. You are a waiter at a restaurant and everyone wants something from you. For each question you hear, write the indirect object pronoun used on the line provided.

Modelo: You hear: Camarero, ¿me trae una hamburguesa, por favor?

You write: *me*

1. __________
2. __________
3. __________
4. __________
5. __________
6. __________

CD 6, Track 7

6-16 El cumpleaños de Pedro en el restaurante. Answer the following questions affirmatively using indirect object pronouns. Then listen and repeat as the speaker gives the correct answer.

Modelo: You see: Sí, ______________________ el restaurante.

You hear: ¿Le están enseñando el restaurante a Irma?

You write and say: Sí, *le están enseñando* el restaurante.

1. Sí, ______________________ el vino.
2. Sí, ______________________ la ensalada.
3. Sí, ______________________ un pastel.

4. Sí, ______________________ el dinero.

5. Sí, ______________________ los helados.

6. Sí, ______________________ langosta.

7. Sí, ______________________ una bebida especial.

2. *Gustar* and similar verbs (Textbook p. 198)

6-17 La pirámide de la alimentación. Based on the drawing, select the items that you like and the ones you dislike and place them under the appropriate column.

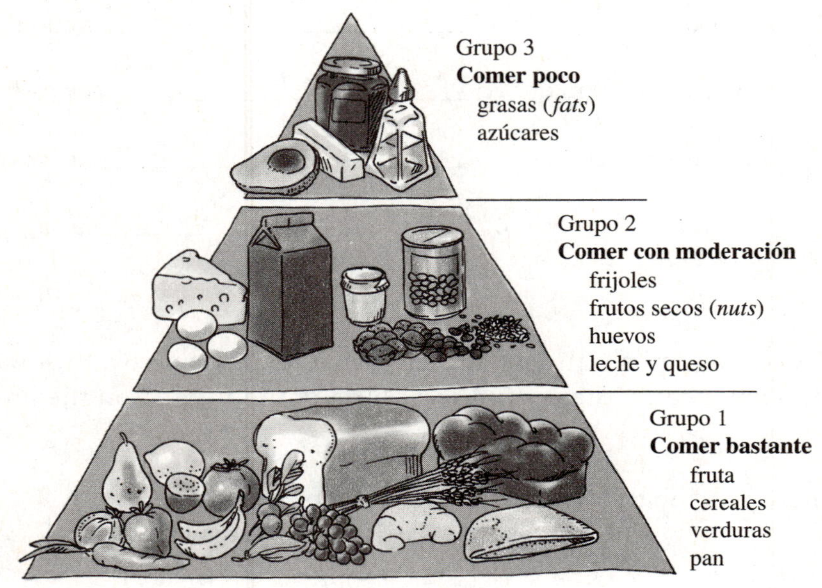

ME GUSTA(N)	NO ME GUSTA(N)
Modelo: *Me gusta la leche.*	*No me gustan los huevos.*
______________________	______________________
______________________	______________________
______________________	______________________
______________________	______________________
______________________	______________________
______________________	______________________

Nombre: ______________________ Fecha: ______________________

6-18 Raúl y Julián. Fill in the blanks in the dialogue between these two friends with the appropriate form of the verb in parentheses.

Raúl: ¿Te (1) ______________ (interesar) las clases de cocina?

Julián: No, no me (2) ______________ (interesar). A mí me (3) ______________ (parecer) aburridas, pero me (4) ______________ (fascinar) ir a restaurantes.

Raúl: ¿Qué tipo de restaurantes te (5) ______________ (gustar)?

Julián: Me (6) ______________ (encantar) los restaurantes japoneses. A mi familia y a mí nos (7) ______________ (encantar) ir a restaurantes exóticos.

Raúl: A mí también me (8) ______________ (encantar) los restaurantes exóticos, pero no me (9) ______________ (gustar) la comida picante.

Julián: Tranquilo, conozco un restaurante que te va a (10) ______________ (fascinar).

CD 6, Track 8

6-19 ¿Qué les gusta? Tell what the following people like, using the cues provided and the verb ***gustar***. Then listen and repeat as the speaker gives the correct answer.

Modelo: You see: ______________ la tarta de manzana.
You hear: a nosotros
You write and say: *A nosotros nos gusta* la tarta de manzana.

1. ______________ las galletas de chocolate.
2. ______________ los camarones.
3. ______________ comer en la terraza.
4. ______________ mucho cocinar.
5. ______________ ese restaurante vegetariano.
6. ______________ los frijoles negros.

CD 6, Track 9

6-20 Las experiencias. Tell what the following people experience based on the cues provided. Then listen and repeat as the speaker gives the correct answer.

Modelo: You see: ______________________ la langosta.
You hear: a nosotros, fascinar
You write and say: *A nosotros nos fascina* la langosta.

1. ______________________ los camareros impacientes.
2. ______________________ ver los ingredientes.

3. ______________________________ comprar los refrescos.

4. ______________________________ Julián.

5. ______________________________ Javier y Anita.

6. ______________________________ el arroz con pollo.

7. ______________________________ la comida chilena.

6-21 Los gustos de los demás. Based on each drawing and following the model, indicate what each person likes using the verb ***gustar.***

MODELO: *A Antonio le gustan las hamburguesas.*

1. ______________________________

2. ______________________________

3. ______________________________

4. ______________________________

5. ______________________________

6. ______________________________

Nombre: ______________________________ Fecha: ______________________

6-22 ¿Te gusta...? Answer the following questions in complete sentences in Spanish.

1. ¿Qué restaurantes te gustan?

____

2. ¿Te interesan las comidas exóticas?

____

3. ¿Qué comida no te gusta?

____

4. ¿Qué comida le encanta a tu familia?

____

5. ¿Qué restaurante les fascina a tus amigos?

____

¿Cuánto sabes tú?

CD 6, Track 10

6-23 Los señores Vega en el mercado. According to the picture below, indicate whether the statements you hear are **cierto** (C) or **falso** (F).

1. ____
2. ____
3. ____
4. ____
5. ____
6. ____
7. ____
8. ____

Nombre: ______________________________ Fecha: ______________________

6-24 ¿Sabes usar los pronombres de objeto indirecto? Read the following sentence and select the letter of the appropriate pronoun to complete each statement.

1. Ellos nunca ____ dan propina al camarero.

   a. le b. les c. me

2. Antonio ____ lee el menú del día a ti.

   a. me b. le c. te

3. Ellos ____ compran el almuerzo a Javier y a mí.

   a. me b. le c. nos

4. Yo ____ preparo la cena a mi familia.

   a. me b. le c. les

5. Ricardo ____ pide un refresco a sus amigos.

   a. les b. le c. te

6-25 ¿Sabes usar los verbos como *gustar*? Fill in the blanks with the appropriate pronoun and form of the verb in parentheses.

1. A Rosa y a Pedro ________________ ________________ (fascinar) la langosta.
2. A mí ________________ ________________ (encantar) los camarones.
3. A Rodrigo y a mí ________________ ________________ (molestar) los clientes impacientes.
4. A Laura ________________ ________________ (aburrir) cocinar.
5. Y a ti, ¿qué ________________ ________________ (parecer) las clases de cocina?

CD 6, Track 11

6-26 Preguntas personales. Answer the questions you hear in complete sentences in Spanish.

1. ____.
2. ____.
3. ____.
4. ____.
5. ____.
6. ____.

Nombre: ______________________ Fecha: ______________________

Segunda parte

¡Así es la vida!

CD 6, Track 12

6-27 La cena de Mamá, Papá y Lola. Listen to the following conversation and indicate whether the statements are **cierto** (C) or **falso** (F) according to what you hear.

1. La mamá preparó el desayuno. _____
2. Papá ayudó a preparar la ensalada. _____
3. Lola y sus padres comen pollo. _____
4. Comen también arroz y frijoles. _____
5. Lola encontró el café en el congelador. _____
6. Tienen pan. _____
7. Hay flan para mañana. _____
8. Papá está calentando los frijoles a fuego alto. _____
9. La torta está en el horno. _____
10. Papá tapó el arroz. _____

6-28 La cocina de tía Julia. Reread the transcript of tía Julia's cooking show on page 202 of your textbook, and answer the following questions.

1. ¿Cómo se llama el programa de televisión?

   a. "La paella"

   b. "La tía Julia cocina"

   c. "Arroz con pollo"

2. ¿Qué les enseñó la tía Julia a los televidentes ayer?

   a. a hacer arroz con pollo

   b. a hacer paella

   c. a hacer un flan

3. ¿Qué ingrediente no hay en la paella?

   a. mariscos

   b. arroz

   c. queso

4. ¿Qué va a cocinar la tía Julia hoy?

   a. una paella

   b. arroz con pollo

   c. bistec con arroz

5. El arroz con pollo es un plato…

   a. caro.

   b. barato.

   c. fenomenal.

¡Así lo decimos! Vocabulario (Textbook p. 203)

CD 6, Track 13

6-29 En la cocina. Complete the sentences you hear with the most logical response.

1. a. el horno.
   b. la sartén.
   c. la cafetera.
2. a. pelamos.
   b. echamos.
   c. desayunamos.
3. a. un litro de leche.
   b. una pizca de sal.
   c. una cucharada de jugo de limón.
4. a. un kilo de pan.
   b. una cucharadita de azúcar.
   c. un pedazo de manzana.
5. a. la cazuela.
   b. la receta.
   c. la tostadora.
6. a. de la receta.
   b. a fuego mediano.
   c. en el congelador.

Nombre: ______________________ Fecha: ______________________

6-30 Vamos a completar. How well do you know your way around the kitchen? Complete each statement below with a word from the word bank.

cafetera	congelador	receta	pizca
pelar	tostadora	sartén	estufa

1. Guardamos el helado en el ______________________.
2. Para preparar el café, necesitas usar la ______________________.
3. Para calentar el agua, ponemos la cazuela en la ______________________.
4. Para freír los alimentos, usamos la ______________________.
5. La lista de ingredientes y las instrucciones para preparar una comida se llama la

   ______________________.
6. Siempre le añado una ______________________ de sal al arroz.
7. Para tostar pan, ponemos el pan en la ______________________.
8. Hay que ______________________ la banana antes de comerla.

6-31 Muchos cocineros. The Spanish Club at the university is having a party and everyone is helping in the kitchen. Complete each sentence describing what the club members are doing. Use the present tense of the correct verb from the word bank.

echar	calentar	freír	pelar	hervir	tostar

Modelo: Anita *prepara* los bocadillos.

1. Ramón y Ricardo ______________________ las papas.
2. Carlos le ______________________ un poco de sal a la ensalada.
3. Julio y Yolanda ______________________ los huevos en la sartén.
4. Yo ______________________ el agua para las papas en la estufa.
5. Tú ______________________ el pan en la tostadora.
6. Jorge y Ángela ______________________ la leche en el microondas.

Nombre: ______________________________ Fecha: ______________________

6-32 **Los utensilios de la cocina.** Write six complete sentences combining food vocabulary from the **Primera parte** and the utensils and appliances that appear in the drawing. Follow the model.

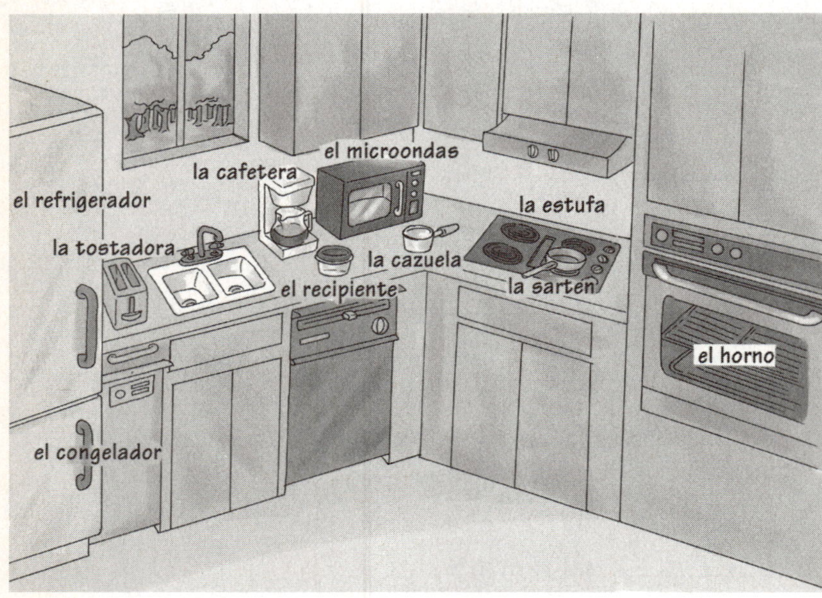

Modelo: *Yo caliento la leche en el microondas.*

1. ____
2. ____
3. ____
4. ____
5. ____
6. ____

Letras y sonidos (Textbook p. 204)

CD 6, Track 14

6-33 **Las "c", "s", "z".** Identify whether the words you hear begin with **"c," "s,"** or **"z"** by selecting the correct letter.

1. c s z
2. c s z
3. c s z
4. c s z
5. c s z

Nombre: ______________________ Fecha: ______________________

6. c s z

7. c s z

8. c s z

9. c s z

10. c s z

CD 6, Track 15

6-34 La "c". Identify the words that contain **"c"**.

1. a. b. c.
2. a. b. c.
3. a. b. c.
4. a. b. c.
5. a. b. c.
6. a. b. c.

CD 6, Track 16

6-35 La "s". Identify the words that contain **"s"**.

1. a. b. c.
2. a. b. c.
3. a. b. c.
4. a. b. c.
5. a. b. c.
6. a. b. c.

CD 6, Track 17

6-36 La "z". Identify the words that contain **"z"**.

1. a. b. c.
2. a. b. c.
3. a. b. c.
4. a. b. c.
5. a. b. c.
6. a. b. c.

Nombre: ______________________________ Fecha: ______________________

¡Así lo hacemos! Estructuras

3. The preterit of regular verbs (TEXTBOOK P. 207)

6-37 ¿Qué hicieron en la clase de cocina? Find out what everyone did during a cooking class. Complete each sentence with the correct preterit form of the verbs in parentheses.

1. Alfredo (pelar) ____________________ las papas.
2. Ana y Silvia (escribir) ____________________ una receta.
3. El chef le (echar) ____________________ sal al pollo.
4. Yo (comprar) ____________________ los ingredientes.
5. José (cocinar) ____________________ los huevos.
6. Tú (tapar) ____________________ la cazuela.
7. Carlos y yo (preparar) ____________________ el pescado.
8. Nosotros (calentar) ____________________ el agua en la estufa.

6-38 El almuerzo de ayer. What happened yesterday at lunch? Complete the paragraph with the correct preterit form of the verb in parentheses.

Ayer yo (1) ____________________ (almorzar) en un restaurante. (2) ____________________ (llamar) a mi amiga Silvia y la (3) ____________________ (invitar) a almorzar. Nosotros (4) ____________________ (llegar) al restaurante a la una. Silvia y yo (5) ____________________ (pedir) la especialidad de la casa, bistec con papas fritas. El cocinero (6) ____________________ (preparar) mi bistec muy bien y yo le (7) ____________________ (añadir) una pizca de sal. Yo (8) ____________________ (beber) un refresco con la comida y Silvia (9) ____________________ (tomar) una taza de café con leche. Nosotros le (10) ____________________ (dejar) una buena propina a la camarera.

Nombre: ______________________ Fecha: ______________________

6-39 ¿Qué pasó? Use the preterit tense of the verbs you hear to complete the following sentences. Then listen and repeat as the speaker gives the correct answer.

CD 6, Track 18

MODELO: You see: Ellos ______________ la carne en el supermercado.
You hear: comprar
You write and say: Ellos *compraron* la carne en el supermercado.

1. Yo ______________ mucho la semana pasada.
2. ¿Tu ______________ los camarones en el mercado?
3. Nosotros ______________ dos kilos de tomates.
4. Ustedes______________ las papas en la cocina.
5. Yo ______________ la receta esta mañana.
6. Ella ______________ en un restaurante famoso.

6-40 ¿Qué hicieron? Fill in the missing parts of each sentence you hear. Then listen and repeat as the speaker gives the correct answer.

CD 6, Track 19

MODELO: You see: Preparamos ______________.
You hear: Preparamos una merienda.
You write and say: Preparamos *una merienda.*

1. Comimos ______________.
2. Salimos a comer ______________.
3. Caminamos ______________.
4. Compré ______________.
5. Compró ______________.

6-41 Preguntas de los padres. Answer the questions you hear affirmatively. Then listen and repeat as the speaker gives the correct answers.

CD 6, Track 20

MODELO: You see: Sí, ______________.
You hear: ¿Compró tu mamá los recipientes?
You write and say: Sí, *ella los compró.*

1. Sí, ______________.
2. Sí, ______________.
3. Sí, ______________.

4. Sí, ______________________.

5. Sí, ______________________.

6. Sí, ______________________.

CD 6, Track 21

6-42 Preguntas de mi mamá. Answer the questions you hear using the negative form.

Modelo: You see: No, ______________.
You hear: ¿Llegaste tarde a la clase?
You write: No, *no llegué tarde a la clase.*

1. No, ______________________.

2. No, ______________________.

3. No, ______________________.

4. No, ______________________.

5. No, ______________________.

6. No, ______________________.

7. No, ______________________.

6-43 Oraciones (*Sentences*) en el pretérito. Using elements from the three columns below, write six complete sentences using the past tense of the verbs.

yo	tapar	café con leche
tú	comer	pescado con papas
Graciela	cenar	sal a la comida
usted	desayunar	la cazuela
Memo y yo	añadir	la cuenta en el restaurante
ustedes	pagar	en un restaurante
Nacho y Tere		comida picante

1. ______________________________

2. ______________________________

3. ______________________________

4. ______________________________

5. ______________________________

6. ______________________________

Nombre: ______________________________ Fecha: ______________________

4. Verbs with irregular forms in the preterit (I) (TEXTBOOK P. 210)

6-44 La primera cita. Juan invited Julia over for dinner at his apartment. He did all the cooking but got a little help. Fill in the blank with the appropriate preterit form of the verb in parentheses to explain what Juan did.

1. No (dormir) ____________________ la noche anterior.
2. (Sentirse) ____________________ nervioso todo el día.
3. (Leer) ____________________ las instrucciones en la receta.
4. (Seguir) ____________________ todas las instrucciones de la receta.
5. (Pedir) ____________________ ayuda a su madre.
6. (Servir) ____________________ la cena en la mesa.

6-45 Una mala experiencia. Read the following paragraph and fill in the blank with the appropriate preterit form of the verb in parentheses.

El viernes pasado fuimos al nuevo restaurante chileno. A mí me gustan los restaurantes mexicanos, pero mis amigos (1) ____________________ (preferir) ir a un restaurante chileno. En el restaurante, Carlos no (2) ____________________ (leer) el menú, pero Menchu y Lupe sí lo (3) ____________________ (leer). Carlos (4) ____________________ (pedir) pescado y ellas (5) ____________________ (pedir) carne. El camarero no nos (6) ____________________ (servir) bien y Carlos (7) ____________________ (pedir) hablar con el encargado (*person in charge*). El encargado no le (8) ____________________ (creer) a Carlos. ¡Fue un desastre! Por la noche Carlos no (9) ____________________ (dormir) bien y Menchu y Lupe no (10) ____________________ (sentirse) bien tampoco.

CD 6, Track 22

6-46 Lo que pasó. Complete the following with the preterit form of the verb you hear, according to the subjects provided. Then listen and repeat as the speaker gives the correct answer.

1. Yo ______________________ crema para el café.
2. Paco ______________________ el pan francés.
3. Usted ______________________ mucho después del almuerzo.
4. El abuelo de Raúl ______________________ en septiembre.
5. Yo ______________________ el ejercicio.
6. Tú ______________________ estudiando por la noche.
7. Ella ______________________ hambre.
8. Los camareros ______________________ los mariscos.

CD 6, Track 23

6-47 Anoche en el restaurante. Complete the following with the preterit form of the verb you hear, according to the subjects provided. Then listen and repeat as the speaker gives the correct answer.

1. Susana ______________________ el menú rápidamente.
2. Tú ______________________ el menú en español.
3. Los niños no ______________________ el menú.
4. Yo ______________________ música en la cocina.
5. Marcos ______________________ el teléfono.

CD 6, Track 24

6-48 Durante el almuerzo. Answer the questions you hear using the cues provided. Then listen and repeat as the speaker gives the correct answer.

Modelo: You hear: ¿Quién se durmió durante el almuerzo?
You see: (mi amigo Luis)
You write and say: *Mi amigo Luis se durmió durante el almuerzo.*

1. (Juan) ____.
2. (solamente seis horas) ______________________________________.
3. (agua mineral) ____.
4. (José y María) ____.
5. (mi papá) ____.
6. (sí) ____.

Nombre: ______________________________ Fecha: ______________________

6-49 Tu última visita a un restaurante. Answer the following questions related to your last experience dining out with a friend.

1. ¿Almorzaste o cenaste en el restaurante?

   ____

2. ¿Qué comiste?

   ____

3. ¿Qué te gustó del restaurante?

   ____

4. ¿Qué pidió tu amigo/a para beber?

   ____

5. ¿Qué prefirió comer tu amigo/a?

   ____

6. ¿Cómo fue el servicio del camarero/a?

   ____

Nombre: ______________________ Fecha: ______________________

¿Cuánto sabes tú?

6-50 ¿Sabes usar el pretérito de los verbos regulares? Match each sentence with the corresponding drawing to explain what each person did yesterday.

1. _____ Mario

4. _____ Dolores

2. _____ Lola

5. _____ Estela

3. _____ El señor Barroso

6. _____ Pilar

a. preparó el café en la estufa.

b. cocinó el bistec en la sartén.

c. cocinó el pollo en el horno.

d. guardó la leche en el refrigerador.

e. cortó la zanahoria.

f. peló las papas.

Nombre: ______________________________ Fecha: ______________________

6-51 ¿Sabes usar el pretérito de los verbos irregulares? Complete each statement by selecting the letter of the correct irregular preterit form.

1. Los camareros ____________________ el almuerzo en el restaurante.

   a. sirven b. servimos c. sirvieron

2. Mi amiga ____________________ vino con la cena.

   a. pidió b. pedí c. pide

3. Ellas ____________________ comer en un restaurante mexicano.

   a. preferimos b. prefieren c. prefirieron

4. Raúl ____________________ mal antes de la cena.

   a. se sintieron b. se sintió c. se siente

5. Ricardo y Lucho ____________________ mucho anoche.

   a. duermen b. dormimos c. durmieron

CD 6, Track 25

6-52 Felicia preparó una cena para dos. Listen to how Felicia prepared dinner and select the letter of the answer that best completes each sentence.

1. Primero Felicia calentó…

   a. el agua.

   b. la sartén a fuego alto.

   c. las papas.

2. Ella peló…

   a. los huevos.

   b. las naranjas.

   c. las papas.

3. Felicia hirvió las papas…

   a. en la sartén.

   b. con mantequilla.

   c. por quince minutos.

4. Felicia sirvió el pollo con…

   a. arroz y frijoles.

   b. pimientos, zanahorias y tomates.

   c. maíz.

5. Felicia tostó el pan en…

   a. la tostadora.

   b. el horno.

   c. el congelador.

6. Felicia preparó toda la cena…

   a. en veinte minutos.

   b. en treinta minutos.

   c. en quince minutos.

CD 6, Track 26

6-53 Otras preguntas personales. Write your response to each question about the last time you went out to eat.

1. ____.

2. ____.

3. ____.

4. ____.

5. ____.

6. ____.

Nombre: ______________________________ Fecha: ______________________

Observaciones

Antes de ver el video

6-54 ¿Qué pasa? Select the letter of the question or statement that best answers each question.

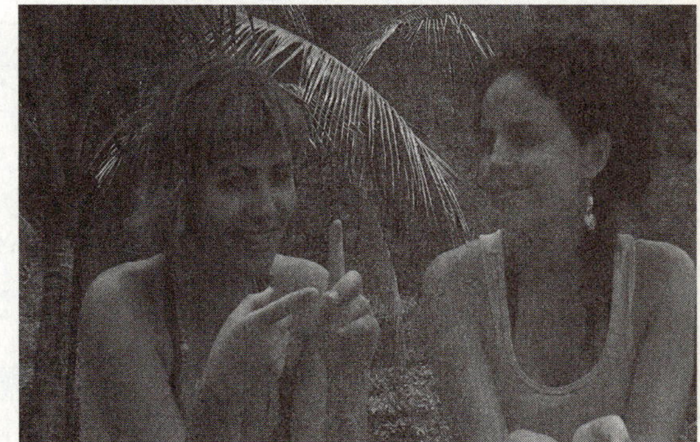

1. Silvia is naming the ingredients she used when making the food she brought to the picnic. What might she say?
   a. Es uno de los platos más comunes de España.
   b. En España eso es una empanadilla.
   c. Lleva patatas, cebolla, sal y huevos.

2. What might Patricio ask Hermés to do with the tortilla?
   a. Hermés, ¿me pasas un poco?
   b. Hermés, ¿y eso qué es?
   c. ¿Quieren uno?

3. What would be Hermés' logical response?
   a. No lo sé.
   b. Claro. Toma.
   c. Mmm, ¡Qué bueno!

4. How would Felipe describe what he brought?
   a. Empanada criolla. Es muy fácil de hacer.
   b. Tenía casi todos los ingredientes en casa.
   c. Ya veo que te gustó. ¿Quieres más?

5. What might Felipe say that his dish is typically served with?
   a. Usé medio kilo de carne que había en el refrigerador.
   b. Se lo comieron todo.
   c. Esto es una salsa que se llama "chimichurri".

A ver el video

6-55 ¿Qué comida llevaron? Write the name of the food item that each person brought to the picnic.

Silvia: ______________________

Marcela: ______________________

Hermés: ______________________

Felipe: ______________________

6-56 La conversación. Fill in the blanks with the missing words according to the video segment.

Silvia: ¿Probaste su (1) ______________________?

Marcela: ¡Claro! Intenté hacerla en casa también.

Patricio: Hermés, ¿me pasas un poco?

Hermés: Claro. Toma.

Patricio: Bueno, en México también se hace (2) ______________________ ¿verdad Marcela?

Marcela: Sí, pero en México es de (3) ______________________.

Patricio: ¿Y eso qué es?

Marcela: Son tacos de (4) ______________________ con (5) ______________________ picante. ¿Quieren uno?

Felipe: Mmm, ¡Qué bueno! ¿Cómo los preparaste?

Marcela: Ayer almorcé en el mejor restaurante mexicano de la ciudad. Los vi en el (6) ______________________ y los compré. Llevan pollo, (7) ______________________, (8) ______________________ y (9) ______________________. ¿Y eso de allí?

Hermés: Pues yo preparé un (10) ______________________.

Nombre: ______________________________ Fecha: ______________________

Después de ver el video

6-57 La acción y los personajes. Determine whether the following statements are **cierto** (C) or **falso** (F) and write the correct letter on the lines provided.

1. En el lugar donde tienen el picnic Patricio encontró una serpiente la semana pasada. ____
2. Patricio se llevó un pedazo de la serpiente a casa. ____
3. Silvia preparó la tortilla con maíz. ____
4. Cuando Marcela estaba en Madrid, siempre iba al bar Los Caracoles. ____
5. La tortilla mexicana es de patata. ____
6. Marcela llevó unos tacos deliciosos. ____
7. Silvia dice "empanadilla" y Felipe dice "empanada criolla". ____
8. El postre que preparó Hermés tiene leche de coco. ____

NUESTRO MUNDO

Panoramas

6-58 ¡A informarse! Based on the information from **Panoramas,** decide if the following statements are **cierto** (C) or **falso** (F).

1. El vino chileno es uno de los mejores del mundo. ____
2. Chile exporta productos agrícolas a los Estados Unidos y al Canadá. ____
3. Chile tiene unos diez mil kilómetros de desierto. ____
4. En este país la pesca es muy importante. ____
5. A los chilenos no les gustan los mariscos. ____
6. El desierto de Atacama es importante por el cultivo de frutas y verduras. ____
7. El desierto de Atacama es rico en minerales. ____
8. Punta Arenas es una ciudad que está al norte de Chile. ____
9. El invierno chileno es de noviembre hasta marzo. ____
10. El volcán Osorno está en el Parque Nacional Vicente Pérez Rosales. ____

6-59 Un poco de historia. Augusto Pinochet is an important name in contemporary Chilean history. Go to **http://www.prenhall.com/arriba** and based on the information found on the web site, pair each date with the letter of an important event in Pinochet's life.

1. _____ 1915	a. golpe de estado
2. _____ 1973	b. Constitución Política
3. _____ 1974	c. Patricio Aylwin, presidente de Chile
4. _____ 1980	d. encarcelado en España
5. _____ 1990	e. Presidente de la República
6. _____ 2000	f. nace en Valparaíso, Chile

Ritmos

6-60 El tren de "Los Prisioneros". Answer the following questions based on the lyrics of "Tren al sur" found in the **Ritmos** section of Chapter 6 in your textbook.

1. ¿A qué hora sale el tren?

   a. 12:30   b. 7:30   c. 2:00

2. ¿En qué carro del ferrocarril está sentado el personaje?

   a. el primero   b. el segundo   c. el tercero

3. ¿A dónde va el tren?

   a. a Valparaíso   b. a Santiago   c. al sur

4. ¿Cómo se siente el personaje?

   a. feliz   b. triste   c. cansado/a

5. ¿A qué hora llega el tren?

   a. 12:30   b. 7:30   c. 2:00

Nombre: ______________________ Fecha: ______________________

Páginas

6-61 La guía *Zagat*. In the **Páginas** section of your text, you read a restaurant review. Now visit **www.prenhall.com/arriba** and decide if the statements below are **cierto** (C) or **falso** (F).

1. El servicio en los restaurantes en Europa es peor que el en los Estados Unidos. ____
2. El tabaco es el gran problema de los restaurantes europeos. ____
3. La cocina italiana es la favorita en Europa. ____
4. En Moscú no hay buenos restaurantes. ____
5. La comida francesa y la mediterránea son muy populares. ____
6. El servicio en los restaurantes en Italia es excelente. ____

Taller

6-62 Los anuncios. Read the following restaurant ads and answer the questions.

1. ¿En qué país y ciudad están estos restaurantes?

____

2. ¿Qué restaurantes tienen el pescado como especialidad?

____

Nombre: ______________________ Fecha: ______________________

3. ¿Qué restaurantes tiene la carne como especialidad?

____

4. ¿Cuáles son las especialidades de "La casa de los tres hermanos"?

____

6-63 Tu restaurante. Now, create your own ad for a restaurant you know or for a restaurant you would like to visit. Try to include as much vocabulary from the chapter as possible.

____

____

____

____

____

____

____

____

____

Nombre: ______________________ Fecha: ______________________

7 ¡A divertirnos!

PRIMERA PARTE

¡Así es la vida!

7-1 El fin de semana. Reread the conversation on page 224 of your textbook and choose the most appropriate answer.

1. Ricardo quiere ir a...

   a. un partido de básquetbol. b. la playa. c. ver una película.

2. Susana no quiere ir al partido de básquetbol porque...

   a. no le gusta el básquetbol. b. no quiere salir con Ricardo. c. hace sol.

3. Susana quiere ir a...

   a. un partido de béisbol. b. la playa. c. ver una película.

4. En la playa, ellos van a...

   a. dar un paseo. b. nadar en la piscina. c. hacer un pícnic.

5. Susana y Ricardo...

   a. quieren ir solos a la playa. b. no van a la playa. c. van a invitar a unos amigos.

Nombre: ______________________ Fecha: ______________________

CD 7, Track 1

7-2 Dos amigos. As you listen to the following conversation, select the letters corresponding to all statements that are correct according to what you hear.

1. Los amigos quieren...
   a. salir esta noche.
   b. caminar por el centro.
   c. hacer un pícnic.
2. Andrea quiere...
   a. ver la televisión.
   b. ir a un partido.
   c. pasear y caminar por el parque.
3. Andrea...
   a. piensa que Ricardo tiene una buena idea.
   b. quiere hacer un pícnic.
   c. dice que va a ser un día perfecto para leer.
4. Ricardo dice que...
   a. prefiere ir al cine.
   b. puede comprar las bebidas.
   c. va a llevar la sombrilla.
5. Andrea...
   a. lleva la heladera.
   b. prepara el almuerzo.
   c. piensa que puede hacer mal tiempo.
6. Si llueve, Ricardo y Andrea...
   a. no hacen el pícnic.
   b. hacen el pícnic por la tarde.
   c. hacen el pícnic debajo de la sombrilla.

¡Así lo decimos! Vocabulario (Textbook p. 225)

CD 7, Track 2

7-3 ¿Lógico o ilógico? Listen to the following short dialogues. Based on your knowledge of the vocabulary in **¡Así lo decimos!,** indicate whether each one is **lógico** (L) or **ilógico** (I).

1. ____
2. ____
3. ____
4. ____
5. ____
6. ____
7. ____
8. ____

Nombre: ______________________________ Fecha: ______________________

7-4 Los pasatiempos. On the line next to each drawing, write the letter of the leisure activity from the right column that it represents.

1. _____

2. _____

3. _____

4. _____

5. _____

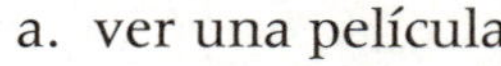

a. ver una película
b. dar un paseo
c. hacer ejercicio
d. ir a una discoteca
e. nadar en el mar

Nombre: ______________________________ Fecha: ______________________

7-5 ¿Qué tiempo hace? Complete the sentences by choosing the letter of the most logical option.

1. En diciembre…

   a. hace frío. b. nado en el mar. c. hace mucho calor.

2. En otoño…

   a. hace mucho calor. b. hace fresco. c. nieva mucho.

3. Cuando voy a la playa…

   a. nieva. b. nado en el mar. c. hay mucha contaminación.

4. Cuando llueve…

   a. hace mal tiempo. b. nieva mucho. c. hace mucho sol.

5. En la primavera…

   a. hace mucho calor. b. hace mucho frío. c. llueve.

6. En el verano…

   a. nieva mucho. b. hace mucho calor. c. hace fresco.

7-6 ¡A completar! Complete each statement with the most appropriate word from the word bank below.

toalla	bolsa	hielo
heladera	sombrilla	traje de baño

1. Hace mucho sol; necesito una ______________________.
2. Paco quiere nadar en el mar; necesita un ______________________.
3. Para secarse después de nadar, necesita una ______________________.
4. Los refrescos están en la ______________________.
5. Los refrescos están fríos porque hay ______________________ en la heladera.
6. Las toallas están en la ______________________.

Nombre: ______________________ Fecha: ______________________

CD 7, Track 3

7-7 Hablamos del tiempo. For each sentence you will hear three possible weather expressions. Complete the sentences with the most logical one. Then listen and repeat as the speaker gives the correct answer.

1. Por lo general, solamente ______________________ aquí en invierno.
2. Salgo a tomar sol en la playa porque ______________________.
3. Hace mal tiempo hoy. Hace mucho viento y ______________________.
4. El día está perfecto porque ______________________.
5. Está nevando. ______________________.

7-8 Preguntas y respuestas. Answer the following questions in complete sentences in Spanish.

1. ¿Qué tiempo hace hoy?

   ____

2. ¿Qué bebes cuando hace mucho frío?

   ____

3. ¿Qué haces tú cuando hace calor en la playa?

   ____

4. ¿Nieva o llueve mucho en tu ciudad?

   ____

5. ¿En qué estación hace mucho frío?

   ____

6. ¿En qué estación hace mucho calor?

   ____

Nombre: ______________________________ Fecha: ______________________

¡Así lo hacemos! Estructuras

1. Irregular verbs in the preterit (II) (Textbook p. 229)

7-9 ¿Qué hiciste ayer? Complete the following dialogue with the appropriate preterit form of the verbs in parentheses. Use the **yo** and **tú** forms only.

1. ¿A quién ____________________ (ver) tú ayer?

   ____________________ (ver) a mis amigos.

2. ¿Adónde ____________________ (ir) con tus amigos?

   ____________________ (ir) a un pícnic.

3. ¿____________________ (tener) que comprar refrescos?

   Sí, ____________________ (tener) que comprar refrescos.

4. ¿____________________ (estar) en la playa?

   Sí, ____________________ (estar) en la playa y ____________________ (dar) un paseo.

5. ¿Con quién ____________________ (dar) un paseo?

   ____________________ (dar) un paseo con mis amigos.

Nombre: ______________________________ Fecha: ______________________

7-10 ¿Qué pasó? To find out what happened to the following people during the past week, complete each paragraph with the correct preterit forms of the indicated verb.

1. **ir**

La semana pasada yo ______________ a un concierto. Mi novia no ______________, pero mis amigos ______________ conmigo. Después, nosotros ______________ a un restaurante a comer.

2. **tener**

Ayer nosotros ______________ que ir a la playa. Yo ______________ que comprar refrescos y mis hermanas ______________ que hacer bocadillos. Nosotros ______________ que comprar bolsas y papá ______________ que comprar una sombrilla.

3. **dar**

Yo le ______________ la sombrilla a mi novia y mis amigos le ______________ la bolsa. Mi hermano le ______________ una heladera. Todos nosotros le ______________ cosas para llevar a la playa.

4. **estar**

Anoche yo ______________ con mis amigos en un restaurante y nuestros profesores también ______________ con nosotros. Nosotros ______________ allí por dos horas. La comida ______________ muy buena. Luego, mis amigos y yo ______________ en casa de mi hermano. ¿Dónde ______________ tú anoche?

CD 7, Track 4

7-11 Anoche. Complete the sentences with the subject you hear and the correct preterit form of the verb in parentheses. Then listen and repeat as the speaker gives the correct answer.

1. ______________ me ______________ las toallas. (dar)
2. ______________ ______________ que comprar un traje de baño. (tener)
3. ______________ ______________ en el cine. (estar)
4. ______________ ______________ al partido. (ir)
5. ______________ ______________ una película de Antonio Banderas. (ver)
6. ______________ ______________ el mejor actor de la película. (ser)

CD 7, Track 5

7-12 Tú y yo. Answer the questions you hear in complete sentences by using the cues provided. Then listen and repeat as the speaker gives the correct answer.

MODELO: You hear: ¿Fueron ustedes al cine?
You see: nosotros sí / Paco no
You write and say: *Nosotros fuimos al cine, pero Paco no fue al cine.*

1. yo sí / Raúl no ______________________.
2. Daniela y Wanda sí / yo no ______________________.
3. Luisa y yo sí / Margarita no ______________________.
4. nosotros sí / Jaime y Rosa no ______________________.
5. yo sí / ellas no ______________________.
6. yo sí / mis amigos no ______________________.

Nombre: ______________________ Fecha: ______________________

7-13 En el teatro. Your friend Sonia has invited you to the theater. Based on the information on the ticket, answer the questions below.

TEATRO HISPANIOLA

"DIATRIBA DE AMOR CONTRA UN HOMBRE SENTADO"
TEATRO LIBRE DEL CARIBE

JUEVES, 25 DE OCTUBRE, 2004

HORA: 21:00
PRECIO: 600 PESOS

BUTACA
FILA: 3 **ASIENTO: 10**

TEATRO HISPANIOLA
C/ DE ALBATROS 42
CABARETE, REPÚBLICA DOMINICANA
(809) 571-0290
201303549 REF: 1222546051

CAJA DE CABARETE CAJA DE CABARETE CAJA DE CABARETE CAJA DE

1. ¿Para qué teatro te dio Sonia la entrada (*ticket*)?

____

2. ¿Qué obra de teatro viste con ella?

____

3. ¿Cuánto tuvo que pagar Sonia por la entrada?

____

4. ¿En qué asiento (*seat*) estuviste?

____

5. ¿Que día fueron al teatro?

____

6. ¿A qué hora fue la obra de teatro?

____

2. Indefinite and negative expressions (Textbook p. 231)

7-14 Conversaciones. Complete each conversation with appropriate affirmative and negative expressions from the word bank.

nada	ninguno	ni... ni	algún	algo
siempre	nadie	alguien	nunca	ningún

1. ¿Quieres refrescos o agua mineral para el pícnic?

   No quiero ____________ refrescos ____________ agua mineral.

2. ¿Deseas ____________ para llevar al pícnic?

   No, gracias. No deseo ____________.

3. ¿Tienes ____________ bocadillo en la heladera?

   No, no tengo ____________.

4. ¿Hay ____________ tomando el sol en la playa?

   No, no hay ____________ tomando el sol en la playa.

5. ¿Vamos al cine esta noche?

   No chico, ¿por qué no vamos a la discoteca? ____________ vamos al cine por la noche.

6. Bueno, ¿qué quieres hacer?

   No sé. ¿Vamos a un concierto? ____________ vamos a ____________ concierto.

Nombre: ______________________ Fecha: ______________________

7-15 Ana y Paco riñen (*argue*). Ana and Paco are quarrelling because Ana has a number of complaints against Paco. Play the role of Paco and change Ana's statements from negative to affirmative, as in the model.

Modelo: **Ana:** Tú *nunca* quieres ir a un concierto conmigo.
Paco: *Siempre quiero ir a conciertos contigo.*

Ana: Nosotros nunca vamos a la playa.

Paco: (1) ______________________________

Ana: Tú nunca me das ningún regalo.

Paco: (2) ______________________________

Ana: Nosotros nunca vamos ni a la discoteca ni al cine.

Paco: (3) ______________________________

Ana: Tú tampoco me invitas a dar un paseo.

Paco: (4) ______________________________

Ana: Nosotros nunca vemos a ningún amigo.

Paco: (5) ______________________________

Ana: Tú no quieres a nadie.

Paco: (6) ______________________________. Te quiero a ti.

CD 7, Track 6

7-16 Al contrario. Change each sentence you hear to its opposite, following the model. Then listen and repeat as the speaker gives the correct answer.

Modelo: You hear: Alguien está cocinando.
You write and say: *Nadie está cocinando.*

1. ______________________________.
2. ______________________________.
3. ______________________________.
4. ______________________________.
5. ______________________________.
6. ______________________________.

CD 7, Track 7

7-17 El pícnic que nadie quiere. Answer the questions you hear negatively, using indefinite and negative expressions. Then listen and repeat as the speaker gives the correct answer.

Modelo: You hear: ¿Debo traer algo para el pícnic?
You write and say: No, no *debes traer nada para el pícnic.*

1. No, no ____________________________.
2. No, no ____________________________.
3. No, ______________________________.
4. No, no ______________________________.
5. No, no ______________________________.
6. No, no ______________________________.

7-18 Tus pasatiempos. Answer the following questions based on the activities you do in your leisure time. Pay attention to indefinite and negative expressions and the possible changes in your answers.

1. ¿Vas a dar un paseo con alguien los fines de semana?

____

2. ¿Haces algún pícnic en la montaña en el invierno?

____

3. ¿Vas a alguna discoteca los sábados por la noche?

____

4. ¿Nadas en el mar en el verano, o en la piscina cubierta (*indoor*) cuando nieva?

____

5. ¿Ves alguna película hispana en el cine?

____

6. ¿Lees siempre el periódico por la mañana?

____

Nombre: ______________________ Fecha: ______________________

¿Cuánto sabes tú?

7-19 ¿Sabes usar las expresiones indefinidas y negativas? Choose the letter of the most appropriate indefinite or negative expression.

1. No me gusta ______________ película de terror.

   a. algo b. nadie c. ninguna d. siempre

2. ______________ voy a la playa cuando llueve.

   a. Nunca b. Nada c. Alguien d. Algo

3. Me gusta hacer pícnics y ______________ me gusta ir a conciertos.

   a. tampoco b. ni… ni c. algún d. también

4. No estuvo ______________ en mi casa el viernes pasado.

   a. alguien b. algo c. nadie d. siempre

5. ¿Tienes ______________ toalla para ir a la playa?

   a. algún b. alguno c. alguna d. ningún

CD 7, Track 8

7-20 El fin de semana. You will hear responses to each of the questions or statements below. First read the following, and then write the letter of the most appropriate response on the line provided.

1. ¿Qué tal si llueve? ____
2. ¿Hace buen tiempo hoy? ____
3. Es un día perfecto para ir a la playa. ____
4. No fui al concierto. ____
5. ¿Dónde pusiste los bocadillos? ____
6. ¿Adónde fuiste anoche? ____

7-21 ¿Sabes usar el pretérito de los verbos irregulares? (1) Fill in the blanks with the most appropriate preterit form of the verbs from the word bank.

dar	ver	ser	estar	tener	ir

1. Ayer nosotros ______________ que leer una novela para la clase de inglés.
2. Yo ______________ un paseo por la playa con Susana.

3. ¿Tú __________________ la última película de Joaquín Phoenix?

4. Pedro __________________ al partido de baloncesto con sus amigos.

5. Yo __________________ en la playa ayer, pero no nadé en el mar.

6. Celia Cruz __________________ una famosa cantante cubana.

CD 7, Track 9

7-22 En el tiempo libre. Write answers to the questions you hear, based on your own preferences.

1. ____

2. ____

3. ____

4. ____

5. ____

6. ____

Segunda parte

¡Así es la vida!

7-23 Hablando de deportes. Reread the passages on page 236 of your textbook and indicate whether each statement is **cierto** (C) or **falso** (F).

1. Muchas personas practican deportes en el Estadio Francisco Montaner. ____

2. Se puede practicar el atletismo y el béisbol. ____

3. Se puede jugar al tenis y al vólibol también. ____

4. El boxeo no es violento. ____

5. Se puede asistir a un partido de fútbol americano los domingos. ____

6. Muchas personas se mantienen en forma practicando deportes. ____

CD 7, Track 10

7-24 ¡El primer día de la temporada de vólibol! Listen to Ramón Fonseca's radio report on the first day of volleyball season at his university. Complete the sentences with all possible answers based on what you hear.

1. El partido es...
   a. en el Estadio Central.
   b. hoy.
   c. de hockey.
2. A los aficionados les gusta...
   a. animar a su equipo.
   b. empatar con el otro equipo.
   c. practicar el esquí acuático.
3. Los jugadores aprenden mucho de...
   a. los árbitros.
   b. los aficionados.
   c. los entrenadores.
4. En la práctica de esta mañana...
   a. patinaron.
   b. levantaron pesas.
   c. vieron boxeo.
5. El equipo de vólibol...
   a. ganó.
   b. hizo ejercicio esta mañana.
   c. quiere ganar.

¡Así lo decimos! Vocabulario (TEXTBOOK P. 237)

7-25 Asociaciones. Write the letter of the word or expression that best associates with each word in the first column.

1. _____ correr	a. no ganar ni perder
2. _____ empatar	b. la piscina
3. _____ gritar	c. pesas
4. _____ nadar	d. el atletismo
5. _____ levantar	e. el hockey
6. _____ patinar	f. el/la aficionado/a

CD 7, Track 11

7-26 Los deportes. Listen to the following descriptions and write the letter of the description that corresponds to each picture.

1. ____

2. ____

3. ____

4. ____

5. ____

7-27 Más deportes. Explain some sports terms to someone unfamiliar with them by completing each statement with the following words or expressions from **¡Así lo decimos!**

árbitro	entrenador	aficionados
equipo	gritar	empatar

1. Los ______________ se ponen contentos cuando el equipo gana.
2. Los aficionados ______________ mucho durante los partidos.
3. El ______________ sabe muy bien las reglas del juego.
4. Un grupo de jugadores son un ______________.
5. Cuando dos equipos ______________, ni ganan ni pierden.
6. El ______________ es la persona que enseña a todos los jugadores.

Nombre: ______________________________ Fecha: ______________________

7-28 Crucigrama. Read the following names of famous sports stars and write the sport that is associated with each in the appropriate squares.

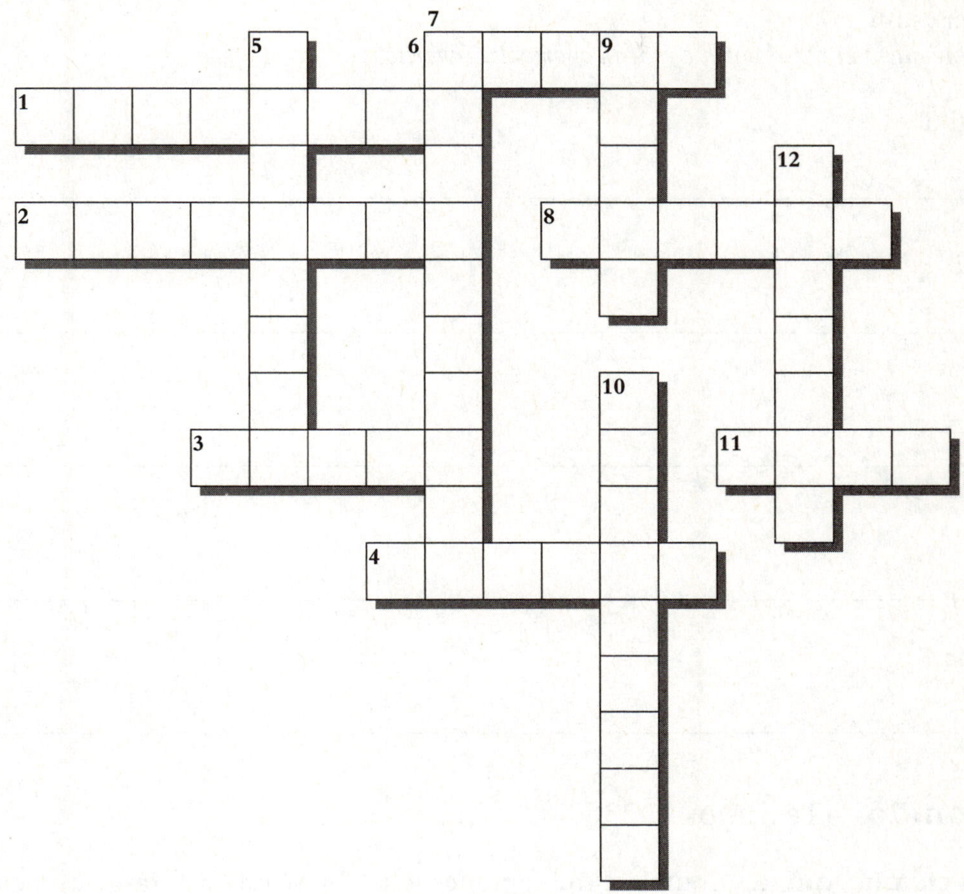

Across

1. Mary Lou Retton
2. Lance Armstrong
3. Andre Agassi
4. Wayne Gretzky
6. Óscar de la Hoya
8. Diego Maradona
11. Jack Nicklaus

Down

5. Michelle Kwan
7. Shaquille O'Neal
9. Picabo Street
10. Justin Gatlin
12. Holly McPeak

Nombre: ______________________ Fecha: ______________________

7-29 ¿Te gustan los deportes? Describe your likes or dislikes of the following sports. Begin each sentence with ***Me gusta*** or ***No me gusta*** and give a reason why.

MODELO: el esquí
Me gusta el esquí porque es un deporte de invierno.

1. el básquetbol

____

2. el atletismo

____

3. el ciclismo

____

4. el hockey

____

5. la gimnasia

____

Letras y sonidos (TEXTBOOK P. 238)

CD 7, Track 12

7-30 Ca, co, cu, que, qui, k. Complete the sentence with the word or phrase you hear. Each one contains the letters **ca, co, cu, que (qué), qui,** or **k.**

1. Me gusta el ____________________.
2. Mi deporte favorito es ____________________.
3. Hace ____________________.
4. No hace ____________________.
5. No te ____________________.
6. Vamos a bailar en la ____________________.

Nombre: ______________________ Fecha: ______________________

CD 7, Track 13

7-31 Más sonidos. Complete the following words you hear with the missing letter.

1. periódi____o
2. ____ué
3. ____ilo
4. ____ontaminación
5. ____uién
6. ____oncierto

¡Así lo hacemos! Estructuras

3. Irregular verbs in the preterit (III) (TEXTBOOK P. 241)

7-32 El partido de anoche. Complete the paragraph with the correct preterit form of the verbs in parentheses.

Ayer (1) ______________ (haber) un partido de béisbol en Fenway Park. Yo (2) ______________ (poder) ver a mi equipo favorito, los *Red Sox* de Boston, y (3) ______________ (ponerse) muy contento de verlos. Mis amigos (4) ______________ (venir) de otra ciudad para ir al estadio conmigo y ellos (5) ______________ (traer) sus entradas (*tickets*). Durante el partido nosotros (6) ______________ (saber) que había cuarenta mil personas en el estadio porque un aficionado nos lo (7) ______________ (decir). Nosotros (8) ______________ (ponerse) muy contentos porque los *Red Sox* ganaron el partido. ¿(9) ______________ (poder) tú ver el partido también?

7-33 Una carta. Find out what Ramiro says in a letter to his friend by using the correct preterit form of the verb in parentheses.

20 de enero

Querido Rafael:

El mes pasado yo (1) ______________ (ir) de vacaciones a casa de Manuel Vargas en la República Dominicana. Allí nosotros (2) ______________ (poder) visitar muchos lugares de interés. Nosotros (3) ______________ (ir) a la capital, donde yo

(4) ______________ (poder) ver monumentos históricos. Luego, Manuel y yo (5) ______________ (ir) a visitar el interior de la isla. Nosotros (6) ______________ (estar) en la playa de Sosúa y también en la ciudad de Santiago de los Caballeros. Por la noche los amigos de Manuel (7) ______________ (venir) a la casa para ir a ver un partido de béisbol y ellos (8) ______________ (ir) al estadio. El partido (9) ______________ (ser) muy emocionante. Desafortunadamente, yo no (10) ______________ (poder) conocer a Sammy Sosa. Después de estar una semana en Santo Domingo, yo (11) ______________ (venir) para los Estados Unidos, pero no (12) ______________ (traer) regalos para nadie.

Un saludo de

Luis Alberto

CD 7, Track 14

7-34 El partido de ayer. Complete the sentence with the correct preterit forms of the verbs that you hear in the infinitive. Then listen and repeat as the speaker gives the correct answer.

1. Ellos ______________ a las tres y tú ______________ a las cuatro.
2. Yo ______________ la heladera y mi novia ______________ las toallas.
3. Ellos ______________ gritar, pero yo no ______________ gritar.
4. Nosotros ______________ "¡Fabuloso!", pero los aficionados del otro equipo ______________ "¡Qué mala suerte!"
5. En el partido de vólibol ______________ 500 espectadores, pero en el partido de hockey ______________ 600 espectadores.
6. En aquel momento, el árbitro ______________ correr y los entrenadores ______________ correr también.

Nombre: ______________________ Fecha: ______________________

7-35 ¡Absolutamente no! Answer the following questions negatively using the preterit and including the direct object pronouns. Then listen and repeat as the speaker gives the correct answer.

CD 7, Track 15

Modelo: You hear: ¿Pusiste los libros en la mochila?
You write and say: No, no *los puse* en la mochila.

1. No, no ______________ ______________ en el baño.
2. No, no ______________ ______________.
3. No, no ______________ ______________.
4. No, no ______________ ______________.
5. No, no ______________ ______________.
6. No, no ______________ ______________.

7-36 Un partido de la Copa Mundial. Luis and Arturo have tickets to one of the World Cup games. Based on the ticket information below, answer the following questions in complete sentences.

Copa Mundial de Fútbol, 2006

HOY

ALEMANIA
VS.
COLOMBIA

Hora: 7:00 PM
Lugar: Estadio Olímpico de Berlín
Boletos: $125

1. ¿Adónde fueron Luis y Arturo?

____

2. ¿Qué partido pudieron ver Luis y Arturo?

____

3. ¿Dónde fue el partido?

____

Nombre: ______________________________ Fecha: ______________________

4. ¿Cuánto pagaron Luis y Arturo por una entrada?

____

5. ¿A qué hora fue el partido?

____

4. Double object pronouns (TEXTBOOK P. 244)

7-37 Un día de pícnic. Read what each person does to get ready for a pícnic. Replace all nouns in the sentences below with direct and indirect object pronouns.

MODELO: Le sirvo la comida a la familia.
Se la sirvo.

1. Les traigo la bolsa a mis padres.

   _____ _____ traigo.

2. Les pido la heladera a mis amigos.

   _____ _____ pido.

3. Le compro un refresco a mi hijo.

   _____ _____ compro.

4. Les preparo los bocadillos a los niños.

   _____ _____ preparo.

5. Me hago una ensalada.

   _____ _____ hago.

6. Le pongo sal a la ensalada.

   _____ _____ pongo.

7. Mi hermano le echa hielo a mi refresco.

   Mi hermano _____ _____ echa.

8. Mi madre nos da la receta de la carne asada.

   Mi madre _____ _____ da.

Nombre: ______________________ Fecha: ______________________

CD 7, Track 16

7-38 ¿Me lo escribes, por favor? Complete the sentences with double object pronouns. Substitute the indirect object you hear and the direct object you see with the corresponding pronouns. Then listen and repeat as the speaker gives the correct answer.

MODELO: You see: Sirven limonada. ____ ____ sirven.
You hear: a sus amigos
You write and say: *Se la* sirven.

1. Compro hielo. ____ ____ compro.
2. Enseña los periódicos. ____ ____ enseña.
3. Leen el nombre del programa de televisión. ____ ____ leen.
4. Traes la heladera. ____ ____traes.
5. Dicen los nombres de los equipos. ____ ____ dicen.
6. Dan las toallas. ____ ____ dan.
7. Buscan un partido en la televisión. ____ ____ buscan.
8. Preparo bocadillos para el pícnic. ____ ____ preparo.

7-39 Muchas preguntas. Answer the following questions affirmatively using double object pronouns. Be sure to follow the model.

MODELO: ¿Te trajo Pedro la novela?
Sí, me la trajo.

1. ¿Les hizo Ricardo los bocadillos para el pícnic a Uds.?

____

2. ¿Te compró Teresa el periódico?

____

3. ¿Te pusieron ellos la toalla en la bolsa?

____

4. ¿Nos dijeron la verdad en la televisión?

____

5. ¿Les trajeron a Uds. el hielo para los refrescos?

____

6. ¿Te pudieron comprar la comida?

____

7-40 Las entradas. Rewrite the following sentences using object pronouns to avoid repetition.

1. Raúl compró las entradas para Rubén.

____

2. Raúl le dijo a Rubén algo de las entradas.

____

3. Rubén no quiso aceptar las entradas.

____

4. Rubén le pagó las entradas a Raúl.

____

5. Rubén nos dio las entradas a nosotros.

____

6. Rubén nos trajo las entradas a la casa.

____

CD 7, Track 17

7-41 Sí, te lo escribo. Answer the questions affirmatively using double object pronouns. Answer informally where possible. Then listen and repeat as the speaker gives the correct answer.

1. ____
2. ____
3. ____
4. ____
5. ____
6. ____

Nombre: ______________________ Fecha: ______________________

¿Cuánto sabes tú?

CD 7, Track 18

7-42 Ignacio y Mónica. Listen to the dialogue between these two friends, and complete each sentence by selecting the letter of the most logical response.

1. La hermana de Enrique practica…
   a. ciclismo.
   b. hockey.
   c. vólibol.
2. Hoy la hermana de Enrique…
   a. tiene el último partido de la temporada.
   b. va a la playa con Ignacio.
   c. tiene que levantar pesas.
3. Fernanda prefiere…
   a. ver un partido de béisbol.
   b. ir a la playa.
   c. hacer ejercicio.
4. Después del partido, los amigos…
   a. van a esquiar.
   b. piensan ir a patinar.
   c. van a comer algo.
5. …lleva los sándwiches.
   a. Fernanda
   b. Ignacio
   c. Mónica
6. Van a nadar porque…
   a. tienen trajes de baño nuevos.
   b. va a hacer muy buen tiempo.
   c. Enrique lleva la música.

7-43 ¿Sabes usar los pronombres de objeto indirecto y directo juntos? Read the following sentences and fill in the blanks with the correct pronouns according to the context.

te	la	los	nos	me	se	lo	las

1. Anita compró unos esquís y ____ ____ dio a su hijo.
2. Yo leí el periódico y después ____ ____ di a ti.
3. Yo quiero una ensalada y mi amigo ____ ____ prepara.
4. Queremos unas cervezas y Ricardo ____ ____ trae.

Nombre: ______________________ Fecha: ______________________

7-44 ¿Sabes usar el pretérito de los verbos irregulares? (2) Fill in the blanks with the most appropriate preterit form of the verbs from the word bank below.

conocer	saber	poner	ser	estar	haber	poder

1. Ayer Jorge ______________ que su padre ______________ boxeador profesional.
2. Teresa, ¿dónde ______________ la toalla? Tengo que ir a nadar y no la encuentro.
3. ______________ una excursión a las montañas el fin de semana pasado, pero yo no ______________ ir.
4. Fernando y Raúl ______________ a Sammy Sosa cuando (ellos) ______________ en Chicago. ¡Fue una experiencia inolvidable!

CD 7, Track 19

7-45 ¿Qué pasó ayer? Answer the questions you hear based on the cues provided. Use pronouns when possible. Then listen and repeat as the speaker gives the correct answer.

1. Sí, ______________.
2. ______________ a las once.
3. ______________ "¡Qué mala suerte!"
4. Sí, ______________.
5. ______________ en la heladera.
6. Sí, ______________.
7. Julio ______________.
8. Yo ______________.

Nombre: ______________________________ Fecha: ______________________

Observaciones

Antes de ver el video

7-46 ¿Qué pasa? Select the letter of the question or statement that best answers each question.

1. How might Marcela describe what she has just been doing?

   a. No pasa nada.

   b. Estuve en la playa surfeando.

   c. Ayer llovió todo el día y toda la noche.

2. How might Silvia explain why she feels the way she does?

   a. Ayer fui a bailar a la discoteca y creo que bebí demasiado.

   b. Nadie supo qué hacer hasta muy tarde.

   c. Es que decidimos ir a última hora.

3. What would Felipe say to indicate that he is upset?

   a. Argentina perdió el partido de ayer.

   b. Pusieron el partido en la televisión.

   c. Es que España siempre pierde, pero Argentina no pierde nunca.

4. Both Marcela and Silvia dislike soccer. What statement does NOT support their opinion?

   a. A mí tampoco me gusta el fútbol.

   b. En España ponen fútbol a todas horas.

   c. No soy aficionada al fútbol.

5. As Felipe tries to determine the name of a particular Argentine soccer player, what might he ask?

   a. ¿Es que nadie lo vio?

   b. ¿Era alto o bajo? ¿De dónde era?

   c. Y a ti, ¿qué te pasa?

A ver el video

7-47 La conversación. Fill in the blanks with the missing words according to the video segments.

Silvia: Hola, Marcela. ¿Ya no (1) ______________?

Marcela: No, no. ¡Menos mal! ¡Qué tal ayer! Llovió todo el día y toda la noche, pero ahora (2) ______________ un (3) ______________, ¡magnífico!

Silvia: ¿De dónde vienes?

Marcela: Estuve en la (4) ______________ surfeando. Fue increíble.

...

Marcela: No soy (5) ______________ del fútbol. Y tampoco me gusta ver la televisión. Lo que más me gusta es estar al (6) ______________ libre.

Silvia: A mí tampoco me gusta el (7) ______________. ¡Qué deporte más aburrido! Prefiero mil veces cualquier otro deporte... incluso el (8) ______________.

7-48 ¿Quién fue? On the lines provided, write the letter of the character that matches each action or description.

1. _____ Vio el partido de fútbol en la televisión.
2. _____ Fue a la playa a surfear.
3. _____ Fue a bailar y bebió demasiado.
4. _____ Baila genial.
5. _____ Le gusta estar al aire libre.
6. _____ Fue a una fiesta el viernes.

a. Hermés
b. Felipe
c. Marcela
d. Silvia

Nombre: ______________________________ Fecha: ______________________

Después de ver el video

7-49 El tiempo libre. Select the letter of the word or phrase that best completes the sentence or answers the question.

1. Anoche Silvia salió…
   a. al restaurante Nuestra Tierra.
   b. al cine.
   c. a una discoteca.

2. Marcela cree que el boxeo es un deporte…
   a. espléndido.
   b. violento.
   c. aburrido.

3. Un lugar donde Marcela surfea es…
   a. el Parque Nacional Braulio Carrillo.
   b. el Mercado Central.
   c. la playa.

4. Hermés fue a un concierto de…
   a. salsa.
   b. merengue.
   c. bachata.

5. A Marcela no le gusta…
   a. bailar.
   b. surfear.
   c. ver la televisión.

6. … ganó la final de la Copa de América hace unos años.
   a. Argentina
   b. Brasil
   c. Perú

7. Felipe quiere saber el nombre...
   a. de la hermana de Silvia.
   b. del futbolista argentino.
   c. del novio de Silvia.

8. ¿Cómo se llamaba el novio de la hermana de Silvia?
   a. Chuqui
   b. Diego Maradona
   c. Kily González

Nombre: ______________________________ Fecha: ______________________

Nuestro mundo

Panoramas

7-50 ¡A informarse! Based on the information found in **Nuestro mundo,** relate each item to one of the Caribbean countries.

1. La isla más grande de las Antillas:

   a. Cuba b. República Dominicana c. Puerto Rico

2. Un estado libre asociado de los Estados Unidos:

   a. Cuba b. República Dominicana c. Puerto Rico

3. Agua tibia y cristalina, y bellas playas:

   a. Cuba b. República Dominicana c. Puerto Rico

4. El merengue:

   a. Cuba b. República Dominicana c. Puerto Rico

5. Coco-taxi:

   a. Cuba b. República Dominicana c. Puerto Rico

6. La fortaleza de El Morro:

   a. Cuba b. República Dominicana c. Puerto Rico

7. Depósitos de ámbar:

   a. Cuba b. República Dominicana c. Puerto Rico

7-51 Los deportes en el Caribe. The most popular sport in the Caribbean is baseball. Some of the baseball stars in the Major League are of Caribbean origin. Look at the following list of current and all-time players and write the name of the country where each player is / was from. You can use **http://www.prenhall.com/arriba** as a source of information.

1. Tony Pérez ____________________
2. Orlando Cepeda ____________________
3. Juan Marichal ____________________
4. Martín Dihigo ____________________
5. Roberto Clemente ____________________
6. Sammy Sosa ____________________
7. Alex Rodríguez ____________________
8. Pedro Martínez ____________________

Ritmos

7-52 Juan Luis Guerra. In the **Ritmos** section of your textbook, you heard a salsa rhythm by Puerto Rican artist Tito Nieves. Juan Luis Guerra is also one of the most internationally recognized Caribbean artists. Visit **http://www.prenhall.com/arriba** and answer the questions below.

1. Juan Luis Guerra nació en…

   a. Cuba. b. La República Dominicana. c. Puerto Rico.

2. Guerra estudió música en…

   a. la Universidad Autónoma de Santo Domingo. b. la Universidad de La Habana.

   c. Berklee College of Music.

3. Su primer álbum se llama…

   a. *Soplando.* b. *Mudanza y acarreo.* c. *El original 4.40.*

4. Su primer álbum de fama internacional fue…

   a. *Mudanza y acarreo.* b. *Ojalá que llueva café.* c. *No he podido verte.*

5. El álbum más exitoso de su carrera es…

   a. *Ojalá que llueva café.* b. *Soplando.* c. *Bachata Rosa.*

6. En febrero de 2006, Guerra tocó en Puerto Rico con…

   a. Rubén Blades. b. Rolling Stones. c. Carlos Santana.

Páginas

7-53 Nicolás Guillén. Review the information on Nicolás Guillén from the **Páginas** section of your textbook and decide if the following statements are **cierto** (C) or **falso** (F).

1. Nicolás Guillén es puertorriqueño. ____
2. Guillén es de origen africano y español. ____
3. La poesía de Guillén no tiene compromiso social. ____
4. Según Guillén, en Cuba no hay discriminación racial. ____
5. Guillén defendió la revolución cubana. ____

Nombre: ______________________ Fecha: ______________________

Taller

7-54 Un fin de semana. Interview three students to find out how they spent last weekend. Fill in the following chart based on your interviews. Remember to ask if they ate out, saw a movie, went shopping, or did other activities. Include your activities in the chart as well.

ESTUDIANTE	ACTIVIDADES	¿CON QUIÉN?	¿DÓNDE?

7-55 Una comparación. Use the information from the previous activity to write a brief paragraph comparing what you and the other students did last weekend.

Modelo: *Ana, Esteban y Rosa fueron a ver una película. Yo no fui al cine, pero salí a cenar en un restaurante muy bueno con unos amigos...*

____

____

____

____

____

____

Nombre: ______________________ Fecha: ______________________

8 ¿En qué puedo servirle?

PRIMERA PARTE

¡Así es la vida!

8-1 De compras. Reread the conversation between Manuel and the sales associate on page 258 of your textbook and decide whether each of the following statements is **cierto** (C) or **falso** (F).

1. Manuel va de compras. ____
2. Manuel quiere ver los zapatos. ____
3. Las chaquetas están en la sección de caballeros. ____
4. Las camisas son una ganga. ____
5. Manuel usa la talla treinta y nueve. ____
6. Manuel decide no probarse la chaqueta. ____

CD 8, Track 1

8-2 Las compras de Rita. Listen to the following conversation and select the letters for all statements below that are correct according to what you hear.

1. Luisa y su amiga Rita van a una tienda...
   a. por la mañana.
   b. por la tarde.
   c. a comprar ropa.
2. Rita quiere ver...
   a. unos pantalones de cuero.
   b. un cinturón de cuero.
   c. una blusa.
3. Hoy están en rebaja...
   a. las blusas.
   b. los pantalones.
   c. los guantes.
4. Rita usa... de blusa.
   a. talla mediana
   b. talla grande
   c. talla 44

5. Los pantalones...
   a. le quedan estrechos.
   b. tienen un descuento.
   c. le quedan muy bien.
6. La blusa...
   a. es de cuadros.
   b. le queda estrecha.
   c. es muy cara.
7. Rita compra...
   a. una blusa de seda.
   b. un bolso de cuero.
   c. los pantalones de cuero.
8. Los zapatos...
   a. están cerca de los probadores.
   b. están en rebaja también.
   c. están en la sección de ropa para hombres.

¡Así lo decimos! Vocabulario (TEXTBOOK P. 259)

8-3 ¿Cómo se visten? Look at the drawing and make a list of all the clothing items you see. Remember to include the definite article for each.

1. ____________________ 5. ____________________
2. ____________________ 6. ____________________
3. ____________________ 7. ____________________
4. ____________________ 8. ____________________

CD 8, Track 2

8-4 La tienda *La Moda*. Listen to the following sentences and put a check mark on all the items in the picture below that you hear mentioned.

Nombre: ______________________ Fecha: ______________________

8-5 La ropa. Complete each statement with the most logical word from the word bank below.

caja	manga corta	material	abrigo
ganga	rebaja	probador	tarjeta de crédito

1. Cuando hace mucho frío, necesito un ______________________.
2. Yo voy a la ______________________ para pagar el vestido.
3. Los pantalones en esta tienda están muy baratos; ¡son una ______________________!
4. Cuando voy al centro comercial, me pruebo la ropa en el ______________________.
5. Para pagar siempre uso la ______________________.
6. Cuando hace mucho calor, llevas una camisa de ______________________.
7. El algodón es un ______________________.
8. Cuando la ropa está barata es porque está en ______________________.

8-6 El cliente y el dependiente. On the line next to each question, write the letter of the response that best answers it.

1. _____ ¿En qué puedo servirle?
2. _____ ¿Qué número calza?
3. _____ ¿Qué talla usa?
4. _____ ¿Cómo me queda la blusa?
5. _____ ¿Cómo quiere pagar?

a. Uso la talla 40.
b. Necesito una corbata para mi esposo, por favor.
c. Pago con tarjeta de crédito.
d. Calzo el número 7.
e. Le queda muy bien.

CD 8, Track 3

8-7 En la tienda. Complete the following dialogues with words and expressions from **¡Así lo decimos!** Then listen and repeat as the speaker gives the correct answer.

1. Buenos días, ¿______________________?

   ¿Me puede mostrar el vestido de rayas azules y rojas?

   Sí, se lo muestro ahora mismo.

2. ¿______________________?

   Uso la talla grande.

3. ¿______________________?

   Calzo número 9.

4. ¿Qué tal le queda?

   ______________________ estrecha.

Nombre: ______________________ Fecha: ______________________

8-8 ¿Qué ropa llevas? What do you wear on the following occasions? Begin each statement with **llevo** and use colors or other adjectives that describe your clothing.

MODELO: Para ir a clase, *llevo vaqueros y una blusa azul. También llevo sandalias marrones.*

1. Para ir a una celebración familiar, ____

   ____.

2. Para ir al centro estudiantil, ____

   ____.

3. Para ir a un partido de básquetbol, ____

   ____.

4. Cuando hace mucho frío, ____

   ____.

5. Cuando hace mucho calor, ____

   ____.

¡Así lo hacemos! Estructuras

1. The imperfect of regular and irregular verbs (TEXTBOOK P. 262)

8-9 ¿Qué hacían cuando iban de compras? Describe what the following people used to do when they went shopping. Complete each sentence with the correct imperfect form of the verb in parentheses.

1. Cuando Ana iba de compras, ____________________ (comprar) la ropa en unos grandes almacenes.
2. Mis padres ____________________ (pedir) el recibo (*receipt*) de la compra.
3. Juan nunca ____________________ (saber) cuál era su talla.
4. Los niños ____________________ (jugar) en el tercer piso del centro comercial.
5. Mis amigos ____________________ (probarse) la ropa en el probador.
6. La dependienta nos ____________________ (atender) muy amablemente.
7. Yo no ____________________ (pagar) con tarjeta de crédito.
8. Tú siempre ____________________ (encontrar) gangas.

Nombre: ______________________________ Fecha: ______________________

8-10 Los recuerdos de mi abuela. Your grandmother is telling you stories of how things were in her day. Describe the customs of the past by changing each statement from the present indicative to the imperfect.

MODELO: Ahora bailamos rock.
Antes, *bailábamos* vals.

1. Ahora trabajamos cincuenta horas a la semana.

   Antes ____________________ cuarenta horas a la semana.

2. Ahora vemos mucha televisión.

   Antes no ____________________ mucha televisión.

3. Ahora las mujeres llevan pantalones.

   Antes las mujeres ____________________ sólo faldas.

4. Ahora compramos mucho.

   Antes no ____________________ mucho.

5. Ahora comemos en restaurantes.

   Antes ____________________ en casa.

8-11 La vida de la dependienta. Complete the store representative's memories with the correct imperfect form of each verb in parentheses.

Cuando yo (1) ____________________ (trabajar) de dependienta, nosotros (2) ____________________ (llegar) a la tienda temprano. Yo (3) ____________________ (hablar) con los otros dependientes mientras nosotros (4) ____________________ (tomar) café. Nuestra tienda siempre (5) ____________________ (abrirse) a las nueve de la manaña. Los clientes siempre (6) ____________________ (ser) amables, pero a veces, ellos (7) ____________________ (ponerse) nerviosos si no (8) ____________________ (encontrar) gangas. A nosotros nos (9) ____________________ (gustar) mucho trabajar en la tienda porque (10) ____________________ (divertirse) todos los días.

Nombre: ______________________ Fecha: ______________________

8-12 Mis recuerdos. Complete the paragraphs with the correct forms of the indicated verbs in the imperfect.

ser

Cuando yo (1) ______________ dependiente, (2) ______________ muy amable con los clientes. Mis compañeros también (3) ______________ muy amables. Nuestra supervisora (4) ______________ muy simpática con los clientes. Nosotros (5) ______________ un equipo muy bueno.

ir

Cuando mi familia y yo (6) ______________ de vacaciones, yo (7) ______________ a los museos. Mis hermanos (8) ______________ a dar un paseo por la mañana y por la noche ellos (9) ______________ al centro. Los domingos todos nosotros (10) ______________ de pícnic.

ver

Cuando trabajaba en un almacén, yo (11) ______________ a muchos clientes. En el almacén, mientras un cliente (12) ______________ la ropa en rebaja, otro cliente (13) ______________ las gangas. Bueno, nosotros (14) ______________ muchas cosas en los grandes almacenes.

CD 8, Track 4

8-13 ¿Qué hacían ustedes? Complete the sentences with the correct form of the verb you hear, according to the subject provided. Then listen and repeat as the speaker gives the correct answer.

Modelo: You see: Luis ____ los pantalones, y sus hermanas ____ faldas.
You hear: probarse
You write and say: Luis *se probaba* los pantalones, y sus hermanas *se probaban* faldas.

1. Yo ______________ las blusas, y mis primas ______________ los pantalones.
2. Tú ______________ en el centro comercial, y nosotros ______________ en un restaurante cerca de la tienda.
3. Leticia ______________ del probador, y yo también ______________ del probador.
4. Ustedes ______________ talla grande, y nosotros ______________ la mediana.
5. Tú ______________ contenta, y nosotras ______________ cansadas.

Nombre: ______________________ Fecha: ______________________

8-14 Nuestra familia antes. Form sentences using the subjects you hear and the correct imperfect forms of the verbs in parentheses. Then listen and repeat as the speaker gives the correct answer.

CD 8, Track 5

1. ______________ ______________ muy introvertida. (ser)
2. ______________ ______________ la televisión todas las tardes. (ver)
3. ______________ ______________ a México cada año. (ir)
4. ______________ ______________ buenas amigas. (ser)
5. ______________ ______________ buen jugador de fútbol. (ser)
6. ______________ ______________ de compras de vez en cuando. (ir)
7. ______________ ______________ dependienta en la tienda. (ser)
8. ______________ ______________ el centro comercial desde nuestra casa. (ver)

8-15 Ayer por la tarde. Look at the drawings and say what each person was doing yesterday afternoon using the imperfect of the verbs under the drawings. Be sure to follow the model.

MODELO: (escuchar música)

Ayer por la tarde, *Jacinto escuchaba música.*

1. 

(ver la television)

Ayer por la tarde, ____.

Nombre: ______________________ Fecha: ______________________

2. (estudiar química)

Ayer por la tarde, ____.

3. (dar un paseo)

Ayer por la tarde, ____.

4. (comprar una blusa)

Ayer por la tarde, ____.

5. (hablar por teléfono)

Ayer por la tarde, ____.

Nombre: ______________________ Fecha: ______________________

8-16 Cuestionario. What were you like when you were a child? What were the things you used to do then? Answer the following questions in complete sentences in Spanish.

1. ¿Cómo eras cuando eras niño/a?

   ____

2. ¿A dónde ibas con tus amigos?

   ____

3. ¿Dónde vivías?

   ____

4. ¿Qué hacías en la escuela?

   ____

5. ¿Veías mucho a tus tíos y a tus primos?

   ____

2. Ordinal numbers (Textbook p. 266)

8-17 Números, números. Complete each statement with the ordinal number corresponding to the number in parentheses. Remember to watch for correct agreement.

Modelo: Los trajes formales están en el (2) *segundo* piso.

1. Ana prefiere la (3) ______________ chaqueta, la verde.
2. La sección de ropa para hombres está en el (8) ______________ piso.
3. ¡Es la (5) ______________ tienda en la que entramos hoy!
4. Puede ir Ud. al (7) ______________ probador.
5. Es el (6) ______________ par de zapatos que compro hoy.
6. Es la (2) ______________ venta-liquidación del año.
7. Los abrigos están en el (4) ______________ piso de la tienda.
8. Hoy es el (1) ______________ día de rebajas.

8-18 ¿Dónde está? On which floor of the department store will you find the following items? Complete each statement with the ordinal number of the correct floor.

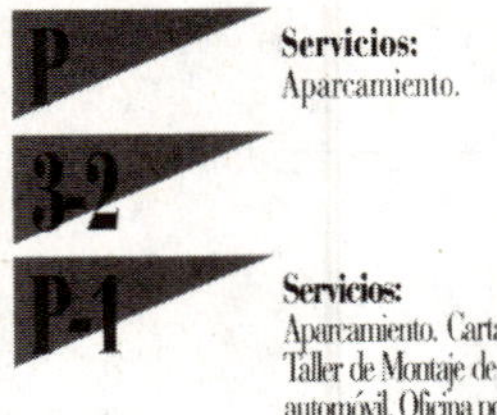

Servicios: (P)
Aparcamiento.

Servicios: (P-1)
Aparcamiento. Carta de compra. Taller de Montaje de accesorios de automóvil. Oficina postal.

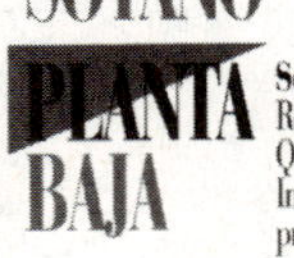

Departamentos:
Librería. Papelería. Juegos. Fumador. Mercería. Supermercado de Alimentación. Limpieza.

Servicios:
Estanco. Patrones de moda.

PLANTA BAJA

Departamentos:
Complementos de Moda. Bolsos. Marroquinería. Medias. Pañuelos. Sombreros. Bisutería. Relojería. Joyería. Perfumería y Cosmética. Turismo.

Servicios:
Reparación de relojes y joyas. Quiosco de prensa. Optica 2.000. Información. Servicio de intérpretes. Objetos perdidos. Empaquetado de regalos.

Departamentos:
Hogar Menaje. Artesanía. Cerámica. Cristalería. Cubertería. Accesorios automóvil. Bricolaje. Loza. Orfebrería. Porcelanas. (Lladró, Capodimonte). Platería. Regalos. Vajillas. Saneamiento. Electrodomésticos.

Servicios:
Listas de boda. Reparación de calzado. Plastificación de carnés. Duplicado de llaves. Grabación de objetos.

2.a PLANTA

Departamentos:
Niños/as. (4 a 10 años). Confección. Boutiques. Complementos. Juguetería. **Chicos/as.** (11 a 14 años) Confección. Boutiques. **Bebés.** Confección. Carrocería. Canastillas. Regalos bebé. Zapatería de bebé. **Zapatería.** Señoras, caballeros y niños. **Futura Mamá.**

Servicios:
Estudio fotográfico y realización de retratos.

Departamentos:
Confección de Caballeros. Confección ante y piel. Boutiques. Ropa interior. Sastrería a medida. Artículos de viajes. Complementos de Moda. Zapatería. Tallas especiales.

Servicios:
Servicio al Cliente. Venta a plazos. Solicitudes de tarjetas. Devolución de I.V.A. Peluquería de caballeros. Agencia de viajes y Centro de Seguros.

Departamentos:
Señoras. Confección. Punto. Peletería. Boutiques Internacionales. Lencería y Corsetería. Tallas Especiales. Complementos de Moda. Zapatería. Pronovias.

Servicios:
Peluquería de señoras. Conservación de pieles. Cambio de moneda extrajera.

Departamentos:
Juventud. Confección. Territorio Vaquero. Punto. Boutiques. Complementos de moda. Marcas Internacionales. **Deportes.** Prendas deportivas. Zapatería deportiva. Armería. Complementos.

Departamentos:
Muebles y Decoración. Dormitorios. Salones. Lámparas. Cuadros. **Hogar textil.** Mantelerías. Toallas. Visillos. Tejidos. Muebles de cocina.

Servicios:
Creamos Hogar. Post-Venta. Enmarque de cuadros. Realización de retratos.

Departamentos:
Oportunidades y Promociones.

Servicios:
Cafetería. Autoservicio "La Rotonda". **Restaurante** "Las Trébedes".

ANEXOS

Preciados, 1. Tienda de la Electrónica: Imagen y Sonido. Hi-Fi. Radio. Televisión. Ordenadores. Fotografía. **Servicios:** Revelado rápido.

Preciados, 2 y 4. Discotienda: Compact Disc. Casetes. Discos. Películas de vídeo. **Servicios:** Venta de localidades.

MODELO: Busco una blusa para mi hermana. Voy a la *cuarta* planta.

1. Necesito comprar un regalo para el bebé de mi hermana. Voy a la ______________________ planta.
2. Deseo una corbata para mi papá. Voy a la ______________________ planta.
3. Necesito unos zapatos. Voy a la ______________________ planta.
4. Me gusta leer y quiero comprar un libro. Voy al ______________________.
5. Mi madre quiere comprar toallas. Ella va a la ______________________ planta.
6. Tengo hambre. Voy a la cafetería en la ______________________ planta.
7. Necesito una falda. Voy a la ______________________ planta.
8. Quiero una tarjeta de crédito. Voy a la ______________________ planta.

Nombre: ______________________________ Fecha: ______________________

8-19 Muchos números. You will hear a cardinal number. In the spaces provided, write the corresponding ordinal number, as in the model. Then listen and repeat as the speaker gives the correct answer.

CD 8, Track 6

Modelo: You hear: tres
You see: Los zapatos están en ____ ________________ piso.
You say and write: Los zapatos están en *el tercer* piso.

1. Ésa fue ____ ________________ tienda que visité hoy.
2. El Sr. Ramos trabaja en ____ ________________ piso.
3. Es ____ ________________ saco de lana que compro.
4. Quería ir de compras en ____ ________________ Avenida en Nueva York.
5. Aquí estoy, en ____ ________________ probador a la derecha.
6. Es ____ ________________ vez que compro en esta tienda.
7. Compré los vaqueros en ____ ________________ piso.
8. Es ____ ________________ persona que se prueba este vestido.

¿Cuánto sabes tú?

8-20 ¿Sabes los números ordinales? You need to shop for a pair of pants. First, read the list of sentences. Then, on the line next to each ordinal number, write the letter of the corresponding sentence, establishing a logical order.

1. ____ primero
2. ____ segundo
3. ____ tercero
4. ____ cuarto
5. ____ quinto

a. Me pruebo los pantalones.
b. Salgo de los grandes almacenes.
c. Busco el departamento de ropa de hombres.
d. Pago con tarjeta de crédito.
e. Entro en los grandes almacenes.

Nombre: ______________________________ Fecha: ______________________

CD 8, Track 7

8-21 El trabajo de mi mamá. Listen to the following story. Then select the letters corresponding to all the statements that are correct according to what you hear.

1. Mi mamá trabajaba en una tienda de ropa para hombres cuando…
   a. ella tenía tiempo.
   b. yo era joven.
   c. necesitábamos dinero.
2. Empezaba a trabajar…
   a. por la mañana.
   b. por la tarde.
   c. por la noche.
3. Mamá…
   a. se ponía nerviosa en el trabajo.
   b. compraba ropa elegante.
   c. miraba los catálogos.
4. A los clientes les gustaba ir a la tienda cuando mamá trabajaba porque…
   a. les daba muchos descuentos.
   b. les daba el mejor servicio.
   c. sabía mucho de la ropa.
5. Mamá salía del trabajo…
   a. a las seis de la tarde.
   b. cuando la tienda cerraba.
   c. después del almuerzo.
6. Cuando mamá regresaba de casa, …
   a. yo la esperaba.
   b. ella estaba cansada.
   c. cenábamos.

8-22 ¿Sabes usar el imperfecto? Fill in the blanks with the appropriate imperfect form of the verb in parentheses.

1. Mientras Julio ____________________ (pagar) la camisa, nosotros ____________________ (comprar) zapatos.
2. Nosotros siempre ____________________ (leer) el periódico por la mañana.
3. Cuando ellos ____________________ (ir) de compras, ____________________ (gastar) mucho dinero.
4. Tú siempre ____________________ (encontrar) las rebajas.
5. Marina ____________________ (trabajar) de dependienta en los almacenes.

Nombre: ______________________ Fecha: ______________________

CD 8, Track 8

8-23 En el pasado. Write your answers to the questions you hear based on your own past experiences.

1. ______________________
2. ______________________
3. ______________________
4. ______________________
5. ______________________

SEGUNDA PARTE

¡Así es la vida!

8-24 ¿Qué compraste? Reread the conversation on page 270 of your textbook and decide if the following statements are **cierto** (C) or **falso** (F).

1. Lucía llamó tres veces a casa de Victoria. _____
2. Victoria contestó el teléfono. _____
3. Victoria fue a la biblioteca porque tenía que terminar un trabajo. _____
4. Victoria fue de compras. _____
5. Victoria fue a la farmacia primero. _____
6. Ella quería comprar una cadena de plata para su mamá. _____
7. Victoria llegó a casa a las dos. _____

CD 8, Track 9

8-25 En el centro comercial. Inés and Marcela run into each other while walking out of a shopping center. Listen to their conversation and select the letters of all statements that are correct according to what you hear.

1. Marcela ...
   a. va al centro comercial.
   b. va a devolver unos aretes.
   c. va a la joyería.

2. Los aretes que Marcela tiene ahora son...
   a. de plata.
   b. de oro.
   c. de perlas.

3. Inés...
   a. va a comprar desodorante.
   b. está en la tienda con su mamá.
   c. necesita comprar pasta de dientes.
4. La mamá de Inés...
   a. está enferma.
   b. llegó esta mañana.
   c. trabaja en la farmacia.
5. Marcela necesita comprar...
   a. maquillaje.
   b. desodorante.
   c. jabón.
6. ... va(n) a la farmacia.
   a. Marcela
   b. Inés
   c. La mamá de Inés

¡Así lo decimos! Vocabulario (TEXTBOOK P. 271)

CD 8, Track 10

8-26 ¿Lógico o ilógico? Listen to the following incomplete statements and select all words or expressions that logically complete them. Then listen and repeat as the speaker gives the correct answer.

1. a. pulseras.
   b. collares.
   c. guantes.
2. a. es de la papelería.
   b. tiene una camisa de algodón.
   c. hace juego con el collar.
3. a. hace juego con el vestido gris.
   b. está de moda.
   c. se devuelve.
4. a. la heladería.
   b. la zapatería.
   c. la farmacia.
5. a. champú.
   b. pasta de dientes.
   c. talco.
6. a. Gasto dinero.
   b. En la farmacia.
   c. En la zapatería.
7. a. La joyería.
   b. Un anillo de plata.
   c. Un reloj de pulsera.
8. a. desodorante.
   b. maquillaje.
   c. pasta de dientes.

Nombre: ______________________ Fecha: ______________________

8-27 Las tiendas. Find 10 words related to names of stores and products from the **¡Así lo decimos!** section.

B	S	A	R	I	F	H	A	R	E	S	L	U	P	U
J	X	M	P	G	L	A	T	L	E	P	N	I	S	F
U	O	F	A	A	O	I	R	D	O	J	E	T	A	B
L	E	Y	P	G	R	L	O	M	T	A	R	I	S	A
L	T	U	E	E	E	O	R	A	A	O	U	L	V	I
O	F	L	L	R	R	U	B	N	I	C	M	A	T	R
A	U	B	E	Z	I	P	Y	I	R	U	I	S	L	E
I	L	P	R	R	A	A	T	T	U	C	A	A	O	M
R	M	O	I	G	A	F	O	M	A	R	C	I	L	U
E	D	R	A	P	T	U	L	I	S	U	V	I	F	F
D	C	U	L	R	O	B	R	C	S	U	Q	T	O	R
A	A	B	R	U	S	E	I	N	C	L	U	A	S	E
L	O	V	O	P	T	A	T	N	I	F	E	C	H	P
E	M	A	M	A	Q	U	I	L	L	A	J	E	I	C
H	B	L	P	N	J	A	T	I	G	U	B	R	A	Z
M	A	A	U	L	B	L	O	P	U	R	N	O	L	U
O	Z	T	L	I	P	E	T	G	I	T	A	L	C	O

8-28 Unos regalos. It seems like everyone you know had a birthday last month! Use words or expressions from **¡Así lo decimos!** to write what you bought for each person and where you purchased it.

Modelo: A mi mamá *le compré su perfume favorito en la perfumería.*

1. A mis hermanos/as ______________________.
2. A mi novio/a ______________________.
3. A mi papá ______________________.
4. A mi mejor amigo/a ______________________.
5. A mi profesor/a de español ______________________.
6. A mi primo/a menor ______________________.

Nombre: ______________________ Fecha: ______________________

Letras y sonidos (TEXTBOOK P. 272)

CD 8, Track 11

8-29 ¿"G", "j", o "x"? Decide whether the word you hear contains the sounds **"g", "j",** or **"x"**, and select the correct letter.

1. g j x
2. g j x
3. g j x
4. g j x
5. g j x
6. g j x
7. g j x
8. g j x

CD 8, Track 12

8-30 Palabras con "g", "j", o "x". Complete the sentences you hear with the most logical word or expression below.

1. a. la biología.
   b. el jabón.
   c. las rebajas.
2. a. el jamón.
   b. la página.
   c. la joyería.
3. a. el traje.
   b. el álgebra.
   c. la gimnasia.
4. a. jamás.
   b. el maquillaje.
   c. joven.
5. a. jota.
   b. mujer.
   c. general.
6. a. geología.
   b. página.
   c. ojo.
7. a. gente.
   b. junio.
   c. caja.
8. a. Jorge.
   b. Tijuana.
   c. México.

Nombre: ______________________ Fecha: ______________________

¡Así lo hacemos! Estructuras

3. Preterit versus imperfect (TEXTBOOK P. 274)

8-31 En el mercado. Every Saturday you and your roommates used to go to the market. Complete the following statements by choosing the correct preterit or imperfect form of the verbs in parentheses and writing it on the line provided.

1. María y Elena siempre (iban/fueron) ______________ a la carnicería.
2. A veces, Paco (encontraba/encontró) ______________ los mejores precios del mercado.
3. El sábado pasado por la noche nosotros no (encontramos/encontrábamos) ______________ estacionamiento.
4. Frecuentemente, mientras Jorge (compró/compraba) ______________ las bebidas, Margarita (tomó/tomaba) ______________ café en la cafetería.
5. El fin de semana pasado, nosotros (nos despertamos/nos despertábamos) ______________ tarde y no (pudimos/podíamos) ______________ hacer las compras.
6. Frecuentemente, todos (gastamos/gastábamos) ______________ bastante dinero, pero este fin de semana Paco (gastó/gastaba) ______________ poco dinero.
7. De vez en cuando, los domingos, nosotros (hicimos/hacíamos) ______________ un pícnic después de las compras.

8-32 Ayer fue un día diferente. To find out how yesterday was different from other days, complete each statement with the correct preterit or imperfect form of the verb in parentheses.

1. David siempre ______________ sandalias, pero ayer ______________ zapatos. (usar)
2. Mercedes y Víctor siempre ______________ joyas, pero ayer no ______________ joyas. (ponerse)
3. Todas las mañanas nosotros ______________ de compras, pero ayer no ______________ de compras. (ir)
4. Roberto y Alicia ______________ mucho dinero frecuentemente, pero ayer no ______________ nada. (gastar)

5. Generalmente, a mí no me ________________ bien el color azul, pero ayer me ________________ bien la camisa azul. (quedar)

6. A veces yo ________________ la ropa que compraba, pero ayer no ________________ nada. (devolver)

7. Las botas que me gustan siempre ________________ mucho, pero ayer no ________________ tanto. (valer)

8. Normalmente yo ________________ con tarjeta de crédito, pero ayer ________________ en efectivo. (pagar)

8-33 El verano en Guayaquil. Describe what happened to you and your cousin while shopping in Guayaquil. Complete the following paragraph with the correct preterit or imperfect form of each verb in parentheses.

Todos los veranos yo (1) ________________ (ir) a casa de mis tíos en Guayaquil. Mi primo y yo (2) ________________ (hacer) muchas actividades. Durante el día (3) ________________ (ir) de compras a la ciudad. Generalmente, yo no (4) ________________ (comprar) nada, pero un día en el centro comercial, mi primo Jaime (5) ________________ (ver) una chaqueta que a mí me (6) ________________ (gustar) mucho. Nosotros (7) ________________ (entrar) en la tienda. La dependienta (8) ________________ (ser) muy amable y simpática. Ella me (9) ________________ (decir) que la chaqueta (10) ________________ (costar) $50. Yo (11) ________________ (probarse) la chaqueta y (12) ________________ (pagar) con tarjeta de crédito.

Nombre: ______________________________ Fecha: ______________________

CD 8, Track 13

8-34 Lo que pasó. Form sentences using the verbs you hear. Use each verb in the preterit or the imperfect, as appropriate. Then listen and repeat as the speaker gives the correct answer.

Modelo: You see: Sofía ______________ la televisión cuando su novio ______________.
You hear: ver, entrar
You write and say: Sofía *veía* la televisión cuando su novio *entró*.

1. Pablo ______________ cuando yo lo ______________ por teléfono.
2. Mis abuelos siempre nos ______________ cuando nosotros ______________ vacaciones.
3. Generalmente nosotros ______________ en la biblioteca cuando ______________ un examen.
4. Ayer yo ______________ una tienda fantástica mientras ______________ por el centro.
5. Anoche nosotros ______________ a las nueve, ______________ al centro comercial y ______________ el regalo perfecto para el cumpleaños de Rodrigo.
6. ______________ las cinco de la tarde y ______________ mucho calor.
7. Ellos no ______________ que tú ______________ tan triste.
8. ¿Cuántos años ______________ tú cuando ______________ a Bolivia?

CD 8, Track 14

8-35 Eventos del pasado. Read the following sentences and complete them with the correct preterit or imperfect form of the verb according to the subjects you hear.

1. ¡Qué día tan interesante ______________ (tener) hoy!
2. ______________ (levantarse) temprano porque ______________ (querer) ir al centro comercial con mis amigas.
3. ______________ (ir) a tener la venta-liquidación más grande de todo el año.
4. Normalmente, no ______________ (salir) de su casa tan temprano.
5. Este año ______________ (decidir) que ______________ (ir) a comprar muchos regalos para mis amigos y para mi familia.

CD 8, Track 15

8-36 ¿Compré o compraba? As you listen to the following story, complete the paragraph below with the correct verbs in imperfect or preterit, according to what you hear.

Mientras (1) ______________ unos zapatos que (2) ______________ en rebaja, (3) ______________ por teléfono. Yo le (4) ______________ a mi mejor amiga si

(5) ________________ comprar los zapatos para hacer juego con mi vestido nuevo.

Cuando le (6) ________________ el precio, ella (7) ________________ que

(8) ________________ una ganga. (9) ________________ al mostrador inmediatamente

para comprarlos, y (10) ________________ con tarjeta de crédito.

8-37 El sábado de Lucía. Lucía spent last Saturday afternoon on a shopping spree. Based on the drawing below, answer the following questions in complete sentences.

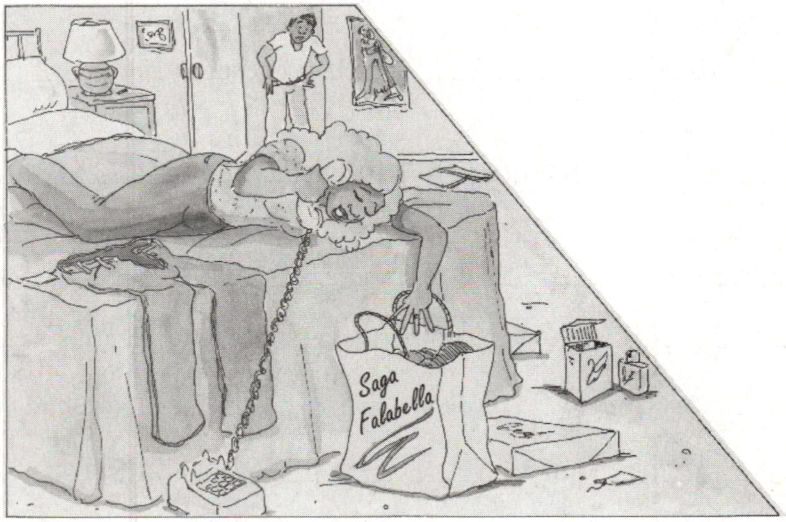

1. ¿Qué hacía Lucía en su dormitorio?

   ____

2. ¿Qué llevaba Lucía?

   ____

3. ¿En qué almacén fue Lucía de compras?

   ____

4. ¿Qué compró en el almacén?

   ____

5. ¿Qué llevaba su novio cuando entró en el cuarto?

   ____

Nombre: ________________________ Fecha: ____________________

4. Impersonal and passive *se* (TEXTBOOK P. 278)

8-38 ¿Qué se hace en cada situación? On the line next to each phrase, write the letter of the corresponding action that best completes the sentence.

1. _____ En la caja	a. se busca gangas.
2. _____ En el probador	b. se gasta mucho dinero en joyas.
3. _____ En la rebaja	c. se paga con tarjeta de crédito.
4. _____ En la zapatería	d. se prueba la ropa.
5. _____ En la joyería	e. se lleva abrigo.
6. _____ En el invierno	f. se compra zapatos.

8-39 ¡La venta-liquidación! Fill in the blanks with the appropriate **se pasivo** expressions using the verbs in parentheses.

(1) ____________________ (decir) que el centro comercial va a tener una venta-liquidación el próximo sábado. En la venta-liquidación (2) ____________________ (regatear) con los dependientes para conseguir la mejor ganga y (3) ____________________ (vender) toda la ropa en rebaja. Normalmente (4) ____________________ (comprar) mucho y (5) ____________________ (pagar) con tarjeta de crédito. Después de comprar, no (6) ____________________ (devolver) la ropa porque en el centro comercial no (7) ____________________ (permitir) devoluciones.

CD 8, Track 16

8-40 Se dice... Complete the sentences with the impersonal **se** using the verb provided. Then listen and repeat as the speaker gives the correct answer.

MODELO: You see: _____ ____________________ que tienen los mejores zapatos.
You hear: Dicen que tienen los mejores zapatos.
You write and say: *Se dice* que tienen los mejores zapatos.

1. _____ ____________________ ver mucha ropa de algodón.
2. _____ ____________________ con tarjeta de crédito.
3. _____ ____________________ español.
4. _____ ____________________ a las diez.
5. _____ ____________________ mucho porque hay descuentos.

Nombre: ______________________ Fecha: ______________________

CD 8, Track 17

8-41 ¿Qué se hizo? Change the sentences below from active to passive by using the passive **se** plus the corresponding singular or plural verb form. Then listen and repeat as the speaker gives the correct answer.

MODELO: You see: ____ ______________ perfumes franceses en esa perfumería.
You hear: Compré perfumes franceses en esa perfumería.
You say and write: *Se compraron* perfumes franceses en esa perfumería.

1. ____ ______________ la tarjeta de crédito.
2. ____ ______________ las venta-liquidaciones ayer.
3. ____ ______________ un anillo en el mercado.
4. ____ ______________ a Bárbara Molina como dependienta del mes.
5. ____ ______________ los vaqueros.
6. ____ ______________ las sandalias.

8-42 Las rebajas en tu ciudad. Answer the following questions about your city using the impersonal and passive **se** forms.

1. ¿En qué tienda o centro comercial se encuentran las mejores rebajas de tu ciudad?

   ____

2. ¿Qué se vende en esa tienda o centro comercial?

   ____

3. ¿Dónde se compra la mejor ropa?

   ____

4. ¿Cuándo se regatea en las tiendas?

   ____

5. ¿Qué idiomas se hablan en los centros comerciales?

   ____

¿Cuánto sabes tú?

CD 8, Track 18

8-43 Una conversación en el centro comercial. Carmen went shopping, but Lucía stayed home sick this time. Listen to their conversation. Then indicate whether the statements that follow are **cierto** (C) o **falso** (F).

1. Carmen gastó mucho dinero. ____
2. Carmen vio a Ricardo y a Estela en la joyería. ____
3. Marcos y Estela querían comprarse unos relojes. ____
4. Carmen salió de la joyería. ____
5. En La Moda tenían una venta-liquidación. ____
6. Carmen compró pantalones y dos blusas. ____
7. Una blusa era de rayas y la otra era de cuadros. ____
8. Se vendían zapatos en la tienda. ____
9. Carmen fue a la farmacia para comprar perfume. ____
10. Carmen llegó a las ocho y media. ____

8-44 ¿Sabes diferenciar el pretérito del imperfecto? Choose the preterit or imperfect forms in parentheses to fill in the blanks.

Cuando yo (1) __________________ (fui / era) pequeño, me (2) __________________ (gustó / gustaba) mucho ir de compras con mis padres. Un día nosotros (3) __________________ (fuimos / íbamos) al centro comercial y yo (4) __________________ (vi / veía) un abrigo. El abrigo (5) __________________ (fue / era) muy caro y yo lo (6) __________________ (quise / quería), pero ellos no me lo (7) __________________ (compraron / compraban).

Nombre: ______________________ Fecha: ______________________

8-45 ¿Sabes usar el *se* pasivo e impersonal? Fill in the blanks with the pronoun **se** and the indicated verbs.

1. En el centro comercial ____________________ (prohibir) fumar.
2. ____________________ (decir) que va a haber buenas gangas en los almacenes el próximo sábado.
3. No ____________________ (vender) sandalias en el invierno.
4. ____________________ (anunciar) las rebajas del centro comercial en la televisión.
5. En la librería de la universidad ____________________ (necesitar) estudiantes para trabajar.

CD 8, Track 19

8-46 En el almacén. Complete the following story using the preterit and the imperfect of the verbs you hear.

(1) ____________________ las ocho y media de la noche cuando yo (2) ____________________ a la joyería. (3) ____________________ mucha gente comprando anillos, collares, aretes y pulseras de muchos estilos. ¡No (4) ____________________ por qué la gente (5) ____________________ comprando tanto! Cuando (6) ____________________ de la joyería, (7) ____________________ que todo (8) ____________________ un increíble descuento del 75%. Ahora entiendo por qué yo también (9) ____________________ mucho dinero y por qué (10) ____________________ tanto para pagar.

Nombre: ______________________ Fecha: ______________________

Observaciones

Antes de ver el video

8-47 ¿Qué pasa? Select the letter of the best answer to each question.

1. How would the market vendor begin her conversation with Silvia?
   a. Señorita, no es mucho dinero.
   b. Mira, Silvia. ¡Mira qué arco!
   c. Dígame, señorita, ¿en qué puedo servirle?
2. What would be a logical response?
   a. ¿Cuánto cuesta esta pieza?
   b. Mire, señorita, diez mil y todo está bien.
   c. No, gracias. Mire, a mí no me gusta regatear.

Nombre: ______________________ Fecha: ______________________

3. How might Silvia ask about the quality of the sandals she sees at the market?

   a. Mira qué sandalias. ¿Son de cuero?

   b. ¿No quieren nada más?

   c. ¿De qué número son?

4. What might Marcela say to convince Silvia that the blouse is perfect for her?

   a. Bueno Silvia, yo quería comprarte algo a ti.

   b. Y ésta, ¿no te gusta? ¡Es lindísima!

   c. ¿Qué talla usas?

5. How would Silvia disagree with Marcela about the blouse?

   a. Pero Marcela, esa ropa no está de moda.

   b. Sí, fenomenal. Muchas gracias.

   c. Mira Marcela, hace juego con tu bolso.

Nombre: ______________________________ Fecha: ______________________

A ver el video

8-48 Se vende... Put a check mark next to the items that are for sale at the market, based on the dialogues in the video.

____ arcos	____ chocolates	____ frutas
____ aretes	____ faldas	____ pantalones
____ blusas	____ figuras de madera	____ platos de cerámica
____ botas	____ flautas (*flutes*)	____ sandalias

8-49 La conversación. Fill in the blanks with the missing words according to the video segment.

Silvia: Mira qué sandalias. ¿Son de cuero?

Marcela: Claro que son de (1) ____________________. Aquí todo es auténtico.

Silvia: ¿De qué número son?

Marcela: Son del treinta y siete. Pero son muy (2) ____________________ para mí. Pruébatelas tú.

Silvia: No. Son bonitas, pero no son para mí.

Marcela: Mira qué (3) ____________________. Seguro que te queda muy bien.

Silvia: ¡Qué suave!

Marcela: Claro, es de (4) ____________________. Y eso a (5) ____________________, ¿qué es?

Silvia: Es una (6) ____________________. Es muy bonita. Mira Marcela, hace (7) ____________________ con tu bolso.

Marcela: Sí, pero ya tengo una parecida. Bueno Silvia, yo quería (8) ____________________ algo a ti.

Después de ver el video

8-50 En el mercado. Select the letter of the word or phrase that best completes each sentence.

1. Marcela quiere gastar…
   a. veinte colones.
   b. diez mil colones.
   c. quince mil colones.
2. Marcela cree que los… son bonitos.
   a. aretes
   b. colones
   c. arcos
3. La figura que quiere comprar Marcela es de…
   a. porcelana.
   b. cerámica.
   c. madera de cocobolo.
4. La señora pide veinte mil colones por la pieza, y después de regatear Marcela paga…
   a. diez mil colones.
   b. quince mil colones.
   c. dieciocho mil colones.
5. Silvia le regala la figura a…
   a. su mamá.
   b. su hermano.
   c. Marcela.
6. La falda es de…
   a. cuadros.
   b. rayas.
   c. seda.
7. Marcela quiere regalarle… a Silvia.
   a. una falda de algodón
   b. una blusa de colores
   c. unas sandalias de cuero
8. Silvia cree que la blusa…
   a. no está de moda.
   b. es bonita.
   c. le queda pequeña.

Nombre: ______________________ Fecha: ______________________

8-51 La acción y los personajes. Determine whether the following statements are **cierto** (C) or **falso** (F) and write the correct letter on the lines provided.

1. La madera de cocobolo es de diferentes colores. ____
2. En el mercado se puede regatear. ____
3. Marcela paga con tarjeta de crédito. ____
4. Los precios están más caros ahora porque hay más turismo. ____
5. Las sandalias le quedan estrechas a Marcela. ____
6. La blusa de colores es la talla de Silvia, pero a Silvia no le gusta. ____

Nuestro mundo

Panoramas

8-52 ¡A informarse! Based on the information from **Nuestro mundo,** decide if the following statements are **cierto** (C) or **falso** (F).

1. En las islas Galápagos no existe vida animal. ____
2. El Centro de Investigación Charles Darwin está en las islas Galápagos. ____
3. Charles Darwin era ecuatoriano. ____
4. El galápago y la iguana marina son especies protegidas. ____
5. No hay volcanes en el Ecuador. ____
6. La alpaca tenía importancia religiosa para los incas. ____
7. La lana de la oveja es más fuerte que la lana de la alpaca. ____
8. Según la leyenda, Inti Tayta creó la civilización incaica. ____
9. Las tradiciones incas ya no existen en la actualidad. ____
10. El Camino Inca está a 2.380 metros de altura. ____

Nombre: ______________________________ Fecha: ______________________

8-53 El mapa del Perú y del Ecuador. Look at the map on page 282 of your textbook and the information from **Nuestro mundo** and decide which country each of the places mentioned below belongs to.

1. Lima:

   a. Perú b. Ecuador

2. Quito:

   a. Perú b. Ecuador

3. Guayaquil:

   a. Perú b. Ecuador

4. Cuzco:

   a. Perú b. Ecuador

5. el Lago Titicaca:

   a. Perú b. Ecuador

6. Las islas Galápagos:

   a. Perú b. Ecuador

7. El Camino Inca:

   a. Perú b. Ecuador

8. Machu Picchu:

   a. Perú b. Ecuador

Ritmos

8-54 Yawar. Read the information on the musical group *Yawar* on page 285 of the textbook and decide if the following statements are **cierto** (C) or **falso** (F).

1. El nombre del grupo es de origen inca. _____
2. El grupo Yawar es famoso en toda América del Sur. _____
3. Yawar toca una vez al año. _____
4. Los incas usan un cóndor y un toro para celebrar su independencia. _____
5. El grupo Yawar es un ejemplo de ritmo puramente andino. _____
6. El grupo usa instrumentos tradicionales, como la quena y la zampoña. _____

Nombre: ______________________ Fecha: ______________________

Páginas

8-55 Fábulas de Esopo en español. In your text you read a fable from Perú. Now visit **www.prenhall.com/arriba** and choose one of Aesop's classic fables, written here in Spanish. Then, answer the questions below about the fable you have chosen.

1. ¿Quiénes son los personajes de la fábula?

   ____

2. Describe a uno de los personajes.

   ____

3. Escoge tres eventos de la fábula y ponlos en orden cronológico.

   ____

   ____

   ____

4. ¿Cuál es la lección de la fábula?

   ____

Nombre: ______________________ Fecha: ______________________

Taller

8-56 De compras. Interview four to five students in your class to find out about their last trip to a department store or supermarket. Ask for information that will help you complete the following chart. Fill in information about your last shopping trip as well.

ESTUDIANTE	¿ADÓNDE?	¿CON QUIÉN?	¿CUÁNDO?	¿QUÉ?	¿DINERO?

8-57 Tu descripción. Now write a paragraph describing and comparing the different shopping trips using the information from the chart you completed in the previous activity.

MODELO: *Yo encontré muchas gangas, pero Pedro no encontró ninguna.*

____

____

____

____

____

____

____

____

____

____

Nombre: ______________________ Fecha: ______________________

9 Vamos de viaje

Primera parte

¡Así es la vida!

9-1 Un viaje. First, reread the conversation on page 294 of your textbook. Then complete the following statements by selecting the letter of the correct answer.

1. Susana quiere ir de vacaciones porque…

   a. tiene dinero.
   b. no tiene clases por una semana.
   c. quiere visitar a la familia.

2. El/la agente de viajes les ofrece un viaje a…

   a. Venezuela.
   b. México.
   c. Colombia.

3. El viaje incluye…

   a. tres días en San Andrés.
   b. dos noches en Cartagena.
   c. cinco noches en San Andrés.

4. ¿Dónde hay una playa fabulosa?

   a. la isla de San Andrés
   b. Cartagena de Indias
   c. Bogotá

5. El viaje cuesta…

   a. 800 dólares para dos personas.
   b. 1.600 dólares para dos personas.
   c. 400 dólares por persona.

6. La agencia López tiene las mejores ofertas de…

   a. Cancún.
   b. Venezuela.
   c. Colombia.

Nombre: ______________________ Fecha: ______________________

9-2 El viaje de Silvia y Marcelo. Listen to the following conversation between Silvia and Marcelo as they make plans for their honeymoon. Then select the letters that correspond to all the statements that are correct according to what you hear.

1. Silvia y Marcelo quieren...
   a. ir a Argentina.
   b. un viaje feliz.
   c. ir de viaje.
2. Silvia describe...
   a. dos viajes interesantes.
   b. un viaje a México.
   c. un viaje a España.
3. El viaje a España...
   a. es de dos semanas.
   b. incluye un pasaje de primera clase.
   c. ofrece excursiones a otras ciudades.
4. El viaje a México...
   a. es tan largo como el viaje a España.
   b. es menos largo que el viaje a España.
   c. es más largo que el viaje a España.
5. Las excursiones desde Madrid incluyen...
   a. Barcelona, Sevilla o Santander.
   b. Toledo y Ávila.
   c. Ávila y Valencia.
6. El viaje a...
   a. México es tan caro como el viaje a España.
   b. España es más caro que el viaje a México.
   c. España cuesta menos que el viaje a México.
7. Marcelo prefiere...
   a. un asiento en clase turista.
   b. un asiento de ventanilla.
   c. el viaje a España.
8. Marcelo y Silvia van a tomar el vuelo...
   a. de ida solamente.
   b. que sale por la tarde.
   c. que sale por la mañana.

¡Así lo decimos! Vocabulario (TEXTBOOK P. 295)

CD 9, Track 2

9-3 Jorge y Virginia hacen un viaje. Listen to the conversation between Jorge and Virginia. Then indicate whether the following statements are **cierto** (C) o **falso** (F).

1. Hay mucha demora en el vuelo de Aeropostal. ____
2. Jorge y Virginia facturaron el equipaje y tienen las tarjetas de embarque. ____
3. Jorge y Virginia van a Lima. ____
4. No van en Aeropostal porque no hay asientos y porque el vuelo ya despegó. ____
5. El vuelo de Avianca iba a despegar en menos de media hora. ____
6. Virginia tiene las tarjetas de embarque. ____
7. Jorge y Virginia viajan por tren. ____
8. Ellos son dos viajeros nerviosos. ____

9-4 Fuera de lugar. For each group of words, select the one that does not belong.

1. a. despegar b. aterrizar c. facturar el equipaje d. volar
2. a. el boleto b. el guía c. el folleto d. la tarjeta de embarque
3. a. abordar b. hacer las maletas c. facturar el equipaje d. la sala de reclamación
4. a. el piloto b. el asistente de vuelo c. el inspector de aduanas d. la sala de espera
5. a. la guía b. la aduana c. la sala de espera d. la sala de reclamación
6. a. el asiento de ventanilla c. el agente de viajes
   b. la clase turista d. el asiento de pasillo

9-5 De viaje. Select the letter of the word or expression that best completes each sentence.

1. Para abordar el avión necesito ____.
   a. el folleto
   b. el cinturón de seguridad
   c. la tarjeta de embarque

2. En todos los vuelos hay ____.

   a. demora

   b. hospedaje

   c. asistentes de vuelo

3. Soy estudiante y no tengo mucho dinero. Compro un boleto de ____.

   a. clase turista

   b. aduana

   c. hospedaje

4. Hay demora en el vuelo a Bogotá. Voy a sentarme en la ____.

   a. aduana

   b. sala de espera

   c. tarjeta de embarque

5. Antes de comprar una excursión, es bueno leer el ____.

   a. vuelo

   b. folleto

   c. pasaje

6. Hay mucha gente en la aduana. Tenemos que ____.

   a. facturar el equipaje

   b. hacer cola

   c. hacer un viaje

7. El avión tiene problemas. Vamos a despegar con ____.

   a. aduana

   b. pasaje

   c. demora

Nombre: ______________________________ Fecha: ______________________

9-6 Cuestionario. How do you like to organize yourself when you travel? Answer with complete sentences in Spanish.

1. Cuando viajas en avión, ¿dónde prefieres sentarte, junto a (*next to*) la ventanilla o en el pasillo?

   ____

2. ¿Haces las reservas en una agencia de viaje o en la Red?

   ____

3. ¿Qué haces si hay una demora con el vuelo?

   ____

4. ¿Qué equipaje facturas y qué llevas en el avión?

   ____

5. ¿Prefieres viajar por tren, por autobús o por avión? ¿Por qué?

   ____

Nombre: ______________________ Fecha: ______________________

9-7 Anuncios. Answer the following questions based on the information below.

1. ¿Cómo se llama la agencia de viajes?

____

2. ¿Qué anuncia la agencia?

____

3. ¿Dónde está la agencia de viajes?

____

4. ¿Cuáles son los viajes más caros?

____

5. ¿Cuál es el viaje más barato?

____

6. ¿Cuál de los viajes prefieres y por qué?

____

Nombre: ______________________ Fecha: ______________________

¡Así lo hacemos! Estructuras

1. *Por* or *para* (Textbook p. 298)

CD 9, Track 3

9-8 Respuestas breves. Listen to the following questions and statements. On the lines before each of the idiomatic expressions below, write the letter of the question or statement to which each expression provides a logical answer. Then listen and repeat as the speaker gives the correct answer.

1. ____ Por aquí.
2. ____ Por favor.
3. ____ ¡Por fin!
4. ____ Por supuesto.

9-9 ¡A completar! Fill in the blanks with **por** or **para** in each sentence, keeping in mind their correct uses.

1. Emilio caminaba ______________ el aeropuerto buscando la sala de espera.
2. Julio llegó al aeropuerto ______________ la tarde.
3. Estuvimos en la sala de espera ______________ dos horas.
4. Necesito la tarjeta de embarque ______________ abordar el avión.
5. ¿Compraste los billetes ______________ mil dólares?
6. Ayer fui a la agencia de viajes ______________ los pasajes.
7. Hice la reserva de los pasajes ______________ ti.
8. Nosotros salimos ______________ San Andrés.

9-10 Decisiones. Decide whether to use **por** or **para** based on the context, and fill in the blanks in the following sentences.

1. El avión salió ______________ Colombia.
2. Nuestro viaje es ______________ el martes.
3. El piloto vuela a Caracas dos veces ______________ semana.
4. ______________ ser tan joven, el piloto vuela muy bien.
5. ______________ fin despegó el avión.

6. ¡ ______________ Dios, qué demora!

7. ______________ ir a Colombia hay que tener pasaporte.

8. La luz entraba ______________ la ventanilla del avión.

9. Este folleto es ______________ ti.

10. Tú estudias ______________ ser piloto.

9-11 Actividades durante las vacaciones. To describe your plans for an upcoming vacation, complete the paragraph using **por** or **para.**

El sábado próximo salimos (1) ______________ Venezuela. Fuimos (2) ______________ los boletos ayer. Vamos (3) ______________ avión y vamos a quedarnos allí (4) ______________ dos semanas. El agente de viajes planeó muchas actividades (5) ______________ nosotros. (6) ______________ las mañanas vamos a visitar la ciudad y (7) ______________ las tardes podemos dar un paseo (8) ______________ el Parque Nacional o caminar (9) ______________ la playa. Vamos a Venezuela (10) ______________ descansar un poco.

CD 9, Track 4

9-12 De viaje en Colombia. Complete the following sentences with **por** or **para.** Then listen and repeat as the speaker gives the correct answer.

Modelo: You see: El próximo domingo viajamos ______________ Colombia.
You write and say: El próximo domingo viajamos *para* Colombia.

1. ______________ la mañana hacemos una excursión a Bogotá.

2. Paseamos ______________ el centro ______________ visitar los monumentos.

3. Los pasaportes son ______________ ustedes y van a estar listos ______________ mañana.

4. Pagamos quinientos dólares ______________ los dos pasajes.

5. Fuimos ______________ las maletas.

6. ¿Van a viajar ______________ tren ______________ la tarde o ______________ la mañana?

7. ¿Necesitaron mucho dinero ______________ el viaje?

8. Estuvimos en Colombia ______________ un mes.

Nombre: ______________________ Fecha: ______________________

9-13 Viajes Venezolanos. Answer the following questions based on the advertisement below. Pay special attention to the correct use of **por** and **para.**

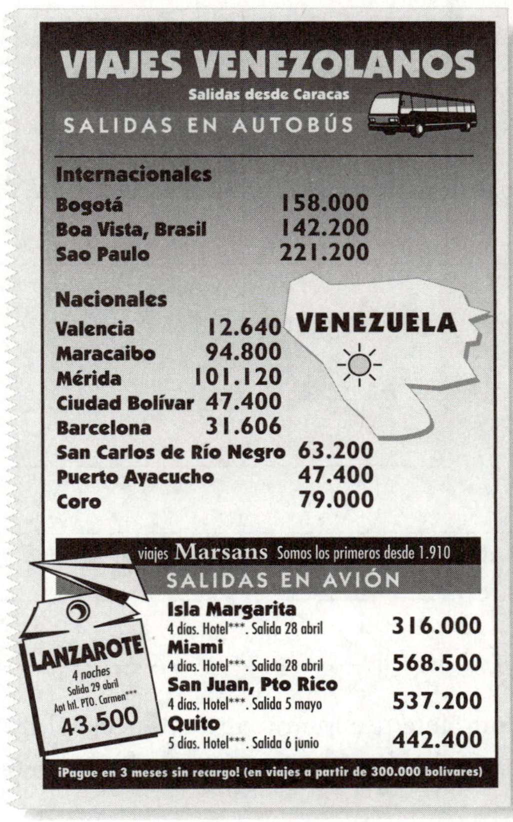

1. El viaje a Valencia ¿es por autobús o por avión?

____

2. ¿Cuánto se paga por un viaje a Sao Paulo?

____

3. ¿Para cuándo es la salida del viaje a Miami?

____

4. ¿Por cuántos días es el viaje a Miami?

____

Nombre: ______________________ Fecha: ______________________

2. Adverbs ending in *-mente* (TEXTBOOK P. 302)

9-14 ¿Cómo lo hacen? Indicate the ways in which the following people do each activity by filling in the blanks with an adverb formed from the adjectives in parentheses.

MODELO: Nora y Luz hicieron una reserva (inmediato) ______________.
Nora y Luz hicieron una reserva *inmediatamente.*

1. Jorge y Juan hacen la maleta (cuidadoso) ______________.
2. El guía camina (lento) ______________.
3. La agente de viajes siempre se viste (elegante) ______________.
4. La piloto habla español (fácil) ______________.
5. Carlos viaja por avión (frecuente) ______________.
6. El avión despega (rápido) ______________.
7. El viajero hace cola (paciente) ______________.
8. El guía hace su trabajo (maravilloso) ______________.

CD 9, Track 5

9-15 Hablando del viaje. Complete the following sentences with the adverb derived from each of the adjectives you hear. Then listen and repeat as the speaker gives the correct answer.

MODELO: You see: Carlos y Ana encontraron la sala de espera ______________.
You hear: fácil
You write and say: Carlos y Ana encontraron la sala de espera *fácilmente.*

1. Carmen y Jorge hablaban ______________.
2. El avión llegaba ______________ al aeropuerto.
3. La asistente de vuelo pasó ______________ por el avión.
4. ______________ los viajeros salieron del avión.
5. Pasamos por la aduana ______________.
6. ______________ los inspectores de aduana pueden entrar aquí.
7. El piloto aterrizó ______________.
8. Carmen espera ______________.

Nombre: ______________________ Fecha: ______________________

9-16 Más adverbios. Answer each question you hear in complete sentences using the adverbial form of the adjective provided. Then listen and repeat as the speaker gives the correct answer.

1. (tranquilo) ______________________
2. (frecuente) ______________________
3. (correcto) ______________________
4. (claro) ______________________
5. (lento) ______________________
6. (fácil) ______________________

9-17 Emparejamientos. Look at the drawings and form logical sentences to describe them. Use verbs from the word bank below and the adjectives in parentheses. You will have to change the adjectives to adverbs.

hablar	cantar	~~caminar~~	hacer cola	vestirse

MODELO: 

Ella ______________________. (lento)
Ella *camina lentamente.*

1. 

Ellas ______________________. (alegre)

2. 

Él ______________________. (claro)

3. Ellos ______________________. (elegante)

4. Ellos ______________________. (paciente)

¿Cuánto sabes tú?

9-18 ¿Sabes usar *por* y *para*? Fill in the blanks with **por** or **para** according to their correct uses.

Hoy (1) ______________ la mañana fui a la agencia de viajes (2) ______________ preguntar el precio de un viaje a la isla Margarita. Quiero ir de vacaciones (3) ______________ una semana y salgo (4) ______________ la isla Margarita la semana que viene. Tengo que pagar el viaje (5) ______________ el lunes, y (6) ______________ supuesto, voy a divertirme mucho.

9-19 ¿Sabes usar los adverbios? Complete the following statements using an adverb formed from the adjectives in parentheses.

1. Pagué el pasaje (inmediato) ______________________.
2. Abordé el avión (tranquilo) ______________________.
3. Me senté en mi asiento (rápido) ______________________.
4. La asistente de vuelo nos trató (amable) ______________________.
5. El piloto aterrizó el avión (cuidadoso) ______________________.
6. Los viajeros salieron del avión (lento) ______________________.

Nombre: ______________________ Fecha: ______________________

CD 9, Track 7

9-20 ¿Quién está en el aeropuerto? Listen to the descriptions of some of the people in the following picture. Then decide who is who, based on the information you hear. Label the picture accordingly with the number of the names provided.

1. Josefina Pereda
2. la familia Peña
3. Dolores Gutiérrez
4. Rosa Romero
5. Ricardo Bello
6. Ema Flores
7. el señor Ramírez
8. Octavio

Nombre: ______________________________ Fecha: ______________________________

CD 9, Track 8

9-21 Preguntas personales. Write appropriate responses to the following questions or statements. Then read your responses to practice communication and pronunciation.

1. ____.
2. ____.
3. ____.
4. ____.
5. ____.

SEGUNDA PARTE

¡Así es la vida!

9-22 Un correo electrónico. Reread the e-mail from Susana to Raquel on page 306 of your textbook and decide if the following statements are **cierto** (C) or **falso** (F).

1. Susana está en Cartagena. _____
2. Llegaron a Cartagena el 22 de junio. _____
3. El hotel de Cartagena es de lujo. _____
4. Susana hizo esquí acuático y buceó en la isla de San Andrés. _____
5. Susana lo pasó mal en San Andrés. _____
6. El hotel de Cartagena tiene un jardín tropical. _____
7. Los dos hoteles tienen buenas vistas. _____
8. Los dos hoteles tienen jacuzzi. _____

Nombre: ________________________ Fecha: ____________________

CD 9, Track 9

9-23 Después de las vacaciones. Listen to the conversation between Gabriela and her mother after Gabriela's vacation in Venezuela. Then select the letters that correspond to all statements that are correct according to what you hear.

1. Gabriela y Jorge...
   a. estuvieron una semana en un parque nacional.
   b. la pasaron regular.
   c. llegaron anoche.
2. Jorge...
   a. estaba muy contento porque pescó mucho.
   b. fue de excursión.
   c. nadaba en el lago a menudo.
3. Gabriela...
   a. tenía una tarjeta de memoria.
   b. pescaba en el lago frecuentemente.
   c. nadó en la piscina del hotel.
4. Desde su habitación tenían una vista...
   a. de la piscina.
   b. del volcán.
   c. de las montañas.
5. A Gabriela...
   a. le gustó recorrer el país.
   b. le gustaron los bosques y las montañas.
   c. le gustó montar en bicicleta.
6. Gabriela y Jorge...
   a. se pusieron impacientes cuando olvidaron el mapa.
   b. la pasaron de maravilla cuando olvidaron el mapa.
   c. recibieron ayuda cuando olvidaron el mapa.
7. La mamá de Gabriela...
   a. también habló con Jorge.
   b. va a ver a Jorge y a su hija el sábado.
   c. no quiere ver a Jorge.

¡Así lo decimos! Vocabulario (TEXTBOOK P. 307)

CD 9, Track 10

9-24 Cosas de las vacaciones. Listen to the following definitions. Then match the letter of each definition with one of the words below.

1. _____ la estadía
2. _____ ir de excursión
3. _____ el lago
4. _____ el mapa
5. _____ la vista
6. _____ un volcán

Nombre: ______________________________ Fecha: ______________________

9-25 ¡A completar! Complete each statement with an appropriate word or expression from the word bank below.

flores	gafas de sol	montar	mapa	rollo
pescar	estadía	isla	vista	bosque

1. Cuando hace mucho sol, tengo que ponerme ________________ para ver bien.
2. Para no perderme en la ciudad miro el ________________.
3. En el jardín hay muchas ________________ en primavera.
4. Nuestra ________________ en el hotel fue por cuatro noches.
5. Quiero sacar más fotos. Necesito comprar un ________________ de película.
6. En el ________________ hay muchos árboles.
7. La ________________ del mar y las montañas desde mi habitación es impresionante.
8. Me gusta ________________ en el lago.
9. No sé ________________ a caballo.
10. San Andrés es una ________________ de Colombia.

9-26 Un crucigrama. Read each statement or description on the following page and write the missing word in the corresponding squares.

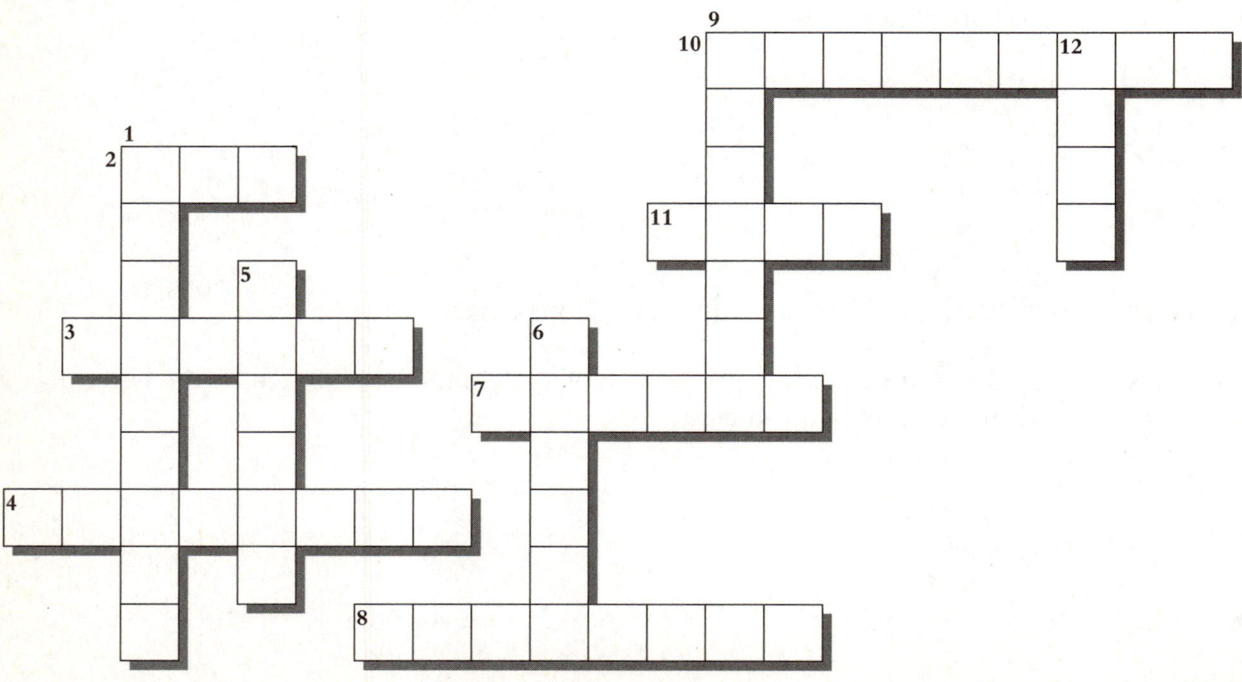

Across

2. Cuando vas a la playa, nadas en el ______________________.

3. Nadar bajo el agua es ______________________.

4. Cuando queremos esquiar, vamos a las ______________________.

7. Un ______________________ es una montaña que produce lava.

8. Una ______________________ es una iglesia grande e importante.

10. Vamos de ______________________ para visitar museos o lugares de interés.

11. El ______________________ Maracaibo está en Venezuela.

Down

1. Machu Picchu es un ______________________ de la cultura inca.

5. Una actividad que puedes hacer en los ríos, los lagos o el mar es ______________________.

6. En el ______________________ hay muchos árboles.

9. La ______________________ de la Libertad está en Nueva York.

12. La ______________________ Margarita está en la costa venezolana.

Letras y sonidos (Textbook p. 308)

CD 9, Track 11

9-27 La "g" de "guía". For each pair of two words, determine which word contains the hard **"g"** sound and write it on the line provided. Then listen and repeat as the speaker gives the correct answer.

Modelo: You hear: guante, lugar
You write and say: *guante*

1. ______________________
2. ______________________
3. ______________________
4. ______________________
5. ______________________
6. ______________________

Nombre: ______________________ Fecha: ______________________

CD 9, Track 12

9-28 La "g" de "despegar". For each question below, you will hear two words. Determine which of the two words you hear contains the soft **"g"** sound and write it on the line provided. Then listen and repeat as the speaker gives the correct answer.

MODELO: You hear: gafas, lago
You write and say: *lago*

1. ______________________
2. ______________________
3. ______________________
4. ______________________
5. ______________________
6. ______________________

¡Así lo hacemos! Estructuras

3. The Spanish subjunctive: An introduction (TEXTBOOK P. 311)

9-29 ¡A practicar! Give the present subjunctive form of the following verbs.

1. NOSOTROS: caminar ______________________
   beber ______________________
   escribir ______________________
2. ELLOS: hacer ______________________
   oír ______________________
   traer ______________________
3. YO: conocer ______________________
   dormir ______________________
   sentarse ______________________
4. USTEDES: llegar ______________________
   seguir ______________________
   sacar ______________________
5. TÚ: sentirse ______________________
   buscar ______________________
   ser ______________________
6. ELLA: dar ______________________
   venir ______________________
   estar ______________________

9-30 Las vacaciones de mamá. Your mother wants to go on vacation and your brother Felipe is in charge. Fill in the blanks with the present subjunctive form of the verbs in parentheses to find out the things he wants everyone to do.

1. Felipe quiere que Ricardo ____________________ (llamar) a la agencia de viajes.
2. Felipe quiere que Ernesto y Carlos ____________________ (leer) el folleto.
3. Felipe quiere que nosotros ____________________ (hablar) con el guía del viaje.
4. Felipe quiere que yo ____________________ (ser) responsable del hospedaje.
5. Felipe quiere que tú ____________________ (hacer) la reserva.
6. Felipe quiere que Ramiro ____________________ (pedir) dos semanas de vacaciones.
7. Felipe quiere que Paula y yo ____________________ (preparar) las maletas.
8. Felipe quiere que papá ____________________ (comprar) una cámara de video.

9-31 Unas recomendaciones. Complete these recommendations by filling in the blanks with the present subjunctive form of each verb in parentheses.

1. El agente de viajes quiere que usted…
   - (reservar) ____________________ el pasaje de ida y vuelta.
   - (cambiar) ____________________ dólares por la moneda local.
   - (tener) ____________________ el pasaporte en regla (*valid*).
   - (pagar) ____________________ con tarjeta de crédito.
2. Los inspectores de aduanas quieren que tú…
   - (hacer) ____________________ cola.
   - (mostrar) ____________________ el pasaporte.
   - (abrir) ____________________ la maleta.
   - (esperar) ____________________ en la sala de espera.

3. El asistente de vuelo quiere que nosotros…

- (abordar) ____________________ el avión.
- (hacer) ____________________ cola al entrar al avión.
- (sentarse) ____________________ en nuestro asiento.
- (darle) ____________________ la tarjeta de embarque.

4. Nosotros queremos que…

- el avión (despegar) ____________________ a tiempo.
- el avión (ser) ____________________ cómodo.
- el piloto (tener) ____________________ mucha experiencia.
- el avión (aterrizar) ____________________ sin problemas.

CD 9, Track 13

9-32 ¿Qué quiere la asistente de vuelo? The flight attendant has advice for all of the passengers. Change the verbs that you hear into the present subjunctive to tell what she wants each passenger to do. Then listen and repeat as the speaker gives the correct answer.

La asistente de vuelo…

1. quiere que yo ____________________ por el pasillo del avión.
2. quiere que tú ____________________ aquí delante.
3. quiere que usted ____________________ toda la comida.
4. quiere que nosotros ____________________ nuestro trabajo durante el vuelo.
5. quiere que los niños ____________________ mucho.
6. quiere que tú ____________________ el volcán desde la ventanilla.
7. quiere que yo ____________________ mi computadora.
8. quiere que nosotros ____________________ en el asiento.

Nombre: ______________________ Fecha: ______________________

CD 9, Track 14

9-33 Los padres. Your parents insist that you and your siblings do certain things while getting ready for vacation. Form sentences using the subjunctive form of the verbs provided. Then listen and repeat as the speaker gives the correct answer.

Los padres...

1. insisten en que yo ______________ en mis clases durante las vacaciones.
2. insisten en que tú ______________ con los niños.
3. insisten en que nosotras ______________ tranquilamente.
4. insisten en que ustedes no ______________ tarde al vuelo.
5. insisten en que nosotros ______________ a comer ahora.
6. insisten en que tú ______________ tu tarjeta de embarque.

9-34 Tus vacaciones. Read the following ad about a hotel in Venezuela and use the information provided to express wishes for your own vacation. Be careful to use the subjunctive where appropriate.

MODELO: Quiero que *el hotel tenga unos jardines bonitos.*

1. Quiero que ____.
2. Quiero ____.
3. No quiero que ____.

4. Necesito que ____.

5. Necesito ____.

6. Espero que ____.

CD 9, Track 15

9-35 Durante las vacaciones. Complete the following sentences using the correct forms of the verbs provided. Then listen and repeat as the speaker gives the correct answer.

Modelo: You see: Yo ______________ que tú ______________ de viaje.
You hear: querer, ir
You write and say: Yo *quiero* que tú *vayas* de viaje.

1. El señor Ureña ______________ que ustedes ______________ el equipaje aquí.

2. Tu madre ______________ en que tú ______________ pronto.

3. Nosotros le ______________ que ______________ a caballo.

4. Yo ______________ que nosotros ______________ de aquí.

5. El guía turístico me ______________ que ______________ en el hotel.

CD 9, Track 16

9-36 Preguntas del guía. Answer the questions you hear in complete sentences, using the phrases provided below. Then listen and repeat as the speaker gives the correct answer.

1. (ir a bucear por la tarde) ____

2. (en dos semanas) ____

3. (montar a caballo) ____

4. (comprar recuerdos) ____

5. (visitar la catedral) ____

4. The subjunctive to express volition (TEXTBOOK P. 314)

9-37 En el hotel. Complete the paragraphs about what the personnel recommends and prefers with the correct present subjunctive form of each verb in parentheses.

1. El recepcionista recomienda que los viajeros ____________________ (dormir) mucho por la noche y que ____________________ (hacer) muchas actividades durante el día. También recomienda que ellos ____________________ (sacar) muchas fotos durante las excursiones. Insiste en que ustedes no ____________________ (quedarse) todo el día en el hotel y que ____________________ (recorrer) las playas.
2. La recepcionista quiere que yo ____________________ (hablar) con ella y que ____________________ (pagar) la cuenta inmediatamente. Me pide que le ____________________ (dar) la tarjeta de crédito. También me aconseja que la ____________________ (llamar) si necesito una reserva para el próximo año.
3. El guía nos aconseja que nosotros no ____________________ (levantarse) tarde y que ____________________ (acostarse) temprano. Nos sugiere que ____________________ (ir) a la playa por dos o tres días y que ____________________ (empezar) a descansar más. También sugiere que ____________________ (montar) a caballo y que lo ____________________ (pasar) de maravilla.

9-38 Recomendaciones. Imagine that a friend wants some advice from you before going on vacation. Give your recommendations by completing the following sentences. Use a different verb in each sentence.

1. Te recomiendo que ______________________
2. Te aconsejo que ______________________
3. Te pido que ______________________
4. Te prohibo que ______________________
5. También te sugiero que ______________________
6. Deseo que ______________________

¿Cuánto sabes tú?

CD 9, Track 17

9-39 El Hostal Margarita. Listen to the following advertisement for *Hostal Margarita.* Then indicate whether the statements below are **cierto** (C) o **falso** (F).

1. En el Hostal Margarita, hay muchos cuartos dobles. _____
2. Los viajeros pueden visitar las playas tropicales. _____
3. En el hostal, les sugieren a los viajeros que lleven las cámaras. _____
4. La isla está a treinta y cinco minutos de Caracas por barco. _____
5. En el hostal, piden que los viajeros hagan las reservas dos semanas antes del viaje. _____
6. En este hostal, consideran las preferencias de los viajeros para preparar unas excursiones ideales. _____

Nombre: ______________________________ Fecha: ______________________

9-40 ¿Sabes usar el presente del subjuntivo? Fill in the blank by choosing the appropriate form of the verb in parentheses and writing it in the space provided.

¡Me encanta ir de vacaciones! En mis próximas vacaciones, espero que todos mis amigos (1) ________________ (poder / puedan) ir conmigo. Deseo que el hotel (2) ________________ (es / sea) grande y lujoso y que (3) ________________ (estar / esté) cerca de la playa. Mis amigos quieren (4) ________________ (montar / monten) a caballo, (5) ________________ (vaya / ir) a la playa y (6) ________________ (sacar / saquemos) muchas fotografías. Ellos quieren que yo (7) ________________ (buscar / busque) información y que (8) ________________ (pregunte / pregunto) los precios en la agencia de viajes. Espero que nosotros lo (9) ________________ (pasar / pasemos) maravillosamente y que (10) ________________ (hagamos / hacemos) muchas actividades.

9-41 Más usos del subjuntivo. Fill in the blanks with the appropriate indicative, subjunctive, or infinitive form of the verbs in parentheses.

1. Necesitamos ________________ (encontrar) boletos baratos para ir de vacaciones.
2. María insiste en que nosotros ________________ (ir) a un lugar cerca de la playa.
3. Yo le sugiero que ella ________________ (buscar) en la Red.
4. Ella me pide que yo la ________________ (ayudar) a buscar un lugar para ir de vacaciones.
5. Quiero que el lugar ________________ (tener) piscina y que ________________ (estar) al lado del mar.

CD 9, Track 18

9-42 Otras preguntas personales. Write appropriate responses to the following questions or statements.

1. ____.
2. ____.
3. ____.
4. ____.
5. ____.

Nombre: ______________________ Fecha: ______________________

Observaciones

Antes de ver el video

9-43 ¿Qué pasa? Select the letter of the statement that best answers each question.

1. What would David respond when asked how his flight was?
   a. ¡Fenomenal! Pero casi pierdo el avión. Cambiaron la puerta de embarque.
   b. En nuestra organización necesitamos gente como tú.
   c. Desde la ventanilla del avión se veían muchos ríos.

2. As Patricio talks about the possibility of seeing a jaguar, what might he say?
   a. No creo que lo veamos ahora. Probablemente esté durmiendo en algún árbol.
   b. Panchito es un jaguar joven. Lo vemos frecuentemente.
   c. Lo importante es que ya estás aquí.

3. How would Patricio describe the weather?
   a. No creo que tarde en llegar, porque este año no hay Niño.
   b. Solamente en esta reserva hay más tipos de pájaros que en toda Europa.
   c. ¿Ven esa niebla? Es vapor del volcán.

4. David believes that Patricio is a skillful tour guide. Which statement does NOT support this opinion?
   a. Veo que conoces bien la fauna. Ahora entiendo porque todo el mundo se apunta a tu grupo.
   b. Ya lo creo. Es evidente que conoces esto mejor que nadie.
   c. Patricio, esto es muy interesante, pero quiero que me enseñes pájaros.

5. What might Silvia say about Patricio regarding his skills as a tour guide?

   a. ¡Sí, es un caimán! ¡Qué lástima no tener mi cámara de video!

   b. Es un apasionado de la naturaleza. No hay nadie más informado que Patricio.

   c. Sí, es una corriente de aire que hace llover excesivamente en algunos lugares.

A ver el video

9-44 La conversación. Fill in the blanks with the missing words according to the video segments.

Patricio: Y hace que otros (1) ____________________ sean terriblemente secos.

David: Bueno, no me parece que el (2) ____________________ esté muy seco. Desde la (3) ____________________ del (4) ____________________ se veían muchos ríos.

Patricio: ¿Qué tal su (5) ____________________?

David: Fenomenal. Pero casi pierdo el avión. Cambiaron la puerta de (6) ____________________ y no me di cuenta.

...

David: ¿Quién es Panchito?

Patricio: Panchito es un jaguar joven.

David: ¿(7) ____________________ a esperarlo?

Patricio: No creo que lo veamos ahora. Probablemente esté durmiendo en algún árbol. ¿Ven esa niebla? Es vapor del (8) ____________________. Sigamos por aquí.

Después de ver el video

9-45 La fauna. Mark the items that refer to the fauna of the jungle.

_____ el caimán	_____ el águila	_____ el apio
_____ el cocodrilo fluvial	_____ la orquídea	_____ el pájaro
_____ el tucán	_____ el árbol	_____ la palma

Nombre: ______________________ Fecha: ______________________

9-46 En la selva. Select the letter of the word or phrase that best completes the sentence or answers the question.

1. … es una corriente de aire que hace llover excesivamente en algunos lugares.

   a. La Niña b. El huracán c. El Niño

2. Desde la ventanilla del avión de David se veía(n)…

   a. muchos ríos. b. los guacamayos. c. la Estación Biológica.

3. En la selva hay… de especies de animales y plantas únicas en el mundo.

   a. cientos b. miles c. cien mil

4. Panchito es…

   a. un jaguar. b. un cocodrilo fluvial. c. un colibrí.

5. En la reserva hay más tipos de pájaros que en toda…

   a. la América del Sur. b. Asia. c. Europa.

6. La organización de David se llama CREFASI,…

   a. Centro de Reforestación y Fincas Sincronizadas. b. Centro de Recuperación de Fauna Silvestre. c. Centro de Ríos, Efluvios y Acueductos de la Sierra.

7. Mucha gente se apunta al grupo de Patricio porque él…

   a. conoce bien la fauna. b. tiene muchos pájaros. c. sabe los nombres de las plantas.

8. En su trabajo Patricio quiere que los turistas…

   a. se entretengan. b. lo ayuden a ganar más dinero. c. aprecien el medio ambiente.

Nombre: ______________________________ Fecha: ______________________

Nuestro mundo

Panoramas

9-47 ¡A informarse! Based on the information from **Nuestro mundo,** decide if the following statements are **cierto** (C) or **falso** (F).

1. Caracas es una ciudad moderna. ____
2. Colombia es un país rico en piedras preciosas. ____
3. Cartagena tiene un puerto muy importante. ____
4. Cartagena de Indias nunca fue una ciudad rica. ____
5. Gabriel García Márquez es un pintor colombiano. ____
6. Gabriel García Márquez ganó el Premio Nobel de Literatura en 1982. ____
7. En la isla Margarita se puede practicar deportes acuáticos. ____
8. La isla Margarita está en el océano Pacífico. ____

9-48 Turismo en Colombia. In your text you learned about the rich cultures of Venezuela and Colombia. Now visit **www.prenhall.com/arriba** and read the information on San Andrés and Providencia. Then select the place where you can find the items or activities listed below.

1. Ritmos como el *reggae*, la soca y el *calipso*:

   a. San Andrés   b. Providencia

2. *Snorkeling* y buceo:

   a. San Andrés   b. Providencia

3. Zona hotelera espectacular:

   a. San Andrés   b. Providencia

4. Playas de Manzanillo:

   a. San Andrés   b. Providencia

5. El rondón:

   a. San Andrés b. Providencia

6. Plaza Marina y conciertos de música en vivo:

   a. San Andrés b. Providencia

7. Puente de los Enamorados:

   a. San Andrés b. Providencia

8. Parque natural marino de 905 hectáreas:

   a. San Andrés b. Providencia

Ritmos

9-49 La cumbia. In your textbook you heard the sounds of the Colombian group *Los Tupamaros*. Now visit **www.prenhall.com/arriba** and read about the origins of ***la cumbia,*** a famous Colombian rhythm. Then decide if the statements below are **cierto** (C) or **falso** (F).

1. La cumbia es un ritmo de origen africano, colombiano y europeo. ____
2. Este ritmo es la fusión cultural de los esclavos y los indígenas en Colombia. ____
3. La cumbia es un ritmo de origen contemporáneo en Colombia. ____
4. La cumbia nació en Panamá. ____
5. Este ritmo tiene mucha aceptación en muchos países latinoamericanos. ____
6. La cumbia contemporánea respeta la cumbia original. ____

Nombre: ______________________ Fecha: ______________________

Páginas

9-50 Las fiestas colombianas. Read about the Colombian festivities on page 323 of the textbook and answer the questions below.

1. ¿Quién empezó el carnaval en Colombia?

____

2. ¿Cuál es el festival más vistoso de Colombia?

____

3. ¿Qué fiesta es una síntesis de tradiciones indígenas y cristianas?

____

4. ¿Dónde se celebran las fiestas de Semana Santa más famosas de Colombia?

____

5. ¿Cuándo se celebra la independencia de Colombia?

____

Taller

9-51 Las vacaciones y los viajes. Colombia and Venezuela have many attractive vacation opportunities. Whether you want lazy days on the beach, an eco-tourist adventure in a rainforest, or a mountain biking expedition through the Andes, you'll find a place in Colombia or Venezuela. Decide what kind of vacation you would like to take if you could travel to either of these countries, and organize your thoughts about each of the following topics in Spanish in the chart below.

PAÍS/CIUDAD	TRANSPORTE	HOTEL	AMENIDADES	ACTIVIDADES	COSTO	MISCELÁNEA

Nombre: ______________________________ Fecha: ______________________

9-52 Tu destino. After filling the chart, decide which destination you would choose and explain why. Use expressions like **quiero que, necesito que, deseo que,** or **insisto en que** followed by the present subjunctive.

Nombre: ______________________ Fecha: ______________________

10 ¡Tu salud es lo primero!

Primera parte

¡Así es la vida!

10-1 ¡Qué mal me siento! Reread the conversation on page 330 of your textbook and answer the questions below.

1. ¿Qué le pasa a don Rafael?

   a. está enojado b. se siente mal c. tiene sueño

2. ¿Qué le duele a don Rafael?

   a. la garganta b. una mano c. la cabeza

3. ¿Cómo se llama la médica?

   a. doña Rafael b. Dra. Estrada c. Dra. Rafael

4. Según la médica, ¿qué tiene don Rafael?

   a. bronquitis b. una infección c. pulmonía

5. ¿Qué tiene que tomar don Rafael?

   a. inyecciones b. jarabe c. pastillas

6. ¿Qué le recomienda la doctora a don Rafael?

   a. que vaya al hospital b. que deje de fumar c. que guarde cama

CD 10, Track 1

10-2 Los síntomas. As you listen to the following conversation between Paula and her mother, select the letters corresponding to all statements that are correct, according to what you hear.

1. A Paula...
   a. le duelen los oídos.
   b. le duele la garganta.
   c. le duelen las piernas.
2. Mamá le pregunta a Paula…
   a. si tiene gripe.
   b. si tose.
   c. si tiene síntomas de una infección.
3. A Paula...
   a. no le gusta ir al médico.
   b. le da un jarabe para la tos.
   c. le duele el pecho.
4. Marcos siempre tiene...
   a. dolor de cabeza.
   b. gripe.
   c. dolor de estómago.
5. A Paula no le gusta cuando...
   a. su hermano se siente mal.
   b. necesita tomarse la presión.
   c. le ponen una inyección.
6. La mamá quiere que sus hijos...
   a. guarden cama.
   b. tomen jarabe.
   c. se mejoren rápidamente.

Nombre: ______________________ Fecha: ______________________

¡Así lo decimos! Vocabulario (Textbook p. 331)

10-3 Fuera de lugar. For each set of words, select the one that does not belong.

1. a. la nariz b. la espalda c. el oído d. la boca
2. a. la garganta b. el brazo c. los dedos d. la mano
3. a. el corazón b. los pulmones c. el estómago d. el pie
4. a. la aspirina b. el jarabe c. la radiografía d. el calmante
5. a. la fiebre b. la gripe c. el resfriado d. el brazo
6. a. el diagnóstico b. la radiografía c. el examen físico d. el antiácido

10-4 El cuerpo. Identify the numbered parts of the body in the illustration below.

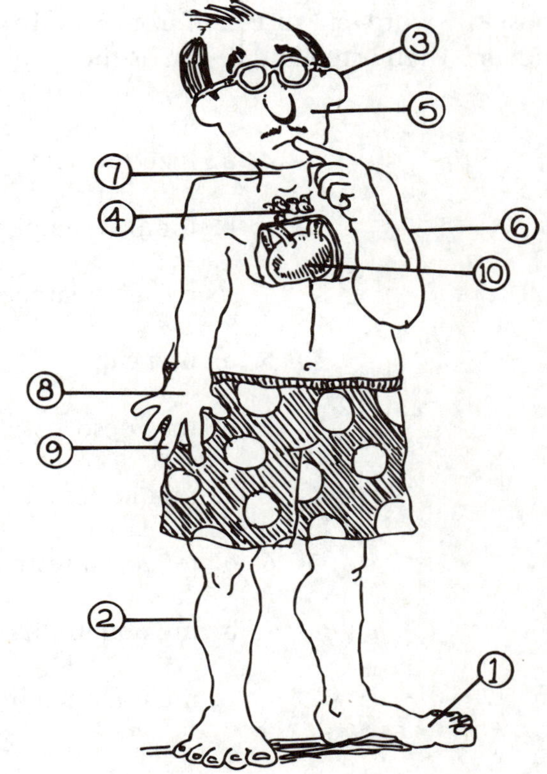

1. ______________________
2. ______________________
3. ______________________
4. ______________________
5. ______________________
6. ______________________
7. ______________________
8. ______________________
9. ______________________
10. ______________________

Nombre: ______________________________ Fecha: ______________________

10-5 ¿Qué me recomienda usted? You are a doctor and need to recommend various courses of action to your patients. Next to each complaint, write the letter of the correct action to be taken.

1. ____ Me duele mucho la garganta.
2. ____ Toso tanto que no puedo dormir.
3. ____ Creo que me rompí el dedo del pie.
4. ____ Comí demasiado y me duele el estómago.
5. ____ Me duele mucho la cabeza.
6. ____ Creo que tengo un resfriado.
7. ____ No puedo respirar bien cuando hago ejercicio.

a. Ir al hospital para una radiografía.
b. Tomarse un jarabe para la tos.
c. Tomarse un antiácido.
d. Guardar cama por dos días.
e. Dejar de fumar.
f. Tomarse dos aspirinas.
g. Tomar un antibiótico.

CD 10, Track 2

10-6 Están enfermos. Choose the word or expression from **¡Así lo decimos!** that best completes each sentence you hear. Then listen and repeat as the speaker gives the correct answer.

1. a. el estómago.
   b. el brazo.
   c. los pulmones.
2. a. te duele la rodilla.
   b. haces ejercicio.
   c. guardas cama.
3. a. un antiácido.
   b. un calmante.
   c. un jarabe.
4. a. hizo una cita.
   b. tomó la temperatura.
   c. recetó el jarabe.
5. a. una cita.
   b. un hueso.
   c. una infección.
6. a. tengo un resfriado.
   b. me ponen una inyección.
   c. me toman la presión.

10-7 ¡A completar! Complete each statement with the correct word or expression from the word bank below.

receta	radiografía	boca	diagnóstico
tomarse la temperatura	dolor de cabeza	los pulmones	

1. Si alguien siente fiebre, debe ___.
2. Después de examinarte, el médico te da el ___.
3. Cuando nos rompemos un brazo, el médico quiere ver una ___.
4. A veces cuando alguien está enfermo, el médico le ___ unas pastillas.
5. Cuando tienes ___, te tomas dos aspirinas.
6. Los dientes y la lengua están dentro de la ___.
7. Los órganos que usamos para respirar son ___.

¡Así lo hacemos! Estructuras

1. *Nosotros* commands (Textbook p. 334)

10-8 La médica y la enfermera. A doctor and a nurse decide together how to treat different patients. Look at the following drawings and match them with the most appropriate **nosotros** command.

1. ___ 

2. ___ 

a. Hagámosles una radiografía.
b. Examinémosle el pie.
c. Démosle aspirina.
d. Tomémosle la temperatura.
e. Recetémosles antiácido.

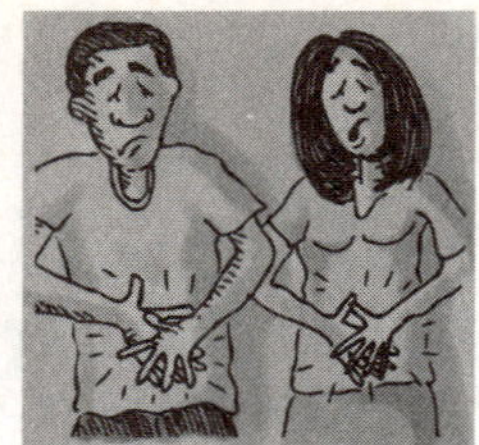

3. ____

4. ____

5. ____

10-9 El profesor de medicina. You are teaching at a university hospital. Complete each statement to your students with the **nosotros** command form of the verb in parentheses.

Modelo: (Levantarse) ______________________ a las cinco.
Levantémonos a las cinco.

1. (Tratar) ______________________ bien a los pacientes.
2. (Hablar) ______________________ mucho con los pacientes.
3. (Ir) ______________________ a las seis al consultorio todos los días.
4. (Estudiar) ______________________ todos los síntomas de los pacientes.
5. (Consultar) ______________________ la información con la enfermera.
6. No (recetar) ______________________ antibióticos frecuentemente.
7. (Visitar) ______________________ a los pacientes dos veces al día.
8. (Poner) ______________________ siempre atención a todo.

CD 10, Track 3

10-10 ¿Qué vamos a hacer? Complete the sentences with the **nosotros** command form of the verbs you hear. Then listen and repeat as the speaker gives the correct answer.

Modelo: You see: ______________ para un examen físico.
You hear: ir
You write and say: *Vayamos* para un examen físico.

1. ______________ al consultorio.
2. ______________ la radiografía.
3. ______________ el diagnóstico.
4. ______________ una cita enseguida.
5. ______________ de fumar.
6. ______________ el antibiótico.

CD 10, Track 4

10-11 Estamos enfermos. You and your roommate think you have food poisoning and plan to go to the doctor tomorrow. What should you do? Respond with **nosotros** commands, completing the sentences with the verbs you hear. Then listen and repeat as the speaker gives the correct answer.

Modelo: You see: ______________ con el médico mañana.
You hear: hablar
You say and write: *Hablemos* con el médico mañana.

1. ______________ para el consultorio.
2. ______________ temprano para no llegar tarde a la cita.
3. No ______________ tarde.
4. ______________ cama y ______________ toda la noche.
5. ______________ qué nos duele.
6. ______________ el antiácido.

Nombre: ______________________________ Fecha: ______________________

10-12 En el hospital. Your new colleague in the hospital where you work is always asking your opinion about what task you should both do next. Answer each of his questions affirmatively, using ***ir***. Use object pronouns when necessary, to avoid repetition.

Modelo: ¿Empezamos la operación?
Sí, vamos a empezarla.

1. ¿Nos preparamos para hacer el examen físico?

   Sí, ____.

2. ¿Estudiamos los síntomas?

   Sí, ____.

3. ¿Escribimos la receta?

   Sí, ____.

4. ¿Leemos el diagnóstico?

   Sí, ____.

5. ¿Recetamos el jarabe?

   Sí, ____.

10-13 El médico en prácticas. You are an intern in a hospital and you ask two medical professors for advice. One responds affirmatively to your questions, and the other responds negatively. Use the **nosotros** command to express their statements and object pronouns to avoid repetition.

Modelo: ¿Preparamos el horario de trabajo?
Profesor 1: *Sí, preparémoslo.*
Profesora 2: *No, no lo preparemos.*

1. ¿Leemos la radiografía?

   Profesor 1: ______________________

   Profesora 2: ______________________

2. ¿Recetamos más pastillas?

   Profesor 1: ______________________

   Profesora 2: ______________________

3. ¿Pedimos la información al enfermero?

   Profesor 1: ______________________

   Profesora 2: ______________________

4. ¿Les ponemos más inyecciones a los pacientes?

   Profesor 1: ______________________

   Profesora 2: ______________________

5. ¿Repetimos el examen médico a don Rafael?

   Profesor 1: ______________________

   Profesora 2: ______________________

6. ¿Operamos al niño?

   Profesor 1: ______________________

   Profesora 2: ______________________

2. Indirect commands (TEXTBOOK P. 337)

10-14 ¡Que todo salga bien! Imagine that you are a doctor and the nurse is listing the health issues of several patients. Give advice using the verb in parentheses as an indirect command.

MODELO: El señor García cree que tiene fiebre. (tomarse la temperatura)
¡Que *se tome* la temperatura!

1. Juan José se rompió el brazo. (hacerse)

   ¡Que ____________________ una radiografía!

2. La señora Ramona tose mucho. (tomarse)

   ¡Que ____________________ un jarabe para la tos!

3. Don Rafael está resfriado. (guardar)

   ¡Que ____________________ cama por dos días!

4. Al señor Ramírez le duele el pecho. (dejar)

   ¡Que ____________________ de fumar!

5. Doña María dice que le duele la garganta. (hacer)

   ¡Que ____________________ una cita conmigo!

CD 10, Track 5

10-15 Situaciones médicas. Answer the questions using an indirect command. Include object pronouns when necessary. Then listen and repeat as the speaker gives the correct answer.

MODELO: You see: ____________________ el doctor Estrada.
You hear: ¿Quién pone la inyección?
You write and say: *Que la ponga* el doctor Estrada.

1. ____________________ Eduardo.
2. ____________________ la enfermera.
3. ____________________ el médico.
4. ____________________ la doctora Iglesias.
5. ____________________ el paciente.

Nombre: ______________________ Fecha: ______________________

CD 10, Track 6

10-16 ¡No quiero! Based on what the speaker does not want to do, indicate who should do each activity instead. Use object pronouns when necessary. Then listen and repeat as the speaker gives the correct answer.

Modelo: You see: ______________ Laura.
You hear: No quiero hacer ese examen.
You write and say: *Que lo haga* Laura.

1. ______________ Manolo.
2. ______________ ellos.
3. ______________ Paco.
4. ______________ Rosalía.
5. ______________ José Antonio.

10-17 Pequeños consejos. Imagine that your friends plan to do the following things. Give them small bits of advice using indirect commands.

Modelo: Van a nadar en el río.
¡Que tengan mucho cuidado!

1. Van a ir de excursión.

____

2. Van a la fiesta de Antonio.

____

3. Van a tener un examen final.

____

4. Van a jugar baloncesto.

____

5. Van a la biblioteca.

____

Nombre: ______________________ Fecha: ______________________

¿Cuánto sabes tú?

CD 10, Track 7

10-18 ¿Cuáles son sus síntomas? Match the letter of the description you hear with the corresponding picture below.

1. ____

2. ____

3. ____

4. ____

5. ____

6. ____

Nombre: ______________________ Fecha: ______________________

10-19 ¿Sabes usar los mandatos? Fill in the blanks with the **nosotros** command form of the verbs in parentheses.

1. Este paciente está muy mal. ______________________ (Operar).
2. Fumar no es bueno para la salud. ______________________ (Dejar) de fumar.
3. Hay que ir al médico por lo menos una vez al año. ______________________ (Hacer) una cita.
4. La salud es muy importante. ______________________ (Cuidarse).
5. Hay que controlar el estrés. ______________________ (Descansar) un poco más.

10-20 ¿Sabes usar los mandatos indirectos? You are talking to your teacher about your friend Roberto, who has not been able to make it to class in the last week due to illness. Complete the conversation with the indirect command forms of the verbs in parentheses.

Tú: Profesor, Roberto está enfermo, pero quiere hacer la tarea. ¿Qué tiene que hacer?

Profesor: Primero, que (1) ________________ (cuidarse).

Cuando se sienta mejor, que (2) ________________ (leer) los capítulos seis y siete del libro y que (3) ________________ (hacer) las actividades del cuaderno.

Tú: ¿Algo más?

Profesor: Sí. Que (4) ________________ (repasar) el capítulo cinco y que (5) ________________ (escribir) un ensayo. Esto es todo.

Tú: Muchas gracias. Se lo voy a decir.

CD 10, Track 8

10-21 Preguntas personales. Answer the questions you hear based on your personal experience.

1. ____.
2. ____.
3. ____.
4. ____.
5. ____.

Nombre: ______________________________ Fecha: ______________________

SEGUNDA PARTE

¡Así es la vida!

10-22 Mejora tu salud. Answer the following questions based on the spa advertisement on page 340 of your textbook.

1. ¿En qué país está Hacienda La Fortuna?

   a. Venezuela b. Bolivia c. el Paraguay

2. ¿Qué plan en el spa puede ayudar a adelgazar?

   a. baño con esencias botánicas b. reflexología c. dieta de baja grasa

3. ¿Qué plan en el spa ayuda a aliviar el estrés?

   a. dieta de baja grasa b. masajes c. acupuntura

4. ¿Qué plan en el spa ayuda con las enfermedades crónicas?

   a. masajes b. acupuntura c. sauna

5. ¿En qué lugar geográfico se encuentra el spa?

   a. cerca del río Amazonas b. cerca del río de la Plata c. cerca del lago Titicaca

6. La piscina del spa es de agua:

   a. termal. b. medicinal. c. fría.

Nombre: ______________________________ Fecha: ______________________

CD 10, Track 9

10-23 "Me duele la espalda..." As you listen to the following conversation, circle the letters corresponding to all statements that are correct, according to what you hear.

1. La doctora Roca...
   a. dice que las radiografías salieron bien.
   b. recomienda pastillas para el dolor de espalda.
   c. insiste en que el problema es el sobrepeso.
2. Carlos...
   a. tiene mucho dolor de espalda.
   b. se siente bien.
   c. necesita comer frutas y beber agua mineral.
3. La doctora...
   a. quiere que Carlos pierda peso lentamente.
   b. prefiere que Carlos haga una dieta muy complicada.
   c. piensa que el plan no va a ser tan horrible.
4. A Carlos...
   a. le sugiere que consuma bebidas alcohólicas.
   b. le aconseja que coma comida con muchas proteínas.
   c. le recomienda que haga ejercicio.
5. La doctora dice que hacer *jogging*...
   a. va a ayudar a Carlos a adelgazar.
   b. ayuda a ponerse en forma.
   c. no es necesario.
6. Carlos tiene que...
   a. correr todas las noches.
   b. hacer una lista de lo que come.
   c. ver a la doctora en dos semanas.

¡Así lo decimos! Vocabulario (Textbook p. 341)

10-24 Los alimentos. Next to each word on the left, write the letter of the food category that it belongs to.

1. _____ cerveza
2. _____ pasta
3. _____ queso
4. _____ pescado
5. _____ mantequilla

a. proteína
b. bebida alcohólica
c. grasa
d. carbohidratos
e. productos lácteos

Nombre: ___________________________ Fecha: ___________________

10-25 ¡A escoger! Select the letter of the most appropriate word or phrase to complete each statement and write it in the space provided.

1. Si alguien desea adelgazar, necesita eliminar de su dieta ____.

   a. las frutas b. la grasa c. las legumbres

2. Para mantenerse en forma, se necesita ____.

   a. fumar b. engordar c. estar a dieta

3. Para subir de peso, se necesita ____.

   a. estar a dieta b. adelgazar c. comer muchos carbohidratos

4. Nosotros necesitamos tener bajo el ____.

   a. cigarrillo b. colesterol c. peso

5. El trabajo, la escuela y las responsabilidades causan ____.

   a. estrés b. proteínas c. diabetes

6. Para ponernos en forma, tenemos que ____.

   a. comer más b. hacer ejercicios aeróbicos c. subir de peso

7. Un alimento rico en proteínas es el ____.

   a. pescado b. azúcar c. aceite

10-26 Nuestra salud. Choose the most logical word or expression to complete each sentence you hear. Then listen and repeat as the speaker gives the correct answer.

1. a. padecer de diabetes.
   b. una bebida alcohólica.
   c. hacer *jogging*.
2. a. la gimnasia.
   b. la grasa.
   c. la diabetes.
3. a. más grasas en la dieta.
   b. bajar de peso.
   c. hacer una cita.
4. a. productos lácteos.
   b. proteínas.
   c. ejercicios aeróbicos.
5. a. hacer *jogging*.
   b. adelgazar.
   c. subir de peso.
6. a. sobrepeso.
   b. la línea.
   c. en forma.

10-27 El menú. Based on the restaurant menu shown below, prepare the menus listed.

Nombre: ____________________ Fecha: ____________________

1. Menú rico en proteínas: ____________________

2. Menú rico en colesterol: ____________________

3. Menú rico en grasas: ____________________

4. Menú rico en carbohidratos: ____________________

5. Menú saludable: ____________________

10-28 Cuestionario. Answer the questions below in complete sentences in Spanish.

1. ¿Cómo guardas la línea?

____

2. ¿Quieres adelgazar o engordar?

____

3. ¿Cómo te pones en forma?

____

4. Cuando haces ejercicio, ¿qué ejercicio haces?

____

5. ¿Qué haces para cuidarte?

____

6. ¿Qué tipo de alimentos comes?

____

Letras y sonidos (Textbook p. 342)

CD 10, Track 11

10-29 The consonants "r" and "rr" in Spanish. Decide whether the **"r"** sound you hear in the following words or word groups consists of a flap or trill, and write **flap** or **trill** on the line provided.

1. __________
2. __________
3. __________
4. __________
5. __________
6. __________
7. __________
8. __________

Nombre: ______________________ Fecha: ______________________

10-30 **¿Cuál es?** Write the words or word groups you hear in the corresponding column, depending on whether they contain the flap or trill **"r"** sound.

CD 10, Track 12

flap	**trill**
______________________	______________________
______________________	______________________
______________________	______________________
______________________	______________________
______________________	______________________

¡Así lo hacemos! Estructuras

3. The subjunctive to express feelings and emotions (Textbook p. 344)

10-31 En el gimnasio. Fill in the blanks with the appropriate present subjunctive form of the verb in parentheses.

Modelo: Espero que tú ______________ (hacer) ejercicio.
Espero que tú *hagas* ejercicio.

1. Me enoja que tú no ______________ (cuidarse) mejor.
2. ¿Temes que ______________ (haber) mucha grasa en la comida?
3. Nosotros sentimos que tú no ______________ (poder) hacer *footing* esta tarde.
4. Ustedes lamentan que el gimnasio no ______________ (estar) abierto.
5. Mis amigos esperan que yo ______________ (hacer) ejercicio con ellos.
6. Pablo está contento de que nosotros ______________ (ir) al gimnasio hoy.
7. ¿Usted se alegra de que yo ______________ (mantenerse) en forma?
8. Me sorprende que tú ______________ (estar) a dieta.

Nombre: ______________________ Fecha: ______________________

10-32 La salud de Luis. Everyone seems to be concerned with Luis's health. Complete the paragraph with the correct present subjunctive, present indicative, or infinitive form of each verb in parentheses, as appropriate.

Los padres de Luis esperan que él (1) ______________ (cuidarse). A ellos les sorprende que Luis (2) ______________ (subir) de peso fácilmente porque él (3) ______________ (hacer) mucho ejercicio. La madre de Luis se alegra de que su hijo (4) ______________ (hacer*) footing* todos los días porque espera que él (5) ______________ (mantenerse) en forma. A Luis le enoja (6) ______________ (estar) a dieta, pero también lamenta (7) ______________ (padecer) de sobrepeso. Yo espero que Luis (8) ______________ (adelgazar) y que (9) ______________ (ponerse) en forma porque temo que (10) ______________ (poder) padecer de otras enfermedades en el futuro.

CD 10, Track 13

10-33 ¿Cómo se siente cuando...? Listen to the following sentences and combine them with the clauses provided to form new sentences. Then listen and repeat as the speaker gives the correct answer.

1. Nos molesta que Susana y Adela ______________.
2. Me enoja que ellos ______________.
3. Sienten que yo ______________.
4. Esperamos que Alejandra no ______________.
5. Me sorprende que Rafael ______________.

CD 10, Track 14

10-34 Deseos. Complete the following sentences based on the verbs you hear. Then listen and repeat as the speaker gives the correct answer.

1. ¡Ojalá no nos ______________ a doler la garganta!
2. ¡Ojalá usted no ______________ alergias a los productos lácteos!
3. ¡Ojalá yo ______________ ir al gimnasio luego!
4. ¡Ojalá ellos ______________!
5. ¡Ojalá tú ______________ en forma!
6. ¡Ojalá les ______________ la dieta!

Nombre: ______________________ Fecha: ______________________

CD 10, Track 15

10-35 ¿Cómo reaccionan? Answer the following questions using the sentence fragments provided. Then listen and repeat as the speaker gives the correct answer.

Modelo: You see: su paciente / cuidarse

____

You hear: ¿Qué espera la doctora Roca?

You write and say: *Espera que su paciente se cuide.*

1. las clases de ejercicio / ser tan caras

______________________.

2. tú / adelgazar tanto

______________________.

3. la dieta / terminar pronto

______________________.

4. el profesor / padecer de diabetes

______________________.

5. tú / tener menos estrés

______________________.

10-36 Tu familia y tu salud. What are the things you fear, hope for, and are happy about regarding your family and your health? Write five sentences using the expressions below.

espero que	me enoja que
estoy triste de que	me preocupa que
lamento que	temo que
me alegro de que	ojalá

Modelo: *Temo que se enferme mi abuela.*

1. ______________________
2. ______________________
3. ______________________
4. ______________________
5. ______________________

10-37 ¿Qué esperas? Write six occurrences that you hope will happen this year. Begin your sentences with **"Ojalá."**

MODELO: *¡Ojalá que tengamos más vacaciones!*

1. ______________________.
2. ______________________.
3. ______________________.
4. ______________________.
5. ______________________.
6. ______________________.

4. The subjunctive to express doubt and denial (TEXTBOOK P. 347)

CD 10, Track 16

10-38 ¿Qué crees? What are your thoughts about the following situations? Choose the correct answer based on the clauses you hear. Then listen and repeat as the speaker gives the correct answer.

1. a. tiene alergias a los productos lácteos.
   b. tenga alergias a los productos lácteos.
2. a. recomiendan tomar muchas bebidas alcohólicas.
   b. recomienden tomar muchas bebidas alcohólicas.
3. a. guardas la línea.
   b. guardes la línea.
4. a. tienen mucho estrés.
   b. tengan mucho estrés.
5. a. se mantiene en forma porque se cuida.
   b. se mantenga en forma porque se cuida.

Nombre: ______________________ Fecha: ______________________

10-39 El estado ideal de salud. Fill in the blanks to make statements about the ideal state of health. Follow the model, and use the **yo** form of each verb.

MODELO: Tal vez este mes ______________ (hacer) más ejercicio.
Tal vez este mes *haga* más ejercicio.

1. Tal vez no ______________ (comer) tanta grasa.
2. Quizás ______________ (controlar) el estrés.
3. Quizás ______________ (adelgazar).
4. Tal vez ______________ (cuidarse) más.
5. Quizás ______________ (ir) al gimnasio todas las mañanas.
6. Tal vez ______________ (levantar) pesas en el gimnasio.
7. Tal vez ______________ (mantenerse) en forma.
8. Quizás ______________ (dejar) de fumar.

CD 10, Track 17

10-40 ¿Dudamos mucho? Form sentences using the verbs provided. Then listen and repeat as the speaker gives the correct answer.

MODELO: You see: Luisa no ______________ que yo ______________.
You hear: creer, cuidarse
You write and say: Luisa no *cree* que yo *me cuide*.

1. Tú no ______________ que ellos ______________ en forma.
2. Ustedes ______________ que María ______________ a dieta.
3. Papá ______________ que los niños ______________ jarabe.
4. Tú ______________ seguro de que Felipe ______________ ejercicio.
5. Los médicos no ______________ que los antiácidos ______________ con el dolor de estómago.
6. Nosotros ______________ que él ______________.
7. La paciente no ______________ que el diagnóstico ______________ bueno.
8. Yo no ______________ que la doctora ______________ cuáles son mis síntomas.

Nombre: ______________________ Fecha: ______________________

CD 10, Track 18

10-41 ¿Qué opinan? State the following opinions based on the comments you hear by writing the appropriate verb forms. Then listen and repeat as the speaker gives the correct answer.

MODELO: You see: No estoy segura de que ______________ de colesterol alto.
You hear: Padeces de colesterol alto.
You write and say: No estoy segura de que *padezcas* de colesterol alto.

1. No creo que ______________ la dieta mañana.
2. Niegan que ______________ mejor.
3. No dudamos que ______________ de peso.
4. Dudas que ______________ para el gimnasio ahora.
5. Mario no piensa que ______________ a tiempo para la cita.
6. Crees que el doctor generalmente ______________ por la mañana.

CD 10, Track 19

10-42 Una vida saludable. Answer the questions you hear using the expressions provided. Then listen and repeat as the speaker gives the correct answer.

MODELO: You see: Tal vez ______________
You hear: ¿Crees que muchos pacientes vienen hoy?
You write and say: *Tal vez muchos pacientes vengan hoy.*

1. Tal vez ______________________________.
2. Quizás ______________________________.
3. Tal vez ______________________________.
4. Quizás ______________________________.
5. Quizás ______________________________.

Nombre: ______________________ Fecha: ______________________

10-43 Unas opiniones. María disagrees with everything Carlos says. Play the part of María and change Carlos's statements from affirmative to negative, as in the model.

Modelo: **Carlos:** Creo que hacer ejercicio es muy bueno.
María: No creo que hacer ejercicio sea muy bueno.

1. **Carlos:** Estoy seguro de que el estrés tiene solución.

   María: ____.

2. **Carlos:** No niego que ponerse en forma es difícil.

   María: ____.

3. **Carlos:** Yo creo que él consigue adelgazar.

   María: ____.

4. **Carlos:** No dudo que ustedes se mantienen en forma.

   María: ____.

5. **Carlos:** Pienso que el médico sabe mucho.

   María: ____.

6. **Carlos:** No niego que los atletas están a dieta.

   María: ____.

7. **Carlos:** Estoy seguro de que Esteban y Rocío guardan la línea.

   María: ____.

8. **Carlos:** Creo que Ramiro hace ejercicio.

   María: ____.

Nombre: ______________________ Fecha: ______________________

10-44 Tu opinión. Guillermo makes many unfounded statements. Set him straight each time he does this by using a verb or expression from the word bank below and by making any necessary changes.

dudar	negar	no creer
no es cierto	no estar seguro/a de	

Modelo: Nosotros siempre vigilamos nuestro nivel de colesterol.
No es cierto que nosotros vigilemos nuestro nivel de colesterol.

1. A él le gusta hacer ejercicios aeróbicos.

   ______________________________.

2. Tengo que subir de peso.

   ______________________________.

3. Nosotros nos cuidamos mucho.

   ______________________________.

4. Hay mucha grasa en la carne.

   ______________________________.

5. Es muy difícil ponerse en forma.

   ______________________________.

6. Pedro es el mejor médico de la ciudad.

   ______________________________.

7. Comer carbohidratos no engorda.

   ______________________________.

8. Todos nosotros siempre hacemos *footing* por la mañana.

   ______________________________.

Nombre: ______________________ Fecha: ______________________

¿Cuánto sabes tú?

10-45 Más subjuntivo. For each sentence, select the letter of the most appropriate verb form.

1. Dudo que ustedes ____ ejercicio.

   a. hacen b. hagan

2. Pienso que ellos ____ a dieta.

   a. están b. estén

3. Estoy seguro de que Marcos ____ *jogging*.

   a. hace b. haga

4. No creo que Andrés ____ la línea.

   a. guarda b. guarde

5. Niego que nosotros ____ de peso.

   a. subimos b. subamos

10-46 ¿Sabes usar el presente de subjuntivo? Fill in the blanks with the correct form of the verbs in parentheses.

Lamento que Roberto (1) ______________________ (estar) enfermo. Espero que

(2) ______________________ (guardar) cama durante dos días y que

(3) ______________________ (tomar) el jarabe que le recetó el médico. Tengo miedo de que

Roberto no (4) ______________________ (seguir) las instrucciones del médico. Ojalá que

(5) ______________________ (mejorarse) pronto y que nosotros

(6) ______________________ (poder) hacer *footing* juntos de nuevo.

Nombre: ______________________ Fecha: ______________________

CD 10, Track 20

10-47 "Doctor, ¿qué puedo hacer?" Listen to the medical statements or questions of the following people and respond using the cues provided. Then listen and repeat as the speaker gives the correct answer. Follow the model closely.

MODELO: You see: (estar contenta / no tener gripe)
You hear: Doctora, creo que no tengo gripe.
You say and write: *Estoy contenta de que no tengas gripe.*

1. (dudar / necesitar una inyección) ______________________.
2. (pensar / deber hacer ejercicio) ______________________.
3. (esperar / volver en dos semanas) ______________________.
4. (alegrarse de / sentirse mejor) ______________________.
5. (molestarme / no mantenerse en forma) ______________________.

CD 10, Track 21

10-48 Otras preguntas personales. Answer the questions you hear based on your personal experience.

1. ______________________.
2. ______________________.
3. ______________________.
4. ______________________.
5. ______________________.

Nombre: ______________________ Fecha: ______________________

Observaciones

Antes de ver el video

10-49 ¿Qué pasa? Select the letter of the statement that best answers each question.

1. What might Patricio say his symptoms are?

   a. Lo único que necesito es descansar. Mañana voy a estar mucho mejor.

   b. Tengo un fuerte dolor de cabeza… y de espalda…y de garganta…

   c. ¡A mí me apasiona el dulce! Pero no puedo tomarlo.

2. According to the symptoms, what does doña María diagnose him with?

   a. ¡Ay, mi hijo! ¡Tú tienes la gripe!

   b. Padeces de diabetes.

   c. Tienes que hacer *jogging*.

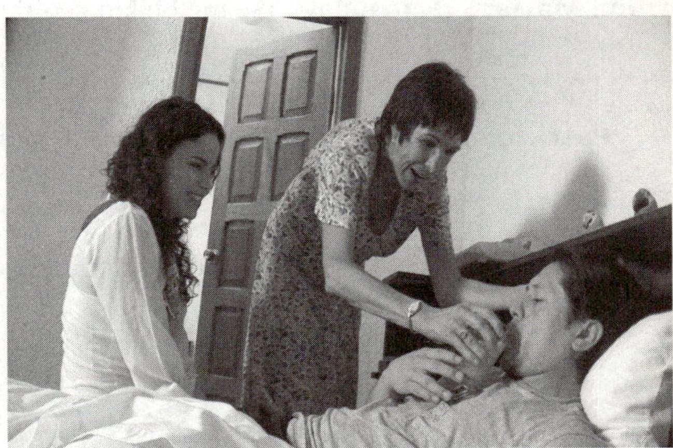

3. What might doña María recommend to Patricio to help him feel better?

   a. Espero que te mejores pronto, mi hijo.

   b. Tienes que guardar la línea.

   c. Anda, mi hijo. Tómate dos. Esta noche te tomas una sopita y mañana como nuevo.

Nombre: ______________________ Fecha: ______________________

4. What might Marcela determine upon touching Patricio's forehead?

   a. Tráeme un poco de apio y unas aspirinas de la farmacia.

   b. ¿Tienes fiebre?... ¡Madre mía! ¡Te quema la frente!

   c. No es muy interesante, pero se trata de ayudar.

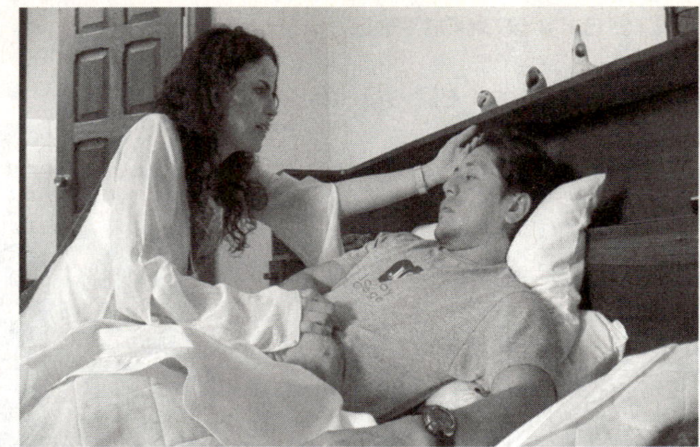

5. How would Patricio let Marcela know that he is not seriously ill?

   a. Lo único que necesito es descansar. Mañana voy a estar mucho mejor.

   b. Felipe y yo tenemos que irnos al parque dentro de una hora.

   c. Ya tomé jarabe, gracias. ¿No tiene una aspirina por ahí?

A ver el video

10-50 La conversación. Fill in the blanks with the missing words according to the video segments.

Doña María: ¡Pero niña!... ¡Se me olvidó pedirle azúcar para hacerte un (1) ______________!

Patricio: No, por mí no, Doña María. Quiero (2) ______________.

Doña María: Sí, mi hijo, tienes que guardar la (3) ______________. Quiero que vayas a tu cuarto. ¡A mí me apasiona el dulce! Pero no puedo tomarlo. (4) ______________ de (5) ______________.

...

Marcela: Patri, ¿cómo estás?

Patricio: ¡Gordo! Tengo que hacer (6) ______________.

Marcela: ¿Tienes (7) ______________? ...¡Madre mía! ¡Te quema la frente!

Patricio: Lo único que necesito es (8) ______________. Mañana voy a estar mucho mejor.

Nombre: ______________________ Fecha: ______________________

10-51 ¿Cómo se mejora? Put a check mark next to the items that correspond with what Patricio does, or wants to do, to get better.

____ Toma aspirina.

____ Toma antibióticos.

____ Toma jarabe.

____ Va al parque.

____ Hace cita con el médico.

____ Toma jugo.

____ Quiere agua.

____ Quiere descansar.

____ Quiere tomar la sopa.

____ Quiere un calmante.

Después de ver el video

10-52 La lista. Identify the items that Doña María wanted Marcela to buy in each of the places indicated.

En el mercado...

____

____

____

En la farmacia...

____

____

10-53 La acción y los personajes. Determine whether the following statements are **cierto** (C) or **falso** (F) and write the correct letter on the lines provided.

1. A Patricio le duele la cabeza. ____
2. Doña María quiere que Patricio se acueste en el sofá. ____
3. Patricio quiere que doña María le traiga un té con limón. ____
4. Marcela llama al médico para saber el diagnóstico. ____
5. Marcela va al mercado a comprar los ingredientes para la sopa. ____
6. Marcela también va a comprar azúcar para hacer un jugo. ____
7. Patricio toma un calmante para ayudarlo a descansar. ____
8. Marcela está segura que Felipe habló con Patricio sobre Elvira. ____

NUESTRO MUNDO

Panoramas

10-54 ¡A informarse! Identify if the following statements are true for Paraguay, Bolivia, or both, and choose the letter of the correct answer.

1. No tiene(n) salida al mar:

   a. el Paraguay b. Bolivia c. el Paraguay y Bolivia

2. Tiene(n) frontera con el Brasil:

   a. el Paraguay b. Bolivia c. el Paraguay y Bolivia

3. La cría de ganado es económicamente importante en…

   a. el Paraguay. b. Bolivia. c. el Paraguay y Bolivia.

4. La Santísima Trinidad de Paraná está en…

   a. el Paraguay. b. Bolivia. c. el Paraguay y Bolivia.

5. La minería es de mucha importancia para la economía en…

   a. el Paraguay. b. Bolivia. c. el Paraguay y Bolivia.

6. La capital situada a una altura considerable está en…

   a. el Paraguay. b. Bolivia. c. el Paraguay y Bolivia.

7. … produce(n) electricidad consumida en el Brasil.

   a. El Paraguay b. Bolivia c. El Paraguay y Bolivia

8. Los sombreros tipo *bowler* son típicos de las mujeres de…

   a. el Paraguay. b. Bolivia. c. el Paraguay y Bolivia.

10-55 De viaje por el Paraguay. In this chapter you learned more about the countries of Bolivia and Paraguay and about issues relating to health. Now visit www.prenhall.com/arriba and read the information given on health issues when traveling to Paraguay. Then, decide if the statements below are **cierto** (C) or **falso** (F).

1. Existe un alto riesgo de contraer malaria en Paraguay. ____
2. Se puede contraer fiebre tifoidea en las zonas rurales. ____
3. El agua en las zonas seguras es buena y se puede beber. ____
4. Se recomienda hervir la leche antes de beberla. ____
5. Se aconseja la vacuna contra la rabia antes de llegar al país. ____
6. No es necesario tener seguro médico para viajar a Paraguay. ____

Ritmos

10-56 El ritmo *taquirari*. Read the following statements and fill in the blanks based on the information on page 354 of the textbook.

1. "Sol de primavera" es representativa del ritmo ____________________.
2. Este ritmo es original de ____________________.
3. El ritmo taquirari es una mezcla de las tradiciones musicales ________________________.
4. La gente ____________________ con este tipo de música.
5. En las ocasiones festivas, las mujeres se visten con ____________________.

Páginas

10-57 La leyenda de la coca. In your textbook you read the legend of **"El ñandutí"** from Paraguay. Now visit www.prenhall.com/arriba and after reading **"La leyenda de la coca,"** answer the questions below.

1. ¿Quiénes son los conquistadores blancos?

   a. los bolivianos   b. los paraguayos   c. los españoles

2. ¿Quién es Kjana-Chuyma?

   a. un conquistador español   b. un indio viejo y adivino   c. el dios de los indios

Nombre: ______________________________ Fecha: ______________________

3. ¿Dónde ocultó el tesoro?

   a. en el templo del sol b. en La Paz c. en una orilla del lago Titicaca

4. ¿Quién es Pizarro?

   a. un conquistador español b. un indio c. el dios de los españoles

5. ¿Quién es el dios de Kjana-Chuyma?

   a. la luna b. el sol c. el lago Titicaca

6. ¿Qué le da el dios Sol a su pueblo?

   a. armas b. la hoja de coca c. el tesoro del lago

Taller

10-58 Nuestra salud este mes. Interview three classmates to find out what health problems they have had in the last thirty days. Use the chart below to record the information. Fill in the same information about yourself as well.

	ESTUDIANTE 1	ESTUDIANTE 2	ESTUDIANTE 3	TÚ
VECES ENFERMO/A				
RESFRIADO				
GRIPE				
FIEBRE				
DOLOR DE ESTÓMAGO				
DOLOR DE CABEZA				
CLÍNICA / HOSPITAL				
¿...?				

Nombre: ______________________ Fecha: ______________________

10-59 Tu resumen. Now, use the information from the chart in the previous activity to write a brief report on the health of the students in your class. Try to make some general assessments, as well as provide specific cases.

MODELO: *Este mes varios estudiantes tuvieron dolor de estómago. Ana tuvo que ir al hospital porque...*

Nombre: ______________________ Fecha: ______________________

11 ¿Para qué profesión te preparas?

Primera parte

¡Así es la vida!

11-1 Los trabajadores. Reread the business cards on page 364 of your textbook and select the letter of the person each statement is describing.

1. Trabajo en Montevideo:
   a. Rafael
   b. Mercedes
2. Trabaja en México:
   a. Rafael
   b. Mercedes
3. Es ingeniero/a industrial:
   a. Rafael
   b. Mercedes
4. Es psicólogo/a clínico/a:
   a. Rafael
   b. Mercedes
5. Trabaja en el Hospital del Instituto Nacional de la Salud:
   a. Rafael
   b. Mercedes
6. Trabaja en el Edificio Díaz de Solís:
   a. Rafael
   b. Mercedes

Nombre: ______________________ Fecha: ______________________

CD 11, Track 1

11-2 Una entrevista. As you listen to the following conversation, select the letters corresponding to all statements that are correct, according to what you hear.

1. Alejandro leyó el anuncio...
   a. en una revista.
   b. en una tarjeta.
   c. en el periódico.
2. La empresa Buen Trabajo publicó...
   a. un solo aviso.
   b. más de un aviso.
   c. tres avisos.
3. Alejandro quiere...
   a. un trabajo de secretario.
   b. un trabajo en la construcción.
   c. un trabajo de arquitecto.
4. Alejandro es...
   a. contador.
   b. carpintero.
   c. electricista.
5. La dirección de Alejandro es...
   a. Calle Valencia 305, tercero, primera.
   b. Calle Valencia 205, tercero, segunda.
   c. Calle Valencia 305, tercero, primero.
6. El horario disponible de Alejandro es...
   a. por la tarde.
   b. de 8:30 a 14:00.
   c. por la mañana hasta las doce.
7. Alejandro tiene…
   a. diez años de experiencia.
   b. tres años de experiencia.
   c. seis meses de experiencia.
8. El jefe de la empresa...
   a. va a llamar a Alejandro.
   b. va a entrevistar a Alejandro.
   c. va a darle el puesto de supervisor a Alejandro.

Nombre: ______________________________ Fecha: ______________________

¡Así lo decimos! Vocabulario (Textbook p. 365)

11-3 Los oficios y los cargos. Select the names of ten professions or job positions in the following puzzle.

S	I	M	V	E	T	E	R	I	N	A	R	I	O	P
C	B	O	P	L	A	V	I	J	A	I	M	U	L	B
O	C	E	R	O	T	I	C	A	M	N	B	O	P	U
N	E	B	L	E	T	N	E	R	E	G	M	U	R	D
T	F	D	O	V	S	I	M	T	L	E	P	T	O	M
A	G	I	M	T	I	D	R	A	R	N	B	E	O	L
D	I	R	F	E	N	U	F	O	J	I	C	R	T	A
O	M	E	D	L	T	C	N	R	L	E	V	U	R	I
R	P	C	O	Z	E	U	M	S	O	R	B	T	I	M
A	C	T	A	L	R	I	B	A	L	A	F	E	J	P
L	B	O	N	I	P	L	O	S	D	E	G	V	N	O
O	M	R	I	D	R	A	L	E	P	S	T	I	R	C
B	L	A	N	R	E	C	U	N	O	T	R	E	S	G
I	N	G	P	A	T	S	I	D	O	I	R	E	P	I
E	S	E	C	R	E	T	A	R	I	O	G	E	F	N
S	E	D	T	A	R	P	N	I	E	F	L	O	P	A

Nombre: ______________________ Fecha: ______________________

11-4 Diferentes oficios. On the line next to each drawing, write the letter of the profession that it describes.

1. ____ 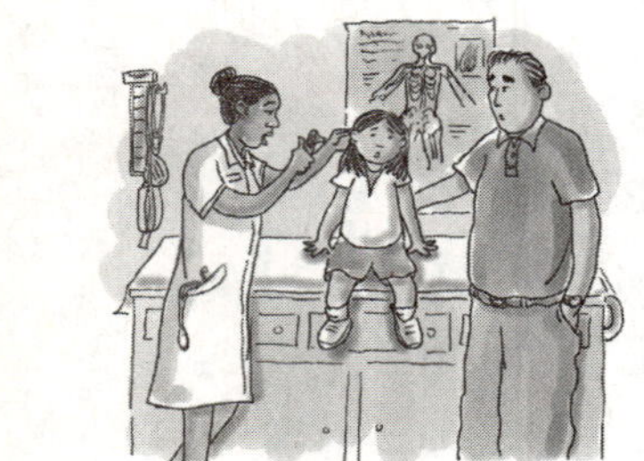 

2. ____ 

3. ____ 

4. ____ 

5. ____ 

6. ____ 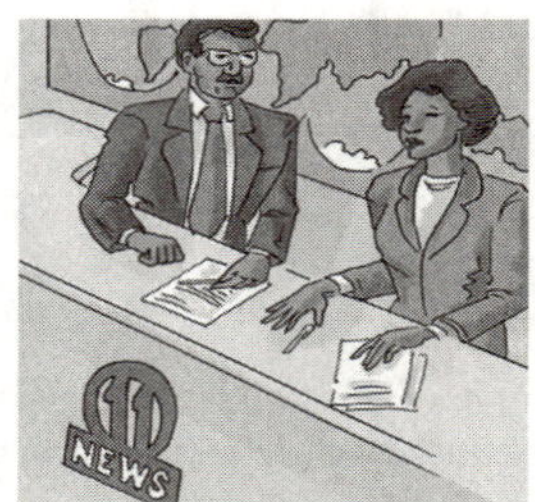

a. contador

b. periodista

c. enfermera

d. cocinera

e. peluquera

f. analista de sistemas

11-5 Palabras relacionadas. On the line next to each occupation, write the letter of the word or phrase that is best associated with it.

1. ____ el/la dentista
2. ____ el/la contador/a
3. ____ el/la cocinero/a
4. ____ el/la viajante
5. ____ el/la peluquero/a
6. ____ el/la enfermero/a

a. la cuenta

b. la receta

c. la pastilla

d. la comisión

e. la pasta de dientes

f. el champú

Nombre: ______________________________ Fecha: ______________________

11-6 ¿A qué profesión corresponde? Listen to the following sentences and choose the letter of the word that best completes each sentence. Then listen and repeat as the speaker gives the correct answer.

CD 11, Track 2

1. a. arquitecto.
   b. dentista.
   c. peluquero.
2. a. analista de sistemas.
   b. electricista.
   c. cocinera.
3. a. plomero.
   b. peluquero.
   c. viajante.
4. a. peluquera?
   b. carpintera?
   c. secretaria?
5. a. veterinario.
   b. psicólogo.
   c. mecánico.
6. a. psicólogo.
   b. periodista.
   c. bombero.
7. a. diseñar casas.
   b. repartir las cartas y los paquetes.
   c. apagar fuegos.
8. a. supervisor.
   b. electricista.
   c. plomero.

11-7 ¡A completar! Fill in the blanks in each statement with a word or expression from the word bank.

carpintero	horario de trabajo	intérprete	arquitecta
meta	veterinaria	contador	entrenamiento

1. Esa ____________________ nos va a diseñar una casa nueva.
2. El ____________________ es el responsable de las cuentas de la empresa.
3. El ____________________ reparó los armarios de mi casa.
4. Mariluz sabe dos idiomas; ella es la ____________________ de su compañía.
5. Los nuevos empleados pasan por un buen programa de ____________________ antes de empezar a trabajar.
6. Los viajantes no tienen un ____________________ fijo y trabajan a comisión.

7. Mi ________________ es obtener ese puesto.

8. La ________________ curó a mi perro.

¡Así lo hacemos! Estructuras

1. The subjunctive with impersonal expressions (TEXTBOOK P. 368)

11-8 Los profesionales. Select the letter of the correct form of the verbs in parentheses.

1. Es urgente que los bomberos _____ el fuego en ese almacén.

   a. apaguen b. apagan c. apagar

2. Es extraño que allí no _____ buenos carpinteros.

   a. haya b. hay c. haber

3. Es obvio que un arquitecto _____ edificios.

   a. diseñe b. diseña c. diseñar

4. Es preciso que la cartera _____ temprano hoy.

   a. venga b. viene c. venir

5. Es difícil _____ dos trabajos diariamente.

   a. haga b. hace c. hacer

6. Es increíble que ese viajante no _____ más.

   a. venda b. vende c. vender

7. Es imposible que los peluqueros _____ dientes.

   a. saquen b. sacan c. sacar

8. Es importante _____ mucho para ser psicólogo.

   a. estudien b. estudian c. estudiar

CD 11, Track 3

11-9 ¿Cierto o incierto? Listen to the following sentences and indicate whether they express certainty or uncertainty by writing the sentence number in the appropriate column, separated by commas.

CIERTO	INCIERTO

Nombre: ______________________ Fecha: ______________________

11-10 El/La jefe/a de personal. You are the personnel director of a large firm and you are describing how you and your staff should conduct yourselves. Fill in the blanks with the correct form of the verbs in parentheses.

1. Es importante que nosotros ______________ (hablar) con los supervisores.
2. Es necesario que tú ______________ (mirar) el horario de trabajo.
3. Es indispensable que ustedes ______________ (conseguir) clientes.
4. Es mejor que todos nosotros ______________ (saber) cuáles son nuestras responsabilidades.
5. Siempre es bueno que usted ______________ (conocer) al gerente.
6. Es urgente que ustedes ______________ (ser) siempre puntuales.
7. Es preciso que yo les ______________ (dar) entrenamiento a todos los empleados.
8. Es importante que nosotros ______________ (trabajar) bien.

11-11 Tres empleados. Miguel, Ricardo, and José work for the same company and Miguel is about to be fired. Ricardo and José argue the fairness of the decision. Complete their dialogue with the correct form of each verb in parentheses.

Ricardo: ¿Oíste lo que le pasó a Miguel?

José: No, ¿qué le ocurrió?

Ricardo: Es seguro que el gerente no (1) ______________ (querer) tenerlo más en la compañía.

José: Bueno, pero es verdad que Miguel (2) ______________ (ser) muy perezoso y muy arrogante.

Ricardo: Es increíble que tú (3) ______________ (decir) eso de Miguel.

José: ¿Cómo es posible que tú (4) ______________ (ser) tan inocente?

Ricardo: Es evidente que tú (5) ______________ (ser) un mal amigo y no (6) ______________ (querer) ayudar a Miguel.

José: Es una lástima que tú (7) ______________ (hablar) tan mal de mí.

Ricardo: Mira, es mejor que tú y yo no (8) ______________ (verse) más.

José: Sí, es obvio que tú y yo (9) ______________ (tener) muchas diferencias. ¡Hasta luego!

CD 11, Track 4

11-12 ¿Un buen puesto? Complete the sentences with the correct form of the verbs you hear. Then listen and repeat as the speaker gives the correct answer.

Modelo: You see: Es necesario que usted ______________ mucho entrenamiento.
You hear: recibir
You write and say: Es necesario que usted *reciba* mucho entrenamiento.

1. Es importante que usted no ______________ durante la entrevista.
2. Es necesario que ustedes ______________ metas claras.
3. Es urgente que nosotros ______________ el horario de trabajo.
4. Es indispensable que ______________ buenas relaciones entre los empleados y los directores.
5. Es una lástima que los empleados ______________ sin trabajo.

CD 11, Track 5

11-13 Responsabilidades del empleado. Answer the questions you hear using the phrases and verbs provided. Then listen and repeat as the speaker gives the correct answer.

Modelo: You see: ______________ (decir) la verdad.
You hear: ¿Qué es importante que haga el director?
You write and say: *Es importante que diga* la verdad.

1. ______________ (pedir) los puestos.
2. ______________ (apagar) todos los fuegos.
3. ______________ (leer) las evaluaciones.
4. ______________ (escribir) la carta.
5. ______________ (diseñar) la casa ahora.
6. ______________ (hablar) de mi formación.

Nombre: ______________________ Fecha: ______________________

11-14 Combinación. Choose one element from each column to form six logical sentences. Be sure to use the correct forms of the present subjunctive or present indicative.

Es bueno	un gerente	atender a los clientes
Es común	una veterinaria	repartir las cartas
Es importante	un mecánico	hacer muebles
Es imposible	un peluquero	reparar el coche
Es necesario	una carpintera	curar a los animales
Es probable	una bombera	contratar a más empleados
Es cierto	un cartero	apagar un fuego
Es obvio	un viajante	cortar el pelo

Modelo: *Es extraño que una psicóloga examine los dientes.*

1. ______________________
2. ______________________
3. ______________________
4. ______________________
5. ______________________
6. ______________________

11-15 Entrevista. Imagine that you are the president of a large corporation and you are being interviewed by a group of students. Answer their questions in Spanish, using complete sentences.

1. ¿Qué es importante para conseguir un buen puesto?

____

2. ¿Qué es indispensable en su compañía?

____

3. ¿Qué es necesario para ser un buen gerente?

____

4. ¿Qué es evidente en un buen empleado?

____

5. ¿Quiénes están mejor preparados?

____

¿Cuánto sabes tú?

CD 11, Track 6

11-16 Las profesiones. Determine whether each of the following statements you hear regarding the workplace and professions is **lógico** (L) or **ilógico** (I) and write the correct letter on the lines provided.

1. ____ 3. ____ 5. ____ 7. ____

2. ____ 4. ____ 6. ____ 8. ____

11-17 A describir. On the lines provided, write the letter of the profession that best fits each description.

1. ____ habla dos o más idiomas a. periodista
2. ____ escribe artículos b. enfermero
3. ____ reparte las cartas y revistas c. cocinero
4. ____ cuida de los enfermos d. intérprete
5. ____ trabaja en un restaurante e. cartero

11-18 ¿Sabes usar el subjuntivo con expresiones impersonales? Fill in the blanks with the correct present subjunctive forms of the verb in parentheses.

En el trabajo...

1. ... es importante que el sueldo ________________ (ser) bueno.
2. ... es necesario que ________________ (haber) un buen gerente.
3. ... es indispensable que tú ________________ (tener) vacaciones.
4. ... es preciso que la empresa ________________ (ofrecer) formación.
5. ... es malo que los empleados no ________________ (estar) contentos.
6. ... es mejor que ustedes ________________ (trabajar) en una gran empresa.

Nombre: ______________________ Fecha: ______________________

CD 11, Track 7

11-19 Preguntas personales. Answer the questions you hear in Spanish, using complete sentences.

1. ______________________.
2. ______________________.
3. ______________________.
4. ______________________.
5. ______________________.

SEGUNDA PARTE

¡Así es la vida!

11-20 En busca de empleo. Reread the interview on page 372 of your textbook and select the letter that best answers the question or completes the sentence.

1. ¿Quién es Juan López?

   a. el director de la empresa   b. el aspirante   c. un estudiante

2. ¿Quién es la Sra. Posada?

   a. la directora de la empresa   b. la aspirante   c. una estudiante

3. La Sra. Posada acaba de examinar…

   a. las cartas de recomendación.   b. el expediente.   c. el currículum vitae.

4. Juan tiene experiencia en…

   a. contabilidad.   b. informática.   c. periodismo.

5. ¿Por qué quiere trabajar Juan en esta empresa?

   a. por el sueldo   b. por el interés en sus empleados

   c. por las vacaciones que ofrecen

6. ¿A quién va a conocer Juan?

   a. al director   b. al jefe de personal   c. a los empleados

Nombre: ______________________ Fecha: ______________________

11-21 Un nuevo trabajo. As you listen to the following conversation, select the letters corresponding to all statements that are correct, according to what you hear.

CD 11, Track 8

1. Carlos Rodríguez fue...
   a. estudiante.
   b. plomero.
   c. ayudante.
2. La señora Peña...
   a. trabaja en una empresa internacional.
   b. acaba de jubilarse.
   c. entrevista a Carlos.
3. Carlos tiene experiencia en...
   a. diseño.
   b. uso de computadoras.
   c. periodismo.
4. El puesto...
   a. es por dos años.
   b. es para una persona justa.
   c. es para una persona que sea amable con la gente.
5. El puesto incluye beneficios de...
   a. plan de retiro para toda la familia.
   b. dos bonificaciones anuales.
   c. seguro médico.
6. La empresa...
   a. hace una evaluación de los empleados dos veces al año.
   b. raramente ofrece aumentos.
   c. asciende a todos sus empleados tres veces al año.

¡Así lo decimos! Vocabulario (Textbook p. 373)

11-22 Relaciones lógicas. On the lines next to each statement, write the letter of the sentence that logically follows it.

1. _____ Rosario acaba de ascender.
2. _____ Tú quieres un aumento de sueldo.
3. _____ Arturo quiere solicitar la vacante en la empresa.
4. _____ Los empleados reciben su bonificación anual.
5. _____ El jefe de personal tiene sesenta y cinco años.
6. _____ Roberto no es honesto en el trabajo.

a. Rellena el formulario.
b. Ha recibido un aumento.
c. A la empresa le va muy bien.
d. Hablas con el gerente.
e. Lo van a despedir.
f. Quiere jubilarse pronto.

Nombre: ______________________ Fecha: ______________________

CD 11, Track 9

11-23 La mejor respuesta. Listen to the following sentences and choose the letter of the word or expression that best completes each sentence. Then listen and repeat as the speaker gives the correct answer.

1. a. la despedida de una carta comercial.
   b. el saludo de una carta comercial.
   c. el título de una empresa popular.
2. a. trabaja poco.
   b. trabaja mucho.
   c. es periodista.
3. a. un expediente.
   b. una solicitud de empleo.
   c. una carta de recomendación.
4. a. la renuncia.
   b. un beneficio laboral.
   c. el puesto.
5. a. solicitud.
   b. agencia.
   c. aspirante.
6. a. la vacante.
   b. la evaluación.
   c. la solicitud.

11-24 La carta de presentación. Complete the letter below with the missing words and expressions from the word bank.

formulario	capaz	currículum vitae
Estimada	entrevista	Le saluda atentamente
vacante	presentación	

(1) ______________ señora:

Le escribo esta carta de (2) ______________ para solicitar la (3) ______________ de contador. Tengo mucha experiencia y mis calificaciones son numerosas, como usted puede ver en el (4) ______________ que adjunto. Soy una persona muy (5) ______________. Incluyo tres cartas de recomendación y el (6) ______________ que me envió su secretaria. Espero poder tener una (7) ______________ con usted.

Esperando su respuesta a la presente.

(8) ______________________,

Rodrigo Rodríguez

Nombre: ______________________ Fecha: ______________________

11-25 Una posibilidad de empleo. Read the following letter and answer the questions below in complete sentences.

20 de julio de 2005

Sra. Jimena Galtieri de Posada, Gerente
Centro de Cómputo, S.A.
Apartado Postal 2225
Montevideo, Uruguay

Estimada señora:
La presente es para solicitar el puesto de analista programadora que anunció su empresa en *La Nación*. Me gradué de la Universidad de la República de Uruguay con especialización en informática y contabilidad. También tengo tres años de experiencia práctica.

Soy bilingüe y me considero una persona entusiasta, responsable y trabajadora. Adjunto mi currículum vitae.

Atentamente,
Isabel Urquiza Duarte
Isabel Urquiza Duarte

Anexo

1. ¿Cómo se llama la gerente de la empresa?

____

2. ¿Cómo se llama la empresa?

____

3. ¿Cuál es la vacante en la empresa?

____

4. ¿Qué adjunta Isabel a la carta de presentación?

____

5. ¿Cómo es Isabel?

____

Nombre: ______________________ Fecha: ______________________

Letras y sonidos (TEXTBOOK P. 374)

CD 11, Track 10

11-26 ¿Cómo se escribe? Determine whether the word or words you hear contain a **"b"** or **"v"** and write the correct letter on the lines provided.

1. ____
2. ____
3. ____
4. ____
5. ____
6. ____
7. ____
8. ____
9. ____
10. ____

CD 11, Track 11

11-27 ¿Cuál es? First, write the word or words you hear. Then determine whether the **"b"** or **"v"** is a hard bilabial or soft bilabial sound and put a check mark on the appropriate line.

	HARD BILABIAL	SOFT BILABIAL
1. ______________	____	____
2. ______________	____	____
3. ______________	____	____
4. ______________	____	____
5. ______________	____	____
6. ______________	____	____
7. ______________	____	____
8. ______________	____	____
9. ______________	____	____
10. ______________	____	____

Nombre: ______________________ Fecha: ______________________

¡Así lo hacemos! Estructuras

2. Formal commands (TEXTBOOK P. 377)

11-28 Las profesiones y los mandatos. Look at the following drawings and write the letter of the formal command that best associates with each profession.

1. _____ Pilar

2. _____ El señor Castillo

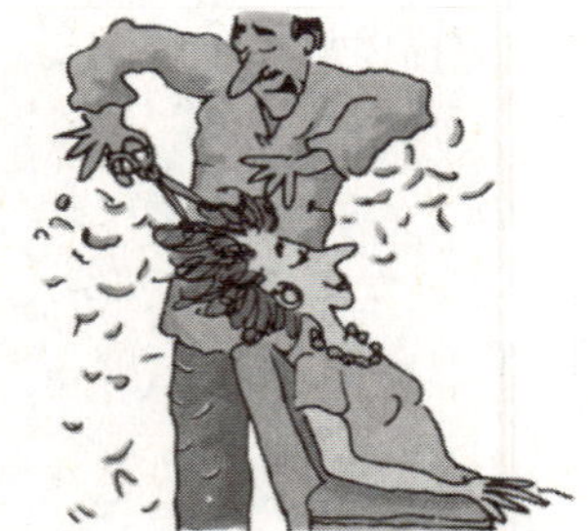

3. _____ Rafael

4. _____ Doña Maruja

5. _____ La doctora Fernández

a. Cure a los animales.

b. No trabaje a comisión.

c. Apague bien el fuego.

d. Cuide a los enfermos.

e. Corte el pelo a la moda.

Nombre: ______________________________ Fecha: ______________________

11-29 Tu jefe. You have a boss who likes to give commands. Complete the orders he gives you by using the correct singular formal command of the verb in parentheses.

1. ____________________ (Seguir) todas mis instrucciones.
2. ____________________ (Llegar) temprano al trabajo.
3. No ____________________ (salir) del despacho temprano.
4. ____________________ (Empezar) a hacer su trabajo.
5. ____________________ (Leer) los nuevos contratos.
6. ____________________ (Rellenar) los formularios.
7. No ____________________ (poner) los expedientes sobre la mesa.
8. No ____________________ (pedir) un aumento de sueldo.

11-30 Rosalía y Felipe. Rosalía and Felipe are about to apply for several jobs, and don Pepe, their grandfather, gives them some advice. Fill in the blanks with the **ustedes** command form of the verbs in parentheses.

1. No ____________________ (trabajar) a comisión y ____________________ (pedir) un buen sueldo.
2. ____________________ (Hablar) con los empleados, pero no ____________________ (conversar) durante el entrenamiento.
3. ____________________ (Tener) metas, pero ____________________ (vivir) su vida al máximo.
4. ____________________ (Recordar) sus responsabilidades y no ____________________ (olvidar) su horario de trabajo.
5. No ____________________ (estar) en el paro y ____________________ (jubilarse) a los sesenta años.

Nombre: ______________________________ Fecha: ______________________

11-31 Recomendaciones para una entrevista. Mr. Fernández, an acquaintance of yours, has certain recommendations for your upcoming job interview. As you ask him questions, he answers affirmatively using the **usted** form. Fill in the blanks with the correct command forms of the verbs provided, following the model.

Modelo: ¿Hablo con confianza?
Sí, *hable* con confianza.

1. ¿Llamo a la empresa para confirmar la entrevista?

   Sí, ____________________ a la empresa.

2. ¿Llevo un currículum vitae conmigo?

   Sí, ____________________ un currículum vitae.

3. ¿Le doy la mano al gerente?

   Sí, ____________________ la mano al gerente.

4. ¿Le muestro mis cartas de recomendación al gerente?

   Sí, ____________________ las cartas.

5. ¿Relleno el formulario antes de ir?

   Sí, ____________________ el formulario.

6. ¿Pregunto acerca del sueldo?

   Sí, ____________________ acerca del sueldo.

Nombre: ______________________ Fecha: ______________________

CD 11, Track 12

11-32 ¡Bienvenida a nuestra empresa! Use formal commands and the sentence fragments provided to give advice to a new employee. Then listen and repeat as the speaker gives the correct answer.

Modelo: You see: (hacer / muchas preguntas) ______________________
You write and say: *Haga* muchas preguntas.

1. (llegar / temprano) ______________________
2. (ser / simpático con el director) ______________________
3. (ir / a la oficina de la secretaria para hablar de un plan de retiro) ______________________
____
4. (hacer / todo el trabajo a tiempo) ______________________
5. (rellenar / los papeles correctamente) ______________________
6. (seguir / el horario indicado en el calendario) ______________________

CD 11, Track 13

11-33 Las entrevistas. Your friends are looking for work and want your feedback on the interview process. Respond to each item with **ustedes** formal commands using the verbs and phrases provided. Then listen and repeat as the speaker gives the correct answer.

Modelo: You see: llegar ______________________
You hear: a tiempo
You write and say: *Lleguen a tiempo.*

1. levantarse
______________________.
2. vestirse
______________________.
3. hacer
______________________.
4. preguntar
______________________.
5. decir(les)
______________________.

CD 11, Track 14

11-34 Mi primer día de trabajo. Answer the questions you hear with formal commands, using the sentence fragments given. Include pronouns when possible. Then listen and repeat as the speaker gives the correct answer.

MODELO: You see: sí / los formularios
You hear: ¿Relleno todos los formularios?
You write and say: *Sí, rellénelos.*

1. no / con estos expedientes

   ____

2. sí / los nombres

   ____

3. no / a las ocho

   ____

4. sí / más responsabilidades

   ____

5. no / en el despacho del director

   ____

6. sí / con nosotros

   ____

7. sí / la información

   ____

8. no / a las cinco

   ____

3. The subjunctive and the indicative with adverbial conjunctions

(TEXTBOOK P. 380)

11-35 Expectativas en el trabajo. Complete each statement below using the present indicative, present subjunctive, or infinitive of the verbs in parentheses.

1. Voy a mandar una solicitud para ______________ (conseguir) empleo.
2. Voy a ir a la entrevista a menos que no ______________ (sentirse) bien.
3. Mis amigos dicen que hable de mis calificaciones para que ellos me ______________ (contratar).
4. Aunque yo ______________ (estar) nerviosa, voy a conseguir el puesto de trabajo.
5. Voy a empezar a trabajar tan pronto como me ______________ (llamar) la empresa.
6. Voy a mandar mi currículum vitae en cuanto el gerente de la empresa me lo ______________ (pedir).
7. Voy a conseguir formación mientras ______________ (trabajar) en esta empresa.
8. Voy a jubilarme después de ______________ (ascender) a la dirección de la empresa.

Nombre: ______________________ Fecha: ______________________

11-36 ¿Cierto o incierto? As you listen to the following statements, decide if each one is **cierto** (C) or **incierto** (I) and write the correct letter on the lines provided.

CD 11, Track 15

1. ____
2. ____
3. ____
4. ____
5. ____
6. ____

11-37 Mis ideales. Complete the following paragraph using the present indicative, present subjunctive, or infinitive of the verbs in parentheses.

Yo (1) ______________ (ser) idealista y (2) ______________ (querer) encontrar el trabajo perfecto tan pronto como (3) ______________ (poder). Primero, voy a llamar a muchas empresas para que ellos me (4) ______________ (llamar) cuando (5) ______________ (haber) vacantes. Luego, voy a mandar mi currículum vitae a todas las grandes empresas, a menos que éstas no (6) ______________ (contratar) a nuevos empleados. Después de (7) ______________ (tener) éxito, espero que la empresa me (8) ______________ (ofrecer) aumentos y un buen plan de retiro.

11-38 ¡Siempre hay condiciones! Fill in the blanks using the present indicative, present subjunctive, or infinitive of the verbs you hear. Then listen and repeat as the speaker gives the correct answer.

CD 11, Track 16

Modelo: You see: Vamos a trabajar para esta empresa, con tal de que ellos nos ______________ un plan de retiro.
You hear: ofrecer
You write and say: Vamos a trabajar para esta empresa, con tal de que nos *ofrezcan* un plan de retiro.

1. Catalina va a aceptar el trabajo a menos que la compañía ______________ muy poco.
2. Reciben los aumentos porque ______________ muy bien.
3. Trabajas por la tarde para ______________ estudiar por la mañana.
4. Vamos a salir del trabajo tan pronto como ______________ las cartas.
5. Francisca y yo vamos a hablar cuando la reunión ______________.
6. Vas a ver si hay vacantes antes de ______________ la solicitud.

Nombre: ______________________________ Fecha: ______________________

11-39 La rutina del trabajo. Using the conjunctions in parentheses, combine each pair of statements to discover what routine Miguel follows at work and how he feels about it. Use the present indicative, present subjunctive, or infinitive and follow the model.

MODELO: Miguel va a ir al banco. Sale del trabajo. (después de)
Miguel va a ir al banco después de salir del trabajo.

1. Normalmente, él llega a la oficina. Son las ocho de la mañana. (cuando)

 ____

2. Hoy él va a hablar con el gerente. Llega a la oficina. (tan pronto como)

 ____

3. Él va a firmar los cheques. Va al banco. (antes de)

 ____

4. Él entrevista a los aspirantes. La empresa tiene los mejores empleados. (para que)

 ____

5. No va a contratar a nadie. Un empleado deja el empleo. (a menos que)

 ____

6. Miguel va a ascender. La supervisora se jubila. (en cuanto)

 ____

7. Él va a trabajar. Él tiene sesenta y cinco años. (hasta que)

 ____

8. Miguel va a estar contento en la empresa. Le aumentan el sueldo cada año. (con tal de que)

 ____

Nombre: ______________________ Fecha: ______________________

CD 11, Track 17

11-40 ¿Cuándo? Answer the questions you hear using the sentence fragments provided, and include direct object pronouns when possible. Then listen and repeat as the speaker gives the correct answer.

MODELO: You see: ascender / luego que / él / buscar más clientes
You hear: ¿Cuándo van a ascender al empleado?
You write and say: *Lo van a ascender luego que él busque más clientes.*

1. ir a apagar / cuando / llegar

 ____

2. reparar / cuando / tener problemas

 ____

3. ir a despedir / antes de que / ella / salir

 ____

4. llevar / cuando / estar enfermo

 ____

5. no deber dejar / sin que / encontrar otro trabajo

 ____

6. ir a estar sin trabajo / en cuanto / empezar el año fiscal

 ____

Nombre: ______________________________ Fecha: ______________________

11-41 Tu futuro trabajo. Talk about the job you may hold after graduation using the conjunctions from the word bank. Follow the model and write five sentences with a different conjunction in each.

en cuanto	hasta que	cuando	mientras que	aunque

MODELO: *Tan pronto como me gradúe, voy a buscar un trabajo en un país de habla hispana.*

1. ____

2. ____

3. ____

4. ____

5. ____

¿Cuánto sabes tú?

11-42 ¿Sabes usar los mandatos formales? Imagine you are a supervisor and have to give commands to the employees. Fill in the blanks with the appropriate formal command form of the verb in parentheses.

1. Elena y Raúl, no ____________________ (llegar) tarde al trabajo.

2. Ricardo, ____________________ (hablar) con el gerente.

3. Rogelio, ____________________ (ser) responsable.

4. Ángeles y Carlos, ____________________ (asistir) al entrenamiento.

5. María, ____________________ (rellenar) el formulario.

6. José y Laura, ____________________ (pedirles) ayuda a sus compañeros.

Nombre: ______________________ Fecha: ______________________

11-43 ¿Sabes usar el subjuntivo con conjunciones adverbiales? Complete the following paragraph with the present indicative, present subjunctive, or infinitive of the verbs in parentheses.

Desde que Arturo (1) ________________ (trabajar) en el banco, no tiene tiempo para sus amigos. Aunque a él le (2) ________________ (gustar) estar con ellos, sus responsabilidades en el banco son muy importantes y tiene que trabajar, a menos que el banco (3) ________________ (estar) cerrado o que su jefe le (4) ________________ (dar) el día libre. En caso de que Arturo (5) ________________ (dejar) el trabajo, no va a estar en paro por mucho tiempo porque todos los bancos lo quieren (6) ________________ (contratar).

CD 11, Track 18

11-44 Puestos y beneficios. As you listen to the following descriptions of these people and their jobs, put a check mark under the heading(s) that describe(s) their salaries and benefits.

NOMBRE	TRABAJA A COMISIÓN	SUELDO FIJO	PLAN DE RETIRO	SEGURO MÉDICO	BONIFICACIÓN ANUAL
ESTEBAN					
LEONARDO					
CARLOS					
SUSANA					

CD 11, Track 19

11-45 Otras preguntas personales. Answer the questions you hear in Spanish, using complete sentences.

1. ____.
2. ____.
3. ____.
4. ____.
5. ____.

Nombre: ______________________________ Fecha: ______________________

Observaciones

Antes de ver el video

11-46 ¿Qué pasa? Select the letter of the best answer to each question.

1. What qualifications might David be looking for in a prospective job candidate?
   a. buenos patrocinadores
   b. gente joven, entusiasta y capaz
   c. experiencia

2. What incentives might David give Patricio?
   a. una gran oportunidad
   b. abrir muchas puertas
   c. una bonificación anual, un plan de retiro y, por supuesto, seguro médico

3. What might David say to recognize Patricio's qualifications?
   a. Es posible que se le abran muchas puertas.
   b. Su formación profesional es brillante.
   c. Lo importante es que esto supone una gran oportunidad para usted.

4. How might Patricio inquire about the hours he would be working?
   a. ¿Y el horario de trabajo?
   b. ¿Y el salario?
   c. ¿Por mi cuenta?

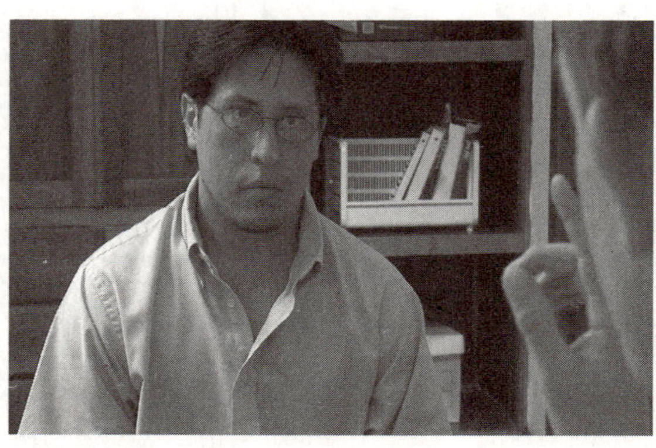

5. What would David's response to Patricio's question be?
   a. Es un trabajo de responsabilidad.
   b. Sí, queremos que sea su propio jefe.
   c. Olvídese de horarios. Éste no es un trabajo de oficina.

Nombre: ______________________________ Fecha: ______________________

A ver el video

11-47 La conversación. Complete the statements with the missing words according to what you hear in the selected video segment.

Patricio: ¿Y qué puedo hacer yo para (1) __________________?

David: Estamos buscando a un (2) __________________ de operaciones. Queremos que (3) __________________ las crías antes de que…

Patricio: ¡Ya entiendo! Antes de que se las lleven los ladrones.

David: Exacto. El coordinador tiene cinco (4) __________________ a su cargo. ¡Queremos que usted les (5) __________________ lo que sabe!

Patricio: Interesante. A situaciones radicales, medidas radicales. ¿Y necesitan un biólogo para hacer eso?

David: Sí. El trabajo requiere la (6) __________________ de un científico. También es (7) __________________ que el coordinador conozca la selva.

Patricio: Si hay algo que tenga es experiencia en la (8) __________________.

11-48 ¿Un nuevo trabajo? Put a check mark next to the items that David and Patricio discuss during the interview.

____ aumento

____ bonificación anual

____ comisión

____ contrato

____ formulario

____ horario de trabajo

____ plan de retiro

____ salario

____ seguro médico

____ supervisión

Nombre: ___________________________ Fecha: ___________________

Después de ver el video

11-49 La entrevista. Select the letter of the word or phrase that best completes the sentence or answers the question.

1. Para recuperar la población de guacamayos, David explica que CREFASI quiere...

   a. curarlos.

   b. quitarlos de sus nidos y criarlos.

   c. verlos en peligro de extinción.

2. Después, la organización va a...

   a. dejarlos en la selva.

   b. venderlos.

   c. convertirlos en mascotas.

3. Si Patricio acepta el trabajo, él...

   a. trabajará en una oficina grande y tendrá muchas responsabilidades.

   b. supervisará a diez empleados.

   c. traerá las crías antes de que se las lleven los ladrones.

4. El salario será...

   a. el doble de lo que Patricio gana ahora.

   b. el mismo que Patricio gana ahora.

   c. un poco más alto de lo que gana ahora.

5. Patricio...

   a. acepta el trabajo porque es un biólogo excelente que conoce la selva.

   b. tiene que pensar si acepta el trabajo porque no le gusta la idea de sacar crías de sus nidos.

   c. no acepta el trabajo porque no le gusta tener mucha responsabilidad en el trabajo.

Nombre: ______________________ Fecha: ______________________

Nuestro mundo

Panoramas

11-50 ¡A informarse! Based on the information from **Nuestro mundo,** decide if the following statements are **cierto** (C) or **falso** (F) and write the correct letter on the lines provided.

1. El tango es un baile popular de la Argentina. ____
2. El tango se originó en la Patagonia. ____
3. Bariloche, Patagonia atrae muchos turistas. ____
4. La Argentina y el Uruguay son países conocidos por la pesca. ____
5. Los argentinos consumen más carne que la gente de cualquier otro país del mundo. ____
6. El gaucho vive en las pampas de la Argentina y el Uruguay. ____
7. Punta del Este es famoso por sus playas. ____
8. El béisbol es más popular que el fútbol en la Argentina y el Uruguay. ____

11-51 ¿Quiénes son? In the text you learned about the geography of Argentina and Paraguay. Now visit **www.prenhall.com/arriba** to find out about these famous Argentinians and match the letter of the correct profession to each name.

1. ____ Jorge Luis Borges	a. primera dama de la Argentina
2. ____ Diego Armando Maradona	b. revolucionario
3. ____ Eva Perón	c. compositor e intérprete del tango
4. ____ Che Guevara	d. músico
5. ____ Astor Piazzolla	e. futbolista
6. ____ Carlos Gardel	f. escritor

Nombre: ______________________________ Fecha: ______________________

Ritmos

11-52 La nueva canción latinoamericana. Reread the information on **la nueva canción latinoamericana** in your textbook. Then decide if the following statements are **cierto** (C) or **falso** (F) and write the correct letter on the lines provided.

1. "Todo cambia" es un ejemplo de tango. ____
2. Este género musical contiene mensajes políticos. ____
3. Lo comercial está presente en la nueva canción latinoamericana. ____
4. La cultura tradicional es importante en la nueva canción latinoamericana. ____
5. Los problemas de la clase alta es un tema importante de este género musical. ____

Páginas

11-53 El autor y sus obras. Argentina is the land of many contemporary authors, one of whom is Julio Cortázar. Go to **www.prenhall.com/arriba** to learn more about him and then list five of his famous works.

1. ______________________
2. ______________________
3. ______________________
4. ______________________
5. ______________________

Nombre: ______________________________ Fecha: ______________________

Taller

11-54 Las carreras. Make a list in Spanish of the expectations you have regarding your career or profession.

____

____

____

____

____

11-55 La agencia. Now, imagine that you are working with an employment agency that will conduct interviews of college students to help build candidate profiles. Based on the categories in the previous activity, write eight questions you might use in the interviews.

Modelo: *¿Para qué profesión te preparas?*

1. ___________________________________
2. ___________________________________
3. ___________________________________
4. ___________________________________
5. ___________________________________
6. ___________________________________
7. ___________________________________
8. ___________________________________

Nombre: ______________________ Fecha: ______________________

11-56 Entrevistas con tus compañeros. Using your list of expectations and the questions you wrote as a guide, interview two classmates and fill all the information in the chart below.

	ESTUDIANTE 1	ESTUDIANTE 2	TÚ
TIPO DE CARRERA QUE BUSCAS			
TRES (TIPOS DE) COMPAÑÍAS QUE TE INTERESAN			
UNA ALTERNATIVA (POR EJ., AUTO-EMPLEO)			
AMBIENTE (*ENVIRONMENT*) DE TRABAJO QUE ESPERAS (POR EJ., OFICINA GRANDE)			
SUELDO QUE QUIERES PARA EMPEZAR			
SUELDO DESPUÉS DE DIEZ AÑOS			
BENEFICIOS QUE QUIERES (POR EJ., MÉDICOS)			
ELEMENTOS ABSOLUTAMENTE NECESARIOS			
ELEMENTOS PREFERIBLES			
ELEMENTOS NO ACEPTABLES			
¿...?			

Nombre: ______________________________ Fecha: ______________________

12 El futuro es tuyo

PRIMERA PARTE

¡Así es la vida!

12-1 El impacto de la tecnología. Reread the paragraph on page 398 of your textbook. Then decide if the following statements are **cierto** (C) or **falso** (F) and write the correct letter on the lines provided.

1. La tecnología ha revolucionado el mundo en que vivimos. ____
2. La tecnología ha impactado las carreras. ____
3. En la universidad, los estudiantes usan la computadora para todos sus diseños. ____
4. No asisten a clase por videoconferencias. ____
5. Usan las hojas electrónicas para mantener tablas. ____
6. Quieren comprarse unos *iPods*. ____
7. Todas las tardes van a la biblioteca a buscar recursos. ____
8. Los estudiantes odian la tecnología y no la usan. ____

CD 12, Track 1

12-2 ¿Por qué lo necesitas? As you listen to the following conversation, select the letters corresponding to all statements that are correct, according to what you hear.

1. Catalina quiere...
   a. una calculadora.
   b. un juego electrónico.
   c. una computadora y una impresora.

2. La mamá cree que Catalina...
   a. no necesita una computadora.
   b. necesita una pantalla grande.
   c. no necesita una impresora.

3. Catalina es...
   a. estudiante.
   b. analista de sistemas.
   c. diseñadora de juegos electrónicos.
4. El precio que ponen en la página web es...
   a. quinientos dólares.
   b. mil dólares.
   c. mil quinientos dólares.
5. El precio incluye...
   a. una videograbadora con pantalla grande.
   b. una computadora y una impresora.
   c. suficiente memoria.
6. Ayer se rompió...
   a. la videograbadora.
   b. el teléfono inalámbrico.
   c. el contestador automático.

¡Así lo decimos! Vocabulario (Textbook p. 399)

12-3 Palabras relacionadas. Next to each drawing, write the letter of the verb that best relates to its function.

1. _____

2. _____

3. _____

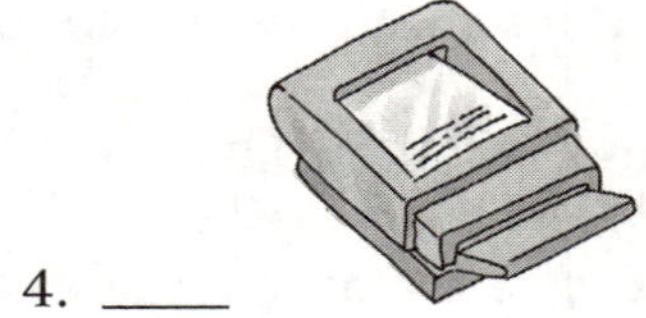

4. _____

5. _____

a. grabar
b. llamar
c. fotocopiar
d. archivar
e. imprimir

CD 12, Track 2

12-4 Escoge la tecnología. Listen to the following sentences and circle the letter corresponding to the word or phrase that best completes each sentence. Then listen and repeat as the speaker gives the correct answer.

1. a. el contestador automático.
   b. el cajero automático.
   c. el teclado.
2. a. los juegos electrónicos.
   b. los ratones.
   c. los discos duros.
3. a. el disco duro.
   b. la hoja electrónica.
   c. el DVD.
4. a. cajero automático.
   b. computadora portátil.
   c. antena parabólica.
5. a. apagada.
   b. instalada.
   c. grabada.

12-5 ***HP photosmart 230.*** Read the following advertisement and select the letter of the word or phrase that best answers each question.

hp photosmart 230

La Impresora HP Photosmart 230

Fotos en menos de 3 minutos

Calidad óptima

Precio razonable

- Vea las imágenes en pantalla antes de imprimirlas.
- Imprima y comparta fotografías sin bordes de 10 x 15 cm, igual que si las hubiera revelado en un laboratorio.
- Imprima directamente desde su cámara digital, sin PC ni Mac.
- Diseño compacto y elegante y funciones sencillas – perfecta para fiestas, bodas y otros acontecimientos.

1. ¿Qué es *photosmart 230*?
   a. un teléfono móvil b. una computadora portátil c. una impresora
2. La *photosmart 230*…
   a. imprime fotos. b. hace fotocopias. c. escanea documentos.

Nombre: ________________________________ Fecha: ________________________

3. ¿Cuánto cuesta la *photosmart 230*?

   a. es muy cara   b. el precio es razonable   c. es muy barata

4. La calidad de las fotografías es…

   a. mejor que en el laboratorio.   b. peor que en el laboratorio.   c. igual que en el laboratorio.

5. Para imprimir las fotografías…

   a. se necesita una PC.   b. se necesita una Mac.   c. no se necesita una computadora.

12-6 ¡A completar! Complete the following statements by filling in the blanks with words from the word bank below.

teléfono inalámbrico	contestador automático	encender
grabar	cajero automático	página web
correo electrónico	apagar	

1. El banco está cerrado, pero puedo usar el ____________________ para sacar dinero.
2. Hoy no es necesario esperar las llamadas telefónicas porque el ____________________ puede ____________________ todos los mensajes.
3. Mi ____________________ favorita es **www.prenhall.com/arriba**.
4. Yo acabo de comprar un ____________________ y me gusta mucho; puedo hablar con mis amigos desde el jardín de mi casa.
5. Cuando llego a la oficina tengo que ____________________ la computadora y cuando me voy por la noche tengo que ____________________ la.
6. A mí me gusta mucho el ____________________ porque puedo mandar mensajes instantáneamente.

Nombre: ______________________ Fecha: ______________________

12-7 Preguntas tecnológicas. Answer the following questions based on your own experience with technology.

1. ¿A quién le escribes por correo electrónico?

____

____.

2. ¿Para qué usas el teléfono móvil?

____

____.

3. ¿Cuándo usas el cajero automático?

____

____.

4. ¿Prefieres una computadora de escritorio o una computadora portátil? ¿Por qué?

____

____.

5. ¿Qué sistema usas para grabar programas de televisión?

____

____.

Nombre: ______________________ Fecha: ______________________

¡Así lo hacemos! Estructuras

1. The past participle and the present perfect indicative (Textbook p. 403)

12-8 ¡Hecho! Complete each sentence with the past participle of the verb in parentheses. Remember to make changes in agreement when necessary.

1. La impresora está ______________ (romper).
2. El cajero automático está ______________ (abrir).
3. El diseño de la página electrónica está ______________ (hacer).
4. Los correos electrónicos están ______________ (escribir).
5. El archivo está ______________ (poner) en el disco duro.
6. El disquete está ______________ (instalado).
7. El correo electrónico está ______________ (enviar).
8. La videograbadora está ______________ (programar).

CD 12, Track 3

12-9 Sí, está hecho. Complete each sentence with the past participle of the verb in the question you hear. Then listen and repeat as the speaker gives the correct answer.

Modelo: You see: Sí, las ventanas están ______________.
You hear: ¿Abriste las ventanas?
You write and say: Sí, las ventanas están *abiertas*.

1. Sí, los ratones están ______________.
2. Sí, el teléfono móvil está ______________.
3. Sí, los juegos electrónicos están ______________.
4. Sí, el DVD está ______________.
5. Sí, las hojas electrónicas están ______________.
6. Sí, las copias están ______________.

Nombre: ________________________________ Fecha: ________________________

12-10 Hay muchas cosas que hacer. Tell what the following people have already done today. Complete the sentences by using the subjects given and the present perfect form of each verb.

Modelo: Francisco / conectarse
Francisco se ha conectado a la Red.

1. nosotros / archivar

   ______________________________ los documentos en el disquete.

2. Fernando / programar

   ______________________________ la computadora.

3. yo / borrar

   ______________________________ los archivos del disco duro.

4. Felipe / imprimir

   ______________________________ los documentos.

5. mis amigos / ir

   ______________________________ al despacho.

6. yo / escuchar

   ______________________________ los mensajes del contestador automático.

7. tú / encender

   ¿______________________________ la impresora?

8. nosotros / comprar

   ______________________________ el teléfono móvil.

Nombre: ______________________ Fecha: ______________________

CD 12, Track 4

12-11 ¿Qué han hecho? Fill in the blanks with the correct present perfect form of the verbs you hear. Then listen and repeat as the speaker gives the correct answer.

MODELO: You see: Susana y Marta ______________ la videograbadora.
You hear: instalar
You write and say: Susana y Marta *han instalado* la videograbadora.

1. Camila ______________ el teléfono móvil.
2. Josefina y Margarita ______________ a la tienda de computadoras.
3. Nosotros ______________ los documentos.
4. Tú ______________ un ratón inalámbrico.
5. Yo ______________ el escáner.
6. Ustedes ______________ la foto.

12-12 ¿Qué han hecho estas personas? Complete each affirmative statement with the correct present perfect form of the verb. Use object pronouns when necessary to avoid repetition.

MODELO: ¿Has apagado la computadora?
Sí, *la he apagado.*

1. ¿Has fotocopiado la carta?

   Sí, ______________________________.

2. ¿Han instalado ustedes la antena parabólica?

   Sí, ______________________________.

3. ¿Ha calculado ella las cuentas?

   Sí, ______________________________.

4. ¿Has archivado los documentos?

   Sí, ______________________________.

5. ¿Han grabado ustedes el programa de televisión?

   Sí, ______________________________.

Nombre: ______________________________ Fecha: ______________________

12-13 En la empresa. Your boss is telling you that the following things need to be done. Respond to each statement by using both the present perfect form of the verb and the past participle as an adjective, following the model.

Modelo: Tienes que enviarle un correo electrónico al programador de computadoras.
Se lo he enviado. Ya está enviado.

1. Tienes que darle el disquete a la Srta. Muñoz.

   ____

2. Tienes que guardar el documento en el disco duro.

   ____

3. Tienes que instalarle el nuevo programa de contabilidad al contador.

   ____

4. Tienes que pedirme un ratón nuevo para mi computadora.

   ____

5. Tienes que hacer una búsqueda en la Red para el Sr. Ortiz.

   ____

Nombre: ______________________ Fecha: ______________________

CD 12, Track 5

12-14 ¿Cómo lo hemos hecho? Rephrase the following actions to indicate the manner in which they have taken place, using the present perfect form of the verb as well as the adverb. Then listen and repeat as the speaker gives the correct answer.

Modelo: You see: Pidieron la carta. ______________________
You hear: electrónica
You write and say: *Han pedido la carta electrónicamente.*

1. Yo le dije mi nombre.

____

2. Tú escribiste el programa.

____

3. Sus clientes volvieron.

____

4. Paco y Raúl vieron la hoja electrónica.

____

5. Ustedes pusieron la información en el disquete.

____

6. Pablo y yo hicimos el trabajo.

____

CD 12, Track 6

12-15 No está hecho todavía. Respond negatively to the questions you hear by using the past participles to say that these things have not yet been done. Then listen and repeat as the speaker gives the correct answer.

Modelo: You hear: ¿Has escrito las cartas?
You write and say: *No, no están escritas todavía.*

1. ______________________
2. ______________________
3. ______________________
4. ______________________
5. ______________________

Nombre: ______________________ Fecha: ______________________

2. The present perfect subjunctive (Textbook p. 408)

12-16 ¿Indicativo o subjuntivo? Select the letter of the verb form that correctly completes each sentence.

1. Ellos esperan que los programadores _____ el sistema operativo.

   a. han instalado   b. hayan instalado

2. Nosotros creemos que Ana _____ un buen trabajo.

   a. ha hecho   b. haya hecho

3. Ojalá que Hugo _____ los documentos que le mandé.

   a. ha imprimido   b. haya imprimido

4. Es bueno que nosotros _____ computadoras nuevas.

   a. hemos comprado   b. hayamos comprado

5. Creo que Manuel va a ser despedido, ahora que _____ documentos importantes del disco duro.

   a. ha borrado   b. haya borrado

6. Desde que Teresa _____ ascensos, no habla conmigo.

   a. ha conseguido   b. haya conseguido

7. Voy a archivar estos documentos tan pronto como _____ de revisarlos.

   a. he terminado   b. haya terminado

8. En cuanto tú _____ la antena parabólica, vamos a ver más canales de televisión.

   a. has instalado   b. hayas instalado

Nombre: ______________________________ Fecha: ______________________

12-17 La jefa incrédula (*incredulous*). An employee is listing all the tasks that have been accomplished at the company throughout the day. However, the boss has room for doubt and does not completely trust him. Fill in the blanks using the present perfect subjunctive to complete her responses.

1. **Empleado:** He contestado todos los correos electrónicos.

   Jefa: Dudo que tú ____________________ todos los correos electrónicos.

2. **Empleado:** He hecho las fotocopias para la reunión de mañana.

   Jefa: Dudo que tú ____________________ las fotocopias para la reunión de mañana.

3. **Empleado:** Fernanda ha archivado todos los documentos.

   Jefa: Dudo que ella ____________________ todos los documentos.

4. **Empleado:** Alex ha instalado los nuevos programas en la computadora.

   Jefa: Dudo que Alex ____________________ los nuevos programas en la computadora.

5. **Empleado:** Rafael y yo hemos arreglado la impresora.

   Jefa: Dudo que ustedes ____________________ la impresora.

6. **Empleado:** Luis y Belén han apagado todas las computadoras.

   Jefa: Dudo que ellos ____________________ todas las computadoras.

CD 12, Track 7

12-18 ¿Funciona la tecnología? Complete the sentence with the correct present perfect subjunctive form of the verbs you hear, according to the subjects in parentheses. Then listen and repeat as the speaker gives the correct answer.

MODELO: You see: Es posible que ____________________ el escáner. (José)
You hear: romper
You write and say: Es posible que *haya roto* el escáner.

1. Esperamos que ____________________ la antena parabólica. (ellos)
2. Dudo que ____________________ la hoja electrónica. (tú)
3. No creo que ____________________ al cajero automático. (Jorge)
4. Es posible que ____________________ el ratón. (nosotros)
5. Ojalá ____________________ un escáner en su despacho. (ustedes)
6. Es una lástima que ____________________ el correo electrónico. (yo)

Nombre: ______________________ Fecha: ______________________

12-19 El accidente. Look at the following drawing and complete the sentences with your own reactions using either the present perfect indicative or present perfect subjunctive.

Modelo: Espero que *ellos hayan llevado un teléfono móvil.*

1. Ojalá que ______________________.
2. Es seguro que ______________________.
3. Es una lástima que ______________________.
4. Es bueno que ______________________.
5. Es necesario que ______________________.
6. Espero que ______________________.

CD 12, Track 8

12-20 Es posible que haya pasado. Complete the answers to the questions you hear using the present perfect subjunctive. Then listen and repeat as the speaker gives the correct answer.

Modelo: You see: Es dudoso que ______________________.
You hear: ¿Ha funcionado la impresora?
You write and say: Es dudoso que *haya funcionado la impresora.*

1. Tal vez ______________________.
2. No es verdad que ______________________.
3. No creen que ______________________.
4. Me sorprende que ______________________.
5. Es imposible que ______________________.
6. Sí, nuestros hijos están contentos de que ______________________.

3. The future and the future of probability (TEXTBOOK P. 410)

12-21 En la oficina. Imagine that you work at an office. Tell which tasks each person is going to do, using the correct future form of each verb in parentheses.

1. Joaquín ____________________ (escribir) cartas en el procesador de textos.
2. Ramiro y Conrado ____________________ (poner) las cuentas en la hoja electrónica.
3. Ella le ____________________ (decir) a la supervisora si hay correos electrónicos.
4. Yo ____________________ (usar) el escáner.
5. Ustedes ____________________ (buscar) la información en la Red.
6. La directora ____________________ (comunicarse) con los clientes por teléfono celular.
7. Enrique y yo ____________________ (ver) los diseños en la pantalla.
8. Todos nosotros ____________________ (preparar) los trabajos en la computadora.

12-22 Mi amiga y yo. In the following paragraph about two friends, rewrite the italicized verb phrases using the future tense.

Mi amiga Marta y yo *vamos a asistir* (1) ____________________ a la universidad. Marta *va a tomar* (2) ____________________ cursos de programación y yo *voy a tomar* (3) ____________________ clases de electrónica. Ella *va a aprender* (4) ____________________ a hacer diseños en la computadora y yo *voy a aprender* (5) ____________________ a reparar computadoras. Marta y sus otras amigas *van a ir* (6) ____________________ a las clases por la mañana, mientras que yo *voy a tener* (7) ____________________ que ir por la noche. *Nos vamos a divertir* (8) ____________________ mucho también.

Nombre: ______________________ Fecha: ______________________

CD 12, Track 9

12-23 ¿Cuándo esperan hacer el trabajo? Complete the answers to the questions you hear using the future tense of the verb. Then listen and repeat as the speaker gives the correct answer.

Modelo: You see: Los ______________ en dos semanas.
You hear: ¿Cuándo van a tener ellos los teclados ergonómicos?
You write and say: Los *tendrán* en dos semanas.

1. Tú lo ______________ mañana.
2. La ______________ esta noche.
3. Los ______________ esta tarde.
4. Las ______________ mañana por la mañana.
5. Usted la ______________ en una hora.

CD 12, Track 10

12-24 En el futuro... Complete the questions in the future tense using the verbs you hear and the subjects provided. Then listen and repeat as the speaker gives the correct answer.

Modelo: You see: ¿______________ el DVD en el lector? (tú)
You hear: poner
You write and say: ¿*Pondrás* el DVD en el lector?

1. ¿______________ ir? (ellos)
2. ¿______________ esta noche? (ustedes)
3. ¿______________ que comprar más memoria? (tú)
4. ¿______________ usar el escáner? (nosotros)
5. ¿______________ recogerlo mañana? (yo)
6. ¿______________ unos diseños originales? (ella)
7. ¿Le ______________ la información por teléfono? (ellas)
8. ¿Dónde ______________ el escáner? (usted)

Nombre: ______________________________ Fecha: ______________________

12-25 El jefe no sabe. Every time you ask your new boss something, he responds with a guess. Complete the dialogues with the future tense of the verbs and the information in parentheses, following the model.

MODELO: **Tú:** ¿A qué hora llegan los empleados al trabajo? (a las ocho)
Jefe: No sé; *llegarán a las ocho.*

1. **Tú:** ¿Quién hace los diseños? (la programadora)

   Jefe: No sé; ____.

2. **Tú:** ¿Quién llama a los clientes? (la secretaria)

   Jefe: No sé; ____.

3. **Tú:** ¿A qué hora almuerzan los empleados? (a la una)

   Jefe: No sé; ____.

4. **Tú:** ¿Quién imprime los documentos? (el asistente)

   Jefe: No sé; ____.

5. **Tú:** ¿Quién enciende las computadoras por la mañana? (el supervisor)

   Jefe: No sé; ____.

6. **Tú:** ¿A qué hora salen los empleados del trabajo? (a las cinco)

   Jefe: No sé; ____.

CD 12, Track 11

12-26 ¿Qué pasará? Answer the questions that you hear using the future tense of probability and the information in parentheses. Then listen and repeat as the speaker gives the correct answer.

1. ______________________________. (4:30)
2. ______________________________. (20 años)
3. ______________________________. (8 euros)
4. ______________________________. (30 personas)
5. No ______________________________. (ninguna computadora)
6. ______________________________. (9:15)

Nombre: ______________________________ Fecha: ______________________

¿Cuánto sabes tú?

12-27 ¿Sabes usar el presente perfecto? Fill in the blanks with the present perfect indicative or subjunctive form of the verb in parentheses.

1. Ojalá que Mariano ya ________________ (terminar) las hojas electrónicas.
2. ¿________________ (ver) tú el nuevo juego electrónico de béisbol?
3. El jefe duda que nosotros ________________ (hacer) bien el trabajo.
4. ¿________________ (tomar) usted alguna vez clases de informática?
5. Es probable que Luciano y Mariela nunca ________________ (escribir) a máquina; siempre lo ________________ (hacer) todo con la computadora.

12-28 ¿Sabes usar el futuro? Complete the following paragraph by filling in the blanks with the appropriate future form of the verbs in parentheses.

La próxima semana Julián y Rosa (1) ________________ (ir) a una conferencia sobre los nuevos usos de la Red informática en San Antonio. Ellos (2) ________________ (reservar) una habitación en el centro de la ciudad y (3) ________________ (visitar) la hermosa ciudad tejana. Yo (4) ________________ (estar) en San Antonio también, aunque no (5) ________________ (asistir) a la conferencia. Nosotros (6) ________________ (cenar) juntos el sábado por la noche.

CD 12, Track 12

12-29 Haremos lo que no hemos hecho. Complete the answers to the questions you hear using the verbs provided. Then listen and repeat as the speaker gives the correct answer.

Modelo: You see: No, no ______________ tiempo pero la ______________ pronto. (tener)
You hear: ¿Rellenaste la solicitud?
You write and say: No, no *he tenido* tiempo pero la *rellenaré* pronto.

1. No, no los ________________, pero los ________________ pronto. (ver)
2. No, no las ________________, pero las ________________ pronto. (terminar)
3. No, ________________ en el Perú, pero lo ________________ pronto. (estar)
4. No, ________________ problemas con la impresora, pero la ________________ pronto. (tener)
5. No, no los ________________, pero los ________________ pronto. (recibir)

CD 12, Track 13

12-30 Preguntas personales. Answer the questions you hear in Spanish, using complete sentences.

1. ____.
2. ____.
3. ____.
4. ____.
5. ____.
6. ____.

SEGUNDA PARTE

¡Así es la vida!

12-31 Hablan los jóvenes. Reread the selections regarding environmental issues on page 416 of your textbook. Then decide whether the following sentences are **cierto** (C) or **falso** (F) and write the correct letter on the lines provided.

1. A los jóvenes de Hispanoamérica les importa el medio ambiente. _____
2. Los gobiernos se han preocupado mucho por proteger los recursos naturales. _____
3. No existen problemas medioambientales en Hispanoamérica. _____
4. El aire en la Ciudad de México está contaminado. _____
5. Los carros y los camiones producen mucha contaminación. _____
6. El humo que producen las fábricas no es un gran problema. _____
7. El humo está poniendo en peligro la vida de todos. _____
8. Todos tenemos que cooperar para resolver estos problemas. _____

CD 12, Track 14

12-32 El programa "Tiempo nuevo". As you listen to the interview, circle the letters corresponding to all statements that are correct, according to what you hear.

1. El tema de la semana es...
   a. la radioactividad.
   b. el medio ambiente.
   c. la energía.
2. El invitado al programa es...
   a. un especialista en el medio ambiente.
   b. un asesor de energía.
   c. un profesor.
3. El doctor Olivares ha...
   a. consumido los recursos naturales.
   b. dedicado mucho dinero a la protección del ambiente.
   c. depositado desechos radioactivos en lugares especiales.
4. Olivares piensa resolver el problema de energía...
   a. creando parques nacionales.
   b. utilizando la energía nuclear.
   c. con el petróleo.
5. Según Olivares, la energía nuclear o sin humo...
   a. produce más contaminación que la energía de petróleo.
   b. es más limpia que la energía de petróleo.
   c. es tan sucia como la energía de petróleo.
6. Las sugerencias de Olivares para proteger los recursos naturales son...
   a. multar las fábricas que arrojen desechos a la naturaleza.
   b. aumentar la deforestación.
   c. comenzar un programa de uso responsable de los recursos.

Nombre: ______________________ Fecha: ______________________

¡Así lo decimos! Vocabulario (Textbook p. 417)

12-33 ¡A emparejar! On the lines next to each word associated with the environment, write the letter of the phrase that best completes the sentence.

1. ____ La energía
2. ____ La multa
3. ____ El medio ambiente
4. ____ La reforestación
5. ____ La radioactividad

a. contamina el aire.
b. se protege.
c. se hace plantando árboles.
d. se pone a las fábricas.
e. se conserva.

CD 12, Track 15

12-34 ¿Cuál es la mejor respuesta? Listen to the following sentences and circle the letter corresponding to the word or phrase that best completes each sentence. Then listen and repeat as the speaker gives the correct answer.

1. a. multa.
   b. energía.
   c. naturaleza.
2. a. la radioactividad.
   b. el aire.
   c. la reforestación.
3. a. deforestación.
   b. medida.
   c. reciclaje.
4. a. produce una escasez de agua.
   b. contamina el aire.
   c. es un recurso natural.
5. a. protegen el medio ambiente.
   b. aumentan la contaminación.
   c. dan multas.

Nombre: ________________________ Fecha: ________________________

12-35 Un crucigrama. Read each description and write the correct word in the corresponding squares.

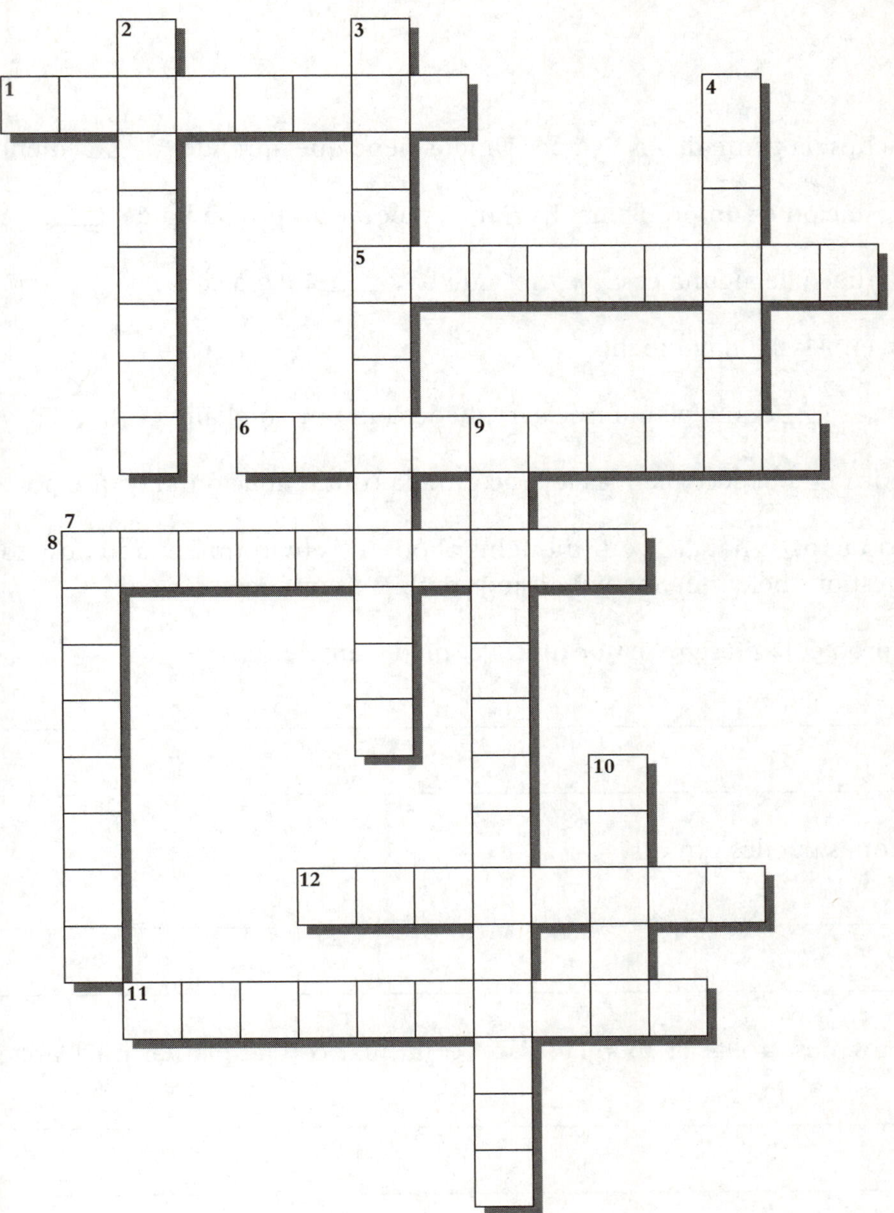

Across

1. Tenemos que _____ el medio ambiente para las generaciones futuras.
5. En vez de arrojar todos los desechos, hay que organizar un programa de _____.
6. El agua, el aire y las selvas forman parte de la _____.
8. Los _____ son productos químicos que se usan en el cultivo de frutas y verduras.

11. El tráfico de una ciudad puede _____ mucho el aire.

12. Hay que _____ los envases de cristal, aluminio y plástico.

Down

2. Según muchos, la gente de los Estados Unidos tiene que aprender a _____ menos.

3. Si la deforestación es un problema, hay que empezar un programa de _____.

4. Si hay muy poco de alguna cosa, se dice que hay _____ de esa cosa.

7. En Texas y en Alaska hay mucho _____.

9. Si se escapa _____ de una planta nuclear, puede contaminar el aire.

10. Si una fábrica no obedece bien las leyes contra la contaminación, hay que ponerle una _____.

12-36 Cuestionario. What are your thoughts about the environment and how to improve it? Answer the questions below in Spanish, using complete sentences.

1. ¿Cuál es el problema más grave que afecta al medio ambiente?

____

____

2. ¿Qué soluciones puedes ofrecer?

____

____

3. ¿Qué prefieres, desarrollar la energía solar o continuar con las plantas nucleares? ¿Por qué?

____

____

4. ¿En qué circunstancias se debe multar a una industria?

____

____

Nombre: ______________________________ Fecha: ______________________

Letras y sonidos (TEXTBOOK P. 418)

CD 12, Track 16

12-37 La "t" en español. For each item, you will hear a word pronounced in two different ways. Select the letter that corresponds to the word pronounced with the Spanish **"t."**

1. a. b.
2. a. b.
3. a. b.
4. a. b.
5. a. b.

CD 12, Track 17

12-38 La "d" en español. Write each word or phrase that you hear. Then decide whether it contains the hard **"d"** or soft **"d"** sound and put a check mark in the correct column.

	Hard "d"	Soft "d"
1. ______________________	____	____
2. ______________________	____	____
3. ______________________	____	____
4. ______________________	____	____
5. ______________________	____	____
6. ______________________	____	____
7. ______________________	____	____
8. ______________________	____	____
9. ______________________	____	____
10. ______________________	____	____

Nombre: ______________________ Fecha: ______________________

¡Así lo hacemos! Estructuras

4. The conditional and conditional of probability (TEXTBOOK P. 421)

12-39 Las promesas del gobierno. Find out what the government promised to do in the new term by writing the conditional form of each verb in parentheses.

El gobierno prometió que…

1. (estudiar) ______________ los efectos del uso de la energía nuclear.
2. (controlar) ______________ la emisión de humos de los carros.
3. (haber) ______________ más medidas contra la contaminación del aire.
4. (multar) ______________ las industrias contaminantes.
5. (proteger) ______________ los bosques.
6. (establecer) ______________ programas de reciclaje.
7. (plantar) ______________ más árboles en los parques.
8. (administrar) ______________ los recursos naturales.

12-40 En la television. Mariluz is a TV reporter concerned about environmental issues and Roberto is a citizen with the same concerns. Complete their dialogue with the correct conditional form of each verb in parentheses.

Mariluz: Roberto, ¿qué (1) ______________ (hacer) usted para mejorar el medio ambiente en la ciudad?

Roberto: Primero, (2) ______________ (informar) a los ciudadanos sobre los principales problemas.

Mariluz: ¿De qué problemas (3) ______________ (hablar)?

Roberto: Les (4) ______________ (explicar) los problemas de la deforestación y la contaminación del aire.

Mariluz: ¿Qué soluciones (5) ______________ (buscar) para estos problemas?

Roberto: (6) ______________ (Promocionar) un programa de reciclaje en toda la ciudad.

Mariluz: ¿Qué (7) ______________ (sugerir) usted para solucionar la contaminación del aire?

Roberto: Los ciudadanos (8) ______________ (deber) usar más el transporte público.

Nombre: ______________________ Fecha: ______________________

CD 12, Track 18

12-41 ¿Qué pasaría? What did the following people say they would do? Complete the sentences using the conditional form of the verbs you hear. Then listen and repeat as the speaker gives the correct answer.

Modelo: You see: Nosotros ______________ menos plástico a la basura.
You hear: echar
You write and say: Nosotros *echaríamos* menos plástico a la basura.

1. Juan me dijo que ______________ a la fábrica.
2. Tú dijiste que ______________ una carta de protesta.
3. Ana dijo que ______________ energía.
4. Mi esposo y yo dijimos que ______________ todo lo posible.
5. Fernando nos dijo que tú ______________ para la planta nuclear.

CD 12, Track 19

12-42 Para un mundo mejor. You are brainstorming topics that address environmental concerns in your area. Create sentences using the correct conditional forms of the verbs and the information you hear. Then listen and repeat as the speaker gives the correct answer.

Modelo: You see: Aurelia ______________.
You hear: proteger/ el medio ambiente
You write and say: Aurelia *protegería el medio ambiente.*

1. Yo ______________.
2. Ustedes ______________.
3. Mis amigos ______________.
4. Nosotros ______________.
5. Tú ______________.
6. Mi ciudad ______________.

CD 12, Track 20

12-43 ¿Qué harían? Answer the questions you hear by using the conditional form of the verbs and the information provided below. Use direct object pronouns when possible. Then listen and repeat as the speaker gives the correct answer.

Modelo: You see: La compañía ______________.
You hear: ¿Quiénes consumieron menos productos?
You write and say: La compañía *consumiría menos productos.*

1. ______________ a las ocho.
2. Los empleados de la fábrica ______________.

3. ______________________ programas de reciclaje.

4. ______________________ en un lugar de reciclaje.

5. ______________________ muchas protestas.

12-44 ¿Qué pasó? The representative of an environmental protection team that you were about to interview did not show up at the last minute. Offer possible reasons using the conditional of probability.

Modelo: olvidarse de la fecha
Él se olvidaría de la fecha.

1. no saber la hora

____

2. tener problemas con su carro

____

3. ir a otra entrevista

____

4. perder la dirección

____

5. no entender a la secretaria

____

12-45 Tu programa medioambiental. Imagine that you are the mayor of your city. Write down six things you would do to protect the environment, as in the model.

Modelo: *Prohibiría echar los desechos industriales en los ríos.*

1. ____
2. ____
3. ____
4. ____
5. ____
6. ____

Nombre: ________________________________ Fecha: ______________________

5. Tú commands (TEXTBOOK P. 424)

12-46 Mandatos para tu hermano. You are giving your younger brother some tips on how to protect the environment. Complete each statement with the **tú** command.

1. (reciclar) __________________ todo el papel.
2. (proteger) __________________ la naturaleza.
3. (poner) __________________ los envases de aluminio en el contenedor de productos reciclables.
4. (comprar) __________________ productos reciclables.
5. No (arrojar) __________________ basura al río.
6. (Pedirles) __________________ a tus amigos que reciclen.
7. No (manejar) __________________ tu carro todos los días.
8. No (cortar) __________________ árboles en el bosque.
9. (hacer) __________________ todo lo posible para proteger los bosques.
10. (ser) __________________ consciente de la importancia de la naturaleza.

12-47 Un amigo consciente. Your friend is very conscious of the environment and asks you several questions about protecting it. Answer his questions with the **tú** command form of the verb in parentheses and the appropriate object pronoun.

MODELO: ¿Son buenos los pesticidas? (no usar)
No, no los uses.

1. ¿Qué hago con los envases de aluminio? (reciclar)

   ____

2. ¿Y con la basura? (no arrojar)

   ____

3. ¿Debería proteger los bosques? (proteger)

   ____

4. ¿Es aconsejable consumir productos no reciclables? (no consumir)

   ____

Nombre: ______________________________ Fecha: ______________________

5. ¿Debería conservar la naturaleza? (conservar)

____

CD 12, Track 21

12-48 ¿Qué hago? As the best salesperson at a gardening store, customers ask you for your advice. Tell them what they should and should not do by using informal commands and the cues provided. Then listen and repeat as the speaker gives the correct answer.

MODELO: You see: Sí, ________________ más árboles.
You hear: ¿Debo comprar más árboles?
You write and say: Sí, *compra* más árboles.

1. Sí, ________________ a ver las flores.
2. No, ________________ pesticidas para la fruta.
3. Sí, ________________ la naturaleza.
4. Sí, ________________ los precios.
5. No, ________________ ahora porque tenemos un plan de crédito.

CD 12, Track 22

12-49 Consejos para tu mejor amigo. Your best friend has decided to become more aware of issues dealing with the environment. Tell him whether he should or should not do the following things, using informal commands and direct object pronouns. Then listen and repeat as the speaker gives the correct answer.

MODELO: You see: conservar ______________________
You hear: agua
You say and write: *Consérvala.*
or
You see: no contaminar ______________________
You hear: el aire
You say and write: *No lo contamines.*

1. no arrojar ____
2. no producir ____
3. observar ____
4. implementar ____
5. no usar ____
6. hacer ____
7. conservar ____
8. poner ____

12-50 ¡Tú mandas! Based on the following drawings, give each person a logical command, as in the model. Be sure to use the **tú** form.

MODELO: 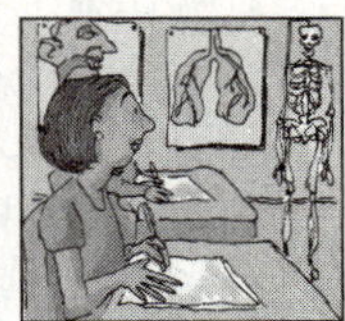

Escucha al profesor.

1. 

____

2. 

____

3.

____

4. 

____

5. 

____

...nto sabes tú?

...51 ¿Sabes usar el condicional? Complete the paragraph by filling in the blanks with the ...ppropriate conditional forms of the verbs in parentheses.

Como presidente, yo (1) ______________ (reducir) los impuestos de los ciudadanos y (2) ______________ (poner) más multas a las industrias más contaminantes. También, (3) ______________ (controlar) el proceso de deforestación de los bosques y (4) ______________ (plantar) más árboles en las ciudades para mejorar la calidad del aire. Como presidente, mi amigo Pedro (5) ______________ (educar) a la gente sobre el medio ambiente y (6) ______________ (combatir) los efectos de la contaminación. El mundo (7) ______________ (ser) un lugar mejor para todos.

12-52 ¿Sabes usar los mandatos informales? Fill in the blanks with the **tú** command form of the verbs in parentheses.

1. ______________ (Escribir) los informes.
2. ______________ (Escuchar) a tu supervisor.
3. No ______________ (jugar) con la computadora.
4. No ______________ (llamar) con mi teléfono móvil.
5. ______________ (Usar) el teléfono inalámbrico de tu oficina.
6. No ______________ (irse) tarde de la oficina.

CD 12, Track 23

12-53 El año próximo. Talk about what would happen next year in ideal conditions, based on what the people you hear are already doing. Use the correct conditional forms of the verbs, and then listen and repeat as the speaker gives the correct answer.

Modelo: You see: Ellos ______________ los problemas del medio ambiente también.
You hear: Resolvemos los problemas del medio ambiente.
You write and say: Ellos *resolverían* los problemas del medio ambiente también.

1. A Paola le ______________ estudiar sobre el medio ambiente también.
2. Nosotros ______________ reciclar mucho también.
3. Tú ______________ que ver la planta nuclear también.
4. Ustedes ______________ menos energía también.
5. Yo ______________ cómo usar menos petróleo también.

Nombre: ______________________ Fecha: ______________________

12-54 Preguntas personales. Write an appropriate response to the following questions or statements in Spanish, using complete sentences.

CD 12, Track 24

1. ____.
2. ____.
3. ____.
4. ____.
5. ____.

Observaciones

Antes de ver el video

12-55 ¿Qué pasa? Select the letter of the best answer to each question.

1. What might Felipe say to indicate that he is having a problem with the Internet?
   a. Voy a poner "camioneta" en el buscador.
   b. ¿Y por qué me sale este mensaje de error?
   c. ¿Tú estás loco?
2. What might Silvia say to help him?
   a. No creo que te la regalen.
   b. Seguro que encuentras una camioneta barata.
   c. Pon uve doble, uve doble, uve doble, punto, Terra punto com.

3. What would Marcela say that indicates she is interested in things other than helping Felipe?
   a. ¡Vaya! ¡Necesito escribir un correo electrónico!
   b. Fíjate, vienen con foto y todo. A mí me gusta esa roja…
   c. ¡Espera! ¡Ahí anuncian una oferta de trajes de baño!

Nombre: ______________________________ Fecha: ______________________

4. If Felipe is unable to print the address he needs, what might he say he must do instead?

   a. Creo que merece la pena.

   b. Tendré que hacerlo según el método tradicional.

   c. Voy a imprimir la información.

5. However, Marcela has a better idea. What might she say?

   a. Te estoy enviando un mensaje con toda la información. Búscala en tu teléfono celular.

   b. Ponte el casco, ¿eh? ¡Ahí van las llaves!

   c. ¡Es igual que la vieja!

A ver el video

12-56 La conversación. Fill in the blanks with the missing words according to the video segment.

Felipe: Tengo el buzón de (1) ________________ ________________ lleno de basura.

...

Marcela: ¿Viste? Ahí tienes una lista de (2) ________________ a (3) ________________ de vehículos usados.

Felipe: ¡Bárbaro! Sólo he (4) ________________ un minuto en llegar a la tienda.

Silvia: La (5) ________________ tienda, mejor dicho. Mira, aquí hay una base de (6) ________________ donde buscar. ¿Por qué no miras ahí?

Felipe: ¡Vamos allá!

Marcela: Fíjate, vienen con foto y todo. A mí me gusta esa roja... Hola, Patricio, ¿qué tal la (7) ________________?

Nombre: ______________________________ Fecha: ______________________

12-57 ¿Quién fue? Write the letter of the character next to the statement that best describes them or their actions.

S: Silvia **M:** Marcela **F:** Felipe

1. _____ Ha tenido que vender su camioneta.
2. _____ Le gusta comprar en la Red.
3. _____ Prefiere usar *Terra* o *Google*.
4. _____ Le dice a Felipe que escriba en la barra de direcciones.
5. _____ Le dice a Patricio que acepte el trabajo que le han ofrecido.
6. _____ Quiere saber dónde está la tienda.
7. _____ Quiere escribir la dirección de la tienda con un lápiz.
8. _____ Envía un mensaje con la información al teléfono de Felipe.

Después de ver el video

12-58 El cíber viaje de Felipe. Select the letter of the word or phrase that best completes the sentence or answers the question.

1. En el correo electrónico de Felipe hay…
   a. un mensaje de Elvira.
   b. muchos mensajes.
   c. mucha basura.
2. Silvia sugiere que Felipe…
   a. busque una camioneta en el Internet.
   b. compre un traje de baño en la cíber tienda.
   c. use *Yahoo!* para leer las noticias.
3. Patricio no sabe si va a aceptar el trabajo porque…
   a. hay algo que no le gusta.
   b. el dinero no es muy bueno.
   c. es un trabajo relacionado con el medio ambiente.

4. Cuando Felipe mira la pantalla, ve…

   a. una ventana.

   b. su camioneta.

   c. mucha ropa.

5. Silvia quiere que Felipe…

   a. mire los detalles, a ver cuáles son las especificaciones.

   b. encuentre otra camioneta.

   c. le pase el ratón.

6. Felipe decide…

   a. ir a la tienda para ver la camioneta.

   b. llamar la tienda para más información.

   c. comprar otro vehículo.

Nuestro mundo

Panoramas

12-59 ¡A informarse! Based on the information from **Nuestro mundo,** decide if the following statements are **cierto** (C) or **falso** (F).

1. Esmeralda Santiago es una escritora puertorriqueña. _____
2. Esmeralda Santiago se mudó a Los Ángeles. _____
3. Los Estados Unidos es la cuarta nación hispanohablante del mundo. _____
4. Los medios de comunicación en los Estados Unidos son sólo en inglés. _____
5. *El Nuevo Herald* es un periódico en español. _____
6. Muchos murales mexicoamericanos sólo muestran el presente del pueblo. _____
7. Los mexicoamericanos compiten y ganan medallas en los Juegos Olímpicos. _____
8. La presencia hispana en los Estados Unidos ha generado miles de negocios. _____

Nombre: ______________________________ Fecha: ______________________

12-60 Los hispanos en los Estados Unidos. In your text, you learned about some of the great contributions Hispanics have made to the culture of the United States, past and present. Now go to **http://www.prenhall.com/arriba** to read more, and select the letter of the correct answers to the following questions.

1. ¿De qué origen es la mayoría de la población latina en los EE.UU.?

   a. cubano b. puertorriqueño c. mexicano

2. La mayoría de la población latina en California es de origen…

   a. cubano. b. puertorriqueño. c. mexicano.

3. La mayoría de la población latina en Nueva York es de origen…

   a. cubano. b. puertorriqueño. c. mexicano.

4. La mayoría de la población latina en Florida es de origen…

   a. cubano. b. puertorriqueño. c. mexicano.

5. ¿En qué estado viven más latinos de origen dominicano?

   a. Nueva York b. Nueva Jersey c. Florida

6. ¿En qué estado hay más latinos originarios de América del Sur?

   a. Nueva York b. Nueva Jersey c. Florida

Ritmos

12-61 Millo Torres y El Tercer Planeta. In your text, you sampled music by this eclectic Puerto Rican musical group. Now visit **http://www.prenhall.com/arriba** and based on the information found on the web page, rewrite the statements below to make them correct.

1. Millo Torres tomó clases de violín, trompeta y guitarra a los seis años.

   ____.

2. Millo Torres estudió el bachillerato de música en Puerto Rico.

   ____.

3. La música de Millo Torres fusiona ritmos afrocaribeños, rock y punk.

   ____.

4. La primera producción de Millo Torres y El Tercer Planeta se llama *Tierra adentro*.

   ____.

Nombre: ______________________ Fecha: ______________________

5. El compacto *Caminando* habla de temas como el amor, la soledad y la muerte.

____.

6. En 2002 Millo Torres y El Tercer Planeta realizaron su primera gira promocional.

____.

Páginas

12-62 Sandra Cisneros. Sandra Cisneros is one of the many *chicanas* who have excelled as writers. Visit **http://www.prenhall.com/arriba** to learn more about her and make a list of five of her well-known works.

1. ______________________
2. ______________________
3. ______________________
4. ______________________
5. ______________________

Taller

12-63 Las costumbres medioambientales. You may not feel like an environmental activist, but even the most "ordinary" citizen does more out of habit to protect the environment now than 30 years ago. Make a list in Spanish of the environmentally friendly actions that you take.

______________________ ______________________

______________________ ______________________

______________________ ______________________

______________________ ______________________

12-64 Ahora... Write a paragraph comparing your environmentally friendly actions with those of the previous generation.

Modelo: *Hoy en día nosotros reciclamos los envases, mientras que en los sesenta se echaban a la basura.*

____

____

____

____

____

Nombre: ______________________ Fecha: ______________________

13 ¿Oíste las noticias?

Primera parte

¡Así es la vida!

13-1 ¿Recuerdas? Reread the horoscopes on page 440 of your textbook. Then decide if each of the following statements is **cierto** (C) or **falso** (F).

1. Los leo van a tener facilidades para sus relaciones personales. ____
2. Los escorpio pueden ayudar a sus amigos. ____
3. Los libra se enfrentan a grandes desafíos. ____
4. Los acuario deben tener prisa para tomar decisiones. ____
5. Los sagitario no están cumpliendo en el trabajo. ____
6. Los cáncer deben confiar en sí mismos. ____

CD 13, Track 1

13-2 El periódico de la mañana. As you listen to the following conversation, circle the letters corresponding to all statements that are correct, according to what you hear.

1. Pablo leía...
   a. los titulares.
   b. la cartelera.
   c. la primera plana.
2. Alejandra quería...
   a. buscar el periódico.
   b. leer el consultorio sentimental.
   c. ver la primera plana.
3. Pablo le dijo a Alejandra que...
   a. viera una telenovela.
   b. mirara la sección financiera del periódico.
   c. leyera la sección deportiva.
4. Pablo y Alejandra leyeron juntos...
   a. la esquela y la crónica social.
   b. el editorial sobre el Perú.
   c. la crónica sobre el Perú.

Nombre: ______________________ Fecha: ______________________

5. Lucas podía leer...
   a. las tiras cómicas.
   b. la esquela.
   c. el consultorio sentimental.

6. Lucas prefiere leer...
   a. la cartelera.
   b. la sección deportiva.
   c. el horóscopo.

¡Así lo decimos! Vocabulario (TEXTBOOK P. 441)

13-3 Los medios de comunicación. Circle ten words related to mass media in the following puzzle.

S	C	A	R	T	E	L	E	R	A	B	O	T	G	A	R
D	R	J	U	H	P	O	M	I	L	Y	R	A	F	B	I
P	R	O	V	I	R	C	S	M	U	L	H	G	J	H	F
E	A	T	I	N	A	U	D	C	B	C	U	I	O	P	G
M	L	S	O	P	D	T	O	U	F	Q	F	R	H	U	E
O	U	H	N	E	E	O	G	H	I	D	O	U	T	A	S
C	T	E	C	F	F	R	U	B	O	S	D	D	A	P	Q
U	I	G	A	B	P	U	I	E	C	M	I	N	E	B	U
J	T	B	I	T	A	V	R	O	T	E	F	S	M	T	E
F	O	R	Q	U	L	I	P	I	D	J	E	O	I	O	L
I	Q	A	L	G	F	O	A	T	M	I	R	L	S	N	A
L	A	N	A	C	J	L	T	E	U	F	S	F	O	V	T
G	R	O	D	O	L	E	J	R	L	A	O	T	R	I	O
T	Y	P	A	T	E	L	E	N	O	V	E	L	A	N	L
S	E	A	M	I	B	A	S	E	I	E	R	A	N	T	A
A	R	T	I	C	U	L	O	J	F	P	I	S	I	O	P

Nombre: ______________________ Fecha: ______________________

13-4 Las secciones del periódico. On the line next to each statement, write the letter of the newspaper section that you would use to obtain the information you need.

1. _____ Buscas un trabajo.
2. _____ Buscas el resultado del partido de béisbol.
3. _____ Tienes problemas con tu novio/a.
4. _____ Quieres ir al cine o al teatro.
5. _____ Deseas saber tu futuro.
6. _____ Necesitas saber la fecha de un funeral.
7. _____ Quieres saber quiénes se casan.
8. _____ Deseas saber la opinión del editor.

a. la esquela
b. el horóscopo
c. el editorial
d. el consultorio sentimental
e. la cartelera
f. la crónica social
g. los anuncios clasificados
h. la sección deportiva

13-5 ¡A escoger! Choose the letter of the word that most logically completes each sentence.

1. A un _____ le gusta escuchar la radio.

   a. televidente b. radioyente

2. Mi _____ favorita es WKGB.

   a. canal b. estación

3. Un _____ da las noticias a las siete de la noche.

   a. comentarista b. lector

4. La _____ transmite sus programas todos los días.

   a. emisora b. telenovela

5. El periodista _____ las noticias del día.

   a. informa sobre b. patrocina

6. Me divierto mucho cuando leo _____.

   a. las esquelas b. las tiras cómicas

Nombre: ______________________ Fecha: ______________________

13-6 Mucha información. Write eight logical sentences about television and newspapers using one word from the left column and one word from the right in each. Be sure to use all words only once.

el / la comentarista	el concurso
el titular	la crónica social
el / la lector/a	la emisora
las tiras cómicas	el noticiero
el / la patrocinador/a	el periódico
el / la radioyente	la primera plana
el / la reportero/a	la televisión
el / la televidente	en directo

MODELO: *La sección deportiva se encuentra en el periódico.*

1. ______________________.
2. ______________________.
3. ______________________.
4. ______________________.
5. ______________________.
6. ______________________.
7. ______________________.
8. ______________________.

Nombre: ______________________________ Fecha: ______________________

13-7 ¿Qué quieres hacer esta noche? Answer the questions you hear in complete sentences, based on the radio and TV guide clippings below.

CD 13, Track 2

MUY ESPECIAL

En la televisión

5:30 p.m.

51 **El niño.** Un programa dirigido a los nuevos padres, con Eva y Jorge Villamar.

8:00 p.m.

HIT **Hablando con el Pueblo.** Armando García Sifredo nos trae un programa para Miami tocando temas de interés para toda la ciudadanía. 90 mins.

8:00 p.m.

DIS **Toy Story 2.** Con las voces de Tom Hanks y Tim Allen. Woody descubre que es seguido por un coleccionista. Tiene que decidir si se queda con los otros juguetes o sigue la fama. 1 1/2 hrs.

9:00 p.m.

51 **El Alburero.** Con Rafael Inclán y Rebeca Silva. Un hombre amable habla en rima y trata de conquistar a las mujeres. 100 mins.

En la radio

Mediodía

WWFE-AM (670) Radio Fe. **La mogolla.** Alberto González en un programa de sátira política y social.

10:00 p.m.

WTMI-FM (93.1) Nocturno. Barber: Concierto de violín, Op. 14; Oliveira, violín; Orquesta Sinfónica de St. Louis; Slatkin, director; Thompson: Sinfonía No. 3 en la menor; Orquesta Sinfónica de Nueva Zelandia; Schenk, director. Brahms: Cuarteto de cuerdas No. 2 en la menor, Op. 51; Cuarteto Janacek.

NOCHE

6:00 p.m.

23 51 Noticiero
HIT La bahía 1 hr.
TEL Topacio Repetición

6:30 p.m.

23 Noticiero Univisión
51 Noticiero Telemundo / CNN
GAL ¡Ándale! Paco Stanley. 1 hr.

7:00 p.m.

23 Paulatina
51 Manuela
HIT Chispita
TEL Tele Perú

7:30 p.m.

GAL T.V.O.
HIT Tremenda corte

8:00 p.m.

23 Buscando
51 Película *El sombrero de tres picos*
GAL La bahía
HIT Hablando con el pueblo
TEL Internacional video "Hit 5/10"

8:30 p.m.

GAL Rosa salvaje

9:00 p.m.

23 Al filo de la muerte
51 Película *El Alburero*. Con Rafael Inclán y Rebeca Silva. Un hombre amable habla en rima y trata de conquistar a las mujeres. 100 mins.
GAL Pepita
TEL Topacio Repetición

9:30 p.m.

GAL Madres egoístas
HIT Clásicos del teatro

10:00 p.m.

23 Viña del mar "Festival de Canciones" (Parte 6 de 7). Desde Valparaiso, Chile. 1 hr.
GAL Valeria y Maximiliano
TEL Estudio abierto Luis Conte

10:30 p.m.

51 Mi vida
GAL La luna

11:00 p.m.

23 51 Noticiero
GAL Vida perdida
HIT Oscar Aguero
TEL Debate Repetición

Nombre: ______________________ Fecha: ______________________

1. ______________________.

2. ______________________.

3. ______________________.

4. ______________________.

5. ______________________.

6. ______________________.

¡Así lo hacemos! Estructuras

1. The imperfect subjunctive (TEXTBOOK P. 445)

13-8 Escogemos. Choose the letter of the present or imperfect subjunctive verb form that completes each sentence correctly.

1. Es bueno que nosotros _____ más periódicos.

   a. leamos b. leyéramos

2. Me alegré de que tú _____ en la televisión.

   a. trabajes b. trabajaras

3. Los comentaristas pedían que les _____ un sueldo mejor.

   a. den b. dieran

4. Yo prefiero que la prensa _____ las noticias antes de publicarlas.

   a. revise b. revisara

5. Preferíamos que el gobierno _____ la libertad de prensa.

   a. proteja b. protegiera

6. Era dudoso que _____ las tiras cómicas.

   a. publicaran b. publiquen

7. Es importante que los reporteros _____ de la noticia.

   a. hablen b. hablaran

8. No creo que _____ un periódico mejor que éste.

   a. haya b. hubiera

Nombre: ______________________________ Fecha: ______________________

13-9 Recomendaciones. You used to work for various mass media companies. Complete the following statements with the imperfect subjunctive forms of the verbs in parentheses to explain the occurrences in each company.

1. El editor le decía al periodista que...
   - ________________ (leer) los artículos de sus compañeros.
   - no ________________ (escribir) sobre temas políticos.
   - ________________ (informar) correctamente a los lectores.
   - ________________ (revisar) el titular del día.
2. El patrocinador del programa insistía en que...
   - la anfitriona ________________ (ser) una mujer.
   - los televidentes ________________ (ver) el nombre de su producto constantemente.
   - el canal de televisión ________________ (transmitir) el programa en directo.
   - el noticiero no ________________ (interrumpir) el programa.
3. Los radioyentes querían que…
   - los noticieros ________________ (explicar) las noticias detalladamente.
   - los locutores ________________ (tener) una voz agradable.
   - los comentaristas deportivos ________________ (estar) preparados para informar puntualmente sobre los resultados deportivos.
   - la emisora de radio ________________ (hacer) programas de radio interesantes.

13-10 ¡A completar! Complete each sentence with the present or imperfect subjunctive form of the verb in parentheses.

1. Los televidentes lamentaron que el canal no ________________ (transmitir) la telenovela hoy.
2. Fue importante que los radioyentes ________________ (oír) la verdadera situación política.
3. El periódico les recomendó a los lectores que ________________ (escuchar) todos los puntos de vista.
4. Tú esperas que las fotos de tu cumpleaños ________________ (estar) en la página social.

5. Dudábamos que las noticias sobre la cumbre hispanoamericana ________________

(aparecer) en la primera plana.

6. Alberto necesita que nosotros ________________ (analizar) la sección financiera.

7. Esperaba que su esposo ________________ (conseguir) trabajo después de leer los avisos clasificados.

CD 13, Track 3

13-11 ¿Qué quería la prensa? Complete the clauses below using the imperfect subjunctive form of the verbs you hear. Then listen and repeat as the speaker gives the correct answer.

MODELO: You see: quería que ellos ________________ las noticias.
You hear: escuchar
You write and say: quería que ellos *escucharan* las noticias.

La prensa…

1. quería que yo ________________ mi opinión.

2. quería que tú ________________ el problema.

3. quería que los reporteros ________________ exactos.

4. quería que nosotros ________________ la crónica.

CD 13, Track 4

13-12 La estación de radio. Change the sentences you hear to the past tense, using the imperfect and the imperfect subjunctive forms. Then listen and repeat as the speaker gives the correct answer.

MODELO: You see: ______________________ el concurso.
You hear: Es posible que presenten el concurso.
You write and say: *Era posible que presentaran* el concurso.

1. ____ del edificio.

2. ____ al público.

3. ____ el programa de radio.

4. ____ la verdad.

Nombre: ______________________ Fecha: ______________________

13-13 **Durante el noticiero.** Answer the questions you hear using the sentence fragments provided. Then listen and repeat as the speaker gives the correct answer.

CD 13, Track 5

Modelo: You see: yo / consumir / poco
You hear: ¿Qué era importante?
You write and say: *Era importante que yo consumiera poco.*

1. tú / escuchar / al meteorólogo

____.

2. nosotros / revisar/ las notas

____.

3. tú / poder / solucionar el problema

____.

4. los editores / poner / más noticias en la primera plana

____.

5. el programa / comenzar / a tiempo

____.

13-14 El futurólogo. The horoscope you see below is from last Sunday's newspaper. Answer the questions in complete sentences, using the imperfect subjunctive.

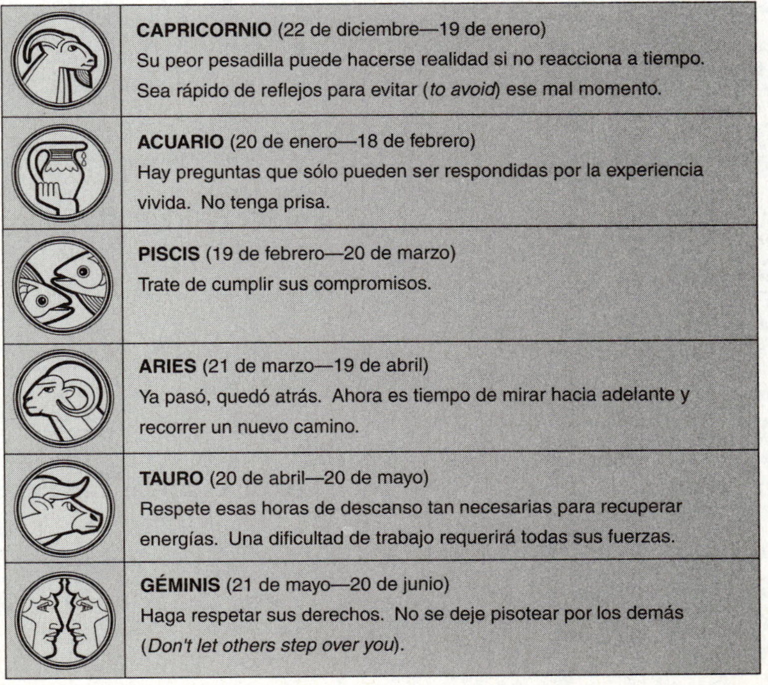

CAPRICORNIO (22 de diciembre—19 de enero)
Su peor pesadilla puede hacerse realidad si no reacciona a tiempo. Sea rápido de reflejos para evitar (*to avoid*) ese mal momento.

ACUARIO (20 de enero—18 de febrero)
Hay preguntas que sólo pueden ser respondidas por la experiencia vivida. No tenga prisa.

PISCIS (19 de febrero—20 de marzo)
Trate de cumplir sus compromisos.

ARIES (21 de marzo—19 de abril)
Ya pasó, quedó atrás. Ahora es tiempo de mirar hacia adelante y recorrer un nuevo camino.

TAURO (20 de abril—20 de mayo)
Respete esas horas de descanso tan necesarias para recuperar energías. Una dificultad de trabajo requerirá todas sus fuerzas.

GÉMINIS (21 de mayo—20 de junio)
Haga respetar sus derechos. No se deje pisotear por los demás (*Don't let others step over you*).

Nombre: ______________________ Fecha: ______________________

Modelo: ¿Qué les recomendó el futurólogo a los capricornio?
El futurólogo les recomendó que fueran rápidos para evitar un mal momento.

1. ¿Qué les recomendó el futurólogo a los acuario?

____

2. ¿Qué les dijo el futurólogo a los piscis?

____

3. ¿Qué les advirtió el futurólogo a los aries?

____

4. ¿Qué les sugirió el futurólogo a los tauro?

____

5. ¿Qué les pidió el futurólogo a los géminis?

____

2. Long form possessive adjectives and pronouns (Textbook p. 450)

13-15 ¿Dónde está(n)? No one can find anything today at the newspaper office. Answer the questions using possessive adjectives, following the model.

Modelo: ¿Dónde está tu titular?
¿El mío? No sé.

1. ¿Dónde están mis tiras cómicas?

¿__________________? No sé.

2. ¿Dónde están tus fotos?

¿__________________? No sé.

3. ¿Dónde está el editorial de Federico?

¿__________________? No sé.

4. ¿Dónde están los avisos clasificados de ustedes?

¿__________________? No sé.

5. ¿Dónde están tus noticias?

¿__________________? No sé.

6. ¿Dónde está nuestro horóscopo?

¿__________________? No sé.

7. ¿Dónde está la crónica social del Sr. Gómez?

¿__________________? No sé.

8. ¿Dónde están las carteleras de Ana y Paula?

¿__________________? No sé.

Nombre: ______________________ Fecha: ______________________

13-16 A cada cual lo suyo. Look at the drawings below and indicate ownership using long form possessive adjectives, as in the model.

Modelo: Los periódicos de nosotros
Los periódicos nuestros

1. 

La pizza de Alberto y Mercedes

____

2. 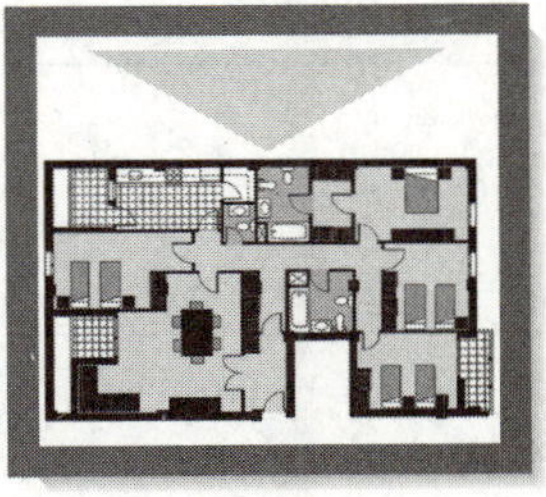

Tu apartamento

____

3. 

Los perros de Tere y Rosario

____

4. 

El coche de Pedro y Susana

____

5. 

Las vacaciones de ustedes

____

Nombre: ______________________________ Fecha: ______________________

13-17 ¿De quién es? Answer Ramón's questions using the possessive adjectives of the names or pronouns in parentheses, following the model.

Modelo: ¿Es tu revista? (ella)
No, no es mía, es suya.

1. ¿Es tu emisora? (Eduardo)

   ____.

2. ¿Son mis estaciones de radio? (nosotros)

   ____.

3. ¿Son los canales de ustedes? (ellos)

   ____.

4. ¿Es mi programa? (yo)

   ____.

5. ¿Es el noticiero de Graciela? (tú)

   ____.

6. ¿Son nuestros radioyentes? (yo)

   ____.

7. ¿Son mis tiras cómicas? (yo)

   ____.

8. ¿Es tu concurso? (él)

   ____.

Nombre: ______________________ Fecha: ______________________

CD 13, Track 6

13-18 ¿Cómo se divide el periódico? Form sentences using the subjects provided and the correct possessive adjectives. Then listen and repeat as the speaker gives the correct answer.

MODELO: You see: el artículo / ella
You write and say: *El artículo es suyo.*

1. la primera plana / nosotros ______________________.
2. las tiras cómicas / tú ______________________.
3. los anuncios / los padres ______________________.
4. el horóscopo / yo ______________________.
5. la sección deportiva / tú ______________________.
6. la cartelera / yo ______________________.
7. el consultorio sentimental / nosotros ______________________.
8. la esquela / los abuelos ______________________.

¿Cuánto sabes tú?

13-19 ¿Sabes usar el imperfecto de subjuntivo? Fill in the blanks with the appropriate imperfect subjunctive form of the verbs in parentheses.

1. El horóscopo me recomendó que ______________ (hablar) más con mis amigos.
2. El comentarista esperaba que la situación política ______________ (cambiar) pronto.
3. El editor quería que el reportero ______________ (escribir) el artículo de nuevo.
4. El periodista quería que el público ______________ (saber) la verdad.
5. Era dudoso que la televisión ______________ (decir) lo que había pasado (*had happened*).
6. El gobierno prohibió que los medios de comunicación ______________ (publicar) el escándalo.

Nombre: ______________________ Fecha: ______________________

13-20 ¿Sabes usar los pronombres y los adjetivos posesivos? Following the model, complete the following sentences with the appropriate long-form possessive adjective or pronoun.

MODELO: Mi televisor es de treinta y dos pulgadas.
El mío es de treinta y seis pulgadas.

1. Mi periódico es muy objetivo en sus editoriales políticas.

   ____________ es muy respetado.

2. Mi padre siempre lee la prensa deportiva.

   ____________ siempre lee la sección de economía.

3. A mí no me gusta lo que dice mi horóscopo sobre mi futuro.

   Pues ____________ dice que voy a tener mucha suerte en el amor.

4. Mis lectores creen que soy el mejor periodista del país.

   ____________ creen que soy imparcial y objetivo.

5. Tus lectores no saben lo que dicen.

   Pues ____________ no entienden nada de periodismo objetivo.

CD 13, Track 7

13-21 En la oficina de los reporteros. Answer the questions that you hear using the possessive adjective that corresponds to the people listed. Then listen and repeat as the speaker gives the correct answer.

MODELO: You hear: ¿De quién es el periódico?
You see: Ana y Héctor
You write and say: *El periódico es suyo.*

1. Alicia ____________.
2. Yo ____________.
3. Vanesa y Julia ____________.
4. Nosotros ____________.
5. Tú ____________.
6. Rosa María ____________.
7. Carlos ____________.
8. Yo ____________.

Nombre: ______________________________ Fecha: ______________________

CD 13, Track 8

13-22 Preguntas personales. Answer the following questions in Spanish, using complete sentences.

1. ____.
2. ____.
3. ____.
4. ____.
5. ____.

SEGUNDA PARTE

¡Así es la vida!

13-23 Jorge Ramos. Reread the passage on page 454 of your textbook. Then indicate whether the statement is **cierto** (C) or **falso** (F).

1. Jorge Ramos ha sido presentador del *Noticiero Univisión* durante veinte años. _____
2. Jorge es un hispano con mucha influencia en los Estados Unidos. _____
3. Su programa sólo se puede ver en Latinoamérica. _____
4. El trabajo de Jorge ha sido reconocido con varios premios. _____
5. La televisión es el único medio de comunicación en el que trabaja Jorge Ramos. _____
6. Jorge es mexicano. _____
7. Jorge Ramos no cree que se pueda ser hispano y buen americano a la vez. _____
8. Según Ramos, los hispanos en los Estados Unidos no tienen fuerza política. _____

CD 13, Track 9

13-24 ¿Te gustó la película? As you listen to the following conversation, circle the letters corresponding to all statements that are correct, according to what you hear.

1. Francisca y Alejandro fueron...
   a. al cine.
   b. a un restaurante.
   c. al teatro.

2. A Francisca le gustó...
   a. el rodaje.
   b. la cinematografía.
   c. el galán.

3. Francisca quiere...
   a. regresar al teatro.
   b. regresar al cine.
   c. cambiar el final.

4. Alejandro también...
   a. leyó el guión.
   b. leyó la novela.
   c. leyó la obra de teatro.

5. A Alejandro le gusta...
   a. el final de la película.
   b. el productor.
   c. el teatro.

6. Alejandro quiere...
   a. volver al cine porque cuesta menos que el teatro.
   b. actuar en varios dramas.
   c. aplaudir a los actores.

¡Así lo decimos! Vocabulario (Textbook p. 455)

13-25 ¡A relacionar! Next to each drawing, write the letter of the word that describes it.

1. _____ 

2. _____ 

3. _____ 

4. _____ 

5. _____ 

a. el galán
b. la cámara
c. los espectadores
d. las noticias
e. el estudio

Nombre: ______________________________ Fecha: ______________________

13-26 ¿Qué es eso? Choose the word or expression that best completes each sentence you hear. Then listen and repeat as the speaker gives the correct answer.

CD 13, Track 10

1. a. el guión.
   b. el galán.
   c. el estudio.
2. a. el guión.
   b. la telenovela.
   c. la productora.
3. a. una comedia.
   b. un protagonista.
   c. una cinta.
4. a. la primera actriz.
   b. el protagonista.
   c. el espectador.
5. a. actuar.
   b. grabar.
   c. representar.
6. a. el estudio.
   b. la obra.
   c. la cinematografía.

13-27 El cine, el teatro y la televisión. Complete each sentence with the correct word from the word bank below.

comedia	final	galán
guión	filmar	protagonista

1. Penélope Cruz va a ____________________ su próxima película en España.
2. Él es muy guapo; es el ____________________ de la telenovela.
3. No me gustó el ____________________ de la película porque el galán se muere.
4. Me divertí mucho cuando fui a ver esa ____________________.
5. ¿Quién escribió el ____________________ de la película?
6. Salma Hayek es la ____________________ de la película *Frida*.

13-28 Preguntas personales. Answer the following questions in Spanish, using complete sentences.

1. ¿Cuál es tu película favorita? ¿Por qué?

____

____

Nombre: ______________________________ Fecha: ______________________

2. ¿Quién es tu actor/actriz preferido/a y por qué?

____

____

3. ¿Cómo tiene que ser una buena película?

____

____

4. ¿Cuál crees que será la película del año? Explica.

____

____

5. ¿Te gustan las telenovelas? ¿Por qué sí o por qué no?

____

____

Letras y sonidos (Textbook p. 456)

CD 13, Track 11

13-29 "Y" o "ll"? Decide whether each word you hear contains the **"y"** or the **"ll"** sound, and write the correct letter on the lines provided.

1. ____
2. ____
3. ____
4. ____
5. ____
6. ____

CD 13, Track 12

13-30 The Spanish "l." In each series, you will hear a word pronounced differently, once by a native English speaker and once by a native Spanish speaker. Decide which is the native Spanish pronunciation and select the correct letter.

1. a. b.
2. a. b.
3. a. b.
4. a. b.
5. a. b.

Nombre: ______________________ Fecha: ______________________

¡Así lo hacemos! Estructuras

3. *Si* clauses (TEXTBOOK P. 459)

13-31 Si... Fill in the blanks with the correct present, imperfect subjunctive or conditional form of the verbs in parentheses.

1. Si ella ________________ (tener) las entradas, la llamaría.
2. Si ________________ (ser) actor, voy a vivir en Hollywood.
3. Si ________________ (poder) ir al teatro, te llamaría a las seis.
4. Si quiero asistir a la obra de teatro, ________________ (tener) que leer la crítica.
5. Si Shakira cantara, yo ________________ (ir) al concierto.
6. Si tú ________________ (querer), nosotros veríamos la película.
7. Si ellas ________________ (tener) amigos, saldrán con ellos al cine.
8. Si hubiera mejores actores, se ________________ (filmar) mejores películas.

13-32 Emparejamientos. Match one clause from the left column with one from the right to form eight logical sentences. Then write them in the spaces below.

1. Si el productor tuviera dinero...
2. Si la película se filma en Europa...
3. Si la obra es de Shakespeare...
4. Si la película fuera una comedia...
5. Si el productor necesita un galán...
6. Si las noticias salen a las seis...
7. Si el estudio estuviera cerrado...
8. Si la comedia es buena...

a. contratará a Antonio Banderas.
b. los espectadores se ríen hasta el final.
c. Jim Carrey sería el actor principal.
d. les pagaría mejor a los actores.
e. habrá escenas en Londres.
f. no se podría filmar la película.
g. necesitarán un presentador.
h. será un drama.

1. ____
2. ____
3. ____
4. ____

Nombre: ______________________ Fecha: ______________________

5. ______________________

6. ______________________

7. ______________________

8. ______________________

CD 13, Track 13

13-33 ¿Cómo sería diferente? Form sentences using the sentence fragments provided to express contrary-to-fact conditions. Then listen and repeat as the speaker gives the correct answer.

Modelo: las compañías teatrales / producir / más obras / el público / ir más frecuentemente al teatro
Si las compañías teatrales produjeran más obras, el público iría más frecuentemente al teatro.

1. el galán / ser / malo / a nadie gustarle / la película

______________________.

2. el programa / empezar / a tiempo / (ellos) tener / menos problemas

______________________.

3. los guiones / estar / en español / ser / más fácil de entender

______________________.

4. la primera actriz / actuar mejor / (nosotros) poder entender su acento

______________________.

5. (nosotros) querer ver / una comedia / ir a ver esta película

______________________.

CD 13, Track 14

13-34 ¡Éxito en las artes! Change the sentences that you hear to reflect contrary-to-fact conditions. Then listen and repeat as the speaker gives the correct answer.

Modelo: You hear: Si los actores actúan bien, reciben muchos aplausos.
You write and say: *Si los actores actuaran bien, recibirían muchos aplausos.*

1. ______________________.

2. ______________________.

3. ______________________.

4. ______________________.

Nombre: ______________________ Fecha: ______________________

13-35 Tus opiniones. Say what you would do in each situation by completing the statements below.

Modelo: Si tuviera dinero, *viajaría a Los Ángeles.* or Yo sería *si estudiara actuación.*

1. Si tuviera más tiempo, ______________________.
2. Si yo llegara más temprano, ______________________.
3. Yo trataría de ser actor/actriz si ______________________.
4. Yo escribiría guiones de películas si ______________________.
5. Yo iría a Hollywood si ______________________.
6. Yo iré al cine si ______________________.

4. The future perfect and the conditional perfect (Textbook p. 462)

13-36 Las órdenes del director. Complete the following exchanges with the correct future perfect form of the verb in parentheses.

Modelo: — ¿*Habrán contratado* (Contratar) ustedes a los actores mañana?
— Claro, nosotros *habremos tenido* (tener) tiempo para contratarlos mañana.

1. — ¿______________ (Aprender) ustedes el guión antes de las once de la mañana?

   — Por supuesto, nosotros ______________ (estudiar) el guión antes de esa hora.

2. — ¿______________ (Filmar) ustedes las escenas peligrosas antes del martes?

   — Sí, ______________ (tener) tiempo para filmarlas antes del martes.

3. — ¿Le ______________ (escribir) usted la carta por correo electrónico al productor en una hora?

   — ¡Cómo no! La ______________ (hacer) en media hora.

4. — ¿______________ (Instalar) ellos las cámaras antes del almuerzo?

   — No sé si ellos ______________ (terminar) de instalar las cámaras antes del almuerzo.

5. — ¿______________ (Poder) recoger el chófer al galán de la película hoy?

   — Seguro, él ______________ (recoger) al galán antes de las nueve de la mañana.

13-37 ¡Una película horrible! The cast has just finished filming a new movie, but they are not pleased. Fill in the blanks with the conditional perfect form of the verbs in parentheses to find out what they would have done differently.

Si el director...

1. hubiera tenido más dinero, ________________________ (contratar) a mejores actores.
2. hubiera encontrado un mejor reparto, ________________________ (grabar) más escenas dramáticas.
3. hubiera contratado un buen productor, la cinematografía ________________________ (ser) mejor.

Si el galán...

4. hubiera tenido un director mejor, (nosotros) ________________________ (actuar) mejor.
5. hubiera estado en otro estudio, (nosotros) ________________________ (tener) más tiempo para filmar.
6. hubiera tenido otros compañeros de reparto, (yo) ________________________ (trabajar) más responsablemente.

Si la primera actriz...

7. hubiera teniendo paciencia, el director ________________________ (conseguir) apoyo del productor.
8. hubiera trabajado con más dedicación, (nosotros) ________________________ (ganar) algún premio.

Nombre: ______________________ Fecha: ______________________

CD 13, Track 15

13-38 ¿Qué habrá pasado en la telenovela? You just found out that you will not be able to record the last episode of the soap opera. You wonder what will have happened. Form questions using the sentence fragments provided. Then listen and repeat as the speaker gives the correct answer.

Modelo: la telenovela / tener mucha acción
¿Habrá tenido mucha acción?

1. Adriana / saber la verdad

____

2. Carina / poner / la evidencia en el auto de Ramón

____

3. Débora y Jaime / casarse

____

4. Todos / estar contentos

____

5. Beatriz / darle/ a Patricio la información confidencial

____

6. Diego / volver de Buenos Aires

____

7. Rosaura / morirse

____

8. Carmen y Rosario / creer / las excusas de sus hijas

____

Nombre: ______________________ Fecha: ______________________

CD 13, Track 16

13-39 Una visita al futurólogo. José is visiting a futurologist because he wants to know what will have occurred by the year 2020. Answer his questions as if you were the futurologist, using the cues provided. Then listen and repeat as the speaker gives the correct answer.

Modelo: You hear: ¿Habitarán los hombres Marte?
You write and say: No, *no habrán habitado Marte.*
or
Sí, *habrán habitado Marte.*

1. Sí, ______________________.
2. No, ______________________.
3. Sí, ______________________.
4. No, ______________________.
5. Sí, ______________________.
6. Sí, ______________________.

13-40 Regreso al pasado. Complete the following clauses by explaining what you would have done differently, using the conditional perfect tense.

Modelo: Siendo primera actriz de una película, *habría trabajado con Antonio Banderas.*

1. Siendo actor/actriz, ______________________.
2. Siendo presidente del gobierno, ______________________.
3. Estudiando en otro país, ______________________.
4. Con más dinero, ______________________.
5. Siendo miembro de la Academia de Hollywood, ______________________
______________________.
6. Siendo director/a de cine, ______________________.
7. Sabiendo hablar español perfectamente, ______________________.
8. En una universidad diferente, ______________________.

Nombre: ______________________ Fecha: ______________________

13-41 Tus expectativas. Using the future perfect, make a list of six goals you think you will have achieved in ten years.

Modelo: *En diez años, yo habré trabajado en tres países diferentes.*

1. ______________________
2. ______________________
3. ______________________
4. ______________________
5. ______________________
6. ______________________

¿Cuánto sabes tú?

13-42 ¿Sabes completar las cláusulas con *si*? Select the letter of the correct verb form to complete the following sentences.

1. Si Antonio Banderas fuera el galán de la película, (nosotros) _____ a verla.

   a. vamos b. iríamos c. fuéramos

2. Penélope Cruz actúa como si _____ una actriz veterana; ¡es muy buena actriz!

   a. fuera b. es c. será

3. Me _____ más la película si el final fuera diferente.

   a. gustará b. gustara c. gustaría

4. Si la televisión muestra la entrega de premios, la _____ juntos.

   a. viéramos b. veremos c. veríamos

5. Pedro Almodóvar será más famoso en los Estados Unidos, si _____ cine más comercial.

   a. hace b. hiciera c. hará

Nombre: ______________________ Fecha: ______________________

13-43 ¿Sabes usar el futuro perfecto y el condicional perfecto? Fill in the blanks with the correct future perfect or conditional perfect form of the verb in parentheses, according to the context.

1. Con más tiempo, ayer (yo) ______________ (ir) al cine con mis amigos.
2. La semana que viene (nosotros) ______________ (ver) la mejor película del año.
3. En diez años Javier Bardem ______________ (tener) mucho éxito en este país.
4. Con estos avances tecnológicos, los actores y actrices del pasado ______________ (ser) mucho mejores.
5. Con más talento, yo ______________ (estudiar) arte dramático.
6. En pocos años el cine latino ______________ (conseguir) mucho reconocimiento.

CD 13, Track 17

13-44 Si yo fuera directora... Tell your friend what would happen if you became a film director, using the sentence fragments provided and the conditional form of the verbs you hear. Then listen and repeat as the speaker gives the correct answer.

Modelo: You see: yo / con John Leguizamo
You hear: trabajar
You write and say: *Yo trabajaría con John Leguizamo.*

1. mi familia y yo / en Hollywood

   ____.

2. mis productores / mucho dinero

   ____.

3. yo / solamente en lugares exóticos

   ____.

4. tú / conmigo en restaurantes famosos

   ____.

5. yo / de ayudar a la gente

   ____.

Nombre: ______________________ Fecha: ______________________

CD 13, Track 18

13-45 ¡El señor dudoso! You are speaking to a friend and doubt that what he asks is true. Answer the following questions with the correct form and tense of the verbs you hear. Then listen and repeat as the speaker gives the correct answer.

Modelo: You see: tener / tantos anuncios en los periódicos
You hear: ¿Crees que los anuncios clasificados son inútiles?
You write and say: *Dudo que sean inútiles. Si fueran inútiles, no tendríamos tantos anuncios en los periódicos.*

1. haber / tanto silencio

____.

2. haber / tantas películas de fantasía

____.

3. ver/ más anuncios en la televisión

____.

4. haber / menos galanes

____.

5. ser / difícil conseguir un trabajo con sueldo fijo

____.

Observaciones

Antes de ver el video

13-46 ¿Qué pasa? Select the letter of the best answer to each question.

1. What might Marcela suggest as she reads the newspaper?

   a. Hay dos películas, una comedia de Juan Cavestany y un drama.

   b. Quiero invitarte, para eso eres mi amigo.

   c. Supongo que te gustará.

2. How might Patricio respond?

   a. Ni hablar, no lo puedo aceptar.

   b. Muy graciosa.

   c. Olvídate de la tele. Esta noche hay partido de fútbol y Felipe querrá verlo.

3. What does Patricio say as he looks at the newspaper?

   a. ¡Mira la foto! ¡Es él! ¡Es él! David Ortiz-Smith.

   b. Según la policía, había más de doscientas crías de guacamayo.

   c. Por eso quería que le ayudara a buscar nidos de guacamayo.

4. Marcela explains what the article is about. Which statement does NOT apply?

   a. "Ciudadano británico detenido por tráfico ilegal de pájaros."

   b. ¿Cómo se puede ser tan horrible?

   c. La policía sospecha que el británico David Ortiz-Smith esté implicado en la operación.

5. What does Marcela say would have happened to Patricio had he accepted the job with CREFASI?

   a. Tu instinto no te engañó.

   b. Bueno, elegiste bien Patricio.

   c. Ahora estarías en la cárcel también.

Nombre: ______________________________ Fecha: ______________________

A ver el video

13-47 La conversación. Fill in the blanks with the missing words according to the video segments.

Marcela: Gracias. Y dime, ¿cuánto tiempo vas a estar fuera?

Patricio: Dentro de un año (1) ________________ terminado el programa y estaré de vuelta.

Marcela: ¿Dónde (2) ________________ de vuelta?

Patricio: Buena pregunta, Marcela. Sé adónde voy, pero la verdad, no sé si (3) ________________ a Costa Rica o a Colombia... o si me quedaré en los Estados Unidos.

Marcela: Quizás ahora no sea el momento de pensarlo. No, ahora es el momento de celebrarlo. ¿Te gustaría hacer algo esta tarde? ¿Quieres que salgamos juntos, al (4) ________________ o al (5) ________________?

...

Patricio: Prefiero ir al cine. Ahora no tengo ganas de meterme en casa.

Marcela: No hay nada interesante en el cine. ¿Por qué no vamos al teatro? Hay una (6) ________________ de teatro (7) ________________ sobre el papel de la (8) ________________ en la sociedad hispanoamericana.

Patricio: ¡Oh, qué interesante!

Marcela: Pues claro que es interesante.

Patricio: Francamente, prefiero una buena película de (9) ________________ marciales, o una de (10) ________________, da igual.

Nombre: ______________________________ Fecha: ______________________

13-48 En el café. Complete the sentence by writing the letter of the most logical word or phrase according to the conversation between Marcela and Patricio.

1. _____ Patricio tiene que aprobar un examen de...
2. _____ Los amigos toman vino porque quieren...
3. _____ Patricio terminará el programa dentro de...
4. _____ El vino cuesta...
5. _____ Una de las películas que ponen es...
6. _____ La policía de aduanas abrió el contenedor en...
7. _____ Piensan que Ortiz-Smith usaba el programa del gobierno para...
8. _____ Muchos animales estaban...

a. el puerto de Limón.
b. muertos.
c. un año.
d. celebrar.
e. inglés.
f. traficar con especies en peligro de extinción.
g. 15.000 colones.
h. *Los pájaros.*

Después de ver el video

13-49 La acción y los personajes. Determine whether the following statements are **cierto** (C) or **falso** (F) and write the correct letter on the lines provided.

1. Patricio podrá hacer investigación en una universidad de Estados Unidos. _____
2. Patricio volverá a Costa Rica después de ir a los Estados Unidos. _____
3. Marcela y Patricio van al cine. _____
4. Marcela y Patricio leen un artículo sobre el tráfico ilegal de pájaros. _____
5. La policía de aduanas piensa que David Ortiz-Smith está implicado. _____
6. La policía de aduanas encontró numerosos animales de Centroamérica. _____
7. Como parte del plan de David, él quería que Patricio le enseñara los nidos de guacamayo para robarse las crías. _____
8. David está ahora en la cárcel. _____

Nombre: ______________________ Fecha: ______________________

Nuestro mundo

Panoramas

13-50 ¡A informarse! Based on the information from **Nuestro mundo,** decide if the following statements are **cierto** (C) or **falso** (F) and write the correct letter on the lines provided.

1. En España hay dieciocho comunidades autónomas. ____
2. El español es el único idioma hablado en el país. ____
3. Galicia, por su idioma, se compara con Escocia. ____
4. Hay influencia celta en Galicia. ____
5. El euskera es un idioma en extinción que no se enseña en las escuelas. ____
6. El origen del euskera es desconocido. ____
7. Cataluña es una región muy importante a nivel artístico y político. ____
8. Andalucía es la región española donde la influencia árabe es más aparente. ____
9. El Alcázar es un palacio árabe que se encuentra en Andalucía. ____
10. El poder de Fernando e Isabel les dio fuerza al catalán y al euskera en toda la península. ____

Nombre: ______________________ Fecha: ______________________

13-51 Las otras comunidades autónomas. In your text you learned about some of the autonomous regions of Spain. Now, using the map below, write the letter of the correct region next to its city.

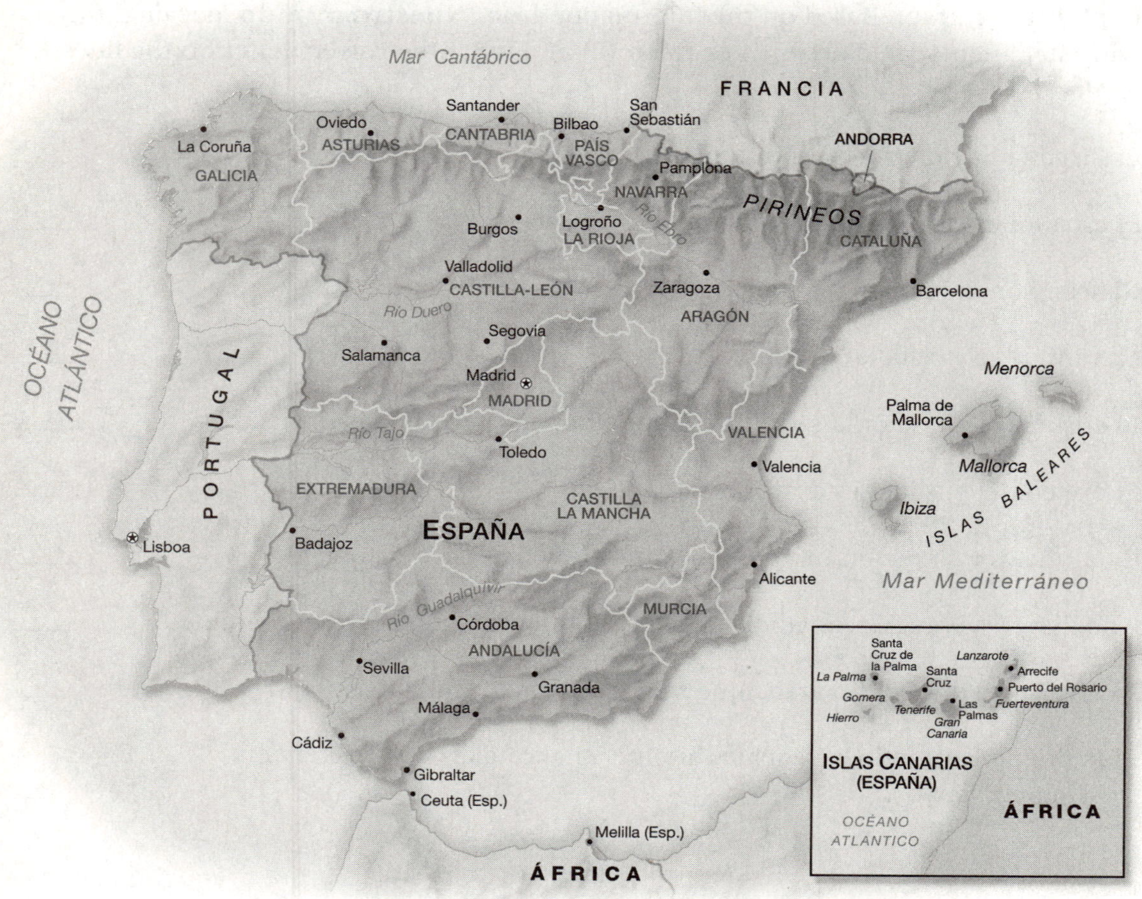

1. _____ Toledo
2. _____ Badajoz
3. _____ Palma de Mallorca
4. _____ Santa Cruz
5. _____ Oviedo
6. _____ Zaragoza
7. _____ Santander
8. _____ Logroño

a. Islas Baleares
b. La Rioja
c. Extremadura
d. Aragón
e. Tenerife
f. Cantabria
g. Castilla La Mancha
h. Asturias

Nombre: ______________________ Fecha: ______________________

Ritmos

13-52 Más rock en español. You have already experienced some music by the band *ADN* from Spain. From the 1980s on, many rock and roll bands have become popular in Spain. Visit **http://www.prenhall.com/arriba** and use the information found on this web site to match the letter of each work with the correct band.

1. ____ Radio Futura
2. ____ Loquillo y Los Trogloditas
3. ____ Duncan Dhu
4. ____ Miguel Ríos
5. ____ Luz Casal
6. ____ El último de la Fila

a. "La canción de Juan Perro"
b. "Astronomía razonable"
c. "A contraluz"
d. "El grito del tiempo"
e. "Rock and Ríos"
f. "Morir en primavera"

Páginas

13-53 Paloma Pedrero. In Chapter 13 of your text, you read a passage by the playwright and dramatist Paloma Pedrero. Now go to **http://www.prenhall.com/arriba** and read Paloma Pedrero's biography. Then, decide if the following statements are **cierto** (C) or **falso** (F) and write the correct letter on the lines provided.

1. Paloma Pedrero estudió en la Universidad Complutense de Madrid. ____
2. Es autora teatral, pero no dirige ni actúa en obras de teatro. ____
3. Su primera obra se estrenó en 1985. ____
4. Su primera obra se llama *Invierno de luna alegre*. ____
5. Paloma Pedrero ganó el Premio Tirso de Molina en 1987. ____
6. Ella ha actuado también en televisión. ____

Nombre: ______________________ Fecha: ______________________

Taller

13-54 Los directores españoles. Pedro Almodóvar, Julio Médem, Alejandro Amenábar, and Isabel Coixet are just a few famous names of Spanish movie directors. Research one of them and select one of his/her movies to watch. Write a brief **reseña** of the movie following the steps listed in the textbook chapter.

Nombre: ______________________ Fecha: ______________________

13-55 Una lista. Make a list of various aspects of a movie that you enjoyed as well as aspects that you believe could be improved.

Aspectos positivos:

____

____

____

____

____

____

____

____

Aspectos negativos:

____

____

____

____

____

____

____

____

Nombre: ______________________________ Fecha: ______________________

13-56 Si fuera yo el/la director/a... If you had been the director, how would you have improved the weaker aspects of the film? Take the weak aspects mentioned in the previous activity and explain what you would have done differently. Be sure to use the conditional perfect correctly.

Si hubiera sido el/la director/a...

____

____

____

____

____

____

____

____

Nombre: ______________________________ Fecha: ______________________

14 ¡Seamos cultos!

Primera parte

¡Así es la vida!

14-1 ¿Recuerdas? Reread the passage about Los Romero on page 478 of your textbook. Then decide whether each statement is **cierto** (C) or **falso** (F) and write the correct letter on the lines provided.

1. Celedonio Romero es el patriarca de "la familia real de la guitarra española". ____
2. Los padres de Celedonio fueron grandes músicos. ____
3. Sus hijos también han destacado en el mundo de la música. ____
4. El Cuarteto Romero fue fundado en Málaga, España. ____
5. La crítica internacional ha apreciado la música de los Romero. ____
6. Celedonio empezó a tocar la guitarra cuando tenía tres años. ____
7. Según Celino, las clases de música no son importantes para aprender. ____
8. Celino aprendió música de su tío y de su abuelo. ____
9. Celino tocó la guitarra con Pink Floyd y Led Zeppelin. ____
10. Un miembro de la familia Romero fabrica excelentes guitarras. ____

CD 14, Track 1

14-2 ¡A la ópera! As you listen to the following conversation, select the letters corresponding to all statements that are correct, according to what you hear.

1. Antonio cree que Catalina...
   a. está elegante.
   b. es alta.
   c. tiene un auto.

2. Catalina está...
   a. entusiasmada.
   b. nerviosa.
   c. enfadada.

3. El señor Villamar quiere que...
   a. Antonio y Catalina se diviertan.
   b. ellos vuelvan muy tarde.
   c. Antonio y Catalina vayan al cine.
4. Catalina y Antonio conversan sobre...
   a. la hora.
   b. la experiencia de ir a la ópera.
   c. el idioma de la ópera.
5. Catalina está preocupada...
   a. por la cantidad de luces.
   b. por el vestido que lleva.
   c. por no entender italiano.
6. Durante el intermedio ellos...
   a. hablan de cuánto les gusta la ópera.
   b. ya quieren irse.
   c. compran refrescos.

¡Así lo decimos! Vocabulario (Textbook p. 479)

14-3 Los instrumentos musicales. Find and circle the names of ten musical instruments in the puzzle.

S	A	X	F	I	N	T	L	O	V	F	L	A	U	T	A
M	A	R	A	C	A	S	A	J	O	L	I	J	E	T	I
O	C	M	G	O	T	L	E	X	G	U	T	C	R	A	S
N	O	L	R	B	U	C	D	E	R	O	P	O	L	I	F
E	R	D	V	I	O	L	I	N	U	T	M	P	E	T	A
R	D	O	L	M	B	A	R	T	O	P	I	C	I	M	S
R	E	N	V	I	O	B	A	T	E	R	I	A	L	O	G
A	O	M	B	O	N	O	C	T	I	R	D	P	U	S	O
L	N	U	X	S	B	L	A	N	C	O	N	A	R	I	N
A	I	R	P	D	A	M	E	G	O	L	R	I	B	F	O
C	L	A	R	I	N	E	T	E	V	R	U	G	A	M	F
O	R	T	B	L	I	C	O	N	A	C	S	F	C	N	O
R	P	A	S	O	M	X	O	T	L	U	M	E	S	I	X
D	U	B	J	R	O	S	I	M	G	R	I	A	R	P	A
E	T	A	B	O	F	U	L	E	R	T	A	S	O	G	S
N	A	R	C	A	G	U	M	T	E	R	O	I	A	N	O

Nombre: ______________________________ Fecha: ______________________

14-4 Emparejamientos. On the line next to each drawing, write the letter of the musical instrument that it depicts.

1. ____

2. ____

3. ____

4. ____

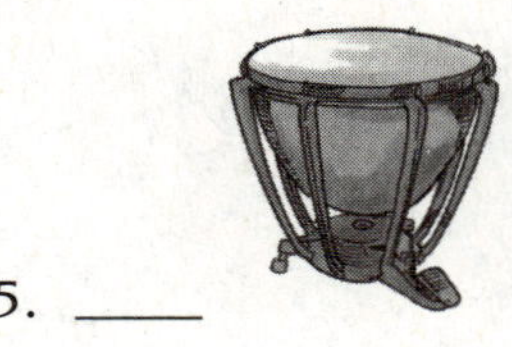

5. ____

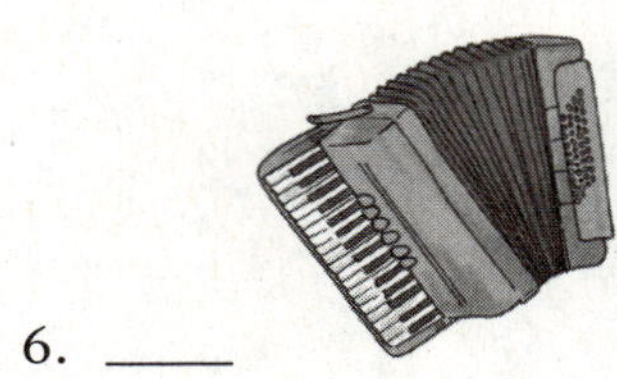

6. ____

a. la flauta

b. el acordeón

c. el saxofón

d. la batería

e. la trompeta

f. el tambor

14-5 ¡Fuera de lugar! In each series of words, circle the letter of the word that does not belong to the group.

1. a. viola	b. violín	c. batería
2. a. trombón	b. maracas	c. trompeta
3. a. clarinete	b. batería	c. tambor
4. a. arpa	b. acordeón	c. guitarra
5. a. sexteto	b. escenario	c. cuarteto
6. a. músico	b. solista	c. sinfonía

Nombre: ______________________ Fecha: ______________________

CD 14, Track 2

14-6 ¿Qué es eso? Select the letter of the word or expression that best completes each sentence you hear. Then listen and repeat as the speaker gives the correct answer.

1. a. aplaudir.
   b. componer.
   c. ensayar.
2. a. improvisar.
   b. representar.
   c. aplaudir.
3. a. corneta.
   b. gira.
   c. arpa.
4. a. la diva.
   b. el escenario.
   c. la batería.
5. a. el compositor.
   b. el director.
   c. el músico.
6. a. el cuarteto.
   b. el violín.
   c. el sexteto.

14-7 ¡A completar! Complete the following statements by filling in the blanks with the correct words from the word bank.

audición	repertorio	músicos
gira	ópera	ensayar

1. El ______________ musical de Plácido Domingo es muy extenso.
2. Muchos grupos musicales hacen una ______________ por diferentes ciudades para presentarle su música al público.
3. Antes de poder tocar en un grupo músical, tengo que presentarme a una ______________ para que me seleccionen.
4. La orquesta tendrá que ______________ por dos semanas para estar lista para el concierto.
5. Un sexteto está compuesto de seis ______________.
6. Los tres tenores cantan su repertorio en la ______________.

Nombre: ______________________ Fecha: ______________________

14-8 Tu experiencia musical. Answer the following questions in Spanish, using complete sentences.

1. ¿Qué instrumento musical tocas / has tocado?

____

2. ¿Cuándo has tomado clases de música?

____

3. ¿Qué cantante popular crees que es talentoso/a?

____

4. En tu opinión, ¿cuáles de las artistas contemporáneas son realmente divas?

____

5. ¿Qué giras musicales van a pasar por tu ciudad o área geográfica en los próximos tres meses?

____

¡Así lo hacemos! Estructuras

1. *Hacer* in time expressions (TEXTBOOK P. 481)

14-9 Hace tanto tiempo... Decide if the following statements need the present or the preterit form of the verb, and select the letter of the correct answer.

1. Fui a un concierto de mi banda musical favorita en el 2000.

   Hace seis años que _____ a un concierto de mi banda favorita.

   a. voy   b. fui

2. Toco el piano desde que tenía seis años. Ahora tengo veintiséis años.

   Hace veinte años que _____ el piano.

   a. toco   b. toqué

3. La diva empezó su gira hace tres meses y terminará la gira en seis meses.

   Hace tres meses que la diva _____ de gira.

   a. está   b. estuvo

4. Mi tía asistió a la ópera por primera vez en 1990 y todavía asiste a la ópera regularmente.

   Hace dieciséis años que mi tía _____ a la ópera.

   a. asiste b. asistió

5. José Carreras cantó en público por primera vez en 1954.

   Hace cincuenta y dos años que José Carreras _____ en público por primera vez.

   a. canta b. cantó

6. Ellos ensayan todos los días hasta que representen la comedia musical en el teatro.

   Hace seis meses que _____ la comedia musical.

   a. ensayan b. ensayaron

7. Al público le fascinó la ópera y no deja de aplaudir.

   Hace cinco minutos que el público _____.

   a. aplaude b. aplaudió

8. Alfredo Kraus, uno de los grandes tenores españoles, murió en 1999.

   Hace siete años que Alfredo Kraus _____.

   a. muere b. murió

CD 14, Track 3

14-10 ¿Habrá espectáculo, o no? Describe how long something has been going on by completing the sentences with the length of time you hear and the correct form of ***hacer***. Then listen and repeat as the speaker gives the correct answer.

MODELO: You see: ____________________ la diva no puede cantar.
You hear: tres días
You write and say: *Hace tres días* que la diva no puede cantar.

1. ____________________ que componemos la música.
2. ____________________ que la directora está enferma.
3. ____________________ que el músico improvisa.
4. ____________________ que la sinfonía toca.
5. ____________________ que no toco una pieza.

14-11 El tiempo vuela. Write sentences using the information provided and the construction ***hace... que*** to find out what happened a while ago.

Modelo: Son las cuatro. El director llegó a las dos.
Hace dos horas que llegó el director.

1. Hoy es sábado. La orquesta ensayó el viernes.

____

2. Son las cinco. La ópera comenzó a las cuatro.

____

3. Son las ocho. La diva cantó a las tres.

____

4. Hoy es el 20 de agosto. La audición terminó el 20 de julio.

____

5. Hoy es martes. El compositor compuso la pieza musical el sábado.

____

6. Hoy es el 3 de mayo de 2006. La banda tocó el 3 de mayo de 2005.

____

7. Hoy es martes 17. La comedia musical se representó el viernes 13.

____

8. Son las nueve. El músico trajo la guitarra a las ocho y media.

____

Nombre: ______________________________ Fecha: ______________________

CD 14, Track 4

14-12 Hace cuánto tiempo que... Answer the questions you hear using the fragments provided and the correct form of ***hacer***. Then listen and repeat as the speaker gives the correct answer.

Modelo: You see: _______________ dos días _______________.
You hear: ¿Hace cuánto tiempo que compraste la viola?
You write and say: *Hace* dos días *que compré la viola.*

1. _______________ tres años _______________________________.

2. _______________ una hora _______________________________.

3. _______________ quince días _______________________________.

4. _______________ diez minutos _______________________________.

5. _______________ seis horas _______________________________.

14-13 ¿Cuánto tiempo hace? Use the time period given in parentheses to answer each question in a complete sentence.

Modelo: ¿Cuánto tiempo hace que escuchas música de acordeón? (dos años)
Hace dos años que escucho música de acordeón.

1. ¿Cuánto tiempo hace que no vas a un concierto? (un año)

____

2. ¿Cuánto tiempo hace que no escuchas una sinfonía? (un mes)

____

3. ¿Cuánto tiempo hace que buscas boletos para la ópera? (un día)

____

4. ¿Cuánto tiempo hace que no ves una comedia musical? (dos días)

____

5. ¿Cuánto tiempo hace que compones esta pieza? (dos semanas)

____

6. ¿Cuánto tiempo hace que tocas el piano? (cinco años)

____

14-14 Las obras de arte. Based on the information given about each work of art, write a sentence with the verb ***hacer*** to express the amount of time that has passed. Be sure to follow the model.

MODELO: *Guernica* (pintura de Pablo Picasso, 1937)
Hace sesenta y nueve años que Picasso pintó "Guernica".

1. *Autorretrato con mono* (pintura de Frida Kahlo, 1938)

   ____

2. *Don Quijote de la Mancha* (libro de Miguel de Cervantes, 1605)

   ____

3. *La Sagrada Familia* (diseño de Antoni Gaudí, 1882)

   ____

4. *Tikal* (construcción de la civilización maya, siglo III a.C.)

   ____

5. *Ópera de Valencia* (diseño de Santiago Calatrava, 2004)

   ____

2. The pluperfect indicative (TEXTBOOK P. 484)

14-15 Luciano Pavarotti. Select the letter of the answer that best completes each sentence about the famous tenor Luciano Pavarotti.

1. El público ____ a Pavarotti en todas las óperas importantes del mundo.

   a. ha aplaudido　　b. había aplaudido

2. Antes de Pavarotti, la ópera nunca ____ tan popular.

   a. ha sido　　b. había sido

3. Luciano Pavarotti ____ la ópera en un género musical popular.

   a. ha transformado　　b. había transformado

4. Antes de debutar en los Estados Unidos en 1965, Pavarotti ya ____ en Europa en 1961.

   a. ha debutado　　b. había debutado

Nombre: ______________________ Fecha: ______________________

5. Pavarotti ____ en el escenario con José Carreras y Plácido Domingo en muchas ocasiones.

   a. ha estado b. había estado

6. Antes de cantar en los Juegos Olímpicos de invierno en Turín en 2006, Luciano Pavarotti ya ____ en la Copa del Mundo de fútbol en Italia en 1990.

   a. ha cantado b. había cantado

14-16 Nunca antes. Fill in the blanks with the pluperfect indicative form of the verbs in parentheses.

1. Carlos nunca antes ______________________ (visitar) un teatro.
2. Nosotros nunca antes ______________________ (conocer) una diva.
3. Miguel nunca antes ______________________ (ver) una comedia musical.
4. Los músicos nunca antes ______________________ (ensayar) esa pieza musical.
5. La diva nunca antes ______________________ (ponerse) un vestido tan feo.
6. El compositor nunca antes ______________________ (componer) una sinfonía.
7. El solista nunca antes ______________________ (enfermarse).
8. El director nunca antes ______________________ (abrir) el teatro por la mañana.

CD 14, Track 5

14-17 Nunca lo habíamos hecho durante una gira. Complete the sentences using the pluperfect tense of the verbs you hear. Then listen and repeat as the speaker gives the correct answer.

MODELO: You see: La diva nunca ______________________ en Buenos Aires.
You hear: cantar
You write and say: La diva nunca *había cantado* en Buenos Aires.

1. Ellas nunca ______________________ en este país.
2. Tú nunca ______________________ un clarinete.
3. Él nunca ______________________ tantos aplausos.
4. Nosotras nunca ______________________ una comedia musical.
5. Yo nunca ______________________ tanto.

Nombre: ______________________ Fecha: ______________________

CD 14, Track 6

14-18 Antes de la gira. Complete the sentences using the pluperfect tense and the fragments provided. Then listen and repeat as the speaker gives the correct answer.

MODELO: You see: ______________ a tocar la trompeta.
You hear: ¿Qué había aprendido Silvia?
You write and say: *Había aprendido* a tocar la trompeta.

1. ______________ los ejercicios.
2. ______________ el artículo.
3. ______________ en México.
4. ______________ en Nueva York.
5. ______________ a Barcelona.

14-19 ¿Qué pasó? Write complete sentences using the words provided. Use the preterit tense in the first clause and the pluperfect in the second, as in the model.

MODELO: cuando / nosotros / recibir / la invitación // ya / empezar / concierto
Cuando nosotros recibimos la invitación, ya había empezado el concierto.

1. cuando / yo / llegar / al teatro // mis amigos / ya / sentarse

____

2. cuando / el director / regresar // la orquesta sinfónica / ya / tocar

____

3. cuando / Luis / comprar / las entradas // Pedro / ya / conseguirlas

____

4. cuando / nosotros / volver // la comedia / ya / terminarse

____

5. cuando / tú / traer / la guitarra // el sexteto /ya / tocar

____

6. cuando Ramón y tú / llegar / al teatro // yo / ya / hablar / con Plácido

____

Nombre: ______________________________ Fecha: ______________________

¿Cuánto sabes tú?

14-20 ¿Sabes usar *hacer* con las expresiones temporales? Fill in the blanks with the correct form of each verb in parentheses.

1. — ¿Cuándo se mudaron tus tíos a Los Ángeles?

   — Hace cinco años que __________________ (vivir) en Los Ángeles.

2. — ¿Cuánto tiempo hace que no ves a tu primo?

   — Hace dos años que no __________________ (ver) a mi primo.

3. — Tu primo es cantante de ópera, ¿verdad?

   — Sí. Hace dos años que __________________ (ser) cantante de ópera.

4. — ¿Conoce tu primo a gente importante?

   — Sí. Hace tres años, en una ópera, __________________ (conocer) a Plácido Domingo.

5. — ¿Cuándo cantó por primera vez?

   — Hace cuatro años que __________________ (cantar) por primera vez.

14-21 ¿Sabes usar el pluscuamperfecto de indicativo? Fill in the blanks with the correct pluperfect form of the verbs in parentheses.

1. Antes de escuchar a los tres tenores, nunca me ________________________ (interesar) la ópera.

2. Antes de escuchar a José Carreras y a Plácido Domingo, nosotros sólo

   ________________________ (escuchar) la música de Luciano Pavarotti.

3. Antes de cantar con Pavarotti, José Carreras ya ________________________ (cantar) en muchas óperas.

4. Antes de ganar el *Grammy* en 1991, Carreras ya ________________________ (ganar) el premio *Emmy*.

5. José Carreras ya ________________________ (debutar) en Barcelona cuando cantó en Nueva York por primera vez.

Nombre: ______________________________ Fecha: ______________________

CD 14, Track 7

14-22 El desfile de modas. Explain what you and your colleagues had already done to prepare for the fashion show, using the pluperfect indicative form of the verbs you hear. Then listen and repeat as the speaker gives the correct answer.

MODELO: You see: Yo ya ______________ al escenario.
You hear: volver
You say and write: Yo *había vuelto* al escenario.

1. Nosotros ya ____________________ los nombres de los diseñadores.
2. Yo ya ____________________ al modelo.
3. Los Ramírez ya ____________________ a la asistente que yo recomendé, pero ella quería un sueldo más alto.
4. Tú ya ____________________ un aumento.
5. Ustedes ya ____________________ los vestidos.

CD 14, Track 8

14-23 Preguntas personales. Answer the questions you hear in Spanish, using complete sentences.

1. ____.
2. ____.
3. ____.
4. ____.
5. ____.

SEGUNDA PARTE

¡Así es la vida!

14-24 Carolina Herrera. Reread the excerpt about the designer Carolina Herrera on page 488 of your textbook. Then select the letter of the correct answer to each of the following questions.

1. Carolina Herrera es…

   a. una figura política. b. una cantante famosa. c. una diseñadora de modas.

2. Se puede comparar a Carolina Herrera con...

   a. Donatella Versace. b. una mujer de Nueva York. c. una mujer de México.

3. La familia de Carolina era…

a. humilde y trabajadora. b. prestigiosa. c. grande.

4. Los diseños de Carolina Herrera…

a. son internacionales. b. son para mujeres de Nueva York. c. son para mujeres de la India.

5. 212 es…

a. el código de teléfono de Nueva York. b. un perfume de Carolina Herrera. c. a y b

6. Carolina Herrera es diseñadora desde...

a. hace veinticinco años. b. hace veinte años. c. hace quince años.

7. Carolina no diseña...

a. casas. b. trajes de novia. c. vestidos de día.

8. Carolina Herrera es la diseñadora para la mujer...

a. simple. b. trabajadora. c. sofisticada.

CD 14, Track 9

14-25 La alta costura. As you listen to the following conversation, select the letters corresponding to all statements that are correct, according to what you hear.

1. La presentación es...

   a. dentro de una semana.

   b. a la una y media.

   c. de ropa de terciopelo.

2. El primer conjunto es...

   a. un vestido de tul.

   b. simple.

   c. un vestido de terciopelo.

3. El diseñador quiere...

   a. viajar a Milán.

   b. ver los conjuntos.

   c. poner una falda de tul.

4. Margarita quiere...

   a. más dinero.

   b. que el esmoquin sea de cuero.

   c. que Óscar no coma tanto.

5. Óscar no...

   a. puede ponerse el esmoquin.

   b. tiene una cita con Calvin Klein.

   c. tuvo problemas en Milán.

6. Pablo...

   a. ha comido demasiado.

   b. quiere estar en Milán con Óscar.

   c. no debería haberse puesto el esmoquin.

¡Así lo decimos! Vocabulario (Textbook p. 489)

14-26 ¡A emparejar! On the line next to each drawing, write the letter of the word that it best depicts.

1. ____

4. ____

2. ____

5. ____

3. ____

a. el disfraz

b. las prendas

c. la sencillez

d. la alta costura

e. la piel

Nombre: ______________________ Fecha: ______________________

14-27 ¿Qué es eso? Choose the letter of the word that best completes each sentence you hear. Then listen and repeat as the speaker gives the correct answer.

CD 14, Track 10

1. a. el conjunto.
   b. el disfraz.
   c. el esmoquin.
2. a. la diseñadora.
   b. la modelo.
   c. la gabardina.
3. a. el poliéster.
   b. la piel.
   c. la paja.
4. a. encantadora.
   b. terciopelo.
   c. prenda.
5. a. el tul.
   b. la paja.
   c. el poliéster.

14-28 ¡A seleccionar! Complete the following statements by filling in the missing word from the word bank below.

tul	modelo	esmoquin	diseñadora	disfraz

1. La ____________ llevaba un vestido diseñado por Carolina Herrera.
2. Carolina Herrera es una ____________ muy famosa.
3. La bailarina llevaba una falda de ____________ blanco.
4. La boda era muy elegante; la novia (*bride*) llevaba un vestido largo y el novio (*groom*) llevaba un ____________.
5. En *Halloween* el niño llevaba un ____________.

Nombre: ______________________ Fecha: ______________________

14-29 Cuestionario. Answer each question in Spanish, using complete sentences.

1. Para ti, ¿qué significa que algo está de moda?

____

2. ¿Cuáles son tus telas favoritas? Explica.

____

3. ¿Prefieres lo sencillo o lo sofisticado en cuestiones de moda? ¿Por qué?

____

4. ¿Qué harías si te invitaran a una fiesta formal y no tuvieras la prenda adecuada?

____

5. ¿Qué diseñadores de moda te gustan? ¿Por qué?

____

Letras y sonidos (TEXTBOOK P. 490)

CD 14, Track 11

14-30 ¿Tiene "ñ"? For each question, you will hear two words in Spanish. Select the letter of the word that contains the **"ñ"** sound.

1.	a.	b.	4.	a.	b.
2.	a.	b.	5.	a.	b.
3.	a.	b.	6.	a.	b.

CD 14, Track 12

14-31 ¿Cuál es? First, write the words you hear. Then decide whether the letter **"n"** in the indefinite article is pronounced as **"n"** or **"m"** and put a check mark in the appropriate column.

		n	**m**			**n**	**m**
1.	________	___	___	5.	________	___	___
2.	________	___	___	6.	________	___	___
3.	________	___	___	7.	________	___	___
4.	________	___	___	8.	________	___	___

Nombre: ______________________ Fecha: ______________________

¡Asi lo hacemos! Estructuras

3. The pluperfect subjunctive and the conditional perfect (TEXTBOOK P. 492)

14-32 ¡A cambiar! Change the following statements from the present to the past, using the imperfect and the pluperfect subjunctive. Be sure to follow the model.

MODELO: Dudo que haya vuelto la diseñadora.
Dudaba que *hubiera vuelto* la diseñadora.

1. Es probable que haya tenido un esmoquin.

   ______________ probable que ______________ un esmoquin.

2. No creo que la modelo haya trabajado allí.

   No ______________ que la modelo ______________ allí.

3. Dudamos que Laura haya hecho el vestido.

   ______________ que Laura ______________ el vestido.

4. Esperas que no hayan vendido todas las blusas de rayón.

   ______________ que no ______________ todas las blusas de rayón.

5. Siento que no hayas conseguido un vestido de lentejuelas.

   ______________ que no ______________ un vestido de lentejuelas.

6. Esperan que tú ya hayas visto el sombrero de terciopelo.

   ______________ que tú ya ______________ el sombrero de terciopelo.

7. Es probable que hayan traído un disfraz a la fiesta.

   ______________ probable que ______________ un disfraz a la fiesta.

8. Es imposible que su hermano haya conocido a Elena.

   ______________ imposible que su hermano ______________ a Elena.

Nombre: ______________________ Fecha: ______________________

14-33 Cambios y más cambios. Change the tenses in the following statements to show contrary-to-fact situations, using the pluperfect subjunctive and the conditional perfect. Be sure to follow the model.

Modelo: Si me regalaran un abrigo de piel, lo devolvería.
Si me *hubieran regalado* un abrigo de piel, lo *habría devuelto*.

1. Si hubiera una camisa de algodón, la compraría.

   Si ______________ una camisa de algodón, la ______________.

2. Si la modelo quisiera salir conmigo, la invitaría.

   Si la modelo ______________ salir conmigo, la ______________.

3. Si no me faltara dinero, iría al desfile de moda.

   Si no me ______________ dinero, ______________ al desfile de moda.

4. Si tuviera talento, sería diseñador/a.

   Si ______________ talento, ______________ diseñador/a.

5. Si fuera rico/a, tendría ropa de alta costura.

   Si ______________ rico/a, ______________ ropa de alta costura.

6. Si pudiera, haría una campaña en contra de los abrigos de piel.

   Si ______________, ______________ una campaña en contra de los abrigos de piel.

CD 14, Track 13

14-34 Dos modelos preocupados. Change the verbs in the sentences that you hear to the pluperfect subjunctive form. Then listen and repeat as the speaker gives the correct answer.

Modelo: You see: ¡Ojalá ______________!
You hear: ¡Ojalá tuvieran las prendas!
You write and say: *¡Ojalá hubiera tenido las prendas!*

1. ¡Ojalá ______________________________!
2. ¡Ojalá ______________________________!
3. ¡Ojalá ______________________________!
4. ¡Ojalá ______________________________!
5. ¡Ojalá ______________________________!

CD 14, Track 14

14-35 Porque estábamos enfermos... Using the conditional perfect form of the verbs you hear, tell what would have occurred to the following people if they had not been sick. Then listen and repeat as the speaker gives the correct answers.

Modelo: You see: La modelo ____________________ el conjunto.
You hear: presentar
You write and say: La modelo *habría presentado* el conjunto.

1. Yo ____________________ la trompeta en el concierto.
2. Tú ____________________ a visitar al diseñador.
3. Los modelos ____________________ el horario de trabajo.
4. Nosotros ____________________ el nombre de la modelo.
5. Usted ____________________ más del desfile de moda.

CD 14, Track 15

14-36 En la oficina de la orquesta. Explain why you and your acquaintances did not follow a certain course of action, using the fragments provided and the correct forms of the verbs you hear. Then listen and repeat as the speaker gives the correct answer.

Modelo: You see: Yo ________________ el puesto si ________________ más experiencia.
You hear: solicitar, tener
You write and say: Yo *habría solicitado* el puesto si *hubiera tenido* más experiencia.

1. Nosotros ________________ las cartas de recomendación si ________________ tiempo.
2. Yo no ________________ al secretario si él ________________ mejor trabajo.
3. Ellos ________________ a la modelo si ella ________________ trabajar más horas.
4. El modelo ________________ un aumento si no ________________ perder su trabajo.
5. Ustedes ________________ al galán si él ________________ al teatro.

Nombre: ______________________________ Fecha: ______________________

14-37 ¿De quién hablamos? Form complete sentences by matching each clause from the left column with the most logical one from the right column and conjugating the verbs in parentheses. Then write your sentences on the lines below.

1. Si Gabriel García Márquez no (escribir) *Cien años de soledad...*
2. Si Cristina Saralegui no (tener) su programa en Univisión...
3. Si Carlos Santana no (tocar) la guitarra tan bien...
4. Si Alejandro Amenábar no (filmar) *Mar adentro...*
5. Si Felipe de Borbón no (ser) hijo de reyes...

a. no (ganar) el Premio Nobel de Literatura.
b. no (ganar) el Óscar.
c. no (ser) príncipe.
d. no (ganar) cuatro *Grammys*.
e. no (ser) tan famosa.

1. ____.
2. ____.
3. ____.
4. ____.
5. ____.

14-38 Si yo hubiera sido... Say what you would have done in the following situations by completing the statements below using the conditional perfect.

1. Si yo hubiera sido modelo,

   ____.

2. Si yo hubiera sido diseñador/a,

   ____.

3. Si yo me hubiera disfrazado en *Halloween*,

   ____.

4. Si yo hubiera sido una persona más extrovertida,

   ____.

5. Si yo hubiera sido una persona más sofisticada,

   ____.

Nombre: ______________________________ Fecha: ______________________

¿Cuánto sabes tú?

14-39 ¿Sabes usar el pluscuamperfecto y el condicional perfecto? Choose the letter of the correct verb form to complete each statement below.

1. Si nosotros _____, no habríamos encontrado boletos.

   a. hubiéramos ido b. habríamos ido c. habíamos ido

2. Si el actor hubiera interpretado mejor su papel, la comedia musical _____ mejor.

   a. había sido b. hubiera sido c. habría sido

3. El público _____ si el cantante hubiera cantado bien.

   a. hubiera aplaudido b. habría aplaudido c. había aplaudido

4. Juanjo habría conseguido ser parte de la banda si él _____ a la audición.

   a. se hubiera presentado b. se habría presentado c. se había presentado

5. Ojalá la gira del tenor _____ por mi ciudad.

   a. había pasado b. habría pasado c. hubiera pasado

14-40 ¿Sabes usar el pluscuamperfecto de subjuntivo con *ojalá*? You wish that some things would never have occurred. Complete the following sentences with the pluperfect subjunctive of the verb in parentheses.

1. Ojalá que no ____________________ (morir) tantos animales a causa de los abrigos de piel.
2. Ojalá que los diseñadores no ____________________ (diseñar) tantos artículos de terciopelo.
3. Ojalá que muchos diseñadores no ____________________ (ser) tan irresponsables.
4. Ojalá que las tiendas no ____________________ (vender) nunca sombreros de paja.
5. Ojalá que los científicos no ____________________ (inventar) artículos de poliéster.

Nombre: ________________________ Fecha: ________________________

14-41 **La ópera habría sido mejor...** Change the sentences that you hear to reflect contrary-to-fact conditions in the past. Then listen and repeat as the speaker gives the correct answer.

CD 14, Track 16

Modelo: You hear: Si la diva practica las arias, la ópera es mejor.
You write and say: *Si la diva hubiera practicado las arias, la ópera habría sido mejor.*

1. ________________________.
2. ________________________.
3. ________________________.
4. ________________________.
5. ________________________.

14-42 **¿Qué habrían hecho?** Listen to the following clauses and complete the sentences, using the conditional perfect to say what the following people in your life would have done.

CD 14, Track 17

1. ________________________.
2. ________________________.
3. ________________________.
4. ________________________.
5. ________________________.

Observaciones

Antes de ver el video

14-43 ¿Qué pasa? Select the letter of the best answer to each question.

1. How might Hermés inquire about Felipe's friend?

   a. ¿A verla? ¿A quién?

   b. ¿Tienes ropa adecuada para el concierto?

   c. ¿Cuánto tiempo hace que la conoces?

2. What would Felipe reply?

   a. Hace casi un año, nos conocimos en un chat y voy a reunirme con ella.

   b. Ahora que ya lo sabe todo el mundo, no tiene sentido ocultarlo.

   c. Se lo quería decir desde hace tiempo.

3. What does Hermés say after giving the jacket to Felipe?

   a. ¿No te gusta?

   b. Caballero, ahora pareces un señor respetable.

   c. ¿No pensarás presentarte con esos pantalones viejos?

4. What does Felipe think?

   a. A ti te toca darme dos.

   b. Es muy bonita.

   c. Claro que sí.

5. Now that Felipe is ready to leave the hostel, how does doña María say good-bye to him?

   a. Buen viaje. Y ya sabes dónde tienes tu casa.

   b. Hasta mañana, mi hijo. Que pases buenas noches.

   c. Adiós, Felipe. Nos vemos la semana que viene.

Nombre: ______________________ Fecha: ______________________

A ver el video

14-44 La conversación. Fill in the blanks with the missing words according to the video segment.

Felipe: Ahora ya lo saben todos. Salgo hoy mismo. Quiero llegar a su debut.

Silvia: ¿Su debut? ¿Es (1) ______________________?

Hermés: ¿O (2) ______________________?

Patricio: ¿O (3) ______________________ de jazz?

Felipe: No, es primera (4) ______________________. El martes que viene (5) ______________________ con la (6) ______________________ Filarmónica de la Ciudad de México. Tengo un (7) ______________________ en primera fila, así que tengo que llegar a México antes del martes.

Silvia: El violín me apasiona.

Felipe: ¿De verdad?

Silvia: Sí, claro. Tengo las mejores grabaciones de Sergui Luca y Midori. Si lo (8) ______________________ sabido, te (9) ______________________ dado un disco compacto para ella.

Felipe: Elvira ha grabado unos cuantos discos con su (10) ______________________. Te los mandaré dedicados.

Después de ver el video

14-45 ¿Quién lo hará? Fill in the blanks with the name of the character who will carry out the following actions.

1. ______________________ recibirá unos disco compactos dedicados.
2. ______________________ irá a un concierto en México.
3. ______________________ necesitará una chaqueta nueva.
4. ______________________ tocará con la Orquesta Filarmónica de la Ciudad de México.

14-46 Felipe y su futuro. Select the letter of the word or phrase that best completes each sentence.

1. Felipe se va…

   a. mañana.

   b. hoy.

   c. en una semana.

2. Patricio dice que Felipe es un hombre…

   a. tímido y reservado.

   b. extrovertido y optimista.

   c. romántico y conservador.

3. Elvira es…

   a. violinista.

   b. bailarina.

   c. cantante.

4. Para que se vea respetable, Hermés le da una chaqueta de… a Felipe.

   a. pana

   b. cuadros

   c. cuero

5. Silvia cree que…

   a. a Felipe le queda bien la chaqueta.

   b. es como llevar un disfraz.

   c. Felipe tiene que ponerse la chaqueta todos los días.

Nombre: ______________________ Fecha: ______________________

Nuestro mundo

Panoramas

14-47 ¡A informarse! Based on the information from **Nuestro mundo,** decide if the following statements are **cierto** (C) or **falso** (F) and write the correct letter on the lines provided.

1. El arte moderno hispano no es conocido internacionalmente. ____
2. Salvador Dalí es uno de los artistas más influyentes. ____
3. Oswaldo Guayasamín se preocupa mucho por los derechos humanos. ____
4. Fernando Botero sólo hace esculturas. ____
5. Las figuras de Botero destacan por su tamaño y voluptuosidad. ____
6. Las obras de Botero se han expuesto exclusivamente en Colombia. ____
7. El estilo del arquitecto Calatrava es clásico. ____
8. Calatrava es uno de los arquitectos seleccionados para el nuevo *World Trade Center.* ____

14-48 De visita a un museo latinoamericano. In your text you have learned about many famous artists, literary figures, and musicians from the Hispanic world. Now go to **http://www.prenhall.com/arriba** and take a virtual tour of the museum. Then, choose the letter of the most appropriate answer to each of the following questions.

1. MALBA es…

   a. el nombre de un artista. b. el nombre de una exposición. c. el nombre del museo.

2. El museo está en…

   a. México, D.F. b. Buenos Aires. c. Bogotá.

3. En MALBA se puede encontrar…

   a. arte contemporáneo. b. arte colonial. c. arte medieval.

4. En MALBA se pueden ver obras de…

   a. Oswaldo Guayasamín. b. María de Mater O'Neill. c. Diego Rivera.

5. Además de pintura, el museo ofrece…

   a. sesiones de literatura y cine. b. clases de pintura. c. clases de danza.

6. El museo está cerrado los…

   a. domingos. b. martes. c. viernes.

Nombre: ______________________________ Fecha: ______________________

Ritmos

14-49 El son montuno. Based on the information about the **son montuno** on page 498 of your textbook, decide if the following statements are **cierto** (C) or **falso** (F) and write the correct letter on the lines provided.

1. El "son montuno" es un ritmo puertorriqueño. ____
2. Este ritmo incorpora elementos de la melódica "trova" española. ____
3. Se hizo popular en el siglo XX. ____
4. La percusión del "son montuno" viene del estilo africano. ____
5. Típica Novel es un grupo musical de Los Ángeles. ____

Páginas

14-50 El microcuento. In your text you read an example of the **microcuento** by Enrique Anderson Imbert. Now visit **http://www.prenhall.com/arriba** and read "La oveja negra" (*Black Sheep*) by another short story writer, Augusto Monterroso. Then answer the questions below.

1. ¿De dónde era la oveja negra?

____

2. ¿Qué le pasó a la oveja negra?

____

3. ¿Qué hizo el rebaño (*herd*) un siglo después de fusilar (*after executing*) a la oveja negra?

____

4. ¿Qué les pasó a las otras ovejas negras? ¿Por qué?

____

____

5. ¿Qué tipo de ironía hay en el cuento?

____

____

Nombre: ______________________ Fecha: ______________________

Taller

14-51 Otro cuento. Select another of Augusto Monterroso's short stories from **http://www.prenhall.com/arriba**. Then explain the meaning of the story you have chosen in a paragraph of your own words.

14-52 Tus ideas. Now make a list of the ideas you want to include in a story of your own and the images you will use to represent them.

Ideas	**Imágenes**

Nombre: ______________________ Fecha: ______________________

14-53 Tu obra literaria. Using the information from the previous activity, write your short story in the space below.

Nombre: ______________________ Fecha: ______________________

15 ¿Te gusta la política?

Primera parte

¡Así es la vida!

15-1 ¿Recuerdas? Reread the interview with Óscar Arias on page 506 of your textbook. Then decide if the following statements are **cierto** (C) or **falso** (F) and write the correct letter on the lines provided.

1. El Dr. Arias ha sido presidente de Costa Rica dos veces. ____
2. La lucha contra el tráfico de drogas es el proyecto más importante, según el Dr. Arias. ____
3. El tráfico de armas pone en peligro la paz mundial. ____
4. Varios ganadores del Premio Nobel de la Paz colaboran en los proyectos políticos del Dr. Arias. ____
5. Una de las metas de Óscar Arias es promocionar el turismo en Costa Rica. ____
6. Otro de los objetivos del Dr. Arias es la lucha contra la corrupción. ____

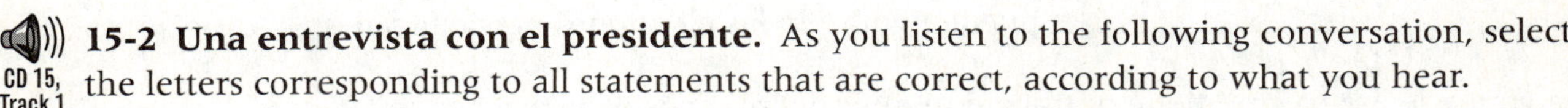

CD 15, Track 1

15-2 Una entrevista con el presidente. As you listen to the following conversation, select the letters corresponding to all statements that are correct, according to what you hear.

1. La reportera quiere...
   a. hablar de su vida social.
   b. que el presidente firme papeles.
   c. entrevistar al presidente.
2. El presidente ofrece...
   a. varias soluciones.
   b. descripciones de los ciudadanos.
   c. algo de beber.
3. El presidente se preocupa por...
   a. la economía.
   b. la pobreza.
   c. los activistas.
4. La entrevista incluye...
   a. una campaña política.
   b. ideas para solucionar varios problemas.
   c. fechas para firmar tratados.

Nombre: ______________________ Fecha: ______________________

5. El presidente le dice a la reportera que...
   a. no será fácil.
   b. fije otra cita.
   c. no tiene tiempo para hablar más.

6. El presidente quiere...
   a. el desarme nuclear.
   b. el periódico.
   c. promover esfuerzos para ayudar a la gente pobre.

¡Así lo decimos! Vocabulario (TEXTBOOK P. 507)

CD 15, Track 2

15-3 Hablando de política. Listen to the following statements. Then decide whether they are **cierto** (C) or **falso** (F) and write the correct letter on the lines provided.

1. ____
2. ____
3. ____
4. ____
5. ____
6. ____

15-4 ¡A completar! Complete the following statements by filling in the blanks with the correct word or phrase from the word bank below.

ejército	desarme	pobreza
ciudadanos	pacifista	país en desarrollo

1. China es un ______________________.
2. Óscar Arias es ______________________ porque quiere la paz mundial.
3. Los ______________________ pueden votar en las elecciones presidenciales.
4. La gente de ese país no tiene ni trabajo ni dinero y muchos de ellos viven en ______________________.
5. El ______________________ tiene en su poder las armas de un país.
6. La comunidad internacional quiere el ______________________ de muchos países para evitar posibles guerras.

Nombre: ______________________ Fecha: ______________________

15-5 La manifestación. Based on the drawing below, answer the following questions in complete sentences.

1. ¿Qué promueven los activistas?

   ____

2. ¿Qué quieren abolir?

   ____

3. ¿Qué quieren fortalecer?

   ____

4. Basándote en la situación actual de los Estados Unidos, ¿qué objetivos han logrado los activistas?

   ____

Nombre: ______________________________ Fecha: ______________________

15-6 Preguntas personales. Answer each question in Spanish, using complete sentences.

1. ¿Se puede hacer un esfuerzo para ayudar a los países en desarrollo? Explica.

____

2. ¿Qué harías tú para terminar con la pobreza?

____

3. ¿Crees que los países deben abolir los ejércitos? Explica.

____

4. En tu opinión, ¿cuáles son los peores conflictos que ocurren en el mundo hoy en día?

____

¡Así lo hacemos! Estructuras

1. The subjunctive with indefinite and nonexistent antecedents

(Textbook p. 509)

15-7 ¡A practicar! Complete the following sentences with the correct present subjunctive form of the verbs in parentheses.

1. Busco un pacifista que ____________ (lograr) hablar con los políticos.
2. ¿Conoces un político que ____________ (querer) terminar con la pobreza?
3. No hay nadie que ____________ (promover) mis ideales.
4. Los ciudadanos necesitamos un presidente que ____________ (fortalecer) el país.
5. Queremos unas leyes que no ____________ (violar) los derechos humanos.
6. No hay ningún país en desarrollo que no ____________ (tener) problemas.

Nombre: ______________________ Fecha: ______________________

15-8 Situaciones. Complete the following statements with the correct subjunctive or indicative form of the verb in parentheses.

1. Nuestro país tiene ciudadanos que __________ (ser) activistas, pero necesitamos unos ciudadanos que __________ (ser) pacifistas también.
2. Conozco al activista que __________ (promover) muchas iniciativas, pero queremos un activista que __________ (poder) lograr más.
3. No hay ninguna campaña que __________ (fortalecer) buenos programas sociales. Hay muchas campañas que no __________ (ser) muy buenas.
4. Hay muchos conflictos que __________ (violar) los derechos humanos. Queremos soluciones que __________ (lograr) acabar con estas violaciones.
5. Éste es el país que __________ (respetar) los derechos humanos. Queremos un país que no __________ (violar) los derechos humanos.
6. Conozco al activista que __________ (querer) eliminar la pobreza. Queremos unas campañas que __________ (ayudar) a abolir la pobreza.
7. —¿Hay algún país que __________ (querer) abolir el ejército?
   —No, no hay ningún país que __________ (poder) hacerlo.
8. Conozco al general que __________ (preferir) el desarme, aunque no hay ningún país que __________ (firmar) un acuerdo para el desarme.

CD 15, Track 3

15-9 El nuevo general del ejército. Complete the sentences using the correct indicative or subjunctive form of the verbs you hear. Then listen and repeat as the speaker gives the correct answer.

Modelo: You see: Buscan un presidente que __________ la paz.
You hear: promover
You write and say: Buscan un presidente que *promueva* la paz.

1. Buscamos un activista que __________ lograr nuestras metas.
2. Conozco a un ciudadano que __________ los derechos humanos.
3. Necesitan un programa de desarme que __________ pronto.
4. Tienen un ejército que __________ su causa.
5. ¿Hay algún ciudadano que __________ pacifista?
6. Queremos una resolución que no __________ violencia.

Nombre: ______________________ Fecha: ______________________

CD 15, Track 4

15-10 ¡Quiero ser activista! Complete the sentences by changing the indicative form of the verb you hear to the subjunctive, as in the model. Then listen and repeat as the speaker gives the correct answer.

MODELO: You see: Buscan un plan que ______________ los esfuerzos del presidente.
You hear: Tenemos un plan que fortalece los esfuerzos del presidente.
You write and say: Buscan un plan que *fortalezca* los esfuerzos del presidente.

1. Buscan un activista que les ______________ acerca de la opresión.
2. Buscan un ejército que ______________ los ciudadanos.
3. Buscan un mapa que ______________ del Ecuador.
4. Buscan una resolución que ______________ inspirar la paz.

15-11 Tus anuncios. You are a newspaper publisher and you need to fill some positions. Write five ads using the information given, and be sure to follow the model.

MODELO: buscar reportera —hablar español e inglés, saber escribir bien, ser simpática
Se busca una reportera que hable español e inglés, que sepa escribir bien y que sea simpática.

1. necesitar periodista —ser decisivo, promover el diálogo, lograr nuestros objetivos

____

____

2. buscar comentarista —tener contacto con los ciudadanos, promover nuestras ideas, fortalecer nuestro mensaje

____

____

3. solicitar secretaria —hablar bien con el público, ser inteligente, llevarse bien con los demás

____

____

4. necesitar empleados —poder vender anuncios, creer en nuestro periódico, querer mejorar las ventas

____

____

5. necesitar artista —poder ilustrar bien, tener nuevas ideas

____

____

CD 15, Track 5

15-12 Cuando era más joven. Answer the questions you hear using the sentence fragments provided and the correct form of the verb. Then listen and repeat as the speaker gives the correct answer.

MODELO: You see: una vida / no tener / conflictos

____

You hear: ¿Qué buscaban?
You write and say: *Buscaban una vida que no tuviera conflictos.*
or
You see: una vida / no incluir / conflictos

____

You hear: ¿Qué tenían?
You write and say: *Tenían una vida que no incluía conflictos.*

1. programas / abolir / la pobreza

____

2. un padre / fortalecerlos

____

3. el gobierno / no promover / hostilidad

____

4. un país en desarrollo / tener / muchos conflictos

____

2. The relative pronouns *que, quien,* and *lo que* (TEXTBOOK P. 511)

15-13 Una conversación. Two friends are having a conversation. Complete their dialogue by filling in the blanks with the relative pronouns **que, quien,** or **lo que.**

Jorge: Allí está el activista con (1) ______________ quiero hablar.

Joaquín: No sabía (2) ______________ lo conocías.

Jorge: No, no lo conozco pero sé (3) ______________ es honesto.

Joaquín: ¿Sabes (4) ______________ trabaja con el presidente?

Jorge: Sí, pero (5) ______________ me gusta son sus ideas.

Joaquín: A mí también me gustan sus ideas, pero (6) ______________ no me gusta es la actitud (*attitude*) del pacifista (7) ______________ está con él.

Jorge: ¿Quién es?

Joaquín: Es un señor (8) ______________ es muy inseguro.

Nombre: ______________________ Fecha: ______________________

15-14 El activista. This activist needs help with his campaign. Complete the paragraph by filling in the correct relative pronouns: **que, quien(es),** or **lo que.**

El activista es muy inteligente. (1) ______________ pasa es (2) ______________ es un poco tímido. (3) ______________ menos le gusta es hablar con las autoridades; por eso, (4) ______________ tiene que hacer es pedir ayuda. Sus amigos, en (5) ______________ él confía y (6) ______________ tienen las mismas ideas, lo ayudan mucho y le dicen (7) ______________ tiene que hacer. Ellos le aconsejan (8) ______________ sea menos tímido y (9) ______________ siempre les diga la verdad. Es muy importante (10) ______________ el activista los escuche.

CD 15, Track 6

15-15 El secretario explica todo. Complete the following sentences using the expressions **que, quien(es),** or **lo que.** Then listen and repeat as the speaker gives the correct answer.

1. El señor ______________ llamó ayer es mi padre.
2. Eso es ______________ no me gusta.
3. Ése es el chico con ______________ viajé.
4. Verte contenta es ______________ me importa.
5. La agencia ______________ vende los pasajes es Costamar.
6. Los pasajeros de ______________ hablamos están allí.
7. Aquella señorita es la persona ______________ me atendió.
8. Aquel señor es el hombre a ______________ le dieron las cartas.

Nombre: ______________________________ Fecha: ______________________

¿Cuánto sabes tú?

15-16 ¿Sabes usar el subjuntivo sin antecedentes? Fill in the blanks in each sentence with the correct form of the present subjunctive or present indicative depending on the context.

1. Busco un ciudadano que ____________________ (ser) responsable y honesto.
2. ¿Conoces a alguien que ____________________ (lograr) unir al pueblo?
3. No hay nadie que ____________________ (poder) acabar con la pobreza.
4. ¿Conoces algún político que ____________________ (preocuparse) por el problema de la violencia?
5. Buscamos al pacifista que ____________________ (defender) sus derechos delante del ejército.
6. Hay un activista que ____________________ (trabajar) para la democracia de su país.

15-17 ¿Sabes usar los pronombres relativos? Fill in the blanks with the correct relative pronoun: **que, quien(es),** or **lo que.**

1. Los esfuerzos ____________________ ellos hicieron para encontrar una solución no sirvieron de nada.
2. José, ____________________ es pacifista, está en contra de una intervención del ejército.
3. La ley ____________________ aprobaron es buena para todos.
4. No nos gustó ____________________ dijo el activista sobre el gobierno.
5. El chico con ____________________ estudio está interesado en la política.
6. ____________________ no entiendo es la violación de los derechos humanos.

CD 15, Track 7

15-18 En la oficina del gobierno. Answer the questions you hear affirmatively or negatively, according to the cues provided. Then listen and repeat as the speaker gives the correct answer.

Modelo: You see: Sí, ______________________.
or
No, ______________________.
You hear: ¿Conoces a alguien que sea de Bolivia?
You write and say: Sí, *conozco a alguien que es de Bolivia.*
or
No, *no conozco a nadie que sea de Bolivia.*

1. No, ____.
2. Sí, ____.

Nombre: ______________________ Fecha: ______________________

3. No, ______________________.

4. Sí, ______________________.

CD 15, Track 8

15-19 Preguntas personales. Answer the questions you hear in Spanish, using complete sentences.

1. ______________________.

2. ______________________.

3. ______________________.

4. ______________________.

5. ______________________.

Segunda parte

¡Así es la vida!

15-20 La política. Reread the excerpt from the electoral campaign of Julián Pérez on page 516 of your textbook. Then decide if the following statements are **cierto** (C) or **falso** (F).

1. Pérez fue candidato a la presidencia de su país. _____
2. Su país afronta problemas muy serios. _____
3. Su oponente puede resolver todos los problemas. _____
4. Pérez promete ayudas sociales. _____
5. Pérez promete aumentar los impuestos. _____
6. El empleo no es parte de las promesas electorales de Julián Pérez. _____
7. Pérez promete combatir el crimen. _____
8. Pérez se va a interesar mucho por el pueblo. _____

Nombre: ______________________ Fecha: ______________________

CD 15, Track 9

15-21 Un debate presidencial. As you listen to the following debate, select the letters corresponding to all statements that are correct, according to what you hear.

1. La moderadora quiere...
   a. hablar de su vida social.
   b. que el presidente firme papeles.
   c. hablar con los dos candidatos.
2. El presidente describe...
   a. ideas para mantener el poder en el mundo.
   b. el proceso de las elecciones.
   c. ideas corruptas.
3. El presidente quiere mejorar los problemas con...
   a. las leyes.
   b. la inflación.
   c. el discurso.
4. El señor Montáñez cree...
   a. que no termina la entrevista.
   b. que es importante controlar el problema de las drogas.
   c. en un gobierno honrado para el pueblo.
5. El señor Montáñez quiere...
   a. establecer un gobierno que mejore la situación nacional.
   b. dar precedencia a los asuntos internacionales.
   c. insistir en aumentar los impuestos.
6. El presidente piensa...
   a. subir los impuestos en el segundo año.
   b. combatir la drogadicción.
   c. preocuparse por la visión global.

Nombre: ______________________ Fecha: ______________________

¡Así lo decimos! Vocabulario (TEXTBOOK P. 517)

15-22 Los cargos politicos. Read each description and write the correct word in the corresponding square.

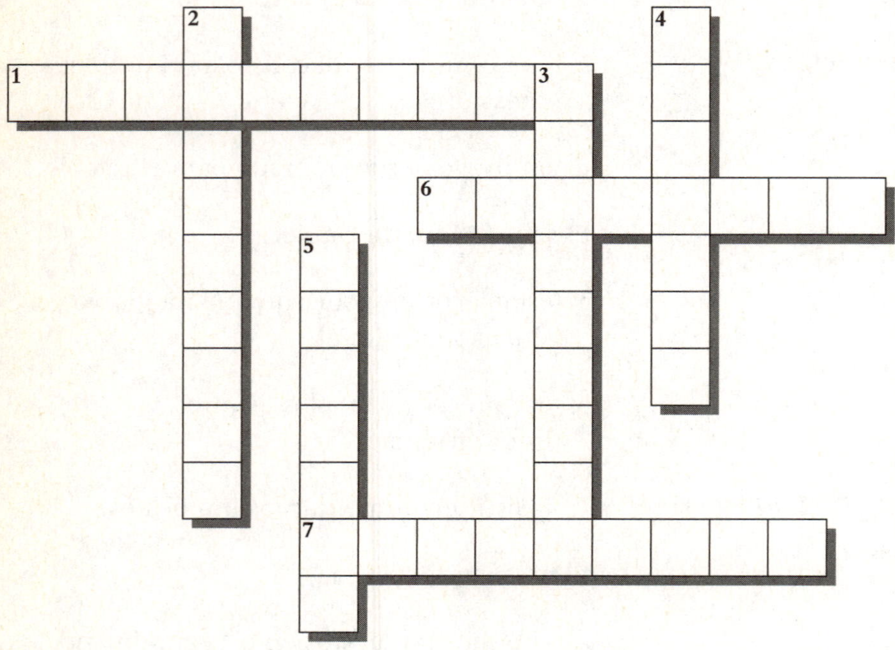

Across

1. Sistema político en el que el pueblo elige a sus representantes.
6. Persona responsable de una dictadura.
7. Sistema político en el que gobierna un dictador.

Down

2. Sistema político que incluye la figura de un rey o de una reina.
3. Mujer que dirige los asuntos políticos de un pueblo o ciudad.
4. Representante en el Senado.
5. Hombre que dirige los asuntos políticos de un pueblo o ciudad.

Nombre: ______________________ Fecha: ______________________

CD 15, Track 10

15-23 Hablemos de política. Complete these sentences with the letter of the most logical word or phrase that you hear. Then listen and repeat as the speaker gives the correct answer.

1. El _____ del ciudadano es votar en las elecciones.
2. El _____ es el gobernante de una ciudad.
3. Las _____ tratan de combatir la corrupción.
4. El rey es el líder de una _____.
5. La _____ es el tipo de gobierno opuesto a la democracia.
6. Los _____ ayudan a mucha gente que tiene poco dinero.

15-24 Un artículo. The following newspaper article is missing some words. Fill in the blanks using the present subjunctive, the present indicative, or the infinitive of each verb in parentheses.

... Todos los políticos dicen que van a (1) ____________________ (afrontar) los problemas del pueblo. También dicen que quieren (2) ____________________ (mejorar) las condiciones de vida de los ciudadanos. Es necesario que ellos (3) ____________________ (combatir) los problemas más graves ahora mismo. También les sugiero que (4) ____________________ (eliminar) el desempleo ahora, dándole trabajo a la gente, ya que el desempleo (5) ____________________ (aumentar) el número de crímenes y causa otros problemas sociales. Si nosotros (6) ____________________ (apoyar) al candidato, es importante que él (7) ____________________ (resolver) algunos de los problemas más graves...

15-25 Las promesas. You are running for an important political office. Write six promises for your campaign platform, using the terms below.

los programas sociales	la drogadicción	la corrupción
los impuestos	el deber	la inflación

Modelo: *Si ustedes me eligen, eliminaré la contaminación del aire.*

1. ____.
2. ____.
3. ____.
4. ____.
5. ____.
6. ____.

Nombre: ______________________ Fecha: ______________________

Letras y sonidos (Textbook p. 518)

CD 15, Track 11

15-26 ¿Conexiones? For each series of words you hear, decide if linking is necessary among any of the sounds and put a check mark under the correct heading.

	Linking	**No Linking**
1.	____	____
2.	____	____
3.	____	____
4.	____	____
5.	____	____
6.	____	____
7.	____	____
8.	____	____

CD 15, Track 12

15-27 ¿Dónde hay conexión? In each sentence you hear, identify and write the two words that require linking.

1. ______________________________
2. ______________________________
3. ______________________________
4. ______________________________
5. ______________________________
6. ______________________________

Nombre: ______________________________ Fecha: ______________________

¡Así lo hacemos! Estructuras

3. *Se* for unplanned occurrences (TEXTBOOK P. 521)

15-28 Diferentes situaciones. On the line next to each drawing, write the letter of the sentence that it best depicts.

1. _____

2. _____

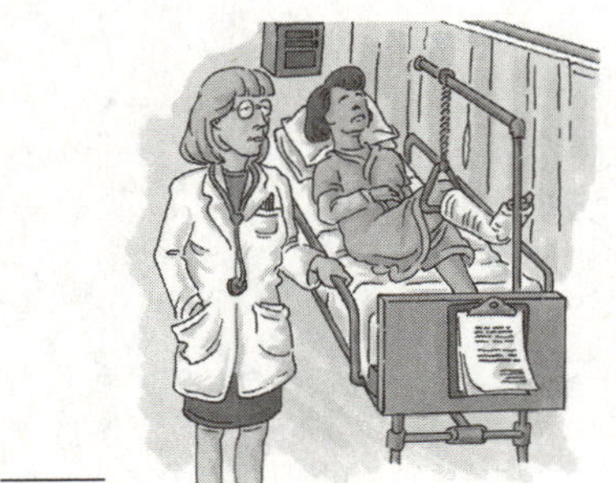

3. _____

4. _____

5. _____

a. Se le fue el autobús.

b. Se le rompió una pierna.

c. No se le perdió ningún niño.

d. Se le olvidó la hora del concierto.

e. Se les acabó la comida.

15-29 La excusa perfecta. On the line next to each situation, write the letter of the sentence that describes the best excuse.

1. _____ No llamaste a un amigo.
2. _____ No le entregaste la tarea al profesor.
3. _____ No compraste el libro para la clase.
4. _____ No llegaste a clase a tiempo.
5. _____ No fuiste a estudiar a casa de un amigo.

a. Se me estropeó la impresora.
b. Se me perdió la dirección.
c. Se me olvidó el número de teléfono.
d. Se me fue el autobús.
e. Se me acabó el dinero.

CD 15, Track 13

15-30 Lo que nos pasó durante el día de las elecciones. Form complete sentences using the sentence fragments provided and the verbs you hear, according to the model. Then listen and repeat as the speaker gives the correct answer.

MODELO: You see: ______________________ una buena idea.
You hear: a él, ocurrirse
You write and say: *Se le ocurrió una buena idea.*

1. ______________________ las llaves.
2. ______________________ el nombre del candidato.
3. ______________________ la cena.
4. ______________________ las elecciones.
5. ______________________ los papeles.
6. ______________________ el periódico en casa.
7. ______________________ los pasaportes.
8. ______________________ el lápiz.

Nombre: ______________________ Fecha: ______________________

15-31 Problemas, problemas. Rewrite the sentences below, substituting the names or pronouns in parentheses.

Modelo: A Ramón se le rompió la silla. (a ti)
A ti se te rompió la silla.

1. Al asesor se le quedó el discurso en casa. (a nosotros)

   ____

2. Se me perdieron los papeles. (a Ana)

   ____

3. Se nos olvidó el lema de la campaña. (a mis asesores)

   ____

4. A Rodríguez y a Martín se les acabó el apoyo del pueblo. (al representante)

   ____

4. The passive voice (Textbook p. 523)

15-32 ¡A cambiar! Rewrite each statement in the passive voice, expressing the agent as in the model.

Modelo: El Senado promovió la ley.
La ley fue promovida por el Senado.

1. El dictador eliminó la democracia.

   La democracia ______________________ por el dictador.

2. El presidente aumentó la tasa de empleo.

   La tasa de empleo ______________________ por el presidente.

3. Los ciudadanos eligieron sus representantes.

   Los representantes ______________________ por los ciudadanos.

4. Los candidatos de ese partido hicieron muchas promesas.

   Muchas promesas ______________________ por los candidatos de ese partido.

5. Los representantes resolvieron el tema de los impuestos.

   El tema de los impuestos ______________________ por los representantes.

6. El Congreso abolió el ejército y la compra de armas.

   El ejército y la compra de armas ______________________ por el Congreso.

7. Los ministros controlaron la inflación.

   La inflación ______________________ por los ministros.

8. La reina visitó Paraguay y Uruguay.

   Paraguay y Uruguay ______________________ por la reina.

CD 15, Track 14

15-33 La campaña. Complete the following sentences by changing the statements you hear to the passive voice. Then listen and repeat as the speaker gives the correct answer.

MODELO: You see: Los impuestos ______________ por el Congreso.
You hear: El Congreso aumentó los impuestos.
You write and say: Los impuestos *fueron aumentados* por el Congreso.

1. Las cartas ______________ por ti.
2. El Senado ______________ por los republicanos.
3. El discurso ______________ por el secretario.
4. Los cheques ______________ por el representante.
5. La presidenta ______________ por la gente.
6. Los candidatos ______________ por el gobernador.

Nombre: ______________________ Fecha: ______________________

15-34 ¿Quién hizo qué? The President wants to know who took care of the following tasks. Answer the questions affirmatively in the passive voice, using the agent in parentheses. Be sure to follow the model.

MODELO: ¿Se redujo la tasa de desempleo? (el ministro)
Sí, la tasa de desempleo fue reducida por el ministro.

1. ¿Se eliminó la drogadicción? (la campaña contra las drogas)

____

2. ¿Se combatió la corrupción? (el senador)

____

3. ¿Se cumplieron las promesas? (la alcaldesa)

____

4. ¿Se controló la inflación? (los asesores económicos)

____

5. ¿Se afrontó el problema del crimen en el estado? (la gobernadora)

____

6. ¿Se aumentaron los impuestos? (el Congreso)

____

CD 15, Track 15

15-35 Después de las elecciones. Change the sentences that you hear to the passive voice. Then listen and repeat as the speaker gives the correct answer.

1. ____
2. ____
3. ____
4. ____
5. ____

15-36 Ante la prensa. Imagine that you are a candidate for the presidency and that you are conducting a press conference. Answer the following questions in Spanish, using complete sentences.

1. ¿Cómo se combatirá el crimen durante su presidencia?

____

____

2. ¿Qué impuestos se eliminarán?

____

____

3. ¿Qué se hará con el ejército?

____

____

4. ¿Cómo se reducirá la tasa de desempleo?

____

____

5. ¿Cómo se podrán aumentar los programas de ayuda social?

____

____

5. *Pero* or *sino* (Textbook p. 526)

15-37 Habla el pueblo. Find out what the people and candidates want by completing each statement with either **pero** or **sino,** as appropriate.

1. Los trabajadores no desean más impuestos, ____________________ más aumentos.
2. Nosotros queremos elegir al presidente, ____________________ no podemos votar.
3. Antonio y Sebastián no pronuncian un discurso, ____________________ que repiten el lema.
4. Mis amigos prefieren más programas sociales, ____________________ no quieren pagar más impuestos.
5. Él quiere ser senador, ____________________ no le gusta pronunciar discursos.
6. Ellos no piensan ser representantes, ____________________ gobernadores.
7. No deseamos la dictadura, ____________________ la democracia.
8. No prefiero a este candidato, ____________________ al otro.

Nombre: ______________________ Fecha: ______________________

15-38 El discurso del candidato. Complete the following candidate's speech appropriately by filling in the blanks with **pero** or **sino.**

Estimados amigos:

Nuestro pueblo busca un nuevo futuro, (1) ______________ tenemos que buscarlo con más esfuerzo. Necesitamos tener más programas sociales, (2) ______________ no queremos pagar más impuestos; no queremos un aumento de impuestos, (3) ______________ una reducción. No queremos más crimen, (4) ______________ más ayuda para combatir el crimen, (5) ______________ el gobierno actual no lo combate. No les pido que voten por mí, (6) ______________ por la democracia.

CD 15, Track 16

15-39 Los resultados. Combine the sentence you hear with the words you see using **pero** or **sino.** Then listen and repeat as the speaker gives the correct answer.

Modelo: You see: ______________ no combatirá la inflación.
You hear: Reducirá la tasa de desempleo.
You write and say: *Reducirá la tasa de desempleo pero* no combatirá la inflación.

1. ______________________________ democracia.
2. ______________________________ no son candidatas.
3. ______________________________ la corrupción.
4. ______________________________ el gobernador.
5. ______________________________ a su contrincante.
6. ______________________________ no sabes dónde hacerlo.

¿Cuánto sabes tú?

15-40 ¿Sabes usar la voz pasiva? Fill in the blanks to give the passive voice of the following sentences.

1. Los ciudadanos eligieron al presidente.

   El presidente ______________ por los ciudadanos.

2. Los diputados discutieron la nueva ley de inmigración.

   La nueva ley de inmigración ______________ por los diputados.

3. El ejército desarmó a los rebeldes.

   Los rebeldes __________________ por el ejército.

4. Los dos países firmaron la paz.

   La paz __________________ por los dos países.

5. El gobierno mejoró los programas sociales.

   Los programas sociales __________________ por el gobierno.

15-41 ¿Sabes usar *pero* y *sino*? Fill in the blanks correctly with **pero** or **sino.**

1. El gobierno quería aumentar los impuestos, __________________ no lo hizo.
2. No hablaron de la paz, __________________ de desarme.
3. No quiero votar, __________________ es mi deber como ciudadano.
4. Apoyo las decisiones del gobierno, __________________ algunas no son correctas.
5. No quiero hablar con el senador, __________________ con el presidente.
6. La paz no debe ser un sueño, __________________ una realidad.

CD 15, Track 17

15-42 De viaje después de las elecciones. Answer the questions you hear negatively with the **se** construction. Then listen and repeat as the speaker gives the correct answer.

Modelo: You see: __________________ la cámara.
You hear: ¿Se te rompieron las gafas de sol?
You write and say: No, *se me rompió* la cámara.

1. No, __________________ los periódicos.
2. No, __________________ la computadora.
3. No, __________________ la maleta.
4. No, __________________ los pantalones en el hotel.
5. No, __________________ el bolígrafo.

Nombre: ______________________ Fecha: ______________________

15-43 Otras preguntas personales. Answer the questions you hear in Spanish, using complete sentences.

CD 15, Track 18

1. ______________________.
2. ______________________.
3. ______________________.
4. ______________________.
5. ______________________.

Observaciones

Antes de ver el video

15-44 ¿Qué pasa? Select the letter of the best answer to each question.

1. What does Hermés say is one of the problems of Latin America?

   a. En América Latina, como en muchas otras partes, mucha gente sigue siendo pobre, con multinacionales o sin ellas.

   b. Los candidatos quieren resolver el problema de la inflación.

   c. Se está celebrando un congreso internacional sobre globalización y desarrollo.

2. What does Patricio say is a problem of free trade?

   a. Necesitamos senadores y representantes cualificados.

   b. Permite que vengan grandes compañías a explotar nuestros recursos naturales.

   c. El mayor reto es acabar con la pobreza…

3. What other problems does Patricio say are facing many Latin American countries?

   a. A lo mejor el problema no es la globalización en sí.

   b. En teoría la globalización hace que los recursos de la tierra se distribuyan por igual.

   c. Pero las poblaciones siguen sin escuelas, sin hospitales, sin infraestructuras.

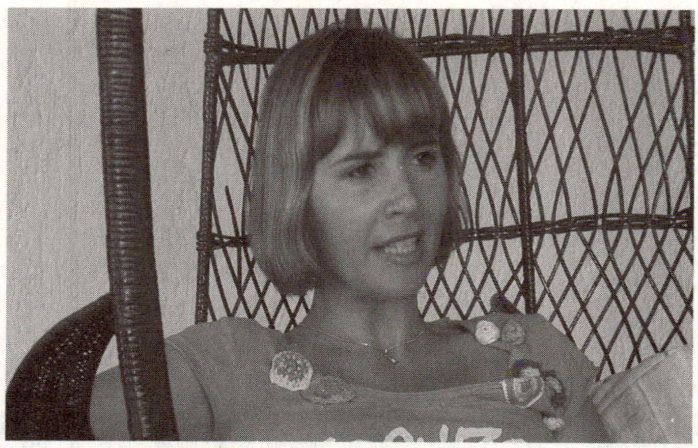

4. What does Silvia say is one of the advantages of globalization?

   a. No, pero la antiglobalización tampoco.

   b. Hay multinacionales de Estados Unidos, Alemania, Francia, Japón. Y hasta de México.

   c. La globalización sirve para crear trabajos y generar nuevas oportunidades…

5. Why does the latest guest, Cristina, say she is at the hostel?

   a. Trabajo en "Papelosa". Es una de las multinacionales de papel más importantes del mundo.

   b. Soy chilena, de Santiago.

   c. ¿Puedo estacionar mi Cayenne en el patio?

Nombre: ______________________________ Fecha: ______________________

A ver el video

15-45 La conversación. Fill in the blanks with the missing words according to the video segment.

Patricio: A lo mejor el problema no es la globalización en sí. Necesitamos (1) ______________ y (2) ______________ cualificados; políticos que se preocupen de verdad por la gente.

Marcela: Si Rigoberta Menchú fuera (3) ______________ a la presidencia de mi país, votaría por ella.

Silvia: Yo creo que la (4) ______________ puede tener sus beneficios. En teoría hace que los (5) ______________ de la tierra se (6) ______________ por igual.

Hermés: Claro, pero hay que controlarla.

Marcela: En Sudamérica se están (7) ______________ gaseoductos que pasan por poblaciones indígenas. ¿Verdad Patricio?

Patricio: Sí, se habló de ello en el (8) ______________. Pero las poblaciones siguen sin escuelas, sin hospitales, sin infraestructuras…

Silvia: ¡Qué horror!

Marcela: El mayor (9) ______________ es acabar con la (10) ______________…

Después de ver el video

15-46 La acción y los personajes. Determine whether the following statements are **cierto** (C) or **falso** (F) and write the correct letter on the lines provided.

1. Silvia cree que la globalización tiene sus beneficios. ____
2. Patricio dice que la globalización no tiene un gran impacto en el medio ambiente. ____
3. Patricio comenta que se necesitan políticos que se preocupen por la gente. ____
4. Cristina es argentina. ____
5. Cristina es representante del gobierno. ____
6. Cristina tiene un Porsche. ____

Nombre: ______________________ Fecha: ______________________

15-47 ¿En qué orden? Put the following events in chronological order, labeling each statement from 1–6.

_____ Cristina explica que ella trabaja para una de las multinacionales del papel más importantes del mundo.

_____ Doña María les ofrece fruta a los amigos.

_____ En la opinión de Hermés, hay que controlar la globalización.

_____ Felipe está muy contento.

_____ Llega Cristina.

_____ Marcela pregunta si la globalización ayuda a la gente común, a los pueblos oprimidos, a los trabajadores o a las grandes multinacionales.

Nuestro mundo

Panoramas

15-48 ¡A informarse! Based on the information from **Nuestro mundo,** decide if the following statements are **cierto** (C) or **falso** (F) and write the correct letter on the lines provided.

1. Todos los idiomas que se hablaban en América antes de la llegada de Colón han desaparecido. _____
2. Los mayas eran los habitantes del sur de México y parte de Centroamérica. _____
3. Los mayas no se distinguieron por su arquitectura. _____
4. Los jeroglíficos fueron usados por los mayas como forma de transmisión de historias y leyendas. _____
5. Los aztecas tenían dos calendarios diferentes. _____
6. El español ha eliminado todas las palabras de origen náhuatl de su vocabulario. _____
7. Los incas eran expertos en la confección de joyas de oro. _____
8. El guaraní todavía es idioma oficial en el Paraguay. _____
9. Las celebraciones hispanas son puramente cristianas. _____
10. La celebración del día de los muertos representa la fusión de la tradición cristiana e indígena. _____

Nombre: ______________________ Fecha: ______________________

15-49 Las celebraciones hispanoamericanas. Many festivities are traditionally celebrated annually all over Latin America. Visit **http://www.prenhall.com/arriba** and review the festivities that are celebrated in Venezuela. Then, on the line next to the name of each festivity, write the letter of the date on which it takes place.

1. _____ San Juan
2. _____ El día de la independencia
3. _____ San José
4. _____ El nacimiento de Simón Bolívar
5. _____ El día del trabajo
6. _____ La declaración de la independencia

a. 5 de julio
b. 19 de abril
c. 1 de mayo
d. 24 de junio
e. 27 de julio
f. 19 de marzo

Ritmos

15-50 Gilberto Santa Rosa. In your text you learned about the salsa music of Gilberto Santa Rosa. Now visit **http://www.prenhall.com/arriba** and review Santa Rosa's biography. Then, select the letter of the answer to each question below.

1. La primera orquesta profesional en la que tocó se llamaba...
   a. Orquesta Los Santa Rosa.
   b. Orquesta Elías López.
   c. Orquesta La Grande.
2. El estilo de Gilberto Santa Rosa...
   a. funde lo clásico y lo tropical.
   b. mezcla salsa y merengue.
   c. es exitoso.
3. Santa Rosa rompió récords de taquillas en...
   a. Nueva York.
   b. Caracas.
   c. San Juan.
4. Gilberto Santa Rosa ha ganado un disco de oro y platino por su álbum...
   a. *Punto de vista.*
   b. *Perspectiva.*
   c. *Nace aquí.*
5. Además de cantar en español, Santa Rosa ha cantado en...
   a. francés.
   b. japonés.
   c. taíno.

Nombre: ______________________ Fecha: ______________

Páginas

15-51 Francisco Jiménez. Based on the information in the **Páginas** section of the textbook, decide if the following statements are **cierto** (C) or **falso** (F).

1. Francisco Jiménez nació en México pero se mudó a los Estados Unidos. ____
2. La vida fue dura en California para la familia de Francisco Jiménez. ____
3. Las obras de Francisco Jiménez hablan de su vida en Guadalajara. ____
4. Francisco Jiménez es la voz de aquellos que buscan el sueño americano. ____
5. Es profesor de español en la Universidad de Santa Clara. ____
6. Francisco Jiménez ha sido nombrado "profesor del año". ____

Taller

15-52 Mi programa electoral y mi lema. Imagine that you are running for an elected office. To help you establish your platform, make a list in Spanish of your position regarding five issues. The issues can be local, national, and/or international.

____

____

____

____

____

15-53 La carta. Using the information from the previous activity, write a letter to your fellow citizens stating the kinds of priorities and changes you will address during your term in office.

Estimados ciudadanos:

____

____

____

____

____

____

NOTAS

NOTAS

NOTAS

NOTAS

NOTAS

NOTAS

NOTAS

NOTAS